INDUSTRIAL MARKETING STRATEGY

Third Edition

FREDERICK E. WEBSTER, JR.

**The Amos Tuck School
of Business Administration
Dartmouth College**

JOHN WILEY & SONS
New York • Chichester • Brisbane • Toronto • Singapore

Copyright © 1984, 1991 by John Wiley & Sons, Inc.

Library of Congress Cataloging-in-Publication Data

Webster, Frederick E.
    Industrial marketing strategy / Frederick E. Webster, Jr.—3rd ed.
      p.   cm.—(Wiley series on marketing management)
    Includes bibliographical references and index.
    ISBN 0-471-61703-2 (cloth)
    1. Industrial marketing—Management.
    I. Title. II. Series.
HF5415.1263.W43   1991
658.8—dc20   90-21501

Printed in the United Stated of America

92 10 9 8 7 6 5 4 3

Printed and bound by Courier Companies, Inc.

This book is dedicated to the loving memory of my son

MARK ANDREW WEBSTER
October 21, 1960–October 2, 1990

*poet and teacher whose writing and love of writing
set a high standard to which his father will always aspire.*

Preface

As industrial firms strive to develop and maintain profitable positions in the global markets of the 1990's, marketing strategy has moved to center stage. For industrial marketers, marketing has become virtually synonymous with business strategy because of the critical importance of market segmentation, targeting, and positioning to the competitive performance and financial success of the firm. We have reached a point where the concept of a customer-focussed, market-driven business is the core value for many industrial firms, rather than something to which a few seemingly enlightened managements pay lip service.

The third edition of *Industrial Marketing Strategy* reflects this emphasis and moves it forward, with a central focus on defining, developing, and delivering superior value in the competitive marketplace. The early chapters develop central concepts of customer analysis, buying behavior, buyer-seller relationships, market segmentation and targeting, and positioning. Special attention is devoted to the increased importance of strategic partnerships with industrial customers and resellers and the management challenges they represent. The middle chapters focus on the development of superior value for customers in products and pricing. The next chapters consider the implementation of the value proposition through distribution and marketing communications, including the sales force. The concept of strategic partnership is an integral part of the discussion of reseller strategy. In the final chapter, the role of marketing is amalgamated into a broader framework of business and corporate level strategic planning in the development of a customer-focused, market-driven enterprise.

Industrial marketing management is a special case within marketing and deserves its own treatment. Industrial marketing, also called business-to-business marketing, is defined by the nature of the customer—a profit-seeking or budget-constrained organization (business, institution, or government) seeking help in achieving its goals through the purchase of goods and services. While the essential elements of marketing strategy and analysis remain the same for all products and services, industrial marketing is unique in its concern for long-term, strategic relationships with customers, the complexity of the buying process, and the mutual dependence that results. Often, the ongoing development of technology is at the core of the buyer-seller relationship. Typically, even standard products must be precisely tailored with a bundle of services for individual customers.

It is assumed that the reader has had a good introduction to the general field of marketing management, as well as some understanding of basic concepts of accounting, financial, and economic analysis. The discussion will emphasize what is unique about industrial marketing. It will focus on strategic management rather than attempt to enumerate or describe in detail the functions and institutions that characterize industrial markets. Instructors using this book in a course in industrial marketing will probably want to supplement it with discussion of case studies to develop and apply the concepts developed in the text.

There has been a significant amount of new research and conceptual development in the academic and professional literature since the second edition appeared in 1904. These new insights have been integrated throughout the third edition. Most are based on careful analysis of company practice as opposed to the development of new theory and sophisticated modeling. At the same time, the heavier modelling emphasis of the 1960's and 1970's has provided a firm foundation and framework for analysis of company practice in the search for improved business performance.

FREDERICK E. WEBSTER, JR.

Etna, New Hampshire
February, 1991

Contents

THREE 9|22

BUYER-SELLER RELATIONSHIPS 66

FOUR 9|15

INDUSTRIAL MARKET SEGMENTATION, TARGETING, AND

POSITIONING   97

FIVE 10|6

PRODUCT STRATEGY AND NEW PRODUCT DEVELOPMENT   124

SIX $10/_6$

DEVELOPING MARKETS FOR NEW INDUSTRIAL

PRODUCTS   158

SEVEN $10/_6$

PRICING STRATEGY   190

EIGHT $^{10}/_{13}$

INDUSTRIAL DISTRIBUTION STRATEGY   219

1 The Nature and Scope of Industrial Marketing

Among industrial firms, recent years have brought a significant increase in the importance attached to marketing as a major source of competitive effectiveness. From computers to machine tools, airfreight to telecommunications, the leaders in industry after industry are urging their organizations to adopt a customer focus and become market-driven. This resurgence of interest in the marketing concept, a management philosophy with its roots in the 1950's, comes at a time when most industrial firms are facing increased foreign competition, slow-growth markets, uncertain economic and political trends in an increasingly "global" marketplace, and an ever-more-demanding and sophisticated customer. Pressures on both the cost and price sides create maximum incentive to manage the business for profit (not just for sales volume and market share) and place real premiums on management skills in market segmentation and targeting as key elements of business strategy.

Marketing is the function by which a firm or other economic organization designs, promotes, and delivers goods and services for customers and clients. The hallmarks of modern marketing are customer orientation and a long-range, or *strategic*, viewpoint that make an organization responsive to its ever-changing environment. Customers' preferences and buying habits are continually evolving and changing in response to changes in *their* environment, including competitive offerings of goods and services. Under the marketing concept, the critical function performed by every economic organization is the creation of customer (or client) satisfaction. Marketing can be defined as *knowing customers and their problems, innovating solutions to those problems, and communicating them to a carefully defined target market.* Profit is a reward for creating a satisfied customer, and marketing is more than a separate business function. It is the whole business seen from the customer's point of view.

CUSTOMER ORIENTATION

Examples of the renewed emphasis on marketing in industrial firms can be seen in the efforts of such leading firms as Deere, DuPont, General Electric, GTE, Hewlett-Packard, IBM, Monsanto, Motorola, and 3M. In each case, the chief executive officer has made a public commitment to reinforcing the company's focus on its customers and markets and to developing the marketing competence of the organization. This commitment requires not only developing and maintaining strong marketing managers, but also, and even more importantly, taking the steps necessary to be sure that all people in the firm understand their roles in serving customer needs and take on those responsibilities. Information and education are key elements in developing a market orientation, as are programs for tracking customer satisfaction and service levels over time. Firms with a strong customer focus will by definition have a core commitment to quality, where quality is defined by the customer. Customer orientation and commitment to quality are really the same thing.

THE ROLE OF MARKETING MANAGEMENT

As a management philosophy, the marketing concept asserts that marketing—putting the customer first—is *every* manager's responsibility. As a practical matter, however, marketing is a distinct set of responsibilities and skills having to do with the customer. Marketing managers must be *expert on the customer,* representing the customer throughout the organization, advocating for the customer's point of view, and helping other managers understand the customers and their needs. The specific role of marketing management depends upon the level of strategic analysis.

It is helpful in this context to think of three levels of marketing strategy. At the *corporate* level, where management is concerned with the question "What businesses should we be in?," marketing management plays a critical role in the assessment of market opportunity, including demand analysis and market trends. A central part of this analysis is development of an understanding of the critical success factors in the business and an evaluation of the firm's strengths and weaknesses *vis-a-vis* market requirements, leading up to a conclusion about the firm's ability to develop a dominant, sustainable competitive position. The results of this analysis are a pattern of resource allocations across businesses in the company's portfolio, with some of those businesses generating resources, especially cash, that will be used in the development of other businesses representing the profit opportunities of tomorrow.

At the *business unit* level, management is trying to answer the question "How should we compete?" in the businesses chosen. Marketing analysis at the business unit level calls for careful assessment of customers, competitors, and the company itself. The result of this analysis will be a detailed understanding of the various segments in the market, the selection of specific segments as market targets, and the development of a *positioning* vs. competition in those market niches. A core concept in the positioning strategy is what we will call the firm's *value proposition,* a statement of how the firm delivers superior value to its chosen customers. It is important to remember, however, that *customer's define value,* and that the customers' definition of value keeps changing in response to their needs, the nature of their buying decision process (most importantly, the actors in the buying process), and competitors' product offerings.

Finally, at the *individual product or brand* level, the principal decisions made by marketing managers include selection of customers, new product development and overall product policy, pricing, choices of distribution channels, and the deployment of promotional resources, including sales representatives, advertising, and other forms of sales promotion such as trade shows. At this level, the marketing manager has responsibility for *implementing* business and corporate level strategy. To make these decisions, the marketing manager relies on analytical tools of the trade like customer surveys, advertising research, product tests, and distribution channel audits. The need for expertise in these analytical tools is one of the major reasons for the existence of a separate marketing function within the industrial firm. Effective marketing management depends heavily upon a steady flow of information about customers, competitors, and market conditions, using data provided by valid and reliable market research methods and analyzed with proven techniques of management science.

Industrial marketing is the marketing of goods and services to industrial and institutional customers. These include manufacturing firms, governments, public utilities, educational institutions, hospitals, wholesalers and retailers, and other formal organizations. Consumer marketing, in contrast, is concerned with marketing to individuals, families, and households purchasing goods and services for their own consumption. The distinguishing feature of industrial and institutional customers is that they use purchased goods and services in their own production of goods and services. Purchased products, such as raw materials, components, and subassemblies, may become part of the customer's final product or may be added to physical facilities, in the form of construction and equipment. In other cases the purchases may be supplies used in operations, repair, and maintenance activities, including such products as fuel, office supplies, and building materials. Resellers, such as retailers, distributors, and wholesalers, purchase products for resale but add value to those products in the form of the services they provide, such as availability, credit, and customer information.

In a real sense, industrial marketing keeps the economy functioning by providing the products and services required by factories, offices, government agencies, hospitals, universities, and other providers of goods and services. It has been estimated that industrial marketing transactions equal in dollar value at least twice the value of consumer purchases. This can be understood by considering the long and complex chain of industrial market transactions preceding the manufacture and sale of a consumer product, such as a shirt or a can of soup, a chain that begins with raw materials from farm, forest, mine, or ocean and almost certainly crosses national borders at several points. Given that all manufacturers depend upon other manufacturers for goods and services, the chain is virtually endless.

These flows are demonstrated in the model of the marketing system shown in Figure 1-1. Such flows are also found in input-output tables used by economists to show movements of products among industrial sectors, usually defined by the Standard Industrial Classification (S.I.C.) code.

THE NATURE OF INDUSTRIAL GOODS AND SERVICES

Industrial goods and services can be categorized in a variety of ways. A typical scheme involves construction, heavy equipment, light equipment, components and subassemblies, raw materials, proc-

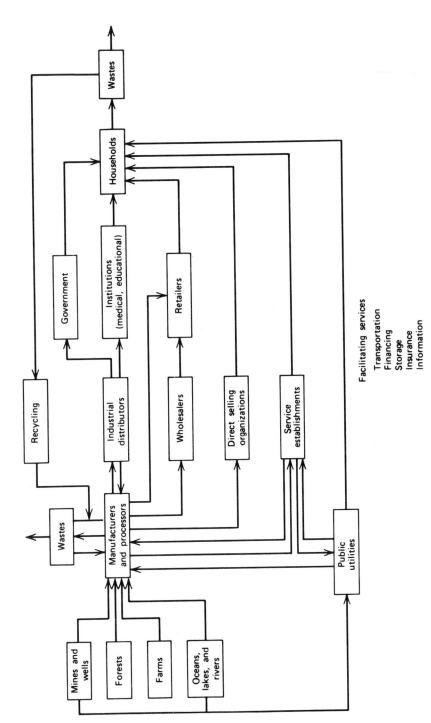

Figure 1-1. The marketing system.

5

essed materials, maintenance, repair, and operating supplies, and services.

Construction includes the design and fabrication of buildings and other structures, such as drilling rigs, chemical processing plants, towers, and cranes.

Heavy equipment involves large machinery, such as machine tools, turbines, supercomputers, locomotives, presses, tugs and barges, and earth-moving equipment. Heavy equipment often denotes "one of a kind" items designed specifically for the needs of a particular user. Construction and heavy equipment almost always are shown on the customer's balance sheet as plant and equipment, fixed assets to be depreciated over a period of years. The purchase of plant and major equipment items is typically financed by borrowing money for a period of time roughly equivalent to the expected life of the asset. Thus, purchases of plant and equipment items have very significant financial dimensions for the customers.

Light equipment consists of smaller pieces of equipment with typically lower purchase prices and, often, shorter lifetimes than heavy equipment. Examples of light equipment include power-operated hand tools, fork-lift trucks, small motors, and dies and jigs. Light equipment purchases may be financed as a current expense with the full purchase price taken as an operating expense in the year purchased, or they may be depreciated over a period of a few years. These products are often available in standard sizes and configurations from several competing suppliers.

Components and subassemblies are fabricated items that become part of the customer's finished product. Small motors, semiconductors and capacitors, integrated circuits, fasteners, instruments and gauges, and glass are examples of components and subassemblies. These are the "parts" of a piece of equipment and may number in the thousands for a finished product. For many equipment manufacturers, the sale of replacement parts is an important source of revenue and profit, not uncommonly producing half of their annual sales volume and more than half of their profits.

For a portion of the manufacturer's requirement for components and subassemblies, there is a choice to be made between manufacturing the item internally or purchasing it from a vendor. It is usually in the buyer's best interest to encourage competition among two or more potential vendors in order to have the possibility of alternative sources of supply and to obtain competitive pricing. However, recent years have seen a tendency toward "sole source" procurements, especially in situations where the vendor's and the customer's operations are highly interdependent, such as "just-in-time" systems used by automobile manufacturers. Suppliers must be able to guarantee uninterrupted availability of products manufactured to stated specifications in order to compete effectively for this type of components and subassemblies business. A components supplier with an established brand name and reputation may secure a marketing advantage because of its product's ability to help the customer, in turn, to sell its product. Examples include Bosch electrical equipment for automobiles, General Electric controls, and Briggs and Stratton small engines.

Raw materials are those basic products of sea, farm, forest, and mine that are at the beginning of every manufacturing chain. Logs, iron ore, corn, fish, and crude oil are obvious examples. Very few firms actually sell such products, since some processing almost always occurs. Raw materials are usually traded in markets where a market price is established by forces of supply and demand, forces that tend to be independent of the actions of individual buyers and sellers.

Processed materials are raw materials that have had their value enhanced by such processes as refining, crushing, and cutting. Processed materials typically come in standard grades and sizes. Many chemical products are good examples of processed materials created by the combination of such basic materials as air, petroleum, and coal. Acids, fats and oils, solvents, fuel oil, and steel are examples of processed materials that are the basic ingredients of many manufacturing activities. It is common in day-to-day discussions to use the term "raw materials" to refer to these basic processed materials as well as to true raw materials.

Processed materials are usually available from several sources of supply, and the products themselves tend to be undifferentiated. Suppliers compete on the basis of their service offerings with an "augmented" product[1]—i.e., a product "augmented" and enhanced by the addition of services such as technical assistance, delivery, and ordering systems using the latest information technology. Customers buy on the basis of these service offerings. Uninterrupted supply and standards of product purity and quality are very important, since a failure in delivery or quality can easily shut down the customer's operations.

Maintenance, repair, and operating (MRO) supplies are con-

[1] Theodore Levitt, *The Marketing Mode* (New York: McGraw-Hill Book Co., 1969), pp. 1–27.

sumed by the organization as part of its normal operations but do not become part of the finished product. These are items that are usually *fungible*, meaning that there are many sources for each item and one brand is easily substituted for another. Their distribution is characterized by broad marketing channels. Common items in this category are lubricants, cutting oils, paper products, office supplies of all kinds, chain, saw blades, grinding wheels and other types of abrasives, fuels, and cleaning supplies. The unit price of MRO items tends to be quite low, and MRO items are likely to be purchased frequently in small quantities, reflecting their fungible nature and widespread availability. On the other hand, even though each purchase may be rather small, MRO items are often bought on the basis of an annual purchase agreement or other purchasing contract where a single vendor is given a blanket order for a stated period of time covering a range of related products in return for quantity discounts and other favorable price and service terms. Such purchasing arrangements may involve the use of a simple computer program to issue orders when supplies fall below a pre-specified level. (Routine re-orders of components and materials may also be managed in this fashion.)

Services include all intangible products, although services may be purchased along with physical products. For example, a service contract may be part of an equipment purchase. When a major piece of equipment, such as a computer or an aircraft, is leased rather than purchased, there is room for debate whether the customer has purchased a product or a service. More obvious services purchased by industrial and institutional customers include liability and property insurance, banking and other financial services, building maintenance services, auditing services, consulting services of all kinds (including architectural and engineering services), common carrier transportation, advertising and marketing research agency services, and data processing. Although services may not be as large a portion of expenditures in industrial markets as they are in consumer markets, where they consume more than half of disposable personal income, they are a very important expense item for most organizations. Services are just as vital to the conduct of the affairs of an economic organization as are tangible goods.

The intangible nature of services adds a complicating dimension to their marketing and procurement. Purchasing specifications are hard to create, and the marketer may find it challenging to develop and maintain a standard of quality. Service quality is often determined by the persons who deliver the service, not only in terms of their skills, but also in terms of their attitudes toward their jobs and other personal characteristics. Thus, people play a central role in services marketing and are the major source of differentiation among service suppliers. The persons who actually deliver the service may also be responsible for selling it. Equally important as the people are the systems that manage these people, including systems for training, supervision, and control, all of which must be assessed carefully by an astute purchaser.

INDUSTRIAL CUSTOMERS

Industrial marketing is distinguished from consumer marketing more by the nature of the customer than by the nature of the product. Industrial markets are made up of organizations that buy many of the same products consumed by individuals and families, such as paper products, automobiles, trucks, tools, and common carrier transportation services.

Industrial customers consist of manufacturing and processing firms (the latter including food, chemical, and petroleum processors) and distributors, who purchase and resell to other industrial and institutional users. A special kind of manufacturer is the so-called OEM, or original equipment manufacturer, who makes equipment incorporating the components of other manufacturers. *Institutional* customers include health care and educational institutions, as well as agencies of government, such as prisons. *Governmental* customers include many agencies at municipal, county, state, regional and national levels. The Federal Government of the United States is the single largest purchaser of goods and services in the world, most notably through its purchases of military equipment and supplies, and of goods and services related to space exploration. For convenience, we will usually use the term *industrial marketing* to apply to all three types of customers—industrial, institutional, and governmental.

There are many other ways of distinguishing between industrial and consumer marketing. For example, industrial customers tend to be relatively few in number for any given supplier compared with the size and scope of consumer markets. Individual transactions, in contrast, typically have a much higher dollar value. Compared with consumer decision making, industrial buying behavior is characterized by the participation of many persons interacting with each other in the context of a formal organization. The buying decision process typically takes a long time and may be more highly structured (but not necessarily less "emotional" or more "rational") than the consumer buying decision process. The unique nature and complexity of the industrial buying process will be explored in Chapter 2.

Derived Demand

Demand for industrial goods and services is derived from the demand for consumer goods and services. Raw materials, components, and subassemblies become part of the customer's finished product, and, therefore, the demand for them is directly determined by the demand for the industrial customer's product. Not so obviously but equally true, the demand for capital equipment, for maintenance and repair items, and for services of various kinds is also determined by the strength of demand facing the industrial marketer's customers.

It is probably more realistic to say that industrial customers' purchases reflect their *expectations* about future demands for their goods and services. Clearly, purchasing decisions must be made in anticipation of the market conditions that the customer company expects to face. The customer's actual need for products, willingness to make commitments to potential suppliers, and ability to pay for these purchases are all a function of the customer's optimism or pessimism about the future.

Information about purchasing agents' expectations has proven to be a useful indicator of economic growth. Surveys of expectations are conducted regularly by McGraw-Hill as well as by the Bureau of Economic Analysis and Census of the U.S. Department of Commerce.[2] Sophisticated analytical techniques have been developed for incorporating such data into forecasts of sales to be used by companies in setting sales budgets, scheduling production requirements, and determining financial needs.[3]

Some purchases may be made in anticipation of hard times rather than good times. For example, cost-reducing capital equipment may become a more attractive purchase if a company expects to face

[2] *Business' Plans for New Plant and Equipment,* Economics Dept., McGraw-Hill Publications, Inc.; *Manufacturers' Inventory and Sales Expectations Survey,* Bureau of Census; *Plant and Equipment Expenditure Survey,* Bureau of Economic Analysis.

[3] See Richard Rippe, Maurice Wilkinson, and Donald Morrison, "Industrial Market Forecasting with Anticipations Data," *Management Science,* **22,** 6 (February, 1976), 639–51.

declining sales and eroding profit margins. Or, to take an opposite situation, a customer operating at full capacity may not have enough organizational slack to permit a program of equipment installation or other innovation requiring a modification of production schedules.

Because demand for industrial products is derived demand, industrial marketers can sometimes stimulate demand for their products by stimulating demand for their customers' products. Figure 1-2 illustrates end-user demand stimulation by a manufacturer of carpet fiber. A somewhat more complex form of end-user demand stimulation is often required to develop markets for truly innovative products. For example, a manufacturer of a high-barrier paper coating material used in food packaging found it necessary to work with paperboard manufacturers, paper coaters, packaging firms, food processors, and retail chains in order to develop the market for its product.

It is therefore true that understanding the nature and scope of industrial markets requires understanding both the nature of demand facing the industrial customer and the customer's customers throughout the marketing channel to actual consumer demand. In addition, it is usually helpful to analyze competition in the customer's industry and perhaps competition among the customers in the markets that customer serves. The need to analyze market activity at all levels between industrial customer and end users/consumers is the most significant implication of the fact of "derived" demand in industrial markets.

HOW INDUSTRIAL MARKETING DIFFERS FROM CONSUMER MARKETING[4]

At the most general level there is a body of theory, knowledge, and practice that cuts across all marketing—industrial and consumer products and services, business and non-profit organizations, and so on. But to understand and intelligently attack industrial marketing problems, a number of substantial differences between industrial and consumer marketing must be recognized. While it may be true that these are often differences of degree rather than kind, the degrees of differences are substantial.

[4] A significant portion of this section first appeared in Frederick E. Webster, Jr., "Management Science in Industrial Marketing," *Journal of Marketing,* **42,** 1 (January, 1978), 21–27, and is used with the permission of the American Marketing Association.

Figure 1-2. An advertisement by a carpet fiber manufacturer prepared for consumer media. Reproduced by courtesy of Monsanto Chemical Company.

Several years ago, B. Charles Ames, a management consultant, noted that the marketing concept, despite lip-service from top management and all the organizational trappings of acceptability, often fell short of full-scale acceptance in industrial companies because of a failure to recognize these differences. He observed that the four key dimensions in applying the marketing concept to industrial marketing were:

1. **Aiming for improved profit performance,** with sales volume and market share *per se* not as important as in consumer marketing.
2. **Identifying customer needs,** which requires understanding the economics of the customers' operations, the structure of the industry within which they operate, and how they compete.
3. **Selecting customer groups for emphasis,** the classic problem of market segmentation, which takes on special meaning in industrial markets because of the high degree of buyer-seller interdependence *after* the sale.
4. **Designing the product/service package,** where there is seldom a standard product, the accompanying bundle of services is often more important than the product itself, and the product must often be "invented."

Ames summarized these observations by noting that,

> From all this, one conclusion is clear: marketing in the industrial world is much more a general management responsibility than it is in the consumer-products field. For in a consumer-goods company major changes in marketing strategy can be made and carried out within the marketing department through changes in advertising emphasis or weight, promotion emphasis or type, package design, and the like.
>
> In an industrial company, on the other hand, changes in marketing strategy are more likely to involve capital commitments for new equipment, shifts in development activities, or departures from traditional engineering and manufacturing approaches, any one of which would have companywide implications. And, while marketing may identify the need for such departures, general management must make the decision on the course the company will take to respond to the market—and it must provide the follow-through to ensure that this course is pursued in every functional area.[5]

[5] B. Charles Ames, "Trappings vs. Substance in Industrial Marketing," *Harvard Business Review*, **48**, 4 (July-August, 1970), 93–102.

Functional Interdependence

In an earlier article exploring reasons for failures in industrial marketing planning, Ames commented that a major distinguishing factor in industrial marketing was that industrial marketing effectiveness depended to a greater degree on other business functions, especially manufacturing, research and development (R&D), inventory control, and engineering.[6] Thus, the first point to be made about industrial marketing is its much closer relationship to overall corporate strategy and its higher degree of *functional interdependence.*

It is worth pausing, before identifying other dimensions of industrial marketing, to observe that in a very real sense industrial marketing calls for and creates conditions leading toward a more complete application of the marketing concept than consumer marketing. By its very nature industrial marketing requires that all parts of the business be customer-oriented and that all marketing decisions be based on a complete and accurate understanding of customer needs. In fact, it can be argued that a marketing-oriented industrial company is often "closer" to its customers and more knowledgeable about their needs than is the typical marketing-oriented consumer company.

Product Complexity

Turning to another dimension of industrial marketing uniqueness, *technical product complexity,* the major barrier to a true marketing orientation in the industrial firm remains excessive product-, engineering-, manufacturing-, and technical-orientation. One class of business strategies available to industrial companies calls for a high degree of technical innovativeness and risk-taking with related high expenditures for research and development. In such companies, top management is likely to have been grown in the engineering and research garden, and technical values may be predominant in management decision making. The real risk in these cases is "loving the product more than the customer," becoming so enamored with a technical accomplishment or particular product parameters that the necessary flexibility for responding to customer needs in a competitive marketplace disappears. As a result, one of the most common marketing sins can be unwittingly committed—trying to change the customer to fit the product.

[6] B. Charles Ames, "Marketing Planning for Industrial Products," *Harvard Business Review,* **46**, 5 (September-October, 1968), 100–11.

Assuming there can be degrees of sin, this sin of product-orientation is more serious in industrial marketing than in consumer marketing. This is caused, normally, by the greater technical complexity of the problem the customer is trying to solve. Therefore, greater supplier flexibility is required, in contrast to consumer marketing.

Professor E. Raymond Corey has addressed this problem by observing that in industrial marketing strategy the product must always be regarded as a variable, not as a given. He offers four key concepts for understanding the nature of industrial market selection and product planning:

1. The basic and most important decisions in planning marketing strategy are those related to the choice of a market or markets to serve. All else follows.
2. The form of the product is a variable, not a given, in developing marketing strategy. Products are planned and designed to serve customers. (In other words, various product options must be evaluated and the best selected to serve the needs of a particular market.)
3. The product is what it does; it is the total package of benefits the customer receives when he buys. [Corey points out that these include not only the functional utility of the product, but also technical assistance, the assurance of dependable supply, product service—the supplier's reputation as a promotable advantage for the customer to use—and a range of personal and technical relationships between buyer and seller organizations.]
4. The product, in this broad sense, will have different meaning to different customers. . . . important with regard to both market selection and pricing.[7]

To summarize this discussion of the unique aspects of product strategy in industrial markets, it can be said that in industrial marketing the product is not a physical entity *per se*. Rather, the product is an array of economic, technical, and personal relationships between buyer and seller. This definition points to a third dimension of uniqueness in industrial marketing—the high degree of interdependence between buyer and seller.

Buyer-Seller Interdependence

From what has already been said about the nature of industrial customers and products, it will be clear that buyer-seller interde-

---

[7] E. Raymond Corey, *Industrial Marketing: Cases and Concepts*, 2nd ed. (Englewood Cliffs, N.J.: Prentice-Hall, Inc., 1976), pp. 40–41.

pendence is indeed a hallmark of industrial marketing, especially for products used in the customer's operations. The buyer becomes crucially dependent on suppliers for many things—an assured supply of raw materials, components, or subassemblies; continued supply of maintenance and repair parts and skilled repair service for capital equipment; efficient order handling, delivery, and, usually, extension of credit terms, and the like. One significant result is that the "sale," the actual transaction, is only one point on the time continuum in industrial marketing, albeit a crucial one, the way most businesses "keep score." By contrast, in consumer marketing the buyer-seller relationship often ends with the sale. In industrial marketing, a significant negotiation process is often the most important regulator of the buyer-seller relationship, whereas consumer marketing usually lacks this, relying instead on an "arm's length" transaction in a more or less competitive and often very impersonal market.

One of the major strategic drivers for both industrial marketers and their customers in the 1990's is the move toward strategic partnerships. Throughout this book, that development will be examined—in analysis of the buying process, in the discussion of buyer-seller relationships, in sales force management, and in strategic planning. Increasingly, customers are looking to vendors for cooperation in reducing costs, improving quality, and exploiting new technologies in the global marketplace. Strategic partnerships with customers may require substantial investments in supporting services and systems, such as electronic data interchange, and these investments must be evaluated in the context of overall marketing strategy.

Buying Process Complexity

A fourth dimension of uniqueness of industrial marketing in contrast to consumer marketing is the greater *complexity of the buying process*. Even when the unit of analysis in consumer marketing is the household rather than the individual consumer, consumer buying behavior never reaches the complexity of industrial buying when we compare like types of buying decisions—straight rebuy or routine purchase, modified rebuy, and new buy, to use the commonly accepted typology. Complexity in the buying decision process reflects several factors: the influence of the formal organization itself; the large number of persons involved; the complex technical and economic factors that must be considered; the environment in which the firm operates; and the frequently large sums of money involved in the transaction. The problem of relating buying response to marketing strategy is made more difficult than in consumer marketing by this complexity, because of the characteristically longer time lags between the application of marketing effort and the resulting buyer response. The nature of the buying process will be examined more carefully in the following chapter.

To summarize, four sources of uniqueness in industrial marketing have been defined: (1) marketing's greater dependence upon other business functions for its effectiveness; (2) product complexity extending to virtually all economic, technical, and personal relationships between industrial buyer and seller; (3) a high degree of buyer-seller interdependence extending well beyond the transaction itself; and (4) the complexity of the organizational buying process.

Complexity is a word often used, appropriately, to summarize the unique features of industrial marketing. Almost as often, complexity is used as an excuse for not developing and adopting more rigorous analytical approaches to problem solving in industrial marketing. There can be little doubt that one reason for the lack of academic interest in industrial marketing is the complexity and apparent intractability of most industrial marketing problems. The foregoing discussion of the uniqueness of industrial marketing has detailed many reasons why management science approaches to industrial marketing must often be different from those found in consumer marketing.

MANAGEMENT SCIENCE IN INDUSTRIAL MARKETING

From a positive perspective, however, it is the very complexity of industrial marketing that makes the introduction of analytical rigor potentially so valuable. Modelling has great potential for helping industrial marketers and students of industrial marketing cope with the complexity of their subject. Then, too, it is clear that there are good and bad models. Good models are those which maintain sufficient reality, while providing the insights that come from simplifying the problem, breaking it into manageable parts. Another way of saying this is that good models are those which are relevant to their users' views of their problems.

Even if good models meet the criteria of realism, relevance, and understandability, they are of little use, either for theory construction or practical problem-solving application, if they do not permit measurement of key variables. Good theories demand empirical verification, and application requires parameterization.

There are only a few signs that current modelling efforts in industrial marketing are sensitive to these requirements, but these few signs are very hopeful indeed. Throughout this book, examples of modelling and measurement techniques of relevance for industrial marketing problem solvers will be integrated into the discussion wherever appropriate. It is through the development and use of such techniques that industrial marketing is developing as a profession.

These observations about the uniqueness of industrial marketing should not be construed as a denial of the basic applicability of the marketing concept and the principles of sound marketing planning to industrial marketing. A failure to do careful market analysis and sound marketing planning is often the root of failure in new product and market development strategies. Inadequate understanding of the functional interdependence of industrial marketing, for example, can lead to an underestimation of relevant costs, such as technical service, manufacturing modifications, and distribution expenses, in planning a new industrial marketing venture. The presence of shared costs among two or more products and questionable allocations of all relevant costs can be major issues in industrial marketing. A failure to appreciate the nature of buyer-seller interdependence can cause inadequate design of the total product and poor understanding of the sources of value in the product for the customer. This, in turn, can lead to poor pricing decisions—decisions that are based solely on costs of manufacturing and that overlook the value of the product in use.

An appreciation of the uniqueness of industrial marketing is, therefore, essential to the application of conventional marketing wisdom and to the development of effective industrial marketing strategy.

THE CONCEPT OF EFFECTIVE MARKETING STRATEGY

A *strategy* is a plan for achieving objectives through the deployment of scarce resources in the face of intelligent competition. Marketing strategy begins with an analysis of the changing environment, especially the part of the environment consisting of potential customers and competitors. All good industrial marketing planning begins and ends with the customer and, as noted earlier, takes the product as a variable, not as a given. The given in industrial marketing is customers and their needs and wants. Selection of customers to be dealt with and markets to be served is the most important decision made by any business firm or other economic organization and is a major determinant of the nature of the business.

The central calculus in the development of marketing strategy is an assessment of the organization's strengths and weaknesses and a matching of those strengths with unsatisfied customer needs in the marketplace. Effective marketing strategy, therefore, depends upon both an honest assessment of strengths and weaknesses and good information about customer needs and wants and the extent to which they are being served by current suppliers. Experience of many industrial marketers suggests that the most common error in this process is the producer's overestimate of the uniqueness of its product and its ability to satisfy customer needs. This is an unfortunate but natural consequence of the common technical-, product-, and production-orientation that characterizes many industrial marketers, especially those with the most innovative technologies.

An effective marketing strategy consists of substrategies for product, price, promotion, and distribution that are consistent with one another and have *synergy*—that is, the impact of the whole is greater than the sum of the parts. For example, pricing policy and strategy are consistent with the firm's product quality and image, providing margins adequate to cover the necessary costs of personal selling, advertising, and sales promotion, and allowing trade margins as required to gain the support of selected middlemen. Product strategy should reflect the true strengths of the firm, including its distribution and promotional capabilities, as well as its technical capabilities. Such strategy must avoid wishful thinking. Promotional strategy should reflect the true level of product quality and should be consistent with the capabilities of the distributor organization. Each element of the marketing strategy depends for its effectiveness on the coordination and support of all other elements of marketing strategy.

The ultimate test of industrial marketing strategy is whether it leads to a valuable differentiation for the industrial marketer, whether it leads to a unique competitive advantage giving potential customers a solid reason for dealing with the industrial marketer rather than with its competitors as summarized in a *positioning* statement. That uniqueness can come from any of the individual elements of marketing strategy—market segmentation, product policy and strategy, pricing policy and strategy, distribution, or promotion. Market segmentation is usually a key element of the strategy of differentiation. Without a true uniqueness in some area, a true "reason for being," the industrial marketer is not likely to realize major success in the competitive marketplace.

SUMMARY

Marketing skill *per se* will be a major source of sustainable competitive advantage for industrial firms in the 1990's. Industrial marketing is pervasive in economic activity and differentiated from consumer marketing in several ways. Industrial products are defined to include construction, heavy equipment, light equipment, components and subassemblies, processed and raw materials, MRO supplies, and services. Industrial customers include manufacturers and processors, institutions, and government agencies at various levels. Industrial markets are characterized by derived demand, a concept that highlights the nature of buyer-seller interdependence in industrial markets and creates the need for careful analysis of the customer's customer. In addition to buyer-seller interdependence, the other elements of uniqueness in industrial marketing are functional interdependence, product complexity (a set of buyer-seller relationships), and buying process complexity. Effective industrial marketing strategy has been seen to require: (1) complete understanding of the customer and its needs, including the requirements of the customer's customer and competitive conditions in the customer's industry; (2) customer orientation at least as strong as the organization's technical orientation; (3) an appreciation of the sources of uniqueness in industrial marketing; (4) an honest assessment of the organization's strengths and weaknesses and a matching of these to customer needs; and (5) an integration of the components of marketing strategy to yield unique competitive advantage through significant differentiation.

Bibliography

Ames, B. Charles, "Trappings vs. Substance in Industrial Marketing," *Harvard Business Review,* **48,** 4 (July-August, 1970), 93–102.

Corey, E. Raymond, *Industrial Marketing: Cases and Concepts*, 3rd ed. (Englewood Cliffs, N.J.: Prentice-Hall, Inc., 1983).

Webster, Frederick E., Jr., "Management Science in Industrial Marketing," *Journal of Marketing*, **42**, 1 (January, 1976), 21–27.

————, "The Rediscovery of the Marketing Concept," *Business Horizons*, **31**, 3 (May-June, 1988), 29–39.

2 Industrial Procurement and Buying Behavior

The new strategic environment of business has had a major impact on the nature of industrial buying behavior and procurement strategy. Customers demand much more complete response to their needs from their vendors and in many instances place greater reliance for quality and delivery, as well as competitive prices, on a small number of suppliers. The nature of the relationship with vendors becomes a subject for strategic analysis and decision making: should the procurement be done as a single transaction, a long-term buyer-seller relationship, or a formal strategic alliance such as a joint venture? Sole-source procurements have become more common in such sophisticated buying arrangements as "just-in-time" and quick-entry production-planning and order-processing systems.

The major drivers in this strategic environment are global competition, cost reduction, concern for quality in its broadest, management-process sense, and the demands being placed on industrial customers by *their* customers. In the words of Wayne Hudgins, Staff Vice President, Marketing & Planning, McDonnell-Douglas Information Systems Group: "It's a whole new world out there, a whole new way of doing business requiring different kinds of commitments and relationships."[1]

In this chapter, we will consider the development of procurement strategy and the role of the procurement, or purchasing, function

[1] In a representation to the Marketing Science Institute Conference on Organizational Buying Behavior, Peachtree City, Georgia, March 9–11, 1988.

within the customer organization, and the nature of the organizational buying process. In the following chapter, we will continue the discussion with an examination of buyer-seller relationships, focusing on the challenges for the marketer in developing and managing such long-term relationships.

THE PROCUREMENT FUNCTION

Buying is the other side of the industrial marketing coin. Just as marketers are seeking customers, so buyers are seeking vendors. The procurement function is one of the critical links between an economic organization and its environment. A firm, government agency, or private institution is absolutely dependent upon suppliers of goods and services for its existence. Fortunately, there is usually more than sufficient competition among potential suppliers of goods and services to ensure that the buyer will always have vendors ready, willing, and able to meet its needs for goods and services. To maintain an adequate flow of goods and services into its operations, the buying firm, agency, or institution must develop a strategy for purchasing and an organization to implement that strategy and to manage the details of that procurement function.

PURCHASING OBJECTIVES

Purchasing objectives are commonly expressed as "buying the right items in the right quantity at the right price for delivery at the right time and place." This simple definition is useful for identifying the major dimensions of the buyer's problem: product specifications and quality; the amount to purchase; price, and delivery. Of course, the management problem is to define what is "right" for each dimension and to manage relationships with vendors in such a way that the desired results are in fact accomplished. The magnitude of the buying task is indicated by the portion of the typical firm's revenue that is expended for purchase of goods and services. One study, conducted several years ago, found that the 100 largest manufacturing firms in the United States spend an average of 52.3% of their sales dollar on purchases.[2]

[2] Cited in Lamar Lee, Jr., and Donald W. Dobler, *Purchasing and Materials Management* (New York: McGraw-Hill, Inc., 1965), p. 10.

The first objective of the procurement function must be to provide for the continuous operation of the organization by ensuring that the purchased goods and services are *available* when and where needed. A corollary of this prime objective is that vendor *reliability* is the most important criterion for evaluating vendors, in most instances. A close second in importance in purchasing objectives is product *quality*. Such quality must be consistent with specifications carefully developed in the purchase planning process. After availability and quality, *price* becomes important in the hierarchy of purchasing objectives. Small percentage improvements in the cost of purchased goods and services can have a major impact on a firm's profit and loss statement. On the other hand, it is possible for a firm to underspend, as well as overspend, and to fail to achieve the desired quality and availability as a result. Needless to say, a low price is meaningless if the product is not delivered when needed or if the quality is unacceptable. A fourth objective for purchasing management is to develop and receive the necessary *services* accompanying the purchase of goods—services such as technical support, applications assistance, repair, and maintenance. A fifth objective is to develop favorable long-term *vendor relationships* and new sources of supply, in order to guarantee the continued availability of goods and services on favorable terms and to make the organization attractive to do business with. These purchasing objectives can be summarized as follows:

1. Availability when and where needed.
2. Product quality consistent with specifications.
3. Lowest price consistent with availability and product quality.
4. Service to maximize the value of the product in use.
5. Good long-term vendor relations and source development.

This brief discussion of purchasing objectives focusses only on the essentials of the procurement function. In typical textbooks on purchasing management, two or three chapters are often devoted to each of these dimensions. In one such text, the opening discussion of purchasing objectives stated the following six objectives:

1. To support company operations with an uninterrupted flow of materials and services.
2. To buy competitively and wisely . . . keeping abreast of the forces of supply and demand that regulate prices and availability . . .

3. To keep inventory investment and inventory losses due to deterioration, obsolescence, and theft at a minimum.
4. To develop reliable alternate sources of supply . . .
5. To develop good, continuing vendor relationships . . .
6. To achieve maximum integration with other departments of the firm . . . [3]

It is difficult to overstate the importance of the procurement function to the efficiency, effectiveness, and survival of the organization.

THE MATERIALS MANAGEMENT CONCEPT

In some firms, the responsibility of the chief purchasing officer goes considerably beyond the procurement function *per se* to include all functions involving the flow of materials from purchase of raw materials through distribution of finished goods. Materials management includes purchasing, inventory control, traffic, receiving, and production control and has the objective of achieving the lowest overall cost of materials for the firm. There are obvious reasons why professional purchasing personnel want to expand their influence within the organization and to control more of the variables in the total materials system.

The materials management concept is a *systems* concept. It recognizes that each of the materials management functions is related to the others in a complex set of interactions. The principles of systems analysis can be summarized in simple terms, as follows:

1. All systems are composed of interdependent subsystems, and these subsystems interact in synergistic fashion—the whole is greater than the sum of the parts.
2. Attempting to maximize the performance of any subsystem can block optimization of the total system.
3. The objective of the system manager should be to optimize total system performance.

Thus, the materials management concept recognizes that focussing on purchasing objectives *per se* could in fact prevent the most effective management of the total materials flow. For example, inventory management costs (including costs of space, capital in-

3 *Ibid.*, pp. 11–12.

vestment, taxes, obsolescence, and deterioration) may be excessive, if the purchasing manager buys a large quantity of a given item in order to realize a favorably low price. The materials management concept recognizes that the purchasing manager's effectiveness depends on close cooperation with other parts of the organization, especially manufacturing, production control, and traffic.

Even in companies not organized along materials management lines, the materials management concept as a philosophy of procurement management is likely to be found to some degree, as purchasing managers attempt to maximize their effectiveness through close cooperation with other departments. This viewpoint has many benefits for the marketer whose product offers the greatest value in use, as opposed to the lowest initial purchase price. In many industrial marketing situations, the true value of the product to the *user* comes about through complex effects on the user's operations, for example by simplifying a step in the assembly process that increases the total flow of manufacturing and reduces labor cost per unit. Such benefits often are accompanied by a higher cost per unit of the purchased parts or materials and would not be attractive to a purchasing manager interested only in reducing the cost of purchases.

It should be noted, however, that the materials management concept does not apply with the same force when *services* are being purchased rather than goods. Indeed, the role of the purchasing department tends to be much less important in the purchase of services. Industrial purchase of services is an area requiring much greater research effort, since there are virtually no studies of this important aspect of industrial purchasing.

Intellectually, the materials management concept is a first cousin to the total distribution cost concept, a view of the firm's distribution cost structure that also emphasizes a systems view.[4] In the total distribution cost concept, distribution costs are defined to include transportation, order processing, cost of lost business, inventory carrying costs (space, capital, taxes, insurance, obsolescence, and deterioration), packaging and materials handling. The total distribution cost concept is relevant in the purchase of transportation services, packaging materials, and related physical distribution services.

[4] Paul Cherington, *The Role of Air Freight in Physical Distribution* (Boston: Graduate School of Business Administration, Harvard University, Division of Research, 1954).

DEVELOPING PROCUREMENT STRATEGY

The first step in planning a procurement strategy is to define the scope of the procurement, especially what is to be purchased. This may not be straightforward, as it requires considerable problem definition and analysis. For example, a malfunction in a manufacturing operation may be traced to a worn-out piece of equipment, or more precisely, a part on the equipment. The first step is to decide whether to repair or replace the part; alternatively, one can decide to replace the entire machine. Beyond that, if the machine is obsolete, it may be economically more sensible to redesign the entire system of which the machine is a part. That may call for retaining the services of a consulting engineer, forming a task force within the manufacturing operation, and consulting with many potential vendors of several different types of equipment and systems. A similar process would be required in the development of a new product and the design and configuration of the purchased components, including the question of whether to make the components internally or to buy them. Many design options would be defined by the availability of standard components from outside vendors, as illustrated by the large number of microcomputers based on the standard processors sold by the computer chip manufacturers.

Having defined the scope of the procurement, it is necessary to develop reasonably detailed specifications for the purchased item or service. Here again there is the choice of designing around standard available products or creating custom specifications. Considerable interaction is typically required among many functional specialists within the customer organization, including manufacturing, finance, engineering, and marketing personnel as well as procurement managers. One of the key strategic considerations in this analysis is the extent to which the firm is willing and able to commit to one or more outside vendors. Is it willing to work on a cost-plus basis with a single vendor to get the necessary product developed, or would it prefer an arm's-length relationship with multiple sources for a standard product? To what extent will it be willing to make long-term purchase commitments in return for a more favorable price and more reliable delivery? Thus scope of procurement involves decisions about both what is to be purchased and how.

A next step in the procurement planning process is to reason through the strategic roles to be played by the vendors and to develop a "sourcing system" in which multiple vendors may play clearly defined roles.[5] For example, a beverage company may want to have multiple sources for its cans and bottles. One vendor may be depended upon for the largest share of the purchases because it provides a superior combination of quality, reliable delivery, technical service, and competitive prices. A smaller vendor may be used primarily because of its technical expertise and ability to develop innovative solutions to specific packaging problems. A third vendor with large production volume and low cost may be used especially because of its low prices and its ability to keep price pressure on the other vendors. Such strategic roles for specific vendors and interactions among them are a key part of planning procurement strategies. The role played by pricing in the strategy, the objectives of vendor negotiations, and the desired type of relationship with vendors, will be derived directly from this planning. In today's competitive marketplace, often defined on a global basis, such careful definition of procurement or "sourcing" strategy is a vital consideration in the search for the combination of low cost and superior performance necessary for survival. The firm's procurement strategy may be the most important ingredient in its ability to deliver superior value to *its* customers.

THE BUYING DECISION PROCESS

Buying decisions do not just happen. They represent a complex set of activities engaged in by many members of the buying organization and result in a commitment to purchase goods and services from a vendor. Buying is not an event. It is an organizational decision-making process, the result of which is a contractual obligation. As part of that process, individual participants in the process must each arrive at their own conclusions and decisions with respect to the purchasing problem.

A purchasing problem arises when someone in the organization observes an opportunity to solve a problem by purchasing goods or services. There are many types of problems where purchasing is only one of several solutions. For example, inefficient office procedures might be due to weak supervisory practices, unskilled personnel, inadequate office space and layout, or ineffective company policies. None of these definitions represents a purchasing

[5] E. Raymond Corey, *Procurement Management: Strategy, Organization, and Decision Making* (Boston: CBI Publishing Co., Inc., 1978), pp. 34–39.

problem or a marketing opportunity. However, an aggressive and competent office equipment sales representative might work with an office manager to analyze the situation and to demonstrate that office efficiency can be improved sufficiently to justify the purchase of a system of office equipment, furniture, and accessories. In this event, the problem has become defined as a purchasing problem— one that can be solved by purchasing something.

Buying Decision Phases

One pathbreaking study of the purchasing decision process in industrial organizations defined eight phases in the process:

1. Need recognition.
2. Definition of the characteristics and quantity of item needed.
3. Development of the specifications to guide the procurement.
4. Search for and qualification of potential sources.
5. Acquisition and analysis of proposals.
6. Evaluation of proposals and selection of suppliers.
7. Selection of an order routine.
8. Performance feedback and evaluation.[6]

The value of this particular description of the organizational buying decision process is that it is based upon field research where these activities were observed as distinct phases in the purchasing process. For example, it was found that phase three, development of the specifications to guide the procurement, was a distinct step involving translating the defined need for purchased goods or services into a detailed and precise description of the desired characteristics for potential vendors. Also, this stage contains a specific opportunity for the industrial marketer to become involved in the procurement process in a way that gives it some competitive advantage, such as when the specifications are developed to include specific product features where a certain potential vendor has unique capability.

An analytical description of the buying decision process is potentially useful to the industrial marketer in developing a selling strategy, since it defines the target for its efforts, the steps through which it must respond to the buyer's needs for information. It is the

[6] P. J. Robinson, C. W. Faris, and Y. Wind, *Industrial Buying and Creative Marketing* (Boston: Allyn & Bacon, Inc., and the Marketing Science Institute, 1967), pp. 13–18.

sequence of activities that must be completed before a buying commitment is made by the purchasing organization and then, perhaps, reaffirmed through repeat purchases.

Types of Buying Situations

The buying decision process will be more or less complex, according to the importance and scope of the purchase being considered. As complexity increases, the amount of time required for the purchase decision and the number of persons involved tend to increase, as do the buying criteria of the purchasing organization and the amount of information required by the decision makers. The Robinson, Faris, and Wind study cited earlier found it useful to think of three distinct types of buying situations: the Straight Rebuy, the Modified Rebuy, and the New Task. These so-called "buyclasses" are similar to those found in Howard's and Sheth's description of buying decisions as Routinized Response Behavior, Limited Problem Solving, and Extensive Problem Solving.[7]

The description of each of the three types of industrial buying situations is relatively straightforward. The Straight Rebuy is the purchase of something purchased before, from the same vendor as before, although purchase terms may vary slightly. Such purchases can be computerized and handled in a completely routine fashion with the triggering mechanism set at a specified inventory level or a certain day of the month.

The Modified Rebuy is the purchase of something purchased before but includes the search for information about alternative sources of supply and terms. Thus, a company purchasing raw materials may systematically ask for bids from several vendors, or the buyer may telephone several potential vendors to seek information about their product offerings.

The New Task involves the purchase of something not purchased before, with all stages of the buying decision process involved, from need recognition through definition of the characteristics and quantity of the needed item, development of specifications, and so on. In these more complex decisions, the earlier stages of the buying process take on relatively greater importance, whereas the later stages receive more emphasis in Straight and Modified Rebuy situations. In the New Task, the buyer's previous experience has limited

[7] John A. Howard and Jagdish N. Sheth, *The Theory of Buyer Behavior* (New York: John Wiley & Sons, Inc., 1969), p. 27

relevance, and she must worry about her purchase goals, as well as defining potential sources of supply and developing criteria and information with which to evaluate alternative sources.

A more recent study by Anderson, Chu, and Weitz provided empirical support for the buyclass framework.[8] In a carefully controlled analysis, the researchers asked experienced field sales managers about their observations on the functioning of buying organizations, especially focussing on the relationships among newness, information needs, and the consideration of new alternatives as characteristics of different types of buying situations. They found a strong association of newness with the amount of information desired and processed by decision makers, but only a weak correlation of these two measures with the tendency for the buyer to consider new sources. Thus, they concluded that task newness and information needs, but not consideration of alternatives, define the buyclasses. They also found that sales forces that frequently encounter New Task buying situations observe the "buying center" (the collection of organizational actors involved in the purchase) to be:

- large
- slow to decide
- uncertain about its needs and the appropriateness of the possible solutions
- more concerned about finding a good solution than getting a low price or assured supply
- more willing to entertain proposals from "out" suppliers and less willing to favor "in" suppliers
- more influenced by technical personnel
- less influenced by purchasing agents

In contrast, the sales forces commonly facing more routine (Straight and Modified Rebuy) buying situations described buying centers with just the opposite characteristics:

- small
- quick to decide
- confident in their appraisal of the problem and possible solutions
- concerned about price and supply

[8] Erin Anderson, Wujin Chu, and Barton Weitz, "Industrial Purchasing: An Empirical Exploration of the Buyclass Framework," *Journal of Marketing*, **51**, 3 (July, 1987), 71–86.

- satisfied with "in" vendors
- more influenced by purchasing agents[9]

Thus, these researchers supported the earlier conclusion of Robinson, Faris, and Wind that the features of the buying situation are more important than the type of product in determining industrial buying behavior. Although other researchers have come to the opposite conclusion,[10] for most observers, including the sales managers who were respondents in the Anderson, Chu, and Weitz study, the buyclass framework has a good deal of face validity.

Procurement Situation Defined by Type of Pricing

Another way of thinking about types of buying situations describes three procurement strategies, which might be thought of best as end- and midpoints on a continuum, with particular emphasis placed on the role of price in the strategy.[11] This scheme also has a time dimension to it that parallels the "buyclasses" or New Buy–Modified Rebuy–Straight Rebuy framework just reviewed.

Cost-based procurement is used for developing and purchasing new equipment, construction, or, less frequently, services. It requires close working relationships with contractor-vendors. Its essential characteristic is that the vendor is paid for time and materials, plus overhead and profit, which are negotiated. The customer usually has direct access to the vendor's accounting data for all relevant costs and the ability to audit these data. For equipment purchases that will eventually become repetitive, price tends to become more fixed over time.

Market-based procurements are used for repetitive buying of such items as processed materials, components and subassemblies, and light equipment, where there are multiple vendors and products available that are more or less substitutable and able to perform the required function. As a result, there is sufficient competition among suppliers to establish a fairly narrow range of "market" prices for similar quality. Under these conditions, the buyer can use multiple sources, and availability may be managed by making long-term commitments that reward good vendor performance on delivery,

---

[9] *Ibid.*, p. 82.

[10] For example, Joseph A. Bellizzi and Phillip McVey, "How Valid is the Buygrid Model?," *Industrial Marketing and Management*, **12**, 2 (February, 1983), 57–62.

[11] E. Raymond Corey, *Industrial Marketing: Cases and Concepts*, 3rd ed. (Englewood Cliffs, N. J.: Prentice-Hall, Inc., 1983), pp. 69–74.

quality, and service. The buyer is likely to negotiate share of purchases (i.e., the percentage of total requirements to go to a particular supplier) rather than price. Development of new vendors may be one key objective in this strategy, as well as an important tactic for maintaining price pressure. It is typically found where both the buying and selling firms are fairly large enterprises.

Competitive bidding is a familiar form of procurement when tight product and performance specifications can be developed and there is a stable base of qualified vendors. Potential bidders are given a tightly drawn description of what is to be purchased, as well as desired quantities, delivery dates, and terms of sale, and asked to submit a price quotation, usually on a confidential basis (often in a sealed envelope). On the appointed date, the bids are opened and the order is awarded to the lowest bidder. A variation on sealed bidding is negotiated bidding, in which further negotiations about price, terms, and conditions are conducted with low bidders following the opening of sealed bids. Raw or semi-processed materials, food items, standard components, automobiles, microcomputers, and some forms of maintenance, financial, and data-processing services are examples of items that can be purchased by competitive bidding. The buyer uses the large volume of purchases to achieve favorable prices, often in the form of discounts from established list prices.

Types of Buying Relationships

Yet another way of characterizing purchase situations looks at the nature of the relationship between the buyer and the seller, once again with time as an important dimension, from extremely short-term to very long-term orientation (See Figure 2-1). Here also the concept is one of a continuum, where we describe the end- and midpoints. As buying relationships move along this continuum from pure transactions through increased buyer-seller interdependence to a true strategic alliance, there are three things to observe. First, note that the movement is from complete reliance on market forces in pure transactions, to achieve lower prices and to minimize cost, to the virtual absence of market forces in strategic alliances. Second, note that the buyer is incurring additional administrative costs and increased dependency in return for a set of benefits relating to quality, reliability, and service. Third, it is interesting to consider that the movement is away from pure "buy" toward the decision to

Transactions ———————→ **Relationships** ———————→ **Strategic Alliances**

Very short term		Very long term
Market control		Bureaucratic control
Independence	Interdependence	Total dependence
Clerical task		Top management position
"Buy"		"Make"

Figure 2-1. The continuum of industrial buying situations.

"make" the product or service within the customer organization itself.

At one extreme, there are pure *transactions*. In this type of procurement, the buying is strictly a "one-shot deal." It may be found for repetitive purchases of highly standardized ("fungible") products that are perfect substitutes for one another. There is virtually no risk for the buyer in terms of product performance or quality and no investment or other costs associated with switching from one vendor to another. Price is the only consideration and the buyer shops for the lowest price, probably using competitive bidding in a routine rebuy. The relationship between buyer and seller is purely adversarial in the sense that one wants the lowest price possible and the other the highest. Within a concept of relationship marketing, what this endpoint defines is the *absence* of a relationship, a fact that may be very important strategically for the actors to note. The assumption is that the seller and the buyer incur no obligation to one another beyond delivering and paying for product that meets the specification, with no precedent or subsequent conditions.[12]

A moment's thought will reveal that there is probably no such thing as a pure transaction, although the concept of a pure transaction is important as a reference point. Real issues arise if one of the parties expects the procurement to lead to a long-term relationship, while the other is operating close to pure transaction mode. The party with the transaction orientation is intent on minimizing the costs associated with this particular procurement, while the one who is thinking in relationship terms is making investments with no

[12] Barbara B. Jackson, *Winning and Keeping Industrial Customers* (Lexington, Mass.: Lexington Books, 1985).

potential for future payoff. Such a relationship will be clearly unstable and both participants will be dissatisfied.

Moving away from pure transactions, one encounters a range of more or less long-term *relationships* between buyers and sellers, moving from a purely adversarial encounter to a strong partnership. In relationship procurements and marketing, each party is aware of their mutual dependence and strives to maximize long-term benefits such as better quality, reliable delivery, and lower total costs. The products or services involved are likely to be quite complex, often developed and tailored, with engineering and other forms of customer service, to meet the needs of the particular buyer. Price is an important consideration, but not as important as product quality, availability, and other dimensions of service. Each party makes investments in developing and maintaining the buyer-seller relationship and there will be costs to both parties if the relationship is terminated.

Relationship marketing is clearly the most common form of procurement situation found in industrial markets. It typically is found in markets where there are several competitors and substantial competition on both price and non-price dimensions. Examples would include mainframe computers, group insurance, industrial chemicals such as fluid cracking catalysts, and trucking services. The customer may rely upon different vendors, changing the portions allocated to each over time according to the record of performance and price. So-called "sole-source" procurements are the extreme case of long-term buyer-seller relationships, in which the customer agrees to purchase its total requirement from a single supplier for a stated time period. In all relationship marketing, the procurement is likely to be of major importance strategically to the customer and the customer is likely be strategically important to the supplier. The relationships must be administered carefully, calling for investments in contracts and procedures to deal with both routine and non-routine aspects of the relationship. Clearly, however, both parties have the ability to terminate the relationship and there will be options available in the competitive marketplace, insuring some degree of control of the relationship by market forces, as well as by bureaucratic and administrative rules, policies, and agreements.

At the far end of the continuum, there are *strategic alliances* that are the most complex and enduring form of buyer-seller relationship, involving virtually total dependence of the customer on the vendor for the procured items. It may require the formation of an entirely new business entity, often in the form of a joint venture. It would typically involve a product or service that was new to both parties. A sole-source procurement would become a strategic alliance if both parties entered into and managed the commitment on a strategic basis, with long-term, contractual commitments. Even more extreme would be the case where the customer bought the vendor, completely incorporating its operations, with the result that there was no longer a buyer-seller relationship but an internal relationship governed by bureaucratic, not market, controls.

Among the characteristics of these long-term buyer-seller relationships are earlier involvement in product design, more sharing of strategic information, and direct linking of manufacturing operations through just-in-time delivery schedules, automatic order entry, electronic data interchange, and relationships across multiple levels of the organization, including top management involvement. The quality management programs of both organizations must be carefully integrated. There are large costs associated with these most complex buyer-seller relationships, which must be offset by improvement in product quality, lower product costs, improved reliability, and superior service. As buying organizations consider their strategic options, it is important to consider whether potential vendors actually have the capability to enter into long-term buyer-seller relationships. The options, rather than a long-term buying-selling relationship, may be either more reliance on market control or substantial investment, requiring a true strategic alliance, in order to enhance limited vendor skills and resources.

In Chapter 3, we will continue to analyze the development and management of buyer-seller relationships.

MODELS OF ORGANIZATIONAL BUYER BEHAVIOR

Several scholar-authors have developed conceptual models of the buying decision process in complex economic organizations. These models offer valuable insights into the buying decision process and are useful to the industrial marketing strategist by describing that process in analytical and conceptual terms. Like all models, those describing the organizational buying decision process are simplifications of the true process but gain their strength and relevance by focussing on the most important variables and relationships among them.

The Sheth Model

Professor Sheth, co-author of the Howard-Sheth model of buyer behavior, has adapted the model to the special case of the industrial buyer.[13] The model has a psychological emphasis, focussing on the mental states and decision processes of individual participants in the buying process. Among the key concepts in this model, summarized graphically in Figure 2-2, are buyers' expectations, perceptions, role orientations, life styles, and perceived risk. Organizational variables are summarized in three constructs: orientation, size, and degree of

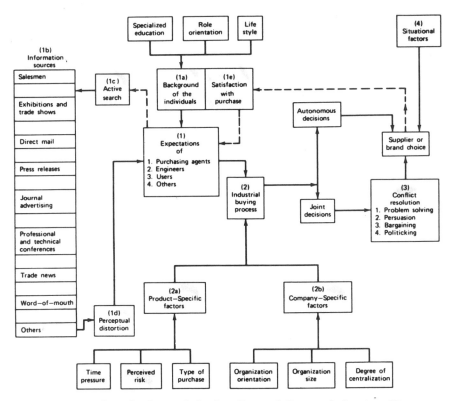

Figure 2-2. The Sheth model of industrial buyer behavior. [Source: *Jagdish N. Sheth, "A Model of Industrial Buyer Behavior," Journal of Marketing, 37, 4 (October, 1973), 50–56, at 51.] Reproduced with permission of the American Marketing Association.*

[13] Jagdish N. Sheth, "A Model of Industrial Buyer Behavior," *Journal of Marketing*, **37**, 4 (October, 1973), 50–56.

centralization. The Sheth model is specifically concerned with joint decision making involving two or more individuals. However, the Howard-Sheth model is specifically a model of individual behavior.

It is a well-known fact, documented by countless studies of industrial buying behavior, that many individuals, in addition to the purchasing agent, are involved in the organizational buying decision process. It is essential that the marketing strategist understand the differences among these participants in the buying process. The Sheth model shows that differences among buyers' expectations are caused by: (1a) the background of the individuals; (1b) their information sources; (1c) active search; (1d) perceptual distortion; and (1e) satisfaction with past purchases.

Background variables include education, organizational role, and life style. Expectations are defined specifically as the individuals' perceptions of the extent to which each vendor or brand can satisfy the individuals' needs and purchasing objectives. Within this framework, it is possible to understand why many research studies have shown that different participants use different buying criteria and rate alternative vendors differently. For example, production personnel are likely to emphasize delivery time and reliability. Engineering personnel are likely to focus on product quality variables, and purchasing personnel are likely to emphasize reliability and price. In the Sheth model, those different expectations and buying criteria lead to conflict among the decision participants, calling for conflict resolution processes, (3) in the model in Figure 2-2.

Industrial market researchers can conduct studies of the buying process aimed at identifying buying expectations and criteria among various decision participants, once these participants have been identified. As Sheth points out, variable (1d), perceptual distortion (the extent to which each participant modifies information to make it consistent with his existing beliefs and previous experience), is the hardest to measure using traditional survey research methods, but more sophisticated techniques, such as perceptual mapping using multidimensional scaling or factor analysis, are available for this purpose.

The Sheth model distinguishes between autonomous decisions, where the buying decision is delegated to a single individual, and joint decisions made collectively by the participants in the decision process. Six situational variables are said to determine whether the decision is autonomous or joint: (2a) product-specific factors, including time pressure, perceived risk, and type of purchase, and (2b) company-specific variables, including size, orientation, and degree of centralization.

The perceived risk variable is of special significance in understanding industrial buying behavior. The original concept was developed by Bauer[14] and first applied to industrial buying decisions by Levitt.[15] Perceived risk is a function of the buyer's level of uncertainty and the seriousness of the consequences associated with various decision outcomes. There are two types of risk—product performance risk associated with the extent to which the product meets the buyer's expectations with respect to actual performance, and psychosocial risk having to do with the way other relevant persons react to the decision, as well as how the buyer himself feels about the outcome. The greater the uncertainty and the more significant the consequences, the higher the degree of perceived risk. Buyers can adopt several tactics for reducing perceived risk, including gathering information, avoiding a decision, passing responsibility on to other decision participants, minimizing the investment of time and money in the decision, or simply reducing goals.

In the Sheth model, low risk decisions are likely to be made autonomously, as are those where time pressures are severe and where the decision is routine and repetitive. Autonomous decision making may also be found where there is one powerful group within the organization, say an engineering group that dominates decision making. The larger the organization and the higher the degree of decentralization, the more likely there will be joint decision making, other things being equal, according to the Sheth model.

In joint decision making, the individual participants gather information, deliberate on it, and engage in a conflict-resolving joint decision making process. Two kinds of rational conflict resolution are posited by Sheth, *problem-solving* in which the key process is information acquisition and deliberation, and *persuasion* in which an attempt is made to influence the opinions of dissenting members by asking them to reduce the importance of the criteria they are using in favor of better overall achievement of organizational objectives. In other words, persuasion is seen as necessary when there is disagreement about relevant criteria rather than about the informa-

[14] Raymond A. Bauer, "Consumer Behavior as Risk Taking," in R. L. Hancock (ed.), *Dynamic Marketing for a Changing World* (Chicago: American Marketing Association, 1960), pp. 389–400.
[15] Theodore Levitt, *Industrial Purchasing Behavior* (Boston: Division of Research, Graduate School of Business Administration, Harvard University, 1965).

tion available with which to evaluate alternatives. Sheth points out that both methods of conflict resolution fit the criterion of rationality. Problem-solving and persuasion are both useful when there is agreement about goals. When there is no such agreement, then *bargaining* must take place. Finally, there can be conflict about the style of decision making, including concern for who is involved in the process and what their relative influence should be. Sheth says that this kind of conflict is resolved by *politicking* and interpersonal tactics. An early study by Strauss defined several tactics used by purchasing agents to extend their influence in the organization, including rule-oriented tactics, rule-evading tactics, personal-polit-ical tactics, educational tactics, and organizational-interactional tactics. The latter involves changing patterns of information flow and interaction within the organization, including organization structure and reporting relationships.[16]

Finally, situational variables in the Sheth model include a variety of factors beyond the individual actors and the organizational charac-teristics and joint decision making process that influence the out-come of the buying decision process, often in an unexpected or unpredictable fashion. Among the situational variables influencing industrial buying behavior are economic conditions, labor disputes, mergers and acquisitions, and the like. Situational variables can be so varied and broad in their influence that the model makes no attempt to explain their impact on the buying process.

The Webster and Wind Model

A somewhat more comprehensive model of the organizational buy-ing decision making process has been developed by Webster and Wind.[17] According to their view, a *buying situation* is created when some member of the organization perceives a problem that can be solved through purchasing action. In response to a buying situation, a *buying center* is created by the organization consisting of those members of the organization who will be involved in the buying decision process. According to the Webster and Wind model, the buying center consists of five *buying roles*: users, deciders, influ-

[16] George Strauss, "Tactics of Lateral Relationship," *Administrative Science Quar-terly,* 7 (September, 1962), 161–86.
[17] F. E. Webster, Jr., and Y. Wind, *Organizational Buying Behavior* (Englewood Cliffs, N.J.: Prentice-Hall, Inc., 1972); for a brief description of the model, see Webster and Wind, "A General Model of Organizational Buying Behavior," *Jour-nal of Marketing,* **36,** 2 (April, 1972), 12–19.

encers, buyers, and gatekeepers. The gatekeepers control the flow of information into the buying center, a role usually occupied by the purchasing agent. Influencers add information or decision criteria to the decision process. Users actually use the product. Deciders select the vendor or brand of product. Buyers execute the contractual arrangements.

Bonoma has expanded the Webster and Wind description of the buying center by adding a sixth buying role, that of *initiator* of the purchase process, the person who is responsible for the definition of the buying situation. While this buying role is implied by the Webster and Wind definition of a buying situation, Bonoma is correct in making it a specific and distinct buying role.[18]

One individual may occupy several roles. The purchasing agent might be an influencer, the buyer, and the gatekeeper, for example, and several individuals might occupy one role, such as influencer. Each member of the buying center is likely to have unique expectations, perceptions, and objectives, as a function of his role in the organization, his background, and the nature of his responsibilities. Developing a sales strategy for an industrial account begins with identification and analysis of the buying center.

The Webster and Wind model specifically considers four sets of variables—environmental, organizational, interpersonal (the buying center), and individual. The relationships among these variables are summarized in Figure 2-3.

Environmental Influences

Environmental variables include political, legal, cultural, technological, economic, and physical environment variables. The influence of these variables is exercised by social and economic institutions, such as governments and labor unions, as well as supplier and competitor organizations. Environmental variables produce information, values and norms, and general business conditions, as well as goods and services. The pervasive influence of environmental variables makes them somewhat hard to identify in any specific situation, but their importance can be readily grasped by recalling, for example, the influence on industrial purchasing plans of economic boycotts in response to international political conflicts. Another illustration is provided by continuing concern for the effects of inflation in the major industrial nations. Now, marketers are trying

[18] Thomas V. Bonoma, "Major Sales: Who *Really* Does the Buying?," *Harvard Business Review*, **60** (May-June, 1982), 111–19.

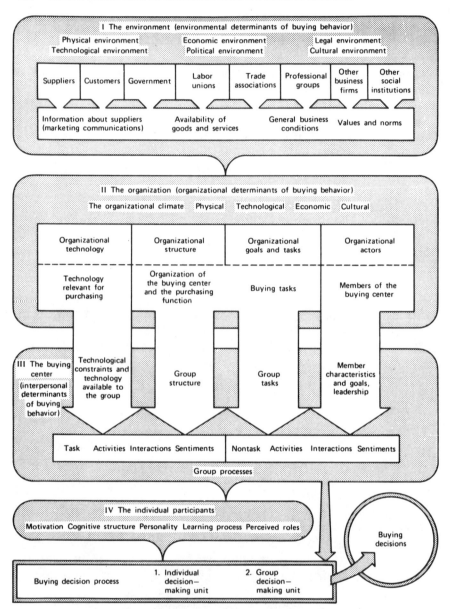

Figure 2-3. A general model of organizational buying behavior. [Source: *F. E. Webster, Jr. and Y. Wind, "A General Model of Organizational Buying Behavior," Journal of Marketing, 36, 2 (April, 1972), 12–19.] Reproduced with permission of the American Marketing Association.*

to assess the likely impact of the consolidation of the European Economic Community in 1992, and the elimination of most European trade barriers, on global markets. These environmental forces shape the direction of markets as well as the buying plans and decisions of individual organizations.

Organizational Variables

Organizational variables are given special prominence in the Webster and Wind model and represent one of the important distinctions from the Sheth model. The Webster and Wind formulation defines four sets of organizational variables—technology, structure, goals and tasks, and actors, using a scheme developed by Leavitt.[19] A subset of each of these four sets of variables is relevant to a particular buying situation, with specific influence in terms of the composition and functioning of the buying center. A major dimension of the organization for analysis of the buying decision process has to do with the relative degree of centralization-decentralization in the purchasing function. Centralization within the buying center influences the buyer's job in at least five ways: by defining his geographical location; by establishing authority relationships between buyers and higher level purchasing executives; by determining the formal nature of communication between buyers and users, and by influencing the informal relationships between buyers and users. An important concept here concerns the individual's "loyalty domain," his sentiments and loyalties to other members of the buying organization. This is one aspect of the degree of centralization-decentralization within the buying organization.

The four organizational subsystems (technology, structure, tasks, and people) interact with one another to determine organizational functioning and define for individuals within the buying center the information expectations, goals, attitudes, and assumptions used in their decision making. Buying tasks can be described in terms of the eight-phase buying decision process presented earlier, and can be further categorized in four dimensions: the organizational purpose served; the nature of demand (seasonality, whether derived from demand for the buyer's products or generated strictly by forces within the organization, etc.); the extent of programming or routinization in the decision process; and the degree of decentralization

---

[19] Harold J. Leavitt, "Applied Organization Change in Industry: Structural, Technical, and Human Approaches," in William W. Cooper, Harold J. Leavitt, and Maynard W. Shelley, II, *New Perspectives in Organization Research* (New York: John Wiley & Sons, Inc., 1964), pp. 55–71.

of buying authority within the organization for this kind of buying problem.

Organization structure is further divided into five subsystems of communication, authority, status, rewards, and work flow, and each subsystem is examined within the Webster and Wind model for its influence on the buying decision process. The marketer must understand the functioning of each subsystem in the specific buying situations that he is trying to influence. For example, the communication subsystem performs four essential functions—information, command and instruction, influence and persuasion, and integration—which must be examined by the sales strategist for their influence on individual members of the buying center and as determinants of the group decision-making process. The authority subsystem defines the power of the organizational actors in the buying decision process in terms of their ability to judge, command, or otherwise act to influence the behavior of other members. The status system assigns persons to buying roles and defines behavior appropriate both in and toward those roles. The rewards system defines payoffs to the individuals for certain behaviors and decision outcomes and, most importantly, interacts with the authority subsystem to determine the responsibilities of actors for evaluating and rewarding other actors. A key question in developing marketing strategy is how the reward and authority systems of the buying organization might interact to determine rewards and punishments to organizational actors for taking the degree of risk implicit in a buying decision. It is often the case that the penalties for being wrong are perceived by organizational actors as greater than the rewards for being right. Finally, the workflow for the organization must be understood as it relates to purchasing procedures and decision-making processes.

Social Influences: The Buying Center
In the Webster and Wind model, the functioning of the buying center is analyzed in terms of models and constructs of interpersonal (social) interaction. The role set of each of the individual participants, which includes role expectations, role behavior, and role relationships, is examined in detail. The nature of group functioning is influenced by individual members' goals and personal characteristics, by the nature of leadership within the group, by group structure and tasks, and by external influences, including both organizational and environmental variables. Group processes involve activities, sentiments, and interactions which relate not only to the

buying task itself, but also, more generally, to nontask dimensions of group functioning as well. Thus, the output of the group decision-making process is not only a solution to the buying problem but also non-task satisfactions and growth for the group and its members.

There are many interesting theoretical and practical issues having to do with the structure and functioning of buying centers. It is generally believed that buying centers become larger and more complex, involving more levels and functions within the organization, as the amounts of uncertainty, novelty, complexity, importance, and investment in the buying situation increase. As buying center complexity increases, buying decisions take longer. Johnston and Bonoma quantified some of the dimensions of buying center structure and interaction, as follows:[20]

Vertical Involvement—the number of organizational levels exerting influence and communicating within the buying center

Lateral Involvement—the number of separate functions, departments, and divisions involved in the purchase decision

Extensivity—the number of individuals involved in the communication network

Connectedness—the number of two-person ("dyadic") interactions among the buying center participants as a percentage of the total possible connections $[n(n - 1)/2]$

Centrality—of the purchasing manager in the buying communication network, defined as total purchase communications sent and received, weighted by the total number of buying center participants

Using these measures, the researchers examined buying centers in 31 companies that had purchased capital equipment and industrial services. They looked at the influence of both organizational structure variables (size, complexity, formalization, and centralization) and purchase situation attributes (importance, complexity, newness, and buyclass) on the structure and interaction patterns of the buying center. While it is not possible to present their detailed findings here (involving 50 separate relationships among the variables examined), an overview of their conclusions is interesting because they confirm the validity and usefulness of the buying center concept.

[20] Wesley J. Johnston and Thomas V. Bonoma, "The Buying Center: Structure and Interaction Patterns," *Journal of Marketing*, **45**, 2 (Summer, 1981), 143–156.

Johnston and Bonoma found that the more formalized the organization, the more extensive the buying center and the higher the degree of lateral involvement. Extensivity and lateral involvement were also positively influenced by buyclass, importance, and complexity in the buying situation. Buying centers for services were "less extensive," i.e., smaller, than those for capital equipment and had less vertical involvement. Vertical involvement was most influenced by purchase situation attributes, especially complexity and importance. Connectedness was influenced by organizational characteristics, especially formalization and centralization, which had the expected positive impact, but not by purchase situation attributes. These results are all in the direction expected based on the concept of the buying center, with the possible exception of the distinction between the findings for capital equipment and those for services, and provide sound support for it.

In another study involving the structure of the buying center, McCabe found that high levels of uncertainty lead to a narrowing of the structure of the buying center.[21] This finding is counter to the common argument that complexity leads to larger buying centers with more lateral and vertical involvement as found by Johnston and Bonoma. McCabe did find that the amount of participation (extensivity) and lateral involvement increased as complexity increased, even though there was also a tendency to centralize buying authority at higher levels of the organization (i.e., less vertical involvement). McCabe's findings agree with those of Corey[22] and Cardozo,[23] who both have argued that centralization of authority accompanies increased purchase uncertainty. McCabe noted that Cardozo, Corey, and others who took this viewpoint defined uncertainty in terms of the product attributes like differentiation, amount of investment, and impact on profits. Others, the so-called "contingency theorists," focussed on the nature of the decision process including decision-making methods, availability of information, and the ability to evaluate outcomes. McCabe looked at 68 buying centers in a sample of 17 domestic airlines and 17 corrugated container manufacturers, focussing on the source selection decision rather than the overall process. He found that, across the board,

[21] Donald L. McCabe, "Buying Group Structure: Constriction at the Top," *Journal of Marketing*, **51**, 4 (October, 1987), 89–98.
[22] E. Raymond Corey, *The Organizational Context of Industrial Buying Behavior*, (Cambridge, Mass.: The Marketing Science Institute, 1978).
[23] Richard N. Cardozo, "Situational Segmentation of Industrial Markets," *European Journal of Marketing*, **14** (June, 1980), 264–276.

higher levels of uncertainty, for both the buying task and product complexity, were associated with higher levels of centralization of buying authority. In general, decisions believed to involve more uncertainty were made by higher level personnel. This finding is counter to a widespread belief that more uncertainty leads to decentralization of buying decision-making authority. McCabe himself noted that he had looked only at the source selection decision, not other phases of the buying decision process, and that while his results are statistically significant, the amount of variation explained in the statistical analysis was only between 4 and 30 percent. The key point in these results is the confirmation of the fact that the structure of the buying center, specifically the level of the key decision influencer, is influenced significantly by the complexity of the buying task and uncertainty about product attributes. Once again, this research underscores the usefulness of the buying center concept in analyzing industrial buying situations and planning marketing strategy.

Individual Behavior

Webster and Wind assert that in the final analysis, however, all organizational buying behavior is *individual* behavior in an organizational and interactional setting. Only individuals can define problems, decide, and act. Furthermore, it follows that all buying behavior is motivated by individual needs and desires, guided by individual perceptions and learning, in complex interaction with organizational goals. Individuals join organizations for the rewards that are available through the organization for the accomplishment of organizational goals and tasks. As a result there is important interaction between individual needs and the individual's perception of how his performance and participation in the buying decision process will be evaluated and rewarded. It follows that individual decision makers must be the target for marketing effort, not the abstract organization.

Individual decision making takes place within the interactional and organizational context and eventually merges into a group decision making process consisting of discussion, bargaining, negotiation, and other forms of persuasion. The Webster and Wind model does not elaborate on these decision processes in any significant way.

The major strengths and weaknesses of the Webster and Wind model are due to its generality. The model is comprehensive and identifies many key variables for consideration by the marketing strategist and provides an analytical framework for thinking about their interaction. But the model is weak on assertions about the specific influence of these variables. One of the major benefits of the model is that, since its introduction several years ago, it has stimulated much high quality research and has provided an integrated framework for interpreting results and relating them to one another in such a way that a reasonably lively body of knowledge about industrial buying behavior has been developing as a result.[24]

The Sheth and Webster and Wind models are both general and comprehensive models. There are, of course, many models of a more specific nature looking at such parts of the total process as the nature of buyer-salesman interaction, the composition of the buying center, decision criteria used by various decision influencers, and so forth.

The Anderson and Chambers Reward/Measurement Model

It is a central assertion of the Webster and Wind model that a key to understanding the functioning of the buying center is to know how the measurement and reward systems of the organization affect the behavior of its members. Anderson and Chambers have developed a model of buying center participants' motivation and decision involvement that extends this central idea more precisely.[25] Using expectancy theory, which sees motivational force as a function of the person's expectations about how behavior and outcomes associated with it will be rewarded or punished, they construct a two-part model. In the motivational component of the model, individuals' job motivation and satisfaction are determined by both "intrinsic" and "extrinsic" rewards, the former being those one grants to oneself while the latter are determined by the performance measurement system of the organization. Intrinsic rewards flow directly from the nature of the work itself and are important in satisfying "higher order" individual needs such as the need for self-esteem and self-actualization. Examples would include the sense of accomplishment

[24] A comprehensive review of the whole field of industrial buying behavior research is provided by Rowland T. Moriarty, *Industrial Buying Behavior*, (Lexington, Mass.: Lexington Books, 1983).

[25] Paul F. Anderson and Terry M. Chambers, "A Reward/Measurement Model of Organizational Buying Behavior," *Journal of Marketing*, 49 (Spring, 1985), 7–23.

in completing a difficult task like developing a set of technical specifications, or the satisfaction of "winning" a negotiation.

In the Anderson and Chambers "reward/measurement" model, a key role is played by the organizational performance measurement system, in which specific performance indexes identify specific behaviors and outcomes that the organization will attend to when evaluating performance. A key issue is the extent to which such indexes are consistent with the person's view of how the job should be performed, whether all aspects of job performance are captured by the indexes, and the amount of error in the respective measurements. To understand industrial buying behavior, the marketer must identify and analyze the functioning of the performance measurement and reward systems and how they are perceived by the individual participants in the buying process.

A key issue relating to the actual functioning of the buying center and the buying decision process resides in the fact that different individuals, especially if they come from different functions and departments within the organization, will be evaluated and rewarded by different performance indexes. This can be a major source of conflict within the buying center, as the participants will be using different criteria in evaluating product offerings and vendors. The second part of the Anderson and Chambers scheme is a "group consensus" model that traces individuals' "advocacy positions" regarding a vendor's offering back to the rewards and measurements offered by their primary work group (i.e., department or function). Participants bring these predispositions into the group interaction and consensus formation process, which may take several forms, along the lines of the Sheth model described earlier.

Another way of conceptualizing the group decision process has been proposed by Choffray and Lilien.

The Choffray and Lilien Model

Choffray and Lilien have also examined the buying center with research into the nature of the process by which individual firms decide to buy new products. While new product adoption is a special case of research in industrial buying, and will be considered in greater detail in Chapter 6, this research is cited here because it is concerned specifically with the nature of the group decision making process, an area not addressed well by the Webster and Wind model, which it extends by introducing a decision-process mechanism.

In the basic model developed by Choffray and Lilien[26] environ-mental and organizational factors are seen as constraints defining a feasible set of product alternatives among which individuals can make choices based on personal preferences. Individual preferences are totaled in the buying center (through processes of negotiation and group problem solving) to produce organizational choices. Choffray and Lilien develop four different models of the multiper-son decision making that produces these organizational choices: a weighted probability model (where weights reflect an individual's power in the buying center); a proportionality model (where all members have equal weight); a unanimity model (where the process keeps going until all members of the buying center agree); and an acceptability model (where the choice is the one least disturbing to individual members' preferences). To make the model operational, standard marketing research techniques can be used to gather data on the preferences of persons occupying particular roles in the buying center—engineers, purchasing managers, production man-agers, and the like. Buying organizations can then be assigned to "microsegments" that have firms with similar buying center compo-sitions. The relative importance of each buying role within these microsegments is assessed empirically or judgmentally. The market-ing manager using this model must specify which model of the multiperson choice process best describes the companies in each microsegment.

This methodology was applied to the specific case of the industrial adoption of solar air conditioning.[27] This study examined how mem-bers of the buying center differed in their perceptions of available product alternatives, how groups of decision participants (i.e., those occupying similar buying roles) differed in their evaluation criteria, and how these criteria influenced actual preferences. Sophisticated research methodology was used to measure participants' percep-tions of product attributes and to assess the differences among the perceptions of various groups. The existence of substantial percep-tual differences was confirmed. Analysis of these differences re-vealed several interesting conclusions, among them that groups with more decision responsibility used more decision criteria and

[26] Jean-Marie Choffray and Gary L. Lilien, "Assessing Response to Industrial Marketing Strategy," *Journal of Marketing*, **42**, 2 (April, 1978), 20–31.
[27] Jean-Marie Choffray and Gary L. Lilien, "Industrial Adoption of Solar Air Conditioning: Measurement Problems, Solutions, and Marketing Implications," unpublished working paper 894–76, Sloan School of Management, M.I.T., June, 1976.

different criteria than those groups with less responsibility. For example, corporate engineers were found to place the most importance on reliability and initial cost, but plant managers felt modernness, fuel savings, and low operating costs were most significant. Another interesting observation was that assumptions appropriate in analyzing consumer preference data (e.g., that consumers use homogeneous evaluation criteria but have different preference parameters) may be inappropriate in analyzing industrial buyers' preferences.

These findings have clear implications for product design decisions and for promotional strategy. For example, they can help management decide on the trade-offs among various product parameters and to design advertising and selling strategies that would be responsive to the information needs of various decision influencers. More important, however, these findings contribute significantly to the development of a methodology for measuring and analyzing industrial buyer preferences and using these data for new product development and marketing communication. This methodology is clearly more appropriate to the complexity of the industrial buying process than any borrowed from consumer marketing.

The models of industrial buying behavior that we have been examining share two serious flaws. First, they assume that the buying center and the buying process exist within the boundaries of a single organization. In fact, the buying center can often include participants from outside the organization such as consultants, government officials, bankers, landlords, or agents. An obvious example would be a buying situation in which the target customer is purchasing products or services to be used in the production of a new product being developed in coalition with another firm. Most construction projects, many capital equipment purchases, and materials that must be disposed of after use would define buying centers with participants outside of the customer organization with significant ability to influence the buying decision as gatekeepers and influencers, placing both information and constraints in the process.

Perhaps more serious as a shortcoming of these models is the fact that they look at buying as a process that occurs without direct input from selling and marketing organizations. Our earlier discussion of buyer-seller relationships indicates the necessity of seeing buying as the result of a process incorporating the selling firm in the decision process of the buying firm in all but the simplest transactions and purely routine buying actions. To what extent, and how, are representatives of the selling organization involved in the buying decision? How can they shape and influence the process to their advantage? Can they influence the scope of the procurement, buying criteria, and the assessment of alternatives?

Some of the most recent attempts to model the organizational buying process are built around the fundamental concept of dyadic (i.e., two-person) interaction between representatives of buying and selling organizations. Even in transactions-oriented marketing with little concern for developing long-run relationships, there is likely to be a multi-person buying center whose members interact not only with the sales representative but also with other members of the selling organization. The exception might be a Straight Rebuy using sealed bidding, but even then there is likely to be some communication between members of the buying and selling organizations. In all other types of buying situations, a model of buyer-seller interaction would seem to be the most realistic view of the organizational buying process.

A first conceptual step in linking the buying and the selling organizations is to think about the role of the sales representative in the communication network of the buying center. The sales representative is an active participant, not just an outsider looking in. At the minimum, the rep is talking with one person, such as a purchasing agent, whose communications with the other members of the buying center are influenced by that input. More likely, the rep has contacts with several members of the buying center, as do other representatives of the selling firm. Each of these two-person interactions has its own antecedents, activities, process, and outcomes that become part of the organizational buying process.

An initial effort at modelling the interaction has been offered by Krapfel,[28] who proposed that members of the buying center who interact with representatives of the selling organization should be perceived as potential advocates for the seller, with the potential to persuade other buying center members of the efficacy of the vendor's offering. Krapfel did not directly model the interaction of the sales representatives with members of the buying center.

Elsewhere, I have developed a model of buyer-seller interaction that emphasizes the role of the field sales representative as a relationship manager. This model, shown in Figure 2-4, summarizes the Webster and Wind model of organizational buying behavior on the

[28] Robert E. Krapfel, Jr., "An Advocacy Behavior Model of Organizational Buyers' Vendor Choice," *Journal of Marketing*, **49** (Fall, 1985), 51–59.

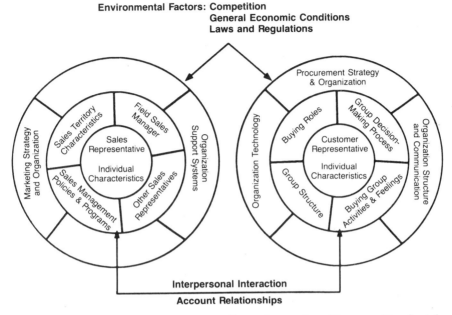

Figure 2-4. A model of the buyer-seller relationship. [Source: *Frederick E. Webster, Jr.,* Field Sales Management, *(New York: John Wiley & Sons, Inc., 1983), p. 230.*] *Reproduced with permission.*

left, depicts the selling organization and the influence of the sales representative on the right, and puts the rep in the center as a key player in three simultaneous *communication* processes: within the selling firm, within the buying organization, and between the two. In Chapter 9, we will explore the implications of this model for the role of the sales rep and the management of the field sales force.

We will continue our discussion of buyer-seller relationships in Chapter 3.

PURCHASING MANAGEMENT ACTIVITIES AND BUYING STRATEGY

While many parts of the buying organization are involved in the buying decision process, that process is usually managed and overseen by professional purchasing personnel in a purchasing department. Within this part of the organization, a number of specific activities and analyses are undertaken that should be understood by the industrial marketer. Strategic planning is as important for the buyer as it is for the seller. Some of these will be examined now and others will be discussed in the next chapter under the heading of buyer-seller relations.

Value Analysis

Value analysis involves analyzing a purchased product in terms of the function that it performs and the economic value of that function, as well as alternative methods of accomplishing the same function. The objective of value analysis is to reduce costs while maintaining the necessary levels of availability and product reliability. In other words, the objective of value analysis is to define "the best buy." Value analysis consists of both design analysis and price analysis.

Value analysis begins by looking at the design of the product in relation to the function it performs. Depending upon the type of item under consideration, this analysis could be performed by members of the purchasing staff, or it might require much more detailed analysis by technical experts from other departments including engineering, production, and quality control. The National Association of Purchasing Agents several years ago published a pamphlet on value analysis for use by its members. Included was a checklist of questions for value analysis as follows:

1. Can the item be eliminated?
2. If the item is not standard, can a standard item be used?
3. If it is a standard item, does it completely fit the application or is it a misfit?
4. Does the item have greater capacity than required?
5. Can the weight be reduced?
6. Is there a similar item in inventory that could be substituted?
7. Are closer tolerances specified than are necessary?
8. Is unnecessary machining performed on the item?
9. Are unnecessarily fine finishes specified?
10. Is commercial quality specified? (Commercial quality is usually most economical.)
11. Can the item be manufactured more cheaply in-house than purchased? If it is being manufactured in-house, can it be bought for less?

12. Is the item properly classified for shipping to obtain lowest transportation rates?
13. Can cost of packaging be reduced?
14. Are suppliers being asked for suggestions to reduce cost?[29]

Clearly, there can be many other questions and dimensions in the value analysis process, but this checklist is adequate to illustrate the nature of the approach. It should be added, however, that value analysis should also consider, in addition to the design dimension, how the product is used in the manufacturing process or in other processes, such as maintenance. Likewise, costs of inventory and other issues of inventory management should be considered. Value analysis as an organizational activity has the potential to bring the purchasing department into direct conflict with other departments wishing to add features to the product that go beyond the basic functions perceived by the purchasing analyst. For example, design engineers are often predisposed to require higher levels of product reliability than necessary and special product features intended to enhance the attractiveness of the finished product. Similarly, marketing personnel in the buying organization may argue for aesthetic values in the product that enhance customer appeal but do not make a functional contribution.

While value analysis should be an on-going activity, it is in fact often stimulated by environmental forces beyond the organization. For example, federal legislation relating to energy conservation caused the automobile industry to perform extensive value analysis in a search for ways to reduce the weight of automobiles and to improve their energy efficiency. Potential vendors have a major opportunity for entrée by performing value analysis on potential customers' purchased products in their specific applications. Then they may be able to show how costs can be reduced, while the other benefits and values of the product in use are maintained or enhanced.

Price analysis is the other part of value analysis. In price analysis, personnel in the purchasing organization attempt to evaluate the purchased product in terms of what it costs the vendor to produce that product. Here, once again, the buying firm's engineers, especially those in production engineering, may be helpful. Accurate

[29] *Basic Steps in Value Analysis*, a pamphlet prepared under the chairmanship of Martin S. Erb by the Value-Analysis-Standardization Committee, Reading Association, National Association of Purchasing Agents, New York, undated, pp. 4–18, quoted in Lee and Dobler, *op. cit.*, p. 250.

estimates of the vendor's costs can be an important assist to the purchasing agent in negotiating price with the vendor.

Value analysis is obviously a process calling for a high degree of creativity, and some authors have advocated the application of creativity-stimulating techniques, such as brainstorming, to the process. The essence of value analysis is to see new ways of performing a product function, and this requires breaking out of the mold of traditional thinking. Because value analysis is time consuming and requires hard work, however, it makes sense for the analyst to concentrate on those products that are used in large volumes, or where there is substantial cost per item and some sense of opportunity for finding improvements. Ultimately, the success of value analysis depends upon the responsiveness of vendors and their willingness to respond to customer needs. Suppliers should be an integral part of any ongoing value analysis program.

Make-or-Buy Decisions

For a wide variety of products and services, the purchasing organization can make a decision whether or not to produce the product or service internally or to purchase it from an outside vendor. The manufacture of components and subassemblies is perhaps the most obvious area for this type of analysis, but many services can also be analyzed in this fashion—for example, whether to own trucks or use common carrier services; leasing is yet another option.

While cost and price considerations are usually paramount, there are a variety of other factors that must be considered in the make-or-buy decision. The viability of competition in the supplier industry may be an important consideration. A firm may decide to make a product rather than purchase it, if that product is available from only one outside source. This would have implications for both availability and price. Level of expertise required to manufacture the product is always a relevant consideration.

In addition to favorable cost considerations, a decision to make a product rather than purchase it may be caused by several factors. Problems of supplier reliability may be paramount, or the buying firm may have excess production capacity or technical skills that are not found in potential suppliers. Making a product is sometimes necessary in order to protect valuable designs from competitive copying (the result of suppliers leaking information to their other customers) or to maintain necessary levels of product quality. One of the real dangers in make-or-buy analysis, however, is failure to estimate realistically the true costs of making the product, including incremental managerial costs, the negative effects on vendor relations with subsequent implications for the availability of other items, and the financial aspects of increased capital requirements for production capability and inventory.

A decision to purchase from the outside, even when the company has its own manufacturing capability, and when there are favorable cost considerations, may be the result of a desire to secure a supplier's technical know-how and research capability for continued product improvement. In other cases, the reason may be the supplier's broad product range and the buyer's preference for purchasing a total system of products from the same source. For example, a buyer of chemical intermediates of a commodity nature may purchase them from a well-known national supplier at a price somewhat higher than the lowest available in the market, in order to achieve that supplier's expertise on fine chemicals and specialty products.

Vendor Evaluation

Many organizations use a more-or-less formal vendor evaluation scheme. There are two major types of evaluations—the qualification of vendors as bidders for a given procurement and the on-going review of present suppliers. Increasingly, vendor evaluation is part of the customer's program for management of a total quality process.

The typical vendor evaluation procedure requires a number of subjective judgments, often expressed in numerical terms, by purchasing officials. Each criterion carries a specified weight, and the products of numerical scores times weights are summed to arrive at an overall vendor score. A minimum score is usually specified for a vendor to remain as a qualified source, and vendors can be compared using their respective scores. Among the most commonly used dimensions for vendor evaluation are reliability, product quality, price, service, and technical competence. Other variables might include the quality of vendor management, labor relations, employee morale, cost consciousness, modernness of production plant and equipment, and so on. Figure 2-5 illustrates one company's vendor evaluation form.

Although such vendor evaluation procedures may be quite simple and subject to criticism for being somewhat arbitrary and subjective, they are not only justified but also necessary as a means of managing vendor relationships and controlling the number and quality of potential suppliers. The ratings can provide an important basis for discussions with vendors about their performance and how to improve it. To the maximum extent possible, vendor ratings should be documented by factual data on vendor performance contained in the buying organization's records. From time to time, most buyers like to visit the production facilities of major suppliers and talk with supplier management as part of the vendor evaluation process. Likewise, a customer-oriented industrial marketer may have a major program for its personnel from many areas, including manufacturing, engineering, and research, to make visits to customer locations in order to better understand their problems and needs and how the marketers' products are used and evaluated. For suppliers of critical raw materials, some customers will require periodic financial statements and other data relating to the vendor's ability to provide an uninterrupted supply.

Requirements Planning

The planning for procurement of major capital items and critical raw materials, components, and supplies is an important purchasing management function. Increased global competition, pressure to reduce costs and improve quality, and environmental uncertainty relating to the performance of the economy and the availability of critical raw materials are a major sources of pressure for better strategic planning for materials requirements. The analyst charged with this responsibility must look at the organization's future requirements, reflecting manufacturing plans and new product development. The analyst must attempt to predict the likely direction of market conditions, since these influence both price and availability.

One outcome of this analysis may be a decision to engage in speculative or forward buying of principal items. In speculative buying, the purchase is made in anticipation of a price increase but without any definite plans for the use of the item. Forward buying, on the other hand, is buying larger quantities than usual in anticipation of a well-defined need, as well as in anticipation of price increases or shortages of supply. Forward buying also offers the advantages of known costs of raw materials as the basis for making pricing decisions and the ability to make commitments to the buying firm's customers.

Figure 2–5. A vendor rating for an on-site review. [Source: Whitney Blake Company of Vermont.] Used with permission of Whitney Blake.

COMPANY X COMMUNICATIONS SECTOR
COMMODITY MANAGEMENT TEAM
WIRE, CABLE, CABLE ASSEMBLIES

Supplier: Whitney Blake   Total Score: 75.75

☐ WIRE   ■ CABLE   ◻ CABLE ASSEMBLIES

CATEGORIES:	POINT VALUE	SCORE
I. QUALITY		
1. Quality Assurance		
A. Responsibilities Clearly Defined	1.0	1.0
B. Manual Exists And Current	1.0	1.0
C. Defect Prevention Program	2.0	1.5
D. Training (Other Than SPC)	1.0	1.0
E. Internal Audit System	1.0	0.25
2. Inspection		
A. Written Instructions Present	1.0	0.75
B. Documentation Legible And Latest Issue	1.0	1.0
C. Adequate Equipment Exists	1.0	1.0
3. Calibration		
A. Procedures Exist For Periodic Calibration	1.0	0.75
B. Proper Calibration Standards Exist, Traceable To Nat'l Bureau Of Standards	1.0	1.0
C. Calibration Documentation	1.0	0.75
4. Material Control		
A. System To Prevent Use Of Uninspected Materials	1.0	1.0
B. Positive Identification Of Raw Material	1.0	1.0
C. Adequate Control Area For Materials	1.0	1.0
D. Certification Of Raw Material (0.5); In House (1.0)	1.0	1.0
5. Material Review		
A. Documented System For Handling Non-Conforming Materials	1.0	1.0
B. Corrective Action System	2.0	1.5
C. System For Removing Non-Conforming Materials From Production Flow	1.0	1.0
6. Housekeeping		
A. Overall Condition	2.0	1.5
B. Plant Layout	2.0	1.5
7. S.P.C.		
A. Implemented On Company X Jobs	2.0	1.0
B. Implemented On Others	1.0	0.0

CATEGORIES:	POINT VALUE	SCORE
C. Training of Employees	2.0	0.0
D. Plan To Implement	1.0	1.0

(A & B Above, Full Credit For Real Time Data Collection And Charting On An Hourly Basis)

	Sub-Total	30.0	22.50

II. TECHNOLOGY

1. Tooling

	POINT VALUE	SCORE
A. In House Tool/Fixture Design	1.0	1.0
B. In House Tool/Fixture Fabrication	1.0	0.75
C. In House Tool/Fixture Maintenance & Repair	2.0	1.5
D. Adequate Outside Tool Shop	1.0	1.0

2. Engineering

	POINT VALUE	SCORE
A. Central Technical Contact For Motorola	1.0	1.0
B. Staff Dedicated To Programs To Increase Productivity, Reduce Costs, Research New Technologies, Etc.	2.0	1.25
C. CAE & CAM	1.5	0.5
D. Test Equipment & Procedures	1.5	1.25

3. Capabilities

	POINT VALUE	SCORE
A. Wire Drawing	0.5	0.0
B. Plating/Coating	0.5	0.0
C. Stranding & Cabling	0.75	0.75
D. Extruding & Jacketing	0.75	0.5
E. Insulation & Jacketing Materials Available	1.5	1.25
F. Continuous Unspliced Length (0.2 Per K Ft)	1.0	1.0
G. Wire & Cable Types	2.0	0.75
H. Short Run	1.0	1.0

4. Process

	POINT VALUE	SCORE
A. Overall Process Setup & Flow	1.0	0.75
B. Trained Operators Capable Of Changing & Adjusting Dies	0.5	0.5
C. Labeling & Marking	0.5	0.25

5. Assembly

	POINT VALUE	SCORE
A. Stripping	1.0	1.0
B. Lugging/Terminating	1.0	1.0
C. Overmolding	1.5	1.5
D. Miscellaneous Equipment	0.5	0.0

	Sub-Total	25.00	18.50

Figure 2–5. (Continued).

CATEGORIES:		POINT VALUE	SCORE
III. CUSTOMER SERVICE			
1. Technical Support			
A. Early Supplier Involvement (ESI)		1.0	0.75
B. Cost Control Concept/Program		2.0	1.5
C. Central Contact For Motorola Jobs		1.0	1.0
2. Quality Support			
A. RMA #'s < 48 Hours		2.0	2.0
B. Response to Corrective Action < 48 Hours		2.0	1.75
3. Customer Service			
A. Material Replacement In Timely Manner		2.0	1.5
B. History Of Service		2.0	1.5
C. Order Entry		1.0	0.25
D. Service Global Markets		2.0	2.0
4. Delivery			
A. Just In Time (JIT) Program		2.0	1.5
B. History Of		2.0	1.75
C. Schedule Sharing (EDI)		2.0	0.0
D. Cycle Time		2.0	1.0
E. Scheduling (Flexibility)		2.0	1.5
	Sub-Total	25.0	18.00
IV. BUSINESS			
1. In House Assembly		1.5	0.75
2. Financially Stable		2.0	2.0
3. Employee Awareness Program		1.5	1.0
4. Diversified Customer Base		2.0	2.0
5. Long Term Plans For Capital Expenditures		1.5	1.5
6. Overall Attitude & Acceptance Of Commodity Management Team		1.5	1.5
7. Low Turnover Rate Of Employees (X < 5% Per Year Of Total Employment)		1.5	0.75
8. Stability Of Upper Management Employment		1.5	1.5
9. Operating Capacity		1.5	1.0
$\quad$ X < 60% = 0.5			
$\quad$ 60 − 70% = 1.5			
$\quad$ 70 − 80% = 1.0			
$\quad$ 80 − 90% = 0.5			
$\quad$ Plans For Expansion = 1.0			
10. Control Of Supplier Base (Or Maintenance)		2.0	2.0
11. Inventory Turns Of WIP & Finished Goods:		1.5	0.75
$\quad$ 5 Turns = 0.5			
$\quad$ 10 Turns = 1.0			
$\quad$ 15 Turns = 1.5			
12. Organization Defined		1.0	1.0
13. Job Responsibilities Defined		1.0	1.0
	Sub-Total	20.0	16.75

Figure 2-5. (Continued).

As noted before, suppliers have an important role to play in helping customers plan their future requirements. In fact, if the customer does a poor job of requirements planning, the supplier may find it necessary to take an active role in that planning to assure that its own production program can be formulated on a rational basis. Needless to say, this can represent a major marketing opportunity and is a key role for a vendor to play in relationship marketing.

There are several advantages to the buying organization from careful planning of material requirements. The most obvious advantage is a lower cost of purchase and more efficiency in the purchasing process itself (and hence lower administrative expense). In addition, there are the benefits of uninterrupted supply, consistent quality, and good supplier relations. Less obvious, perhaps, purchase planning activities are an excellent training ground for developing purchasing management personnel and for developing analyses and records that can assist in the professional management of the purchasing function.[30]

Purchasing Contracts

Much of today's purchasing activity between buyers and sellers takes place under special contractual relationships that have relegated much of the purchasing task to the level of clerical routine. Buying decision making becomes a straight rebuy situation such as described earlier. Many of these contractual innovations in purchasing have been stimulated by the introduction of information technology into the purchasing function and by aggressive marketing on the part of suppliers, especially industrial distributors. For example, the *blanket purchase order* is widely used for small items bought frequently, such as office supplies, and repair and maintenance items. Under a blanket purchase order arrangement, the buyer contracts with a supplier to provide the specified item or items at agreed upon price and other terms. A simple release form, rather than a formal purchase order, is then all that is needed to authorize the vendor to provide the item to a representative of the buying organization.

Under the *annual requirement* purchasing arrangement, a supplier agrees to supply all or a portion of the buyer's requirements for a specified item for a given year at an agreed upon price. Once again,

[30] Dean S. Ammer, *Materials Management* (Homewood, Ill.: Richard D. Irwin, Inc., 1962), pp. 117–18.

items can be released in response to a simple request form, often in predetermined amounts for each transaction. The annual requirement contract often calls for quantity discounts contingent upon the amounts actually purchased by the customer. Like the blanket purchase order, which is most useful for relatively small purchases, the annual requirement contract reduces the cost of purchasing by minimizing the amount of administrative work and negotiation that must be conducted.

So-called *stockless purchasing* arrangements are another frequently found type of purchasing contract. Here the supplier agrees to supply all of the customer's requirements for a given item or set of items at a specified price from an inventory that the supplier agrees to have available at all times for the customer. Some industrial distributors have entered into such agreements with major customers for a large variety of related items. A machine tool manufacturer, for example, might depend upon an industrial distributor to supply small motors, electrical relays, and other electrical controls, in specified combinations and quantities, upon demand as the customer's manufacturing operations require them. When a particular machine tool is scheduled for manufacture, the customer's computer could easily print out a list of materials requirements, or a magnetic tape that could then be sent to the vendor. The vendor could read the tape into its computer and get a print-out of a stocklist to be used by its warehouse personnel for putting up the order to be shipped to the customer. Or, data could be exchanged between the customer's and vendor's computers over telephone lines with little or no human intervention. Such arrangements are in fact quite common and can be highly efficient as well as reducing the customer's inventory investment. The benefit to the supplier is a "captive" customer and a high level of service to the customer resulting in goodwill and a high probability of future orders.

At the extreme, as we discussed in the section on types of buying situations, are just-in-time systems for purchasing and inventory management. These are sole-source procurements in which the vendor agrees to provide precise quantities of materials, as determined by the customer's production planning and scheduling on an on-going basis, delivered to the customer's manufacturing location at exactly specified times. Quantities are usually just sufficient for an eight-hour production shift. The customer is likely to have no incoming inspection and to require that the vendor provide 100 percent usable product, defect-free, meeting all dimensional and performance specifications precisely. Vendor failure on any dimension can shut down the customer's operation and the penalties when that happens are likely to be severe. Thus, such arrangements represent the ultimate in buyer-seller interdependence.

These various types of purchasing contracts tend to "lock in" organizations to their present vendors and have obvious benefits for the vendors who are "in" and represent a major obstacle for the vendors who are "out." Purchasing contracts permit consistent purchasing activities across the many locations of a large diversified organization and bring appropriate cost efficiencies through quantity discounts and other economies of scale.

The purpose of this section has been to suggest some of the longer-term purchasing arrangements that characterize industrial buying and have important strategic implications for the industrial marketer. No attempt has been made to describe the myriad of detailed procedures included in management of the purchasing function. As was mentioned in the discussion of models of the buying decision process, the potential supplier must be completely familiar with the various administrative procedures and policies of the customer organization, a very important part of the basic dictum of "Know Your Customer."

SUMMARY

While the study of industrial marketing typically is focussed upon the problems that the industrial marketer is trying to solve, a thorough understanding requires knowledge of the procurement problems faced by industrial customers and how they attempt to plan for and manage the procurement process. Procurement is a critical area in the strategic planning of the customer organization. Industrial buying behavior has been seen to be a complex organizational decision making process, rather than a single purchase event. Several models of industrial buyer behavior were reviewed. Some of the most interesting features and challenges of industrial marketing relate to the complexity of the industrial buying process, including the many persons involved in the process, the multiple buying criteria they use, their different role perceptions and information needs, and the complex interaction between individual needs and organization goals. In the next chapter, the relationship between customer purchasing and vendor marketing will be explored in terms of buyer-seller relationships.

Bibliography

Anderson, Erin, Wujin Chu, and Barton Weitz, "Industrial Purchasing: An Empirical Exploration of the Buyclass Framework," *Journal of Marketing* **51, 3** (July, 1987), 71–86.

Bonoma, Thomas V., "Major Sales: Who *Really* Does the Buying?," *Harvard Business Review,* **60** (May–June, 1982), 111–119.

Corey, E. Raymond, *Procurement Management: Strategy, Organization and Decision Making* (Boston: CBI Publishing Co., Inc., 1978).

Levitt, Theodore, *Industrial Purchasing Behavior* (Boston: Division of Research Graduate School of Business Administration, Harvard University, 1965).

Moriarty, Rowland T., *Industrial Buying Behavior* (Lexington, Mass.: Lexington Books, 1983).

Sheth, Jagdish N., "A Model of Industrial Buyer Behavior," *Journal of Marketing,* **37, 4** (October, 1973), 50–56.

Webster, Frederick E., Jr., and Yoram Wind, *Organizational Buying Behavior* (Englewood Cliffs, N.J.: Prentice-Hall, Inc., 1972).

Westing, J. H., I. V. Fine, and Gary Joseph Zenz, *Purchasing Management,* 4th ed. (New York: John Wiley & Sons, Inc., 1976).

3 Buyer–Seller Relationships

The nature of the buyer-seller relationship is a major factor distinguishing industrial marketing from consumer marketing. It will be recalled, from Chapter 1, that buyer-seller interdependence and product complexity were also defined as unique aspects of industrial marketing. Product complexity was defined, not in terms of technical complexity, but in terms of the product as a set of relationships—economic, technical, personal—between buyers and sellers. Another dimension of the industrial buyer-seller relationship is that industrial marketing and selling strategies must usually be directed toward individual customer organizations, or relatively small aggregations of customers, not to "typical" customers or mass markets, as is characteristic of consumer marketing. For strategic purposes, the central focus of industrial marketing should not be on products or on markets, broadly defined, but on buyer-seller relationships.

In the previous chapter it was noted that industrial buying-selling situations can be characterized along a continuum from simple transactions to strategic alliances, with a broad range of *relationships* in the middle. Such relationships can vary considerably in their character, complexity, and durability, but in general it is relationships between buyers and sellers that are the hallmark of industrial marketing. These relationships involve mutual interdependence and are strategically important to both parties. They provide continuity, predictability, and security, but they also create unique and important management challenges.

Buyer-seller relationships in industrial marketing develop in the purchasing decision process and continue through negotiation of the sale and consummation of the transaction to post-sale service and repeat orders. Ongoing relationships with customers are a major business asset, albeit difficult to value precisely, of industrial marketers, and especially of industrial distributors without their own product lines and production facilities. In this chapter, we will look at several dimensions of buyer-seller relationships, including buyer-sales representative interaction, influence processes, reciprocal buying arrangements, customer service, and the strategic choice of type of relationship. Not all customers warrant the investments required for relationship marketing.

At the core of every buyer-seller relationship is a series of individual interactions between representatives of the two organizations. It is appropriate, therefore, to begin our analysis of relationships by looking in some detail at the nature of that interpersonal interaction between a sales representative and someone from the customer organization. First, we look at the sales rep as a "boundary role person." Then we look at the interaction process.

THE SALES REP AS A BOUNDARY ROLE PERSON

Important elements of the sales rep's functioning and responsibility are captured in the notion of a "boundary role" within an organization structure. A boundary role is simply an organizational role that is performed on the boundary of the organization at the interface between the organization and the environment (which includes other organizations). This definition clearly applies to the role of sales representative. Likewise, the people in customer organizations with whom the sales rep interacts are also functioning in boundary roles.

The sales rep is responsible both for representing the selling organization to the customer and representing the customer back to the selling organization, in order to develop the best possible marketing response to the customer's needs and problems. People within the customer organization are likely to have expectations that are quite different from those of the selling organization about how the sales rep should perform. Furthermore, the sales rep may very well spend more time interacting with representatives of customer organizations than with members of the selling company. The physical distance that separates the sales representative from the employing organization (and from direct supervision) is also accompanied by psychological distance. The rep may, in fact, develop a sense of identity with customer organizations, especially if they are few in number, that is as strong as his identity with his own firm.

When the sales reps interact with members of their own organizations, it is likely to be in a problem-oriented context. In representing the customer back to the company, the rep will report on problems in the field with products, pricing, delivery, and the like, and will be, implicitly at least, critical of the company's activities. The rep's requests and demands on the capabilities of the company may be regarded as unreasonable and insensitive to the company's needs, problems, objectives, and policies.

These simple facts about the nature of the sales rep's work have some interesting and potentially problematic implications. Because of the fact that the boundary role performers' interactions are primarily with people outside of their organizations, they are the target of a certain amount of distrust and fear from people within the organization. These attitudes are likely to be communicated to the rep in subtle ways and to create a sense of anxiety in the rep. Conflicting role expectations for the sales rep held by members of the two organizations are a further source of tension and anxiety.[1]

BUYER-SALES REPRESENTATIVE INTERACTION[2]

The basic unit of analysis in buyer-seller relationships is the interaction between a representative of the buying organization and a representative of the selling organization. Of course, there may be several persons on either side of the relationship, but the two-person dyad remains the building block of more complex social interactions.

When buyer and sales representative (or "rep") meet, the nature of their interaction can be understood as a form of role-playing. The roles of buyer and sales rep are distinct and definable social roles, each having certain behaviors and expectations associated with it. Furthermore, these behaviors and expectations are specified both for persons in the role and toward the role, that is for "self" and "other." The social role of buyer or sales rep is thus a very important

[1] Robert E. Spekman, "Organizational Boundary Behavior: A Conceptual Framework for Investigating the Industrial Salesperson," in Richard P. Bagozzi (ed.), *Sales Management: New Developments from Behavioral and Decision Model Research*, Report No. 79–107 (Cambridge, Mass.: Marketing Science Institute, 1979), pp. 133–44, esp. 134–35.
[2] The following material is adapted, in part, from F. E. Webster, Jr., "Interpersonal Communication and Salesman Effectiveness," *Journal of Marketing*, **32**, 3 (July, 1968), 7–13 and is used with permission of the American Marketing Association.

source of predispositions (opinions, attitudes, beliefs, values, goals, etc.) influencing the perceptions of persons in those roles.

Sources of Role Expectations for the Industrial Sales Representative

There are two particularly important sources of buyers' role expectations for industrial sales reps. The first is the stereotype of the sales rep. A "stereotype" can be defined as a consensus of role expectations shared by a large segment of the population. It is a well-known fact that there is a stereotype of the sales rep, describing him or her as "talkative," "easy going," "competitive," "optimistic," and "excitable." Kirchner and Dunnette found that sales reps describe themselves in these terms.[3] This stereotype is said to be one of the reasons why the sales rep is not highly regarded by a large segment of the population.[4] Perception is subjective, and it is not important whether or not the stereotype is an objectively accurate one. The industrial buyer who does not have previous experience with a particular sales rep will respond to that rep in terms of the stereotype that she has of sales reps in general, based on the sum total of her experience with sales reps. "Inaccurate" perception of the rep by the prospect may lead to a lack of communication. On the other hand, by virtue of their occupation, all sales reps are regarded as having manipulative intent—they want the prospect to behave in a particular way—and communications theory indicates that the perception of manipulative intent in the communicator leads to certain resistance.[5]

A second important source of "role expectations" held by a prospect for a rep is the reputation of the selling company. This is a special case of the generalized concept of "source credibility" in communications theory. Several research studies have confirmed that the reputation of the source is an important determinant of response to persuasive communication.[6]

[3] Wayne K. Kirchner and Marvin D. Dunnette, "How Salesmen and Technical Men Differ in Describing Themselves," *Personnel Journal*, 37 (April, 1959), 418–19.
[4] John L. Mason, "The Low Prestige of Personal Selling," *Journal of Marketing*, 29 (October, 1965), 7–10.
[5] Carl I. Hovland, Irving L. Janis, and Harold H. Kelley, *Communication and Persuasion: Psychological Studies of Opinion Change* (New Haven: Yale University Press, 1953), p. 295.
[6] Carl I. Hovland and Walter Weiss, "The Influence of Source Credibility on Communication Effectiveness," *Public Opinion Quarterly*, 15 (Winter, 1951–52), 635–50.

Levitt[7] found that industrial purchasing agents' and chemists' responses to sales presentations were influenced strongly by the reputation of the company (source) that the sales rep (communicator) represented. In general, the rep for the company with the better reputation (created through advertising, for example) always obtained a more favorable response to his or her presentation. On the other hand, Levitt also found that respondents tended to rank the rep as lower in "trustworthiness" than they ranked the company that the rep represented. While this finding probably reflects, in part, the low occupational prestige of sales reps, Levitt suggested that there was more involved. He concluded that the prospect's perception of the trustworthiness of the rep was not as closely related to the rep's product knowledge as it was to the overall quality of the sales presentation. Furthermore, a poor sales presentation resulted in a reduction in the perceived trustworthiness of the company. Finally, Levitt's research suggested that for a company with an excellent reputation, the prospect has very high expectations for the kind of sales reps that will represent that company—so high, in fact, that reps may not be able to meet these expectations.

Determinants of How the Buyer "Plays the Role"

Interaction theory explains that the needs of the actors are important determinants of their predispositions and that these predispositions influence their perceptions of the situation. As Jones and Thibaut have stated:

> If we can successfully identify the goals for which an actor is striving in the interaction situation, we can begin to say something about the cues to which he will attend, and the meaning he is most likely to assign to them.[8]

The old "need satisfaction" theory of salesmanship recognized this basic fact, but said little about the true complexity of the prospect's needs. In Chapter 2, our analysis of industrial buyer behavior indicated that both personal needs and organizational goals, as well

[7] Theodore Levitt, *Industrial Purchasing Behavior: A Study of Communications Effects* (Boston: Division of Research, Graduate School of Business Administration, Harvard University, 1965), pp. 31–32.
[8] Edward E. Jones and John W. Thibaut, "Interaction Goals as Bases of Inferences in Interpersonal Perception," in R. Tagiuri and R. L. Petrullo (eds.), *Person Perception and Interpersonal Behavior* (Stanford, California: Stanford University Press, 1958), pp. x–xi.

as social dimensions of interaction in the buying center, are important determinants of buyer response to selling effort.

Every prospective buyer has at least two kinds of needs: personal needs, which motivate behavior, and social needs, which define the kinds of need fulfillment activity acceptable to relevant other persons in the social situation. While this is only a crude cut across the complex set of needs that determine behavior, it makes an important distinction. For example, the industrial buyer may be motivated by a personal need for recognition and advancement and by the social need to satisfy the using department. The buyer's need for the sales rep's product will not exist unless he can see how a buying decision will allow him to satisfy both sets of needs. Those particular personal and social needs will determine: (1) whether the prospect grants an interview to the sales rep; (2) which parts of the presentations she really listens to; (3) the information she will remember; and (4) the influence of the sales presentation on her decision to buy.

An important dimension of how the prospect behaves is her self-confidence in her ability to play the role. The prospect's self-confidence is a determinant of how much risk she perceives in the buying decision she is asked to make. Levitt's research found that the influence of the sales rep's presentation was in part determined by the riskiness of the decision (that is, actual purchase versus recommend for further consideration) and by the self-confidence of the prospect.

Another set of factors determining how the buyer plays her role in a specific sales interaction is other sources of information to which she has been exposed concerning the rep's product. These can be grouped into two categories—impersonal, commercial sources of information, such as media advertising and direct mail, and personal, non-commercial sources such as colleagues, friends, and neighbors. (The rep can be characterized as a personal, commercial source of information.) Generally speaking, personal sources of information are known to be more effective in producing an attitude change than impersonal sources.[9] On the other hand, commercial sources tend to be less effective than noncommercial sources. These general research findings suggest that industrial sales reps would be more effective than advertising but less effective than buyers' peers in developing favorable attitudes toward products.

[9] Elihu Katz and Paul F. Lazarsfeld, *Personal Influence* (Glencoe, Ill.: The Free Press, 1955), pp. 183–84; and Paul F. Lazarsfeld, Bernard Berelson, and Hazel Gaudet, *The People's Choice* (New York: Duell, Sloan, and Pearce, 1944), pp. 49–50.

However, the importance of alternative sources of information varies with the stage of the buying decision process and the product life cycle. As buyers goes through the mental stages of deciding to buy a new product (or the "adoption process"—awareness, interest, evaluation, trial, and adoption), they rely on different sources of information. Furthermore, the people who buy a new product early in its life cycle (the innovators and early adopters) tend to rely upon different sources of information than later adopters.[10] We examine this research area in Chapter 6.

A study of industrial buyers' uses of information sources at various stages of the new product adoption decision process found that sales reps were regarded as the most important source of information at all stages, except initial awareness. For becoming aware of new products, 90 percent of the industrial buyers interviewed reported that advertising was useful to them. Only 84 percent mentioned sales reps. Even at the evaluation stage, reps were more important (mentioned by 64 percent) than buyers and engineers in other companies (mentioned by 28 and 44 percent, respectively). Thus, it was concluded that informal communication in industrial markets may be less common than in consumer markets and that industrial buyers value the information provided by the industrial rep.[11]

The interaction of personal selling with advertising and other forms of mass communication should not be overlooked. Source effects attributable to advertising have already been discussed. In addition, there is good evidence that effective industrial advertising can reduce the cost of selling as a percentage of sales revenue.[12] Another study of industrial buyer's uses of information sources for machine tool purchases found that advertising in trade magazines was the most important source for keeping informed about products and suppliers. Sales reps were second in importance, a finding consistent with the earlier finding that journal advertising is most important at the awareness stage. Machine tool marketing managers, however, ranked sales reps first, followed by catalogues, second, and advertising, third.[13]

---

[10] Everett M. Rogers, *Diffusion of Innovations* (New York: The Free Press, 1962).
[11] Frederick E. Webster, Jr., "Informal Communication in Industrial Markets," *Journal of Marketing Research*, VII (May, 1970), 186–89.
[12] John E. Morrill, "Industrial Advertising Pays Off," *Harvard Business Review*, 48, 2 (March-April, 1970), 4–14, 159–69.
[13] Charles H. Patti, "Buyer Information Sources in the Capital Equipment Industry," *Industrial Marketing Management*, 6, 4 (October, 1977), 259–64.

In reviewing the literature on the adoption of pharmaceuticals by physicians, Bauer and Wortzel found that doctors consistently ranked detailers as the most important source of information.[14] Earlier studies found the detailer was more important as a source of first knowledge than as a source of influence, while colleagues and medical journal articles were more important as sources of influence than as sources of first knowledge.[15] Rogers and Beal found that dealers and sales reps served different functions (awareness, evaluation, etc.) for different adopter categories (early adopters versus later adopters) in the acceptance of new farm products.[16] Thus, the sales rep's influence and effectiveness are determined, in part, by the relative innovativeness of the prospect and the stage of the prospect's buying decision process. The prospect's innovativeness and her buying stage influence how she will use and respond to information provided by the sales rep relative to the other commercial and noncommercial sources of information.

To summarize, how the prospect "plays her role" in the sales interaction and how she responds to the sales rep's efforts is determined by her personal needs and the organization's goals, the interactions within the buying center, her self-confidence, the perceived risk in the buying decision, her innovativeness, the stage of her buying decision process, and her exposure to advertising and other forms of mass communication.

Determinants of How the Industrial Sales Rep "Plays the Role"

Many of the observations made about the buyer apply to the sales rep as well. The sales rep's behavior is determined by his personal needs (for example, his desire to earn a commission on the sale) and his social needs. The sales rep's behavior will be influenced by his desire to meet the expectations of relevant other persons including his manager, his peers, and the prospect herself. The sales rep's

[14] The detailer is a sales rep who calls on physicians to provide information about pharmaceutical products with the objective of encouraging the doctor to write prescriptions for those products. Raymond A. Bauer and Lawrence H. Wortzel, "Doctor's Choice: The Physician and His Sources of Information About Drugs," *Journal of Marketing Research*, **III** (February, 1966), 40–47.
[15] Elihu Katz, "The Social Itinerary of Technical Change: Two Studies on the Diffusion of Innovation," *Human Organization*, **20** (Summer, 1961), 70–82.
[16] Everett M. Rogers and George M. Beal, "The Importance of Personal Influence in the Adoption of Technical Changes," *Social Forces*, **36** (May, 1958), 329–35.

confidence in his own ability to "play the role" of sales rep is important in determining his behavior and is influenced by his knowledge, training, personality, and previous experience.

Because of the importance of the buyer's behavior in determining the success of the sales call, the sales rep's ability to infer the buyer's role expectations of him is a vitally important factor. This ability has been defined as "empathy" or "empathic ability"—the ability to put oneself into the position of another person, a feeling of oneness with the other person. There is an unresolved controversy about empathy: whether it is an inborn personality trait or can be taught and learned; and whether persons who have empathic ability are always more effective or only more effective in interactions with specific types of persons. Nonetheless, the ability to sense how the prospect is reacting to what the sales rep says is an important determinant of how successfully the sales rep plays his role.[17]

The sales rep's behavior will also reflect his perception of how his manager expects him to play the role of sales rep. If these expectations have not been stated clearly by the manager, the sales rep's behavior may not be consistent with management's expectations. Furthermore, management must be sure that its expectations about reps' behavior are consistent with buyers' expectations. Otherwise, the rep is in the difficult position of having to resolve conflicting role expectations. This will lead to some frustration and anxiety, as well as reduction in effectiveness.

The sales rep's effectiveness also depends on his ability to determine the locus of responsibility for buying decisions within the buying organization. Where more than one person is involved in the buying decision (for example, a purchasing agent and an engineer), the sales rep may be faced with conflicting role expectations. Once again, the ability to sense and resolve conflicts in buyers' role expectations is an important determinant of the rep's behavior.

To summarize, how the sales rep plays his role is determined by his ability to infer the expectations of relevant others for how he should play his role. Relevant others include his manager and the buying decision influencers within the buying organization. There is significant potential for role conflict and anxiety inherent in the fact that the sales rep occupies a boundary role in the organization.

[17] David Mayer and Herbert Greenberg, "What Makes a Good Salesman," *Harvard Business Review*, **42**, 4 (July–August, 1964), 119–25.

The Sales Presentation

Of course, a major element in the interaction of buyer and sales rep is the sales presentation itself. Viewing personal selling as interpersonal interaction emphasizes that the presentation should be tailored to fit the needs and expectations of the prospective customer. In addition, communications theory suggests several specific characteristics of effective sales presentations.

The quality of the sales presentation is an important factor both in getting a favorable first hearing for the sales rep and in inducing buying action. Communication theory suggests that the rep should first arouse the interest and identify the needs of the buyer and then show how his product can fill those needs. He should present the buyer with the positive features and arguments first, saving "negative" features such as price for the last stages of the presentation. Wherever possible, he should attempt to get early commitment by taking the buyer through a series of minor decisions first and by encouraging the buyer to agree with a series of statements supporting the value of the product.

In a competitive situation, the sales rep can "insulate" the buyer against competitors' claims by facing up to any limitations of his product and showing the prospect why his product has greater value. Communications theory suggests that a "two-sided" argument can be effective in anticipating and negating the effects of counter-arguments. The sales rep should explicitly point out the advantages of using his product and the need satisfactions to be derived. This conclusion-drawing can avoid the prospect's "missing the point" but must be used cautiously where the buyer is more "expert" than the sales rep.

Finally, emotional appeals are useful in heightening interest and attention but only up to a point. Beyond that point, the buyer's increased anxiety and emotional involvement may actually decrease the effectiveness of the presentation by reducing attention, comprehension, and acceptance. All of these comments on sales presentations are drawn directly from the findings of communications research.[18]

These views of buyer-sales representative relationships as dyadic interaction and as a form of communication have significant implications for the development of account strategies and for management of the selling process. One of the most obvious implications is the

[18] Most of these findings are summarized in Hovland, Janis, and Kelley, op. cit., and in Levitt, op. cit.

recognition that the sales rep has only limited control over the interaction and the outcome. "Salesmanship" views of the selling process often concentrate excessively on the sales rep's personal characteristics, skills, and actions as influences on buyer behavior. Such one-sided views of the selling process are inadequate to provide a full understanding of the nature of the industrial sales rep's activities and responsibilities.

The Buying-Selling Process

Traditional views of selling such as AIDA (Attention, Interest, Desire, and Action), need-satisfaction theory, and the steps-in-the-sale approach all suffer from a common weakness: they view selling as something the sales rep does to the prospect, and the sales rep as having most of the control in the interaction. Even the more modern views of selling as interpersonal communication, which we have just been reviewing, tend to emphasize the sales rep's activities and perceptions as the major determinants of the outcome of the sales interaction. They see the central influence process as one of persuasion, and the sales rep's most important characteristics as those that relate to his ability to listen carefully and turn what he hears into an effective persuasive communication.

Similar observations can be made about the study of the industrial buying process which has also viewed buying as something within the control of the buying organization, passing through several stages of decision making, as outlined in our review in Chapter 2. The outcomes of the buying process are seen as determined by the actors, structure, technology, and goals and tasks of the buying organization, processing information obtained from the environment about buying alternatives (products and vendors).

The most recent conceptual work on industrial buying and selling builds on basic concepts of social interaction and takes the view that buying and selling are the same process, two sides of the same coin. Recognizing that the two-person dyad is the basic unit of social interaction, and using that as the starting point, this view of the buying-selling process as interaction argues that the outcome of the interaction is determined by the total process itself, not by the characteristics and activities of the individual actors. The influence process involved is negotiation, not persuasion. Each actor recognizes that his or her welfare is dependent on the activities and welfare of the other party in the interaction. This perception of

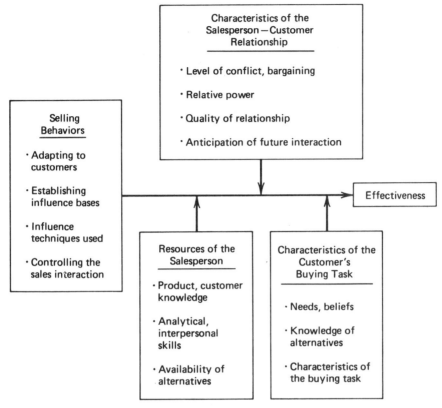

Figure 3-1. A contingency model of sales representative effectiveness.
[Source: *Barton A. Weitz, "Effectiveness in Sales Interactions: A Contingency Framework,"* Journal of Marketing, 45 *(Winter, 1981), 85–103, at 90.] Reproduced with permission of the American Marketing Association.*

mutual interdependence is a key to the nature of the interaction itself.[19]

Weitz has taken these ideas and integrated them into a "contingency model," which is presented in Figure 3-1. The central notion in this model is that the effectiveness of the industrial sales rep is contingent on three sets of variables: (1) the rep's resources (knowl-

[19] Thomas V. Bonoma, "A General Theory of Interaction Applied to Sales Management," in Richard P. Bagozzi (ed.), *Sales Management: New Developments from Behavioral and Decision Model Research*, (Cambridge, Mass.: Marketing Science Institute, 1979), pp. 145–73.

edge, skills, and organizational support); (2) the customer's buying task; and (3) the nature of the interpersonal interaction itself.[20] Such a view of the buying-selling process goes considerably beyond the simple notions of selling as persuasion by the rep and buying as a process controlled by the actors of the buying organization. Within this more complex view of the buying-selling process, we can now turn to look at the influence the type of buying situation has on the interaction. Then we will review different influence processes and their appropriateness in various industrial marketing situations.

TYPES OF BUYING-SELLING SITUATIONS

The nature of the interaction between buyer and sales rep is determined in large part by the type of buying situation (new buy, modified rebuy, or straight rebuy) and the stage in the buying decision process (problem recognition, description of needed item, etc.). A sales rep selling a new product the buyer has never considered before faces a fundamentally different challenge from that of the rep for one of several vendors being evaluated for the repurchase of a standard commodity. Clearly, different selling and marketing strategies are required, depending upon the specific nature of the buying situation.

One classification of buying-selling situations has been proposed by Håkanson, Johanson, and Wootz, who define three types of uncertainty facing buyers:

Need uncertainty, when product need is difficult to define and measure and when product characteristics are hard to measure and specify clearly.

Market uncertainty, when there are many sellers, sellers have markedly different characteristics, and the market changes rapidly, with the result that sellers are hard to compare and there are likely to be high opportunity costs associated with the decision.

Transaction uncertainty, when there are likely to be significant problems of actually getting the product from seller to buyer, such as in cross-border transactions involving cultural differences.[21]

[20] Barton A. Weitz, "Effectiveness in Sales Interactions: A Contingency Framework," *Journal of Marketing*, **45** (Winter, 1981), 85–103.
[21] Håkan Håkanson, Jan Johanson, and Björn Wootz, "Influence Tactics in Buyer-Seller Processes," *Industrial Marketing Management*, **5**, 6 (December, 1976), 319–32.

The authors go on to suggest how the degree of each type of uncertainty determines the buyer's concerns, and they define selling strategies in terms of the type of uncertainty they are intended to change. As a general observation, "in" suppliers are interested in reducing or stabilizing uncertainty. "Out" suppliers will be trying to increase uncertainty to levels where the buyer is willing to consider new alternatives.

When *need uncertainty* is high, buyers are likely to be more concerned with quality than with price and are likely to demonstrate high source loyalty. Within the buying organization, more people will be involved in the buying center. In addition, buyers will likely use more extended sources of information and may use the services of specialists and consultants in the relationship with suppliers. The decision process is likely to take longer, since it involves more people, multiple buying criteria, and more information processing.

When *market uncertainty* is high, buyers can be expected to contact more suppliers and to seek the help of specialists both within the organization and outside who have experience with these high uncertainty markets.

When *transaction uncertainty* is high, the buyer is most likely to insist upon multiple sources of supply. Delivery becomes the most serious consideration in evaluating alternatives. There will likely be several contacts with the supplier before the final buying decision is made, with a focus upon the supplier's ability to deliver the item in necessary quantities and with sufficient reliability.

In Chapter 2, we looked at two other characterizations of buying-selling situations, and we will only summarize those here. We looked at one typology that distinguished three types of procurement situation *based on pricing: cost-based* procurements, *market-based* procurements, and *competitive bidding*. It was in the context of types of buying-selling situations that we also introduced the continuum of *transactions → relationships → strategic alliances*.

STRATEGIC SUPPLIER SELECTION

Increasingly, buyers have come to think about the strategic importance of supplier selection. Driven in large measure by the need to reduce costs and improve quality in order to compete in the global marketplace, buyers are moving away from old, adversarial views of the buying-selling process toward new concepts of strategic partnerships.

Traditional procurement practice was built around an assumption that competition among vendors was good because it resulted in lower prices for a specified level of quality. It was common to have several qualified suppliers for a given item, not only to insure lower prices but also for continuity of supply. The key control element was a tightly drawn set of product specifications that permitted the maximum degree of competition among available vendors. In this fashion, the buyer could depend upon market forces to insure the lowest possible price. Such procurement practice clearly lies toward the *transaction* end of the continuum with the notion of a buyer-seller "relationship" confined to the development and maintenance of a list of qualified bidders in a competitive bidding or market-based procurement. Buyer-seller relationships tended to be adversarial and impersonal.[22] There were multiple vendors for each item; their shares of the customer's business were dependent largely upon their prices.

For the total purchases of a large corporation, many thousands of vendors were common. Hindsight suggests that this was a major cause of poor quality, because different vendors' parts and materials were in fact *not* interchangeable and there was little concern for quality as a total management process on the part of either buyers or sellers. The need to develop and maintain multiple vendors and to manage multiple relationships resulted in higher purchasing costs as well as lower quality.

By the early 1980's, procurement management attention had shifted toward an emphasis on quality and customer satisfaction. Quality was defined from the end-user's perspective, and companies developed more complex specifications that included not only the product itself but terms for delivery, technical service, marketing support, and so on. Fewer vendors were depended upon for a more complete response to the company's requirements, with an emphasis on "doing the right things, the right way, the first time." But relationships were in important respects still adversarial. Vendors were played off against one another using the multiple buying criteria of a more complex specification that they had little or no role in developing.

Interest in a concept of buyer-seller partnership, sometimes in

[22] Roy D. Shapiro, "Toward Effective Supplier Management: International Comparisons," Working Paper No. 9-785-062, Harvard Business School, 1985.

the form of so-called "just-in-time" supply relationships, grew rapidly in the 1980's.[23] These are modelled on the Japanese "kanban" systems of procurement. A few vendors, or perhaps even a sole source, collaborate with the buyer across multiple business functions including manufacturing, engineering, design, procurement, and marketing. The vendor is actively involved in the design of the product and the development of specs. There may be continuous updating and innovation. Blanket contracts and more flexible, less formalized procedures for releasing orders are common. Order quantities are likely to be smaller and shipments more frequent, in order to reduce inventory costs throughout the system. Among the hallmarks of these procurement situations are greater reliance on fewer vendors, a commitment to zero defects, vendor participation in product design, just-in-time delivery, shared communication networks (using advanced information technology), an increased service component, and a much more complex buying decision process, involving multiple functions and management levels.

Problems in Strategic Buyer-Seller Partnerships

Such intense buyer-seller relationships, at or near the *strategic alliances* end of the continuum, are not without their problems and risks.[24] One kind of risk, related to market and transaction uncertainty, may be reduced, but another kind of risk—that which comes from increased dependence—is created. The higher level of trust and commitment between the partners does not mean that conflict will not exist, especially if there is an imbalance of power, which may be inevitable if the parties are of significantly different size.

A particular problem noted by several marketers who have entered into strategic partnerships with customers is the tendency for functional managers, especially purchasing personnel, in the customer organization to "play by the old rules." For example, the buyer may continue to insist on using specifications that are not developed with the collaboration of the partner, may continue to solicit competitive bids, and may emphasize low price to the exclusion of other considerations such as quality and technological innovation.

[23] Gary L. Frazier, Robert E. Spekman, and Charles R. O'Neal, "Just-In-Time Exchange Relationships in Industrial Markets," *Journal of Marketing*, **52**, 4 (October, 1988), 52–67.
[24] Robert E. Spekman, "Strategic Supplier Selection: Understanding Long-Term Buyer Relationships," *Business Horizons*, **31**, 4 (July-August, 1988), 75–81.

It is important that the design of strategic buying relationships anticipate potential conflicts and develop mechanisms for their resolution. Legalistic contractual terms are likely to be inadequate to resolve conflict and keep the partnership on a positive track of mutual trust and cooperation. Experienced managers suggest that people who will be responsible for implementing the relationship should be involved in its design as well. Exchange visits by members of both buying and selling organizations, from multiple levels of management, supervision, and operations, have proven to be valuable in developing and maintaining understanding and creating simple problem-solving mechanisms. Dialogue and joint problem solving replace negotiation as the primary means of exchanging information and resolving conflict.[25]

It has been suggested that the concept of a balanced portfolio of strategic partnerships, with resource commitments and management style tailored to each, can be a useful conceptual tool for management.[26] Customer development can be thought of as an investment, with investment attractiveness determined by the degree of commonality of interest between the customers and the expected value of the long-term relationship. Krapfel, Salmond, and Spekman propose that marketers use a process that consists of first *typing* the relationship and then *selecting a management mode* appropriate to that type. The resulting analysis produces the classifications of customer-partners and the management styles shown in Figure 3-2. In managing the relationship, they suggest that it is important that the buyer and the seller have similar or "matched" management styles. They call this the *matching* process. Clearly, problems will result if one treats the relationship as essentially a single transaction while the other is hoping to develop a strategic partnership. Part of the marketer's analytical task is to determine as clearly as possible, usually with incomplete information, how the buyer perceives the relationship. In the Krapfel, Salmond, and Spekman framework, the fourth step in strategic relationship management is *signaling*—the exchange of information between buyer and seller to monitor and refine the management of the relationship. Signaling can establish the foundation of information and impressions upon which trust, the essential glue in any strategic partnership, can be built.

[25] *Ibid.*, p. 78.
[26] Robert Krapfel, Deborah Salmond, and Robert Spekman, "A Strategic Approach to Managing Buyer-Seller Relationships," Working Paper, University of Maryland, June, 1990.

Types of Relationships

Value of Relationship*

High	Low		
Alliance (Partner)	Relationship (Friend)	**High**	Commonality of Interest
Relationship (Rival)	Transaction (Acquaintance)	**Low**	

* A function of
- "criticality" = degree of differentiation; availability of substitutes; margins, role in company strategy; portfolio
- quantity purchased
- ease with which customers can be replaced, "switching" costs
- cost savings resulting from buyer's practices and procedures.

Management Modes

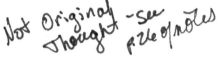

Partner	Friend
High economic investments; high interdependency; high switching costs; customized responses.	Common goals; low (current) economic value; information sharing; limited investment; may *have been* or *become* partners; needs monitoring, joint planning.

Rival	Acquaintanace
High value but low commonality of interests; want to "go-it-alone"; may be competitors as well as customers; do business because they "have to," not "want to"; limit investment and customization; have exit plan; look for other partners.	Market-based relationship; lots of them; standard products and routine producers; minimal investment; serve through distribution instead of direct.

Figure 3-2. Managing strategic buyer-seller partnerships. [Adapted from Robert Krapfel, Deborah Salmond, and Robert Spekman, "A Strategic Approach to Managing Buyer-Seller Relationships," Working Paper, University of Maryland, June, 1990.]

INFLUENCE PROCESSES

The industrial marketer has a number of tactics and strategies available for trying to influence potential customers to buy and to persuade present customers to remain loyal or increase the amount of their purchases. For purposes of analysis, these methods of influence can be summarized in four categories—persuasion, compromise, bargaining, and negotiation. In an actual selling and buying situation, these methods of influence are likely to coexist in varying degrees.

Persuasion

Persuasion as an influence process is seen clearly in the traditional view of salesmanship as the process of convincing customers to buy. In this old-line approach, the sales rep knows her customer and his needs well enough to know how he can be made to buy. The sales interaction is described by a series of buyer mental stages, such as awareness, interest, desire, and action, through which the sales rep deftly moves the buyer. In the last analysis, the intent of persuasion is to impose the seller's will upon the buyer by showing him how the seller's offering can satisfy his needs. The sale is seen as a conquest.

As an influence process, persuasion can be effective in the short-term, but its major weakness is that it leaves the buyer open to counter-persuasion by competitive sales reps. It is not based on a thorough understanding of the customer organization and its needs, and it lacks a long-term orientation of building strong buyer-seller relationships. It concentrates instead on getting the order. The rep is viewed as controlling a number of variables within the sales presentation that, when properly used, can cause purchase behavior and generate a sale. Sales contests and incentive compensation schemes of various kinds typically are based on a persuasion model of influence, one intended to stimulate sales by motivating the sales rep to work harder and to generate sales that would otherwise be lost.

Implicit in the salesmanship view of buyer-seller influence processes is an assumption that the order is a reward to the sales rep, something that she wins for her effort, and something that the buyer gives up. These notions of win and lose, of conqueror and vanquished, seem a bit out of place in the relationship between industrial marketers and their organizational customers. They are equally inappropriate as a view of purchasing tactics, where the buyer is trying to win something from the sales rep and to dominate the interaction with her.

Compromise

The concept of compromise is also negative in its orientation. If persuasion is based on an "I win, you lose" model, then compromise is "I lose something, you lose something." The result is a solution to a problem that is acceptable to both parties but truly satisfying to neither. It is based on an essentially negative view of buyer-seller relationships as an adversary proceeding. In actual industrial selling situations, this view is probably more prevalent than it should be.

Compromise means that both parties feel trapped in a situation where they must make the best of things but cannot achieve all their objectives. It might characterize markets where there are few alternative sources of supply or where products are largely undifferentiated. Compromise as a method of influence takes a long time, since each party tries to hold onto what the other party is asking for. Agreement is difficult, because the essential nature of the process is to give up something rather than to gain something. The outcome often depends on the power of the respective parties, determined by size and the availability of alternative suppliers or customers. If one party is significantly more powerful than the other, then compromise may become a process of the weaker party giving in to the demands of the stronger, a situation that is basically unstable over a period of time, since the weaker party will search for a way out of his predicament.

Compromise and accommodation, like persuasion, is short-term in its orientation and inadequate as a process for developing effective and satisfying buyer-seller relationships.

Bargaining

The bargaining process as an analytical concept recognizes that the two parties in the process are interdependent and that through various combinations of cooperation and competition they can, through their behaviors, influence both the total value of the outcomes and the way in which that value is shared. Bargaining is *strategic interaction*, goal-oriented, interdependent behavior by two or more parties, where the choices of each party are contingent upon his estimate of the actions of the other party or parties.

Bargaining theory distinguishes between situations where the actors are rational and those where they are not. Formal theories of bargaining have not found widespread application in real-world situations, however.[27]

Models of bargaining in industrial marketing often involve the special case of competitive bidding where price is the key strategic variable. This is only one type of bargaining, however, since many variables other than price may be important to the buyer. In the previous chapter, the discussion of purchasing strategy demonstrated that reliability was often more important than price. The discussion of buying situations and their influence on buyer-seller interaction suggested that transaction uncertainty may lead to more emphasis on delivery and reliability than on price.

The basic assumption in bargaining models is that the actors can cooperate for mutual benefit, although cooperation will not maximize the value of outcomes for either party. This set of assumptions is quite appropriate for most, if not all, industrial marketing situations. Buyer and seller can elect to cooperate and can increase the total value of the transaction to themselves, or they can avoid cooperation and each can try to maximize the value to himself. In theoretical terms, buyer-seller interaction can be characterized as a non-zero sum two-person game.

Negotiation

Negotiation is a process that attempts to maximize the value of the interaction to both buyer and seller. It recognizes the fact that the parties are in a bargaining situation of strategic interaction and that cooperation can increase the total value of the interaction. Furthermore, it recognizes the interdependence of buyer and seller and allows each actor to accept a goal of maximizing the total value of the interaction rather than trying to maximize his share. It involves a long-term view of the buyer-seller relationship.

One practice-oriented treatise on negotiation characterizes this process as that of "win/win negotiation" with the objective of maximizing profits for both buyer and seller. According to this view, there are five benefits of negotiation in comparison with other methods of influence: (1) recognition of the buyer as an individual who can through his behavior increase the value of the buyer-seller relation-

---

[27] Oran R. Young, *Bargaining: Formal Theories of Negotiation* (Urbana, Ill.: University of Illinois Press, 1975), p. 408.

ship; (2) the development of a climate of confidence between buyer and seller; (3) the positioning of the sales rep as an advisor and counselor to the buyer, rather than a persuader or adversary as implied by other views of the influence process; (4) the encouragement of information exchange as necessary to develop the best long-term solutions to the buyer's problems; and (5) its contribution to the development of satisfying long-term relationships.[28]

While negotiation is likely to avoid short-term outcomes that have the greatest possible value for one of the two parties, it maximizes the long-term value of the relationships to both and significantly enhances the probability that the outcome will be more than satisfactory to both parties.

Effective negotiation requires both positive attitudes toward the buyer and toward the buyer-seller relationship and a solid understanding of the buyer and his needs and of the buying situation. A conceptual basis for understanding industrial buyers has been developed in Chapter 2 and in the earlier part of the present chapter.

Our conclusion is obviously that negotiation is a more appropriate influence strategy than either simple persuasion or compromise in the complex environment of industrial buyer-seller relationships. Use of negotiation as an influence process requires that the sales rep and the buyer develop different (and higher-order) skills and attitudes toward their work than would be characteristic of the salesmanship view. The sales rep must look beyond getting the order to the development of the best possible environment for future growth of the account. The buyer must think in terms of developing effective suppliers. Each party must think about what he can contribute to the relationship, not just what he can take away from the transaction. The sales rep must avoid the temptation to get the current order at almost any cost and must instead develop the long-term viewpoint that attempts to maximize her value as a supplier to the customer. The relevant questions are not "What will convince you to buy?" but "What are your needs and how can my company serve them best over the long run?" and "How can I make my company and its offerings most attractive to you? What can we do for you?" A negotiation view of buyer-seller relationships has involved in it, implicitly, a willingness and readiness to adapt the selling company's product offering to the needs of the individual customer. In other

[28] Mack Hanan, James Cribbin, and Howard Berrian, *Sales Negotiation Strategies* (New York: AMACOM, 1977).

words, as we have stated before, the product is a variable, not a given, in a strategic (long-term) view of industrial marketing.

Negotiation is a time-consuming process requiring the careful deployment of company resources. A major responsibility for the industrial sales rep is to select her targets carefully and to avoid wasting resources on low expected value situations. Several company executives and specialists will be involved in a significant negotiation, and their roles must be carefully planned. A methodology, called GERT—Graphical Evaluation and Review Technique—has been proposed as a means of estimating expected negotiation costs in a major sales negotiation and for estimating the probability of success. Data for the GERT analysis including costs, times, and estimated probabilities can be obtained from historical records of similar negotiations.[29]

RECIPROCITY

Reciprocity, or reciprocal dealing, is a special case of negotiation in which each party is both a buyer from and a seller to the other party, a system of mutual patronage. Reciprocity is both the use of purchasing power to obtain sales and the practice of preferring one's own customers in purchasing. But the problems and issues relating to reciprocity go considerably beyond the basics of negotiation.

Reciprocal dealing has historically been believed to be widespread in industrial marketing, especially in industries where there is little significant product differentiation, such as petroleum, transportation, paints and coatings, and commodity chemicals. When products are relatively homogeneous, and there is an absence of strong price competition (the two sets of conditions obviously need not occur together), reciprocal dealing is likely to occur. If at least one of the two firms is a major supplier to the other, then there is an additional factor favoring reciprocity. Finally, if at least one of the firms has excess capacity and feels a strong need to fill it, then the probability of reciprocal dealing is quite high.[30]

Other things being equal, there is a reasonable argument to be made in favor of a firm's buying from its own customers. Such values

---

[29] Monroe M. Bird, Edward R. Clayton, and Lawrence J. Moore, "Sales Negotiation Cost Planning for Corporate Level Sales," *Journal of Marketing*, **37**, 2 (April, 1973), 7–13.

[30] Reed Moyer, "Reciprocity: Retrospect and Prospect," *Journal of Marketing*, **34**, 4 (October, 1970), 47–54.

as fairness, helpfulness, and good faith are involved. When one considers the scope and complexity of many of today's largest, multinational, conglomerate firms, then the opportunities for reciprocity are clearly very great, indeed. Unfortunately, although these are the major arguments in favor of reciprocity—it "makes sense"—things are seldom so simple. More often than not, the procedures involved in reciprocal dealing become exceedingly complex and simple reciprocity ("it makes sense to buy from your customers when prices are equal") becomes coercive reciprocity ("buy from us, at favorable—possibly non-competitive—terms, or we will refuse to buy from you.").

At the heart of a reciprocal buying scheme there is often a complex system of recording purchases from a customer, informing sales management of these data, and using this information to coerce proportional orders from that customer. When the requirements of reciprocity become paramount, then the benefits of competition to the purchaser begin to wither. Too often, sellers may use reciprocity as a way of avoiding price competition.

The use of reciprocity, thus, may vary from subtle to aggressive. The more aggressive it becomes, the more illegal it is likely to be. In the past two decades or so, the courts have increasingly viewed reciprocity with suspicion under the antitrust laws. The courts have tended to view the presence of organized systems for monitoring purchases and informing sales management of these data as *per se* evidence of reciprocal dealing. One effect has been to make membership in trade relations associations virtually illegal. On the other hand, the absence of such formal arrangements is likely to be a reasonable defense against charges of illegal use of reciprocal dealings.

The case against reciprocity was succinctly stated by the head of the Justice Department's Antitrust Division, R. L. McLaren, during the period when the government was pursuing the issue most vigorously:

> Particularly where conducted by big, diversified companies, reciprocity programs substitute buying power consideration for the normal and accepted ways of selling, i.e., on the basis of price, quality, and service—with foreclosure effects on smaller or less diversified competitors.[31]

[31] Quoted in the "Notable and Quotable" Column, *The Wall Street Journal*, May 8, 1969, p. 20, and cited in Moyer, *op. cit.*

On the other hand, given the scope of operations of the typical large, industrial corporation, it is almost impossible to avoid dealing with suppliers who are also customers. Reciprocity can therefore never be made illegal. Rather, the problem comes with coercive use of purchasing power to restrict competition.

From the purchasing manager's viewpoint, the central point is that reciprocal dealing reduces price competition. One survey found that a large majority of purchasing managers disliked reciprocity, apparently because of the recognition that it required compromise in which "somebody loses." The same survey found that sales managers were even more opposed to reciprocity, with a majority saying that it should be made illegal.[32]

Reciprocal dealing can become tremendously complex, especially when it involves customers' customers. For example, in a classic legal case, it was charged that E. I. duPont de Nemours' large ownership interest in General Motors limited competition for GM's purchases of fabrics and automotive finishes.[33] In a related case, a competitor of E. I. duPont de Nemours & Company charged that duPont attempted to increase its sales of explosives by putting pressure on Curtis Publishing Company, whose magazines carried duPont advertisements. Curtis was reportedly asked to put pressure in turn, on Castonia Paper Company, its subsidiary, which bought large quantities of coal from Rochester and Pittsburgh Coal Company, to induce them to purchase explosives from duPont.[34]

A late 1970's survey of company practices suggested that the incidence of reciprocal dealing had diminished substantially as a result of more aggressive interpretation and enforcement of the antitrust laws relating to reciprocity. In general, the findings of this study support the notion that reciprocal dealing is inevitable in a world of large diversified corporations and cannot be made illegal, whereas aggressive, anticompetitive reciprocity does clearly run afoul of the antitrust laws. Quoting the author of this report,

> . . . one can say that reciprocal purchasing in a setting which meets the market structure criterion for anticompetitive results and is equipped with the requisite marketing-purchasing data exchange

---

[32] Monroe M. Bird and C. Wayne Shepherd, "Reciprocity in Industrial Buying and Selling: A Study of Attitude," *Journal of Purchasing*, **9**, 4 (November, 1973), 26–35.

[33] United States versus E. I. duPont de Nemours & Co. et al., 366 U.S. 316 (1961) referred to in Moyer, *op. cit.*

[34] Reported in Moyer, *op. cit.*

has almost ceased. Once the enforcement agencies directed their interest to this harmful marketing practice, it became evident that anticompetitive reciprocity is hard to conceal and that it is illegal.[35]

To conclude, reciprocity is a special case of buyer-seller negotiation. Casual reciprocity, buying from one's customers, can probably not be avoided by large industrial firms. But aggressive reciprocity, relying on formal systems for tracking purchases by suppliers, tends to undercut the effectiveness of the purchasing manager and may very well be illegal. Because many firms cannot avoid some reciprocal dealing, reciprocity cannot be judged to be *per se* illegal or undesirable. But caution must be exercised to make sure that it remains a relatively minor consideration both in selecting suppliers and in negotiation with customers.

DEALING WITH CUSTOMERS' CUSTOMERS

It is not uncommon, especially when trying to develop markets for new products, for the industrial marketer to find it necessary to influence the customers of the target purchaser. For example, a fabricator of ice cream cartons, who sells cartons to ice cream producers, might find it necessary to promote its new ice cream package to retailers, and even to consumers, in order to convince the ice cream maker to adopt it. Similarly, aircraft engine manufacturers are likely to direct their principal marketing efforts at aircraft buyers (e.g., airlines) rather than at airframe manufacturers, the installers of the engines. The objective is to have the airline specify a particular engine when placing an order with the aircraft manufacturer.

One of the complexities of industrial marketing is the frequent necessity to sell to a customer's customers and, therefore, to become a competitor of certain customers. This is the common dilemma for the parts manufacturer who sells to both OEM's and end-users. For example, Cummins Engine Company is both a supplier of diesel engines to General Motors and a major competitor of GM's Detroit Diesel division. A truck purchaser may specify either manufacturer's engine when he purchases a General Motors truck.

Dealing with customers' customers can be a very sensitive matter. In some instances the customer may expect the supplier to help it

[35] F. Robert Finney, "Reciprocity: Gone But Not Forgotten," *Journal of Marketing*, **42**, 1 (January, 1978), 54–59, at 56.

develop acceptance for its product among users. In other cases, such "pull-through" marketing efforts may be viewed as interference in the customer's relationships with its customers. If it is done secretively, the latter is likely to be the case. Such marketing efforts are likely to be most effective when they are based on careful planning and coordination with the customer. The nature of these cooperative efforts, which can represent significant investments of sales reps' time, advertising efforts, and technical service, is often the subject of negotiation. To be productive, negotiation should begin with the development of agreement about the objective of the program to influence the customers' customers so that both parties see clearly how they will gain from these efforts.

CUSTOMER SERVICE

We have defined the industrial product as a complex set of relationships between supplier and customer. The service offering supplements the basic physical product to create the total value of the relationship for the customer. Many people and departments in the supplier organization may be involved in the service offering including production, product engineering, applications engineering, traffic, advertising and sales promotion, credit, and repair service.

One of the major responsibilities of the industrial sales rep is to plan and coordinate the roles of all these actors as they interact with her customers. And one of the essential tasks for the marketing manager is to develop and integrate these various elements of the firm's capability into a comprehensive marketing strategy. It will be recalled from Chapter 1 that one of the unique features of industrial marketing is functional interdependence, the dependence of marketing for its effectiveness on many other parts of the business beyond the direct control of the marketing managers.

Service Bundling

An increasingly important issue for many industrial marketers is that of *service bundling*, that is, which services to include with the basic product offering and which to offer, and price, separately. The problem is a very complex one with its roots in the firm's business strategy and its positioning in the marketplace. (*Positioning* will be discussed in detail in the following chapter.) The firm that positions itself as offering a complete service package must create a perception of superior value that will justify a price high enough to cover the costs of providing the full service bundle. In contrast, there will be market nichers whose value proposition to the customer is the availability of services, "as needed and wanted," on an *a la carte* basis, at a lower price. The dilemma is that the firm that uses services as a basis for differentiating its product offering may find that its prices must be so high that it becomes non-competitive because of the costs of those service features, especially if their principal competitors are small specialists with much lower costs for such "overhead" items as administration, marketing, and R&D.

The importance of various components of customer service will vary with the stage in the relationship with the customer, with the stage in the product life cycle, and with the type of product. Too little service can reduce the effectiveness of the marketing program, but too much can prove costly and even unprofitable in a highly competitive market. On the other hand, a solid and attractive service offering can be the key element in a strategy of product differentiation and market segmentation that protects the marketer from aggressive price competition.

For truly new products involving potentially high risk for the customer, technical service and application assistance are likely to be essential components in the marketing mix. Very often, the key to the successful development of a market for a new industrial product is a positive outcome to a joint technical development program with an important customer whose business is important to the supplier and whose credibility is high with other potential customers. A successful outcome to such technical development programs will show that the new product can be used profitably by potential customers. Both technical soundness and economic (cost) viability must be demonstrated. Usually this involves successful use in a production situation, not just in a laboratory test. The true economic impact of a significant new material, process, part, or piece of equipment cannot be assessed until the actual operating situation has been duplicated as completely as possible.

For equipment items, technical cooperation between buyer and seller may lead to refinements of design and the development of operating systems incorporating the item. For components and materials, customer product development and production methods must often be assisted by cooperative efforts. The supplier's technical competence and its credibility are very important elements of its product offering. Because such product and process developments are likely to have competitive value for the customer, the customer will be interested in protecting its investment in their development. A relationship of trust with suppliers and specific supplier personnel is obviously necessary. Beyond that, specific contractual obligations may have to be worked out for sharing the results of the project. Patents may be involved. The customer may ask for exclusive use of components, materials, or processes developed with suppliers, for an agreed upon period of time. Often, the customer may initiate such developments, either as concepts or as actual prototypes taken to the supplier for production.[36] The obligations of both parties must therefore be worked out as carefully as possible to avoid misunderstanding and legal problems.

We will return to this issue of market development programs for new products in Chapter 6.

In mature markets, demand may be still growing or stable, but there will be increased competition with roughly similar products being offered by competing suppliers. The major elements of customer service in mature markets usually are delivery, relatively "minor" (but vitally important) technical improvements, and technical support from a readily available field service organization. When the product is easily available from several competitors with competitive prices, then the nuances of availability, modest differences in product quality, and technical service are very important differences among suppliers' product offerings.

Service for established products is often defined by the geographic location of the customer service organization. For mature products, the service organization may be an integral part of the distribution network, which is likely to be extensive in order to compete on the basis of availability. For customers, both market uncertainty and transaction uncertainty for untried suppliers may be very high.

For equipment, the critical elements of customer service are installation, maintenance, and repair including availability of spare parts and replacement units. For components and supply items, the major dimensions of service are availability of the materials and applications assistance to solve production problems. Delivery may have to be scheduled carefully when customers prefer to hold very small inventories to minimize their investment. This situation puts an important responsibility for inventory on the supplier. For very

[36] Eric von Hippel, "Has a Customer Already Developed Your Next Product?" *Sloan Management Review*, **18**, 2 (Winter, 1977), 63–74.

large customers, components and materials suppliers may build production or distribution facilities right next to the customer. Such arrangements obviously require contractual obligations and build long-term buyer-seller relationships.

SUMMARY

In this chapter we have examined several aspects of buyer-seller relationships, including sales rep–prospect interaction, strategic partnerships, methods of influence, reciprocity, dealing with customers' customers, and the role of customer service. Throughout the discussion, emphasis has been placed on the development of mutually satisfying, profitable, long-term relationships between suppliers and customers. Thus, negotiation with an objective of maximizing the value of the transaction to both parties was said to be preferable to persuasion or compromise as an influence process in industrial marketing.

Personal selling was analyzed as a form of dyadic (two-person) communication using concepts from role theory. Among the factors influencing a buyer's response to a sales rep, we identified the buyer's stereotype of the sales rep based on her previous interactions with sales reps, the reputation of the selling company (source effect), the buyer's perception of the expectations of other members of the buying center, the quality of the sales presentation, the type of uncertainty perceived by the buyer, the stage in the buying decision process, and the stage in the diffusion process. In a word, buyer-sales rep interaction is complex.

Strategic buyer-seller partnerships have become increasingly popular in industrial marketing, offering benefits in terms of both improved quality and lower costs. However, as firms move from one-at-a-time transactions toward more complex relationships, substituting administrative and bureaucratic control of the procurement process for market control, they face new and different management challenges. It is important to tie management practice and financial investment to the type of relationship, and to anticipate the inevitable management conflict in such relationships in their design so that conflict resolution processes will be in place when needed.

Customer service, including helping the customer sell to his customers, is often more important than the physical product itself. The nature of the service offering was seen to vary with the type of product and the stage in the product life cycle. In industrial marketing, customer service is often the key dimension of product differentiation. This fact was recognized in our Chapter 1 definition of the industrial product as "an array of economic, technical, and personal relationships between buyer and seller," and in our statement that buyer-seller interdependence is a salient dimension of industrial marketing.

Bibliography

Dwyer, F. Robert, Paul Schurr, and Sejo Oh, "Developing Buyer-Seller Relationships, *Journal of Marketing,* **51,** 2 (April, 1987), 11–27.

Frazier, Gary L., Robert E. Spekman, and Charles R. O'Neal, "Just-In-Time Exchange Relationships in Industrial Markets," *Journal of Marketing,* **52,** 4 (October, 1988), 52–67.

Hovland, Carl I., Irving L. Janis, and Harold H. Kelley, *Communication and Persuasion: Psychological Studies of Opinion Change.* (New Haven, Conn.: Yale University Press, 1953).

Jackson, Barbara B., *Winning and Keeping Industrial Customers* (Lexington, Mass.: Lexington Books, 1985).

Nierenberg, Gerard I., *The Complete Negotiator* (New York: Nierenberg & Zeif Publishers, 1986).

Raiffa, Howard, *The Art and Science of Negotiations* (Cambridge, Mass.: Harvard University Press, 1982).

Spekman, Robert E., "Strategic Supplier Selection: Understanding Long-Term Buyer Relationships," *Business Horizons,* **31,** 4 (July-August, 1988),   75–81.

Webster, Frederick E., Jr., *Field Sales Management* (New York: John Wiley & Sons, 1983).

4 Industrial Market Segmentation, Targeting, and Positioning

At the heart of every marketing strategy decision is market segmentation, partitioning a large market into smaller, more homogeneous submarkets in order to target customers more effectively and efficiently. The selection of customers is the most important decision any industrial firm makes because commitment to serving the needs of those customers will shape the firm's resources and skills, business strategy, and organization structure. The marketer adapts its product offering, pricing, communications, and distribution systems to the needs, preferences, and buying processes of its customers. Having chosen its market targets, the firm must then decide on its *positioning* in those segments, that is, determine its *value proposition* stating how it wants to be viewed by those customers compared to its competitors.

As a corollary of the strategic importance of customer selection, it follows that there are good and bad customers. "Good" customers are those that stand to benefit most from what the supplier has to offer, those whose needs and buying practices best fit the supplier's capability. They will ask the firm to do things that it can do well and that are consistent with its strategy. They will value the resources that the firm commits to solving their problems, and they will be willing to pay for them.

In turn, these customer relationships are a major source of strength for the supplier's business. If the selling effort is properly conducted, this matching of customer needs and vendor capabilities can assure a mutually profitable long-term relationship. In the case of new product offerings and new market entry, "good" customer opportunities are also defined by the absence of effective relationships with existing suppliers, either because these competitors lack the technical capabilities of the potential supplier or because of other weaknesses in the buyer-seller relationship, such as unrealistic pricing or weak distribution.

"Bad" customers, in contrast, leave the firm weaker rather than stronger. They ask it to do things it cannot or does not want to do well, things that are inconsistent with its business strategy. They do not value the relationship and they are not willing to pay for the resources the vendor firm commits to solving their problems.

Good customers take the firm in directions consistent with its strategy and contribute to the development of its skills and resources. If the firm does not have a clear strategy for business development, it is difficult to tell the difference between good and bad customers.

Ideally, customer selection strategy is based on careful analysis of markets and of company capabilities. Just as a good purchasing strategy, guided by a careful statement of objectives, leads to a reasoned choice among competing suppliers and the development of effective suppliers, so should marketers develop statements of objectives for selecting among potential customers and developing effective long-term customer relationships.

Unfortunately it is the case, however, that customer selection is often opportunistic and unplanned in actual practice. Sales representatives and their managers, guided by current sales goals and a short-term orientation, are happy to get any piece of business available to them. Then comes the problem of trying to satisfy the customer and to develop long-term relationships without the necessary organization capacity to do so. Weaknesses may appear in the form of customer dissatisfaction, unrealistically low prices, product failure, distribution inefficiencies, high marketing costs, and a high rate of turnover in the customer list.

THE CONCEPT OF MARKET SEGMENTATION

Market segmentation is a strategy for selecting customers, for differentiating customers according to differences in the way they respond to marketing effort, for choosing among alternative market opportunities, and for tailoring marketing strategies to those distinctive opportunities. The basic calculus of market segmentation is one of matching company capabilities with unsatisfied customer needs. The common descriptive metaphor is that of firing single rifle shots at the market rather than using a shotgun. The definition of market segments is a creative act, requiring both analysis and imagination, demanding that the marketing manager think in conceptual and abstract terms about the structure of his markets, the nature of potential customers, and the distinctive features of his company's capability. The definition of those variables that will serve as the basis for an operational segmentation is seldom easy or obvious.

Criteria for Segmentation Variables

Segmentation variables are customer characteristics that relate to some important difference in customer response to marketing effort. The selection of those variables that will be used for industrial market segmentation should meet three criteria.

First, the variable should be measurable, otherwise the scheme will not be operational. With an innovative and imaginative segmentation scheme, the marketing manager may find it necessary to use field research to obtain the necessary measurements. Cost considerations, as well as research methodology, may lead to the choice of a less elegant definition of the segmentation variable.

Second, the segmentation variable should be relevant for a substantial grouping of customers. That is, the characteristic chosen should pertain to several customers and should relate to important differences among customers in terms of their response to marketing strategies. Thus, the resulting segments should be substantially large enough to warrant attention and substantially different enough to warrant distinctive marketing strategies. Occasionally, in industrial markets, a single customer may be large enough and distinctive enough to be treated as a unique segment, but, in general, segments make sense only when they have a reasonably large number of customers.

Third, the segmentation variable chosen ought to have operational relevance for marketing strategy. Differences identified among customers should relate to differences in their preferences and buying behavior that require a differentiated marketing approach—unique products, selective pricing, alternative distribution arrangements, different selling approaches, and so on. The risk here is that segments will be defined that are conceptually valid and interesting but that do not have valid strategic implications.

An effective segmentation scheme will create segments that contain customers, within the segment, that are highly homogeneous. Equally important, the segments will be as distinctly different from one another as possible. To use statistical terminology, the objective of a segmentation scheme should be "to maximize among-group variance and to minimize within-group variance."

Benefit Segmentation

As an alternative to segmenting markets based on customers' characteristics such as their demographics and attitudes, benefit segmentation has been proposed. Benefit segmentation simply recognizes that customers buy the same products for different reasons, and place different values on particular product features. In the purchase of a machine tool, for example, some customers may be primarily interested in the quality of the output from that machine in terms of precise machining of metal, others may value most highly its ability to lower production cost per unit, while still others will be most concerned about the initial capital cost for the purchase. The central notion underlying benefit segmentation is that differences among customers in the reasons for purchasing and using products and services are the most basic of all reasons for the existence of market segments.[1]

Benefit segmentation can be made operational if there are identifiable and measurable characteristics of customers that are strongly related to the preference for particular benefits. To continue our example, it might be found that interest in precision machining was a characteristic of small companies serving the aircraft industry, that those firms that weighted cost savings most heavily served only a few, large customers and were subsidiaries of large diversified manufacturers, and that those most concerned with capital cost were either very new firms or those experiencing little growth in sales volume. In the absence of the ability to relate benefits to such observable and measurable characteristics, benefit segmentation is infeasible. The concept and techniques of benefit segmentation have been developed over the past two decades in the area of

---

[1] Russell I. Haley, "Benefit Segmentation: A Decision-Oriented Research Tool," *Journal of Marketing,* **32** (July, 1968), 30–35.

consumer marketing, especially packaged goods, with no published applications in the industrial marketing area.

Moriarty and Reibstein set out to test the viability of benefit segmentation in an industrial marketing context. Their basic research problem was to test whether industrial market benefit segments could be derived from segments developed by more traditional means. Studying the purchase of computer terminals, Moriarty and Reibstein came to a negative conclusion. While they were able to define distinct segments (using the statistical technique called "cluster analysis") based on benefits sought (speed, ease of operation, aesthetics, compatibility, service, etc.), they were unable to relate these benefit segments to traditional segmentation variables of size and S.I.C. classification. Thus, benefit segments could not be identified operationally without first knowing the benefits sought by each customer. The researchers could not find any surrogate measures for benefit segmentation. While more research on benefit segmentation is clearly needed in an industrial marketing context, at the present time it appears that the industrial marketer must continue to rely on more traditional bases of market segmentation.[2]

Strategic Alternatives

There are three distinct types of strategies available to the marketer as a function of its basic segmentation scheme. Competition, the nature of the market, and company resources will determine the strategic posture that is best in a given situation. To repeat a point made earlier, the purpose of segmentation is to deploy company marketing resources against market opportunities in the most effective manner.

Concentrated marketing means focussing all marketing effort on a single, carefully defined segment. The result is likely to be a somewhat narrow product range, usually associated with high quality and high price, along with highly selective promotional and distribution strategies. Examples of concentrated marketing include Hypertherm, a manufacturer of plasma welding torches, Control Data Corporation, which focusses on large systems in the computer field, and Cairns & Brother, specialists in protective clothing for firefighters.

Differentiated marketing is probably the most common type of

[2] Rowland T. Moriarty, and David J. Reibstein, "Benefit Segmentation in Industrial Markets," *Journal of Business Research,* 14 (December, 1986), 463–86.

segmentation strategy, using distinctive marketing approaches in two or more carefully chosen segments. It would not be uncommon for a firm to elect to compete in some segments and to avoid others within a total market. The strategic differences may be organized around distinctive product offerings or they may be primarily promotional differences, offering the same product in multiple segments. Diesel engine builders, for example, have distinct product lines for over-the-road, construction, and marine applications, as well as different sizes in each line. Obviously, promotional, pricing, and distribution policies for these distinct markets are also different. In contrast, manufacturers of light trucks typically sell the same product to such diverse markets as farming, construction, route delivery, and recreation, with similar pricing and distribution. Different promotional strategies are used for reaching these distinct segments.

Undifferentiated marketing is the absence of effective segmentation. It may reflect a lack of management analysis and planning, or it may be a conscious strategic choice due to the lack of meaningful differentiations among customers in terms of their response to marketing effort. While undifferentiated marketing may make sense under these circumstances, it is often a sign of weakness. It is generally agreed that a lack of effective segmentation was a root cause of the failures of General Electric and RCA in the computer business, for example. Neither of these companies was able to define a distinct market niche for itself against giant IBM. IBM, by the way, is an excellent example of differentiated marketing with distinctive product offerings and marketing strategies for a large number of market segments defined along industry lines and within industry by customer size.

POSITIONING

Positioning is an important strategic concept, developed in consumer marketing but with equal applicability for industrial products and services. It is closely related to what we have been referring to as the firm's *value proposition*, the reasons why customers should do business with it rather than with its competitors.

Positioning has been called "the battle for your mind" by the authors of a well known book by that title.[3] More formally, it has

[3] Al Ries and Jack Trout, *Positioning: The Battle for Your Mind*, 1st ed.—rev. (New York: Warner Books, 1986).

been defined as " . . . the act of designing the company's image and value offer so that the segment's customers understand and appreciate what the company stands for in relation to its competitors."[4] A positioning statement can be a very important communication element both for the marketplace and for the marketer's own organization, helping to build consensus about the firm's commitment to serving a well-defined set of customer needs. It is a way of communicating strategy.

A good positioning statement will contain three elements: the target market; the competitive frame of reference; and the unique benefit. These might be thought of as answers to three questions:

1. *Who* is the product for?
2. *What* are we selling?
3. *Why* should the customer buy it?

Logically, positioning must follow segmentation and targeting. The reasons are obvious: positioning is *in the mind of the customer/ prospect* and *in comparison to competition.* Thus, a sandpaper manufacturer might create a positioning that says:

> For auto body paint and repair shops, Gritty brand sandpaper is the surface preparation system that combines all grades needed for the job in a handy dispenser.

Strong positioning is a necessary but not sufficient condition for business profitability. Without it, marketing strategy lacks focus and direction and the company's value proposition cannot be communicated clearly either to potential customers or within the organization. Internally, the positioning statement becomes a key part of the values and beliefs of the company, the "corporate culture," the shared view about how the firm delivers value to customers.

STRATEGIC MARKET SEGMENTATION

McKinsey and Company, international management consultants, have developed and publicized a concept of strategic market segmentation which can be very helpful to industrial marketers. The

[4] Philip Kotler, *Marketing Management: Analysis, Planning, Implementation, and Control*, 6th ed. (Englewood Cliffs, N.J.: Prentice-Hall, Inc., 1988), p. 308.

McKinsey "Strategy Game Board" is a 2 × 2 matrix of answers to the questions "Where to Compete?," where the choices are "Head On" or "Niche" and "How to Compete?," either with "The Same Game" or "A New Game." Strategic market segmentation is the process of moving away from competing "Head On" and toward a well defined market "Niche." The model is outlined in Figure 4-1.

In their work, McKinsey and Company have defined five types of strategic market segments: (1) end-use segments; (2) product segments; (3) geographic segments; (4) common buying factor segments; and (5) customer size segments. They suggest that creative analysis may identify combinations of the above.

Their experience has led them to conclude that industrial marketers in general have difficulty developing and implementing niche marketing strategies for several reasons. There is a reluctance to concentrate effort on a few market segments because of the fear of losing sales volume, and a tendency to focus on sales volume rather than profitability. Short-term profit pressures cause managers to resist a critical appraisal of marketing approaches. Also, the McKinsey experts saw a tendency to place too much emphasis on segmentation *per se* rather than on the development of strategies for competing successfully in those segments. There was also an observed lack of understanding of how to resegment markets, leading to either too few segments and therefore inadequate opportunities to achieve real competitive advantage, or too many segments and therefore confusion and misdirection.[5]

Because industrial buying behavior is fundamentally different from consumer buying behavior, the methodology of market segmentation and the specific variables used for segmentation must also be different. Industrial segmentation at the minimum should recognize that customers are organizations, that the decision-making unit is a group of individuals interacting within the context of the formal organization's structure, and that these individuals occupy unique roles that are major influences on their behavior. Thus, characteristics of the organization, of the buying center, and of organizational actors are all candidates for segmentation variables.

The early literature on industrial market segmentation did not clearly delineate these options. Industrial market segmentation

[5] This description of the McKinsey work on strategic market segmentation is based on a presentation by Mr. Robert Garda, a McKinsey Director, to the Industrial Marketing and Procurement course at the Amos Tuck School of Business Administration at Dartmouth College on January 22, 1991.

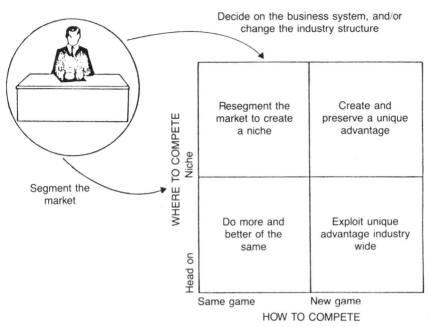

Figure 4-1. The McKinsey & Company Strategic Gameboard. Reproduced with permission.

schemes typically began with the recognition that industrial customers should be segmented according to geographic location and end-use of the purchased product. When describing the buying center, these early approaches tended to mix together behavioral variables that pertained to different aspects of the buying decision process. For example, Robinson, Faris, and Wind proposed segmenting industrial markets according to type of buying situation (straight rebuy, modified rebuy, and new buy) and stage in the decision process (from need recognition to selection of an order routine).[6] Kernan and Sommers proposed segmenting according to the purchaser's primary organizational role and his degree of com-

---

[6] Patrick J. Robinson, Charles W. Faris, and Yoram Wind, *Industrial Buying and Creative Marketing* (Boston: Allyn and Bacon and the Marketing Science Institute, 1967), and Charles W. Faris, "Market Segmentation and Industrial Buying Behavior" in M. S. Moyer and R. E. Vosburgh, *Marketing for Tomorrow . . . Today* (Chicago: American Marketing Association, 1967), pp. 108–10.

mitment to it.[7] Feldman and Cardozo proposed segmentation on the basis of the purchasing strategies used by different buyers (roles) to process information and select suppliers.[8] Yankelovich suggested segmenting on the basis of the type of problem being solved by the buyer (a measure that would be similar to end use) and on the basis of the buyer's self-confidence.[9]

These early papers all helped to establish a new direction in industrial market segmentation, moving away from a traditional focus on the characteristics of the organization, such as size, location, S.I.C. category, and intended use of the product, and toward a behavioral focus on the decision-making process and its participants. In some discussions, there was a tendency to view the traditional and the behavioral as competing view-points. In fact, both kinds of segmentation may be necessary and desirable.

Any specific descriptor of the industrial buying decision process or any hypothetical construct describing that process is a candidate for use as a segmentation variable, provided it can be measured and made operational. Previous chapters have suggested several, and they can be listed as follows:

A. Characteristics of the Buying Organization:

1. Type of organization—manufacturing firm, educational institution, transportation authority, hospital, governmental agency, public utility.

2. Organization "demographics"—e.g., number of employees, annual sales volume, industry affiliation (S.I.C. group), geographic location, number of plants.

3. Product application—end use.

4. Type of buying situation.

5. Degree of source loyalty, and whether the supplier is "in" or "out."

6. The existence of purchasing contracts of various kinds, such

[7] Jerome B. Kernan and Montrose S. Sommers, "The Behavioral Matrix—A Closer Look at the Industrial Buyer," *Business Horizons*, **9**, 2 (Summer; 1966), 59–72.
[8] Wallace Feldman and Richard N. Cardozo, "Industrial Buying as Consumer Behavior," in M. S. Moyer and R. E. Vosburgh, *Marketing for Tomorrow . . . Today* (Chicago: American Marketing Association, 1967), pp. 102–7.
[9] Daniel Yankelovich, "New Criteria for Market Segmentation," *Harvard Business Review*, **42**, 2 (March—April, 1964), 83–90.

as annual requirement suppliers, stockless purchasing, and so on.

7. Presence or absence of reciprocity.

B. **Characteristics of the Buying Center:**
   1. Composition—buying roles.
   2. Stage in buying decision process.
   3. Type of uncertainty perceived in the buying center—need, market, or transaction uncertainty.
   4. Degree of decentralization—locus of buying responsibility within the organization.
   5. The task assigned to the buying center—the specific type of problem being solved.
   6. Amount of time pressure felt by members of the buying center.
   7. Type of conflict resolution characteristically used in the buying center—persuasion, compromise, bargaining or negotiation.
   8. Decision rules and characteristic types of purchasing strategies used.

C. **Characteristics of Individual Decision Participants:**
   1. Demographics—age, occupation, education, industry experience.
   2. Organizational role—position in organization structure and within buying center.
   3. Professional affiliations outside of organization.
   4. Psychographics—attitudes toward and preferences for suppliers and brands; degree of self-confidence.
   5. Perceptions of rewards, or punishments, for risk taking.
   6. The individual's "loyalty domain," his interactions with and sentiments toward other members of the buying center.
   7. Buying criteria used—reliability, price, product quality.

The foregoing lists are not intended to be exhaustive but should illustrate the relationship between market segmentation strategy and the many aspects of industrial buyer behavior mentioned earlier, including organizational, social-interactional, and individual variables.

UNIQUE ASPECTS OF INDUSTRIAL MARKET SEGMENTATION

Consumer markets are typically segmented on the basis of demographic variables, such as age, sex, stage in family life cycle, number of children, occupation, income, education, or psychographic variables, such as attitudes, personality characteristics, preferences, and values. In earlier chapters we have seen that industrial buying behavior is fundamentally different from consumer buying behavior. Obviously, the industrial customer is not an individual but a number of interacting individuals in a decision-making unit of a formal organization.

Should industrial market segments consist of organizations or individuals? Given the fundamental differences between consumer and industrial buyer behavior, are variables such as age, income, education, personality measures, and attitudes appropriate segmentation variables in industrial markets?

A TWO-STAGE APPROACH TO INDUSTRIAL MARKET SEGMENTATION

How can an industrial marketing decision maker select among these various approaches to market segmentation and determine those variables most relevant for its unique strategic problems? Wind and Cardozo have proposed a useful and straightforward distinction between macrosegmentation and microsegmentation[10] Their approach is presented graphically in Figure 4-2. Wind and Cardozo combine characteristics of both individuals and buying centers in their conceptualization of microsegments.

Macrosegmentation

Macrosegments consist of organizations with similar characteristics and with such characteristics having a direct relationship to response to marketing effort. These are the traditional, non-behavioral industrial market segments defined by organization type, size, S.I.C., and so on. In differentiated marketing, different products are sold through different distribution channels with distinct promotional methods. Such macrosegmentation strategies are often reflected in a "market" form of organization, with several "market

[10] Yoram Wind and Richard Cardozo, "Industrial Market Segmentation," *Industrial Marketing Management*, **3**, 2 (April, 1974), 153–66.

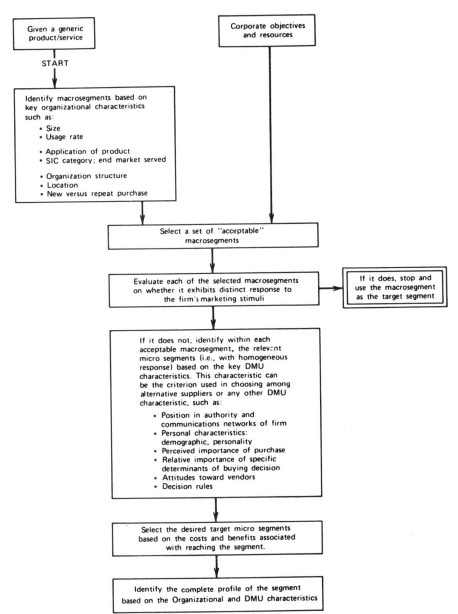

Figure 4-2. An approach to segmentation of organizational markets. [Source: *Yoram Wind and Richard Cardozo, op. cit., p. 156.*] *Reproduced with permission.*

managers," each responsible for selling the company's products to a distinct class of customer.

Macrosegments define target markets. Organizational character-istics such as size, location, and S.I.C. group may be adequate to explain differences in buying behavior. The next step, microseg-mentation, may, therefore, be unnecessary. The marketer can follow either concentrated or differentiated strategy with these macroseg-ments. Data for macrosegmentation are available from secondary sources such as the Census of Business for minimal expenditures of time and money. More detailed data are required for the next step, microsegmentation.

Microsegmentation

Microsegments are homogeneous groups of buyers within the mac-rosegments. Segmentation variables defining microsegments are *behavioral* variables characterizing buying centers and their mem-bers. Thus, within a given macrosegment, defined by S.I.C. group and size of firm, microsegments might be defined by composition of the buying center, principal buying criteria used, and degrees of perceived risk.

Obtaining data for developing microsegmentation strategy is more complex than for macrosegments. The company's sales force is an obvious place to begin, since sales representatives are usually good sources of information about customer characteristics and buying behavior. For sophisticated measures of organizational buy-ing behavior, such as buyer's self-confidence and degree of per-ceived risk, professionally conducted market research studies may be necessary. One of the most obvious benefits of this two-stage approach to market segmentation is that the cost of such research programs can be reduced and the expenditures made more efficient by concentrating only on those macrosegments with sufficient po-tential to warrant the expense of more detailed microsegmentation analysis.

The strategic implications of microsegmentation lie primarily in promotional strategy and to a lesser extent in product, price, or distribution refinements. Decisions influenced by segment differ-ences at the micro level include selecting individuals in the buying organization upon whom to make sales calls, design of sales pres-entations to stress specific product features relevant for the decision criteria used by these individuals, selection of advertising media to reach decision influences, budgeting the total amount of selling effort required as a function of degree of perceived risk, and so on.

A number of empirical studies have been made showing the viability of microsegmentation and segmentation based on behavioral variables characterizing industrial markets. A study of buying decisions for industrial protective coating materials, for example, showed eight distinct macrosegments based on product use and S.I.C. grouping and, within each macrosegment, from two to five microsegments defined by composition of the buying center, relative influence of group members, and buying criteria used. One microsegment was defined by the major role played by the purchasing managers, their reliance on information from their company's laboratory evaluations, and the use of price as the major decision criterion. In another microsegment, the major influence was the production foreman, who depended heavily upon the advice of production engineering, and who was concerned primarily about application characteristics and odor.[11]

Cardozo reported some preliminary findings that microsegments could be defined on the basis of purchasing strategies used, with each purchasing strategy requiring a different marketing strategy. He described two strategies used by purchasing managers: *simultaneous scanning*, which is used when the dollar expenditure is high, when the probability of a supplier's inability to meet specifications is moderate to high, when the major perceived risk is paying a premium price, and when management resources are available; and *sequential evaluation* of alternative suppliers, used when expenditure is low, the probability of failing to meet specifications is low, the major perceived risk is interruption of supply, and management resources for the decision process are limited.[12] It has been suggested that buyers may develop different purchasing strategies to respond to different types of perceived risk, an assertion similar to the analysis of different types of buying-selling situations (need, market, and transaction uncertainty) developed by Håkanson, Johanson, and Wootz and reported in our previous chapter.[13] These

---

[11] Frederick E. Webster, Jr., "Modeling the Industrial Buying Process," *Journal of Marketing Research*, **II**, 4 (November, 1965), 370–76.

[12] Richard N. Cardozo, "Segmenting the Industrial Market," in R. L. King (ed.), *Marketing and the New Science of Planning* (Chicago: American Marketing Association, 1968), pp. 433–40.

[13] Håkan Håkanson, Jan Johanson, and Björn Wootz, "Influence Tactics in Buyer-Seller Processes," *Industrial Marketing Management*, **5**, 6 (December, 1976), 319–32.

studies suggest that there is value, whenever possible, in seeking relationships among behavioral segmentation variables and incorporating these relationships into a single model, rather than treating them as independent variables offering, in a sense, competing explanations for differences in buying behavior. For example, individual buyer characteristics, such as self-confidence, may be major determinants of the degree of perceived risk that is directly related to the type of purchasing strategy employed. The purchasing strategy employed may, in turn, exert a major influence on the composition of the buying center.

An illustration of this more complex view of microsegmentation is given in research reported by Wilson, Matthews, and Sweeney. They used measures of four personality variables—generalized self-confidence, need for certainty, need to achieve, and perceived risk—to predict whether purchasing agents would follow a "normative" or "conservative" decision style. Normatives were defined by their use of an expected monetary value criterion in evaluating buying alternatives. Conservatives did not. Using discriminant analysis with the discriminant function consisting of the four personality variables, the authors were able to correctly classify, as normatives or conservatives, 75 percent of their research subjects, 132 Canadian purchasing agents. However, only "need for certainty," among the four personality variables, had a statistically significant impact. Only about 30 percent of the subjects could be characterized as normatives, using the "rational" approach in their decision making. The authors argued that normatives and conservatives need different marketing communication approaches with information aimed at their unique decision styles.[14]

Another example of microsegmentation based on behavioral variables is provided by the research of Choffray and Lilien, mentioned in Chapter 2.[15] Using data on the differing preferences and decision criteria of persons occupying specific buying roles within a buying center, buying organizations were assigned to microsegments composed of firms with similar buying centers. Marketing managers using this approach were called upon to judge which of four models of the multiperson choice process best characterized each microsegment. The relative influence of each of the buying roles was deter-

[14] David T. Wilson, H. Lee Matthews, and Timothy W. Sweeney, "Industrial Buyer Segmentation: A Psychographic Approach," in 1971 Conference Proceedings of the American Marketing Association, pp. 327–31.
[15] Jean-Marie Choffray and Gary L. Lilien, "A New Approach to Industrial Market Segmentation," Sloan Management Review, 19, 3 (Spring, 1978), 17–29.

mined empirically, and the resulting microsegments were shown to require significantly different marketing approaches, both in terms of product features and promotional approaches.

In a more generalized approach to the market segmentation problem, Choffray and Lilien developed a segmentation methodology consisting of five steps, following the Wind and Cardozo approach:

Step 1: Develop macrosegments of organizations that are likely to react to a product offering differently, because of their industry, geographic location, or other observable characteristics.

Step 2: Use a sample of firms in the potential market to determine the structure of decision-making units in each macrosegment by developing a "decision matrix," in which the columns correspond to phases of the decision process and the rows are categories of individuals (buying roles) involved in the decision process; the entries in the matrix are percentages of task responsibilities in each buy phase associated with each buying role.

Step 3: Develop an index of inter-organizational similarity using a mathematical coefficient of association and remove from the analysis those firms that are "outliers," those significantly different from the large majority of organizations in the sample in their decision process.

Step 4: Use cluster analysis to develop microsegments, groups of organizations homogeneous in the composition of their buying center.

Step 5: The composition of the resulting clusters—microsegments—is examined to assess qualitatively the relationship between microsegment membership and other, external and observable, characteristics of the organizations in the microsegment.[16]

Choffray and Lilien applied their methodology in a large scale study of the industrial market for solar air conditioning.

In summary, a two-stage approach to the industrial market segmentation process has been shown to be both desirable and practical. Recent research studies have concentrated on demonstrating the viability of microsegmentation strategies using a variety of sophisticated behavioral measures relating to individual decision makers and to the buying center as a decision making unit. It can be seen that industrial market segmentation is approaching the level of sophistication that has characterized consumer marketing. The two-

---

[16] *Ibid.* An appendix to the article describes the methodology in greater detail including the formula used as a measure of dissimilarity.

stage approach recognizes that industrial buying behavior is a unique combination of individual motivation and decision-making behavior and organizational decision processes in the context of formal organization structure, tasks, and technology. Macrosegmentation relates differences in response to marketing effort with organizational variables, such as product end-use, type of buying situation, size, S.I.C. grouping, and geographic location. Microsegmentation examines the individual characteristics and activities of the members of the buying center. Macrosegmentation may be sufficient, if it relates to important differences in response to marketing efforts. But microsegmentation is likely to add a degree of analytical sophistication of great value to the industrial marketer by suggesting refinements in selling strategy that are responsive to the needs of each microsegment.

A "NESTED APPROACH" TO INDUSTRIAL MARKET SEGMENTATION

Bonoma and Shapiro have developed a more detailed approach to industrial market segmentation which they call a "nested approach."[17] They argue that the distinction between macrosegments (based on traditional measures of firm characteristics such as location, size, and S.I.C. classification) and microsegments (based on behavioral characteristics) leaves out a number of potentially valuable segmentation variables. Their approach advocates segmentation on the basis of demographics, operating variables, purchasing approach, situational factors, and personal characteristics, as diagrammed in Figure 4-3. They equate macrosegmentation with demographics and microsegmentation with personal characteristics, whereas other authors would likely incorporate some aspects of situational factors and purchasing approach into a definition of microsegmentation while including at least some aspects of operating variables into the definition of macrosegmentation. Furthermore, as the following discussion will show, distinctions among the variables—called operating variables, purchasing approach, and situational factors by Bonoma and Shapiro—are often hard to make in practice. Despite these potential difficulties, however, the "nested approach" serves the very useful purpose of expanding our thinking

[17] Thomas V. Bonoma and Benson P. Shapiro, *Segmenting the Industrial Market* (Lexington, Mass.: Lexington Books, 1983).

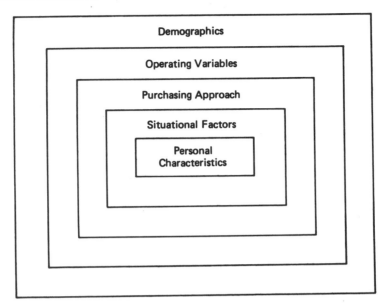

Figure 4-3. A "Nested Approach" to industrial market segmentation. [Source: *Thomas V. Bonoma and Benson P. Shapiro,* Segmenting the Industrial Market *(Lexington, Mass.: Lexington Books, 1983), p. 10.*] *Reproduced with permission.*

about the bases upon which industrial markets may be segmented and presenting them in an organized framework.

Included in *demographics* are the familiar variables of industry (S.I.C. classification), company size, and geographic location. These variables are easily measured and often have direct relationships to customer needs and usage patterns.

Operating variables are defined to include technology, user-nonuser status, and the customer's operating, technical, and financial capabilities. Compared with more traditional segmentation schemes, this is where the nested approach makes perhaps its greatest contribution. Technology includes the customer's product, production, and distribution technology. Companies in the same industry may in fact make use of quite different technologies in producing the same products and these differences in technology may be a highly relevant basis for segmentation. Whether the potential customer is presently a user or nonuser of the type of product being offered by the marketer may also be a very important distinction. An example would be a computer-based order-picking system designed to be added onto the existing warehouse racks made by the manufacturer but also adaptable to other brands of racks. Potential customers would obviously constitute two distinct segments: those with the manufacturer's rack installed and those with competitors' installations. Each competitor's customers may constitute a distinct segment if the technical characteristics of the installations are distinctly different.

The customer's operating, technical, and financial capabilities may also be highly relevant bases for segmentation. The basic question being asked concerns the ability of customers to purchase and use the product or service being offered. Segments might be defined by the ability of the customer to purchase equipment outright, for example, vs. those who must make leasing arrangements in order to afford the investment. Companies with several manufacturing locations, some producing parts and others doing assembly work, might constitute unique market segments for regularly scheduled transportation services, for example. Such detailed information about the customer's capabilities might be available in published sources such as trade journals and annual reports, but the company's sales representatives may be the most important source of this type of information.

Purchasing approach includes such variables as organization of the purchasing function, power structure within the purchasing operation, the nature of existing relationships with vendors, general purchasing policies, and purchasing criteria. Contrary to the assertion of Bonoma and Shapiro that these variables are not included in the traditional macro-microsegmentation schemes, our previous review of the subject has described a number of instances in which these types of variables were considered in the microsegmentation approach. They are suggested in the model of industrial buying behavior developed by Webster and Wind[18] and reviewed in Chapter 2, as well as in the approach of Choffray and Lilien that was described in the previous section. Purchasing approaches and organization have also been studied extensively by Corey.[19] Benefit segmentation, described earlier in this chapter, is closely related to the concept of segmentation based on decision criteria, one aspect of the purchasing approach.

[18] Frederick E. Webster, Jr., and Yoram Wind, *Organizational Buying Behavior* (Englewood Cliffs, N.J.: Prentice-Hall, Inc., 1972).
[19] E. Raymond Corey, *Procurement Management: Strategy, Organization, and Decision Making* (Boston: CBI Publishing Co., Inc., 1978).

Situational factors include such things as the urgency of the purchase, the specific application planned for the product, and the size of the order. Whereas the previous nests of segmentation variables have applied to particular customers (either organizations or individuals), situational factors could result in the definition of distinct segments within a given customer organization. Situational factors also have a close similarity to the concept of benefit segmentation and may be one practical way of making that concept operational. Data about such variables as urgency, application, and size should be easily obtainable by the industrial sales representative as part of the communication in any reasonably well-developed buyer-seller relationship.

At this level of specificity, one can ask whether we are still talking about market segmentation or whether we are now dealing with issues in the planning and execution of key account selling strategies. Should we think of specific buying situations within a given customer organization as a special case of market segmentation or should segments be defined to include organizations and individuals within organizations? Situational factors can be a reasonable basis for market segmentation if they lead to definitions of segments that include several customers. For example, customers who need overnight delivery of cutting tools may constitute one segment, served through industrial distributors, whereas those who plan their purchases and place orders days or weeks in advance of needed delivery can be served directly by the tool manufacturer. On the other hand, a unique buying situation within a given customer organization is hardly adequate to constitute a true market segment; in an important sense, all buying situations are unique. Carried to the extreme, situational factors could lead to the definition of an infinite number of market segments. One must always be sure that the segments defined satisfy the basic criterion of being substantial and large enough to be an important basis for making distinctions in marketing strategy.

Another problem with the nested approach is that there is not a clear-cut distinction between purchasing approaches and situational factors. (These two categories are both included in "organizational" variables described in the Webster and Wind model.) Nor is the distinction between situational factors and demographics completely clear; industry affiliation may determine the type of application, for example. Bonoma and Shapiro are aware of these overlaps and argue that the nested approach is intended to be used flexibly and with a good deal of managerial judgment applied to the definition of specific variables at each level.

Personal characteristics of members of the buying organization are the last or "inner" nest. Situational factors are called the "middle" nest, whereas demographics, operating variables, and purchasing approach are lumped together as "the three outer nests" by Bonoma and Shapiro. Included among personal characteristics are individual buyer motivation, personal strategies for reducing risk, individual perceptions, and measures of similarity between the individual representatives of the buying and selling organizations. Compared with the Webster and Wind model, these would be similar to the "individual" variables in that model. As our earlier review of several examples of microsegmentation suggested, individual characteristics can be a very useful basis for market segmentation.

What appears to be missing from the nested approach is any careful consideration of the nature of the buying decision process occurring within the buying center, especially the nature of interpersonal interaction among the members of the buying center. Bonoma and Shapiro include the buying center in what they call "the power structure" within the purchasing approach, but it may be more appropriately identified as a unique set of factors. It would seem to be more clearly identified with "inner nest" than "outer nest" considerations. It is not just a feature of the organization but also a social and psychological phenomenon characterizing the individual actors. In other words, variables relating to interpersonal interaction, both within the buying center and between representatives of the buying and selling organizations, are important enough to be singled out for analysis, most appropriately located between personal characteristics and situational factors rather than lumped together with other characteristics of the purchasing organization.

As with the basic macro-microsegmentation approach, the nested approach proceeds from the most general (demographics) to the most specific (personal characteristics). One need go no further in developing the necessary data than is justified by the payoff of more precise tailoring of marketing strategies to the truly important differences among substantial groupings of potential customers. Despite some overlap in the definition of segmentation variables and the fact that much of what is contained in the nested approach has also been defined by earlier studies, the nested approach makes a solid contribution to our thinking about industrial market segmentation because it pulls many important ideas together into an organizing framework. It is also consistent with the evolving view of industrial buying and selling as an integrated process and with our emphasis on the buyer-seller relationship as the basic unit of analysis in the study of industrial marketing.

VERTICAL MARKET SEGMENTATION

Vertical market structures define the path followed by a product from its point of origin to the end-user. If the product is a raw material and its final form is a part of a consumer product, then the vertical market structure can be very complex. Along the way, a large number of buyer-seller relationships form a chain of transactions. For a particular product seller, market entry at any of several points in that chain may be a strategic possibility. An important type of segmentation decision in industrial markets is the selection of the point in the chain of transactions at which to enter the market. From an operations management view, the problem is how much value to add to the product in its raw form before entering into a market transaction.

Vertical market segmentation, or the market entry level decision, obviously relates to the issue of product policy and strategy. As the marketer adds more value to the product, it is performing functions that would be performed by those market intermediaries. In that sense, it is competing with potential customers, a situation that has obvious negative features, especially if the marketer is already selling certain products to the affected firms.

The materials or components producer may elect to move up in the chain, despite these problems, for several reasons, including a desire to maintain control over product quality, the opportunity to earn greater profits, the possibility of strengthening long-term relationships with end users, and the assessment that intermediaries are either unwilling or unable to promote the new product aggressively. The materials or components producer may have the ability or incentive lacked by market intermediaries to make the necessary investments in plant or equipment.

In other cases, the materials or components supplier may assume responsibility for market development and promotion while working with intermediaries to strengthen their ability to respond to end-user demands. For example, Owens Corning Fiberglass Corporation for many years invested heavily in technical development work and selling effort for the automotive industry. The company was trying to expand the use of fiberglass-reinforced plastics in automobile parts, while continuing to rely upon custom molders to supply the parts. Owens Corning regarded the custom molders, not the automobile companies, as its customers. When one auto maker decided to buy its own presses, because of unresolved quality control problems with its parts supplier, Owens Corning was asked to supply material direct to the automobile company and, thus, found itself competing with its own customers, a common problem in industrial markets.

Vertical market segmentation, therefore, poses some unique competitive and strategic problems, but the basic calculus of segmentation remains the same—to define a profitable market niche where the company's unique capabilities are best matched with customer needs. Other things being equal, that niche is determined by the company's ability, defined by its technical, financial, and marketing capabilities, to add greater value, or to add value at lower cost, than market intermediaries. Stated differently, the optimal entry level is that point at which the company's offering will have the greatest value and benefit for customers and at which customers will be most eager and receptive, given competitive conditions and the relationships among market intermediaries.

SEGMENTATION IN PRACTICE

The foregoing material has presented a normative, somewhat idealistic, view of segmentation in industrial markets, suggesting what is both desirable and possible, but not necessarily describing the actual practices of industrial marketers.

Reviews of actual industry practice show a less sophisticated approach to market segmentation. Wind and Cardozo interviewed marketing managers in a sample of large industrial firms to determine the extent to which segmentation strategies were used and the types of segmentation variables employed.[20] Their major conclusion was that industrial marketers do use differentiated marketing, but it is not often based on a careful analysis of market segments. Rather, the approaches followed tended to be intuitive, not based on careful data collection and analysis. Most frequently, products were modified to fit the needs of different customers, especially through differentiated service offerings. Next most frequent were adjust-

[20] Wind and Cardozo, *op. cit.*, pp. 160–64.

ments in prices for different segments, followed by differences in promotion and distribution.

Because these modifications were made in response to customer demands rather than planned selections of customers based on careful analysis of marketing opportunities, these modifications probably should not be regarded as evidence of conscious market segmentation strategies. These findings do, however, lend credence to our basic assertion that the product is a variable, not a given, in industrial marketing strategy. Such "segmentation strategies" disclosed by the Wind and Cardozo research seem to be based more on sales representatives' intuition than on good marketing planning.

Wind and Cardozo found that macrosegmentation, using variables such as size, S.I.C. category, product end use, and geographic location, was much more frequently used than microsegmentation based on such behavioral measures as characteristics of the buying center. Marketers were found to use two different criteria for evaluating segmentation variables—appropriateness and ease of implementation. The latter is a function of the cost of identifying segments and differentiating marketing programs, the acceptance of the segmentation variable by marketing personnel, and ease of identifying segments and differentiating marketing programs. In actual practice, ease of implementation appears to be more important than appropriateness. These authors concluded that most industrial marketers, by not developing careful segmentation strategies, were losing profit opportunities and leaving themselves open to competitive inroads while, in other cases, where segmentation was *ad hoc* and intuitive, practicing uncontrolled segmentation. In other words, without carefully planned segmentation strategies, effectiveness and efficiency both suffer.

AN APPLICATION OF INDUSTRIAL MARKET SEGMENTATION

As noted, there are surprisingly few published applications of industrial market segmentation. Clearly, one reason is that good segmentation strategies represent an important source of competitive advantage, and therefore might be regarded as proprietary information. It is certainly also true, however, that industrial marketers have been slow to realize the benefits of sound segmentation studies.

One interesting study was reported by Doyle and Saunders, involving a basic raw material producer that was moving into a specialty chemicals market, requiring more careful market targeting and positioning.[21] They outlined a seven-step procedure:

1. Define objectives
2. Determine market segments
3. Evaluate the attractiveness of alternative segments
4. Select target markets
5. Develop a positioning strategy
6. Develop the marketing mix
7. Validate the strategy

The core of this analysis was a set of multivariate statistical procedures, including various forms of factor analysis and clustering techniques. Recognizing that a major reason that industrial marketing managers have not made heavy use of such segmentation techniques is their unwillingness to use techniques that they do not understand, the process began with a three-day briefing session for management on these techniques and their application. Following that, data were collected on both customers and competitors. Factor analysis was used to group the choice criteria used by customers into a smaller set of simpler dimensions, determined to be perceived strength of the supplier, breadth of application of product range, and technical characteristics determining the product's use.

Using these factors, clustering methods were then employed to determine distinct market segments in terms of the importance of these factors to the customers in those segments. The results yielded 12 segments based on customer preference. Next, segments were evaluated in terms of their attractiveness, given their size, rate of growth, amount and quality of competitive activity, and the company's own capabilities. This step called for combining managerial judgment with the statistical data and concluded that seven of the 12 segments were potentially viable and that four were particularly attractive.

The company then developed unique marketing approaches for each of these four primary segments and the company was able to achieve the profit margin and market share objectives established for each segment. The result was a successful demonstration of the use of rigorous analytical techniques, combined with careful manag-

[21] Peter Doyle and John Saunders, "Market Segmentation and Positioning in Specialized Industrial Markets," *Journal of Marketing* **42**, 2 (Spring, 1985), 24–32.

erial judgment, to decompose the competitive environment and develop an effective positioning strategy.

SUMMARY

Selection of customers is probably the critical strategic decision made by any industrial firm. Most firms appear to follow an *ad hoc* approach to market segmentation, taking whatever business may be available to them, rather than selecting carefully among alternative customer strategies. A two-stage approach to market segmentation, beginning with macrosegmentation based on organization characteristics and proceeding, only if necessary, to microsegmentation based on behavioral characteristics of the buying center and its members, was developed in some detail, and its appropriateness to industrial marketing was discussed. The discussion frequently referred to earlier chapters to show the relevance of various models of industrial buying behavior to the strategic task of market segmentation.

It is through strategies of market segmentation and differentiated marketing that industrial marketers apply the marketing concept, characterized by customer orientation, integrated marketing programs, and a long-term viewpoint. The result is a selective approach to the market, finding a market niche where the company's capabilities are best matched with customer needs.

Bibliography

Bonoma, Thomas V., and Benson P. Shapiro, *Segmenting the Industrial Market* (Lexington, Mass.: Lexington Books, 1983).

Choffray, Jean-Marie, and Gary L. Lilien, *Market Planning for New Industrial Products* (New York: John Wiley & Sons, 1980).

Doyle, Peter, and John Saunders, "Market Segmentation and Positioning in Specialized Industrial Markets," *Journal of Marketing*, **42**, 2 (Spring, 1985), 24–32.

Frank, Ronald E., William F. Massy, and Yoram Wind, *Market Segmentation* (Englewood Cliffs, N.J.: Prentice-Hall, Inc., 1972).

Ries, Al, and Jack Trout, *Positioning: The Battle for Your Mind*, 1st ed.-rev., (New York: Warner Books, 1986).

Wind, Yoram, "Issues and Advances in Segmentation Research," *Journal of Marketing Research*, **XV**, 3 (August, 1978), 317–37.

———, and Richard N. Cardozo, "Industrial Market Segmentation," *Industrial Marketing Management*, **3**, 2 (April, 1974), 153–66.

5 Product Strategy and New Product Development

New products are the lifeblood of any business. They energize the company's marketing, sales, and distribution activities and provide new opportunities in the face of declining markets for existing products. Because of the inexorable forces of the product life cycle, the old products gradually lose their ability to generate profits. This creates a requirement for new products to regenerate profit margins. New products provide new hope, promise, and challenge for the industrial marketing organization.

At the same time, it must be recognized that one third of all commercialized new products fail in the marketplace, for a variety of reasons.[1] Most notably, they fail because they do not meet the sales volume and profit expectations of those managers introducing the product. The reasons for this failure are sometimes obvious, after the fact, although not at all obvious during the struggle to achieve the expectations that had been established for the product. Management of new products is one of the most challenging tasks in marketing, and new product development and commercialization can be a very risky business, indeed.

If the probability and the costs of new product failure are so high, it is legitimate to ask why firms devote such significant resources to the tasks of new product development. The answer should be obvious. New products must continually refresh the product mix, if the company is to maintain and, hopefully, enhance its profitability.

[1] Booz · Allen & Hamilton, Inc., *New Products Management for the 1980s* (New York, 1982), p. 7.

New products are a necessary response, if the firm is to retain its marketing effectiveness, to changing customer preferences and dynamic competition in the marketplace. A stagnant product line is good evidence that an industrial firm has failed to keep up with advancing technology and the state-of-the-art in its industry.

Earlier chapters have developed several basic concepts relevant to understanding the issues of product strategy in industrial markets. It has been said that the product is a variable, not a given, in industrial marketing. Different customers are likely to have different needs requiring some adjustment of the product. The industrial product was defined not as a physical entity but as a complex set of economic, technical, legal, and personal relationships between buyer and seller. (In this broad sense, price is an extremely important dimension of the firm's product offering.) This means that the selection of customers, market segmentation strategy, is the key, long-term strategic choice for the industrial firm. Product strategy, then, is a more flexible and dynamic area of strategic planning. Market segmentation should logically precede new product development, and information about both macro- and microsegment characteristics should be the important input. The dynamic and variable nature of product strategy in industrial marketing must not be regarded as a random, unplanned, or an opportunistic response to the marketplace. New product failure can be caused by lack of careful, long-term product planning just as surely as by product line stagnation and the absence of a flexible and dynamic response to changing market needs and competition.

In this chapter, we will concentrate on the new product development process. In the following chapter, our focus will shift to the development of markets for new industrial products, with special consideration given to the process by which potential customers respond to innovations.

THE PRODUCT LIFE CYCLE

The product life cycle is a hypothetical concept describing how a typical product's sales volume and profit margin are likely to behave over time. Figure 5-1 depicts the product life cycle and defines the five stages commonly used to describe it. Slight variations in the description of the stages are sometimes found, resulting in a four-stage model, but these variations are insignificant (except to those who enjoy arguing about such details for the sake of argument).

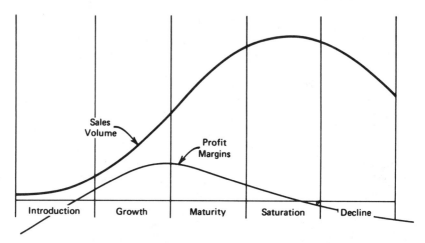

Figure 5-1. The product life cycle.

In this five-stage model it is significant that there is an inflection point in the sales volume curve at the dividing line between the growth and maturity stages. At this point, the profit margin curve is at its peak. In the maturity stage, sales volume continues to increase although at a decreasing rate, but profit margins are falling.

The behavior of the product life cycle is caused by three forces over which management has little or no control: changing customer needs and preferences, advancing technology, and changing competition. In the introductory stage, the company may have a virtual monopoly with the new product, but profit margins are low, reflecting costs of product and market development, even though prices may be as high as they will ever be. Market introduction takes time and sales develop slowly at first. Profit margins improve with significant growth in sales volume, since production and marketing efficiencies permit lower costs per unit, and the rate of market acceptance continues to grow. In the maturity stage, sales continue to grow, but profit margins decline as the result of competition, which may require lower prices, increased promotional expense, and, perhaps, the additional expense of product improvements or product line extensions resulting in smaller production quantities of more specialized items. Distribution expense and other service cost items may also increase. These forces, and especially price pressures, will continue through the saturation stage. There the company faces a stagnant market demand until falling sales bring profit to the bare minimum.

There are marketing experts who discount the value of the product life cycle concept, pointing out that seldom does a new product actually follow the proscribed route of sales volume and profitability.[2] Such criticisms may be justified, although the central tendency described by the product life cycle concept is valid, but they really miss the point. The product life cycle concept should be regarded as a forward-looking, conceptual tool for strategic planning, not a backward-looking description of a basic marketing truth. It is a description of forces at work in the market that will influence product sales and profit margins. It is not a prediction of outcomes, which depend on marketing actions, but it is highly normative.

In this light, then, the product life cycle concept is an important planning tool and has three very significant implications for marketing management. First, it shows clearly the need for a continuous stream of new product ideas. Second, it suggests that different marketing strategies are needed at different stages of the product life cycle. In other words, the marketing program should contain an appropriate mix of product quality, price, distribution, and promotional features to reflect the nature of competitive forces at each stage. Third, the product life cycle shows the importance of planning for the total life of the new product at the time the product is being developed and its market introduction planned. Without such a long-term view, encompassing the realities of competition and tight margins in the later stages of the product life cycle, estimates of long-run profitability and return on investment may be exceedingly optimistic.

There is one other fact about the product life cycle that should be noted. Firms seldom have careful procedures and systems for evaluating old products and deciding to eliminate them when they begin to consume resources instead of contributing to the firm's profitability and growth. But, just as new products are the lifeblood of a business, old products can be a major drain on the resources of the firm, requiring excessive management attention, selling effort, and other life-sustaining resources. Systems for the evaluation and euthanasia of old, sick products have as much potential for sustaining company profitability as those whose purpose is to develop and introduce new products.

[2] See, for example, Nariman K. Dhalla and Sonia Yuspeh, "Forget the Product Life Cycle Concept!," *Harvard Business Review*, **54**, 1 (January-February, 1976), 102–12. Their analysis is based on the experience of several consumer brands, however, and may not pertain to industrial products. This is generally true of all critical analyses of the product life cycle concept.

CHANGES IN COMPETITIVE MARKET STRUCTURES

It has been noted that the so-called *product* life cycle is really a *market* life cycle, and that the driving forces are customer preferences, technology, and competition, all interacting with one another. We have also noted in earlier chapters that customer preferences or "value structures" keep evolving in response to changes in suppliers' product offerings. Behind the product life cycle facing a particular marketer, then, is a set of complex, interacting environmental forces including technology, the economic climate, government regulations, suppliers of materials and components used in the manufacture of the product, competitors and their product offerings, competitive conditions in the customers' industries, and more. Each potential supplier, competitor, and customer firm can be characterized by its current economic performance, the business environment it is facing, its cost structure, its business and corporate strategies, and its management style and culture—all interacting with one another![3]

The result is a continuously changing marketplace in terms of the number of competitors, their strategies, product lines, pricing, and profitability. In developing marketing strategy, it is useful to think about stages in the product life cycle in terms of such changes in the competitive market structure. These changes in competitive market structure can be summarized briefly as follows.

In the *Introductory* stage of the product life cycle, the market is small and growing, there are very few competitors, and the market will tend to be undersupplied once it begins to develops. The firm's major marketing problems are finding customers, creating awareness and trial, and building distribution on a selective basis.

In the *Growth* stage, the market has become much larger and is growing rapidly. There are many more competitors and their numbers are increasing. The market is likely to fluctuate between being over- and under-supplied as new firms enter the business and new capacity comes on line in large increments. The marketer's principal concerns include forecasting the rate of market growth and capacity expansion, building and holding market share, creating brand differentiation and customer preference, developing product line extensions, continuing to stimulate trial by new users but also

[3] Mary Lambkin and George S. Day, "Evolutionary Processes in Competitive Markets: Beyond the Product Life Cycle," *Journal of Marketing*, **53**, 3 (July, 1989), 4–20.

gaining repeat and expanded usage by existing customers, and broadening distribution.

In the *Maturity* and *Saturation* stages, the number of competitors reaches a maximum and begins to decline. The market remains oversupplied with excess capacity, which will continue to expand through the mature stage but at a slower rate. Marketing strategy focusses on maintaining share in an increasingly segmented and fragmented market with multiple models, brands, and product line extensions. Marketing communications attempt to create product differentiation and to build trade support. Distribution may be consolidated and become more selective, especially in the saturation stage as the firm is likely to focus on fewer market segments. In the saturation stage, all competitors are likely to be fighting to reduce their costs and there is likely to be significant price erosion as firms fight to hold market share, resulting in very low or even negative levels of industry profitability.

Finally, in the *Decline* stage, there may be only a few surviving competitors. Market prices may be defined by the cost structure of the least efficient surviving producer. The remaining firms will have reduced their expenditures on marketing and R&D in order to improve profit margins, instead of attempting to grow the size of the market or to steal customers from competitors. Costs per customer served may be at their lowest level in the history of the industry, with a declining number of distributors and marketing concentrated on a smaller set of market segments. The market will be oversupplied and capacity will continue to shrink slowly. The remaining firms are likely to enjoy substantial positive cash flow from these products as prices stabilize and marketing and manufacturing costs continue to decline.

The product life cycle concept is an attempt to summarize the effect of these interacting market forces in terms of their impact on the rates of sales growth and profitability. In the next chapter, we will look at closely related models of market adoption and diffusion processes that consider in greater detail the underlying competitive processes in both supplier and customer industries.

INDUSTRIAL PRODUCT LIFE CYCLES AND MARKET STRUCTURE

Using data on 1,148 industrial businesses from the Profit Impact of Marketing Strategy (PIMS) studies of the Strategic Planning Institute, Thorelli and Burnett tested the extent to which industrial products, specifically, fit the descriptions of sales and profit growth contained in the product life cycle model.[4] They also looked at several variables describing the changes in the structure of a market, especially the number of competitors and rates of product innovation and competitive entry, that logically are related to the stages in the product life cycle. While the data were not complete enough to allow analysis of the earliest (Introduction) and latest (Decline) stages of the cycle, the study confirmed that industrial products typically follow the pattern of sales and profit growth, maturity, and decline depicted by the product life cycle concept. In general, it appeared that industrial product life cycles are longer than are those for consumer goods.

The number of competitors entering a market was found to increase as products moved through the growth stage and into maturity. This was accompanied by a decline in market concentration, defined as the combined market shares of the four largest competitors. Conversely, all measures of product innovation declined over the product life cycle, as competitors appear to cut back on expenditures for marketing and research and development for product and process improvements in order to maintain profit margins. Gross margin as a percentage of revenue declined as a function of product age, but return on sales and return on investment were not significantly related to age of product. Reducing marketing and R & D expenditures as a percentage of sales was apparently a common tactic for maintaining overall profitability in the face of declining profit margins. Cash flow, on the other hand, was positively associated with product age. As products mature, industrial companies cut back on investment in those products in order to maintain rates of return and improve cash flows.

Finally, in the area of international trade, some patterns originally hypothesized by Wells were confirmed.[5] As products mature in domestic markets, industrial marketers seek export markets in order to maintain growth rates in sales and profits. This underscores the basic fact that the product life cycle really describes a market,

[4] Hans B. Thorelli and Stephen C. Burnett, "The Nature of Product Life Cycles for Industrial Goods Businesses," *Journal of Marketing*, **45**, (Fall, 1981), 97–108. For a description of the PIMS data base, see Robert D. Buzzell, Bradley T. Gale, and Ralph G. M. Sultan, "Market Share—A Key to Profitability," *Harvard Business Review*, **53** (January-February, 1975), 97–106.
[5] Louis T. Wells, Jr., "A Product Life Cycle for International Trade?," *Journal of Marketing*, **32** (July, 1968), 1–6.

not a product. Putting a seasoned product into a new foreign market is one way of "restarting" the product life cycle. At first, the product will have a unique position in the foreign market, but as its sales grow it will likely attract domestic competition. As these domestic competitors grow, they are likely to attain cost advantages due to growing experience and lower transportation costs. At this stage, the original producer's exports are likely to begin to decrease in the face of increasingly effective foreign competition. In time, these foreign producers may very well decide to export back to the home market of the original firm, exploiting the advantage of lower production cost and the size of the original producer's home market. Severe price competition and declining profit margins can be expected. Although Thorelli and Burnett were not able to examine behavior in the decline stage, their analysis did confirm this basic pattern of international competition. As products aged, it was found that exports decreased while import competition increased.

The Thorelli and Burnett analysis serves the useful purpose of confirming the basic existence of product life cycles in industrial markets and underscores the managerial usefulness of the model. It should be seen not as a model of some immutable laws of market behavior but as a pattern of marketing strategies, changes in market structure, and resulting sales and profit performance over time. Product life cycles are not "caused" by time. Rather, they reflect specific strategic choices and actions by managements contending for the customer's preference with investments in technology and market development.

PRODUCT PORTFOLIO ANALYSIS

From time to time, it makes sense for a company to review its product portfolio. Such a review can usefully be conducted once or twice per year. Grouping products according to approximate stage in the product life cycle may be a useful first step: new products; growth products; mature products; and declining products. Different marketing objectives and strategies are required for products in these stages. Also it is important to realize that it may be possible to alter significantly a product's position in the life cycle through changes in marketing strategy. The life cycle concept should really be called the market life cycle, since the concept describes changes in markets, not changes in products themselves. Thus, to the extent that marketing strategies have an effect on conditions in the market, they influence the product life cycle. Effective marketing may be successful in retarding the inevitable progress of the product life cycle and, in the extreme case, may bring the market back to an earlier stage, such as moving from maturity back to growth. The development of new technology for electrical storage batteries promises such a scenario, for example.

The concept of the product portfolio stresses the importance of viewing products not individually but as parts of a total system. In this context, different products have different roles to play in the game plan for achieving the firm's short-range and long-range objectives. For some products, current cash generation may be the most important and realistic goal. For others, longer-term return on investment may be the major contribution. Still others may be looked on as complements to major products, enhancing their marketability in the face of strong customer brand preference.

The basic concept of the product portfolio was first put forth by the founder of the Boston Consulting Group, Mr. Bruce Henderson, in a pamphlet on the subject published in 1970.[6] It looks at a company's range of products as a mix of businesses that interact and influence one another strategically, principally in terms of their uses of resources and the deployment of those resources against opportunities in a competitive marketplace. These product/market commitments, or "businesses," are described and evaluated in terms of three dimensions:

1. The attractiveness of the market, especially the rate of growth in that market and the stage of market development (i.e., stage in the product life cycle);

2. The firm's competitive position in that market, most especially its share of market compared with the share held by the largest competitor;

3. The company's strengths and weaknesses, especially in the context of market trends.

A major purpose of product portfolio analysis is to develop a long-run, dynamic, strategic focus on the business. It was intended, among other things, as a kind of antidote for the short-run orientation that is inherent in a decentralized, profit-center approach to a business that focusses on achieving current sales and profit budgets

[6] Boston Consulting Group, "The Product Portfolio," *Perspectives on Experience*, 1970.

and significantly discounts longer-term performance. Product port-folio analysis was very much a part of the almost faddish interest in, and acceptance of, strategic planning that characterized the 1970's. It was completely consistent with the basic SWOT analysis—Strengths, Weaknesses, Opportunities, and Threats—that was the foundation of all strategic planning approaches.

The outcome of the analysis of the product portfolio was a pattern of resource allocations unique to the firm, focussing primarily on the cash-generating or cash-using needs of various product/market or "business" combinations. Financial, marketing, and production commitments were based on a view of competitive factors as well as the interdependence within the portfolio. Each business had a specific set of strategic objectives that assigned it a particular role within the portfolio.

The results of the analysis are characteristically presented as positions in the four quadrants of a two-by-two matrix, as illustrated in Figure 5-2. One dimension of the matrix is market growth rate, a measure of the attractiveness of the market and a proxy measure for the stage in the product life cycle. The other dimension is the measure of market share dominance—market share relative to com-petition—a measure of the firm's competitive strength. Products in each of the four quadrants were called, clockwise from the upper left, Stars, Problem Children (also called Question Marks), Dogs, and Cash Cows. These colorful labels helped to popularize the product portfolio concept.

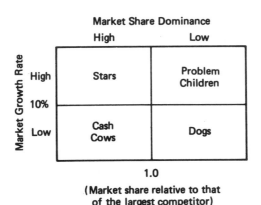

Figure 5-2. The Boston Consulting Group growth-share matrix.

This simple analysis has a number of advantages and benefits:

1. It is simple and easy to comprehend. It puts the various businesses into a strategic perspective.

2. It is an effective way to analyze not only the firm's businesses but those of competitors; competitors can be put into the matrix as a way of generating insights into their competitive positions and likely future moves; it is a way of inferring and predicting competitive moves.

3. As noted, it introduces a long-run, dynamic, strategic viewpoint that specifically takes account of market attractiveness and competitors' positions.

4. It provides a hard-nosed look at those businesses that are demanding resources in markets that are not growing and where the firm's competitive position is weak, and identifies them as candidates for divestiture.

Several different strategic options may be possible for products in each of these four states. "Dogs" can be re-positioned in more carefully defined market segments, for example, at modest expense for product refinement and carefully targeted promotional efforts, or they can be "harvested" by cutting back on all marketing support including selling effort, technical service, advertising, and so on. "Dogs" can also be eliminated entirely. A choice among strategic options for products in a particular state will be determined by many factors, including the availability of marketing resources, the demands of products in other states, the firm's financial resources and need for cash, and an estimate of how the market will respond to marketing efforts. Needless, to say, a firm with several "stars" will not spend significant time and effort trying to reposition a "dog." At the other extreme, a firm that has not been diligently developing new products may have no choice but to reinvest in "problem children" and "dogs." On the other hand, successful new product development usually requires the presence of "cash cows" and "stars" generating the necessary funds to support the development effort. A healthy firm will have products in each state, as well as new products.

The central focus in the product portfolio approach is on cash flow; businesses are viewed in terms of their use or generation of cash. Thus, one major advantage of the approach is that it makes the necessary connections between financial objectives and resources and overall corporate and marketing strategic analysis.

While the Boston Consulting Group growth-share matrix was the first widely known product portfolio model, others have subsequently been developed by McKinsey & Company working with the General Electric Company, by Arthur D. Little, Inc., and by Shell Chemical International (Royal Dutch Shell Company), among others. We will return to a further consideration of the use of such models for strategic planning purposes in Chapter 11.

MARKET SHARE AND THE EXPERIENCE CURVE

The logic of the product portfolio approach is based on a fundamental assertion or assumption—namely that market share is a key strategic variable because the competitor with the highest sales and production volume has the advantage of being the low-cost producer. This is due to two principal sources of cost advantage: "scale effects" and "the experience curve." Scale effects are the commonly recognized "economies of scale" due to size and volume of production and purchasing. The experience curve, first recognized as a phenomenon in the production of military aircraft and used as the basis for price negotiation in military procurement, reflects "learning." Cost per unit declines over time as a function of the cumulative volume of production up to that point. More specifically, cost per unit declines by a constant, predictable percentage each time volume doubles.

Day and Montgomery took a critical look at some of the principal assumptions and issues of application in the use of experience curve analysis as the basis for strategic planning.[7] Their principal conclusions stressed the errors in strategic reasoning that can result from unthinking application of the experience curve concept with its single-minded emphasis on the importance of production volume and market share. First of all, there are several different experience curves, relating to both costs and prices, and to the various components of cost. Whereas the Boston Consulting Group model assumed that all competitors face the same experience curve (and hence relative cost is very simply a function of market share and volume), Day and Montgomery pointed out that there are a number of reasons why this assumption is very likely to be invalid. Later entrants into a market are likely to benefit from improved technol-

[7] George S. Day and David B. Montgomery, "Diagnosing the Experience Curve," *Journal of Marketing*, **47**, 2 (Spring, 1983), 44–58.

ogy, learning from the pioneer's mistakes. Thus, even if the first firm into the market has the largest cumulative volume and the highest market share, it may not have the lowest cost per unit. All competitors may benefit from the (experience-based) cost improvements of a common supplier of a key component or subassembly. As markets mature, current rankings of competitors with respect to market share may be a poor indicator of relative cumulative output. Thus, there are many reasons for caution in assuming that the key to profitability is the effect of the experience curve in lowering producers' costs.

How important is market share? Several researchers have confirmed a positive association between market share and company profitability. Most notably, Schoeffler, Buzzell, and Heany discovered that market share, among 37 variables examined in the PIMS data base, had the strongest correlation to profitability, measured as return on investment.[8] The major sources of this relationship appear to be economies of scale in purchasing (i.e., larger discounts based on volume from suppliers) and in marketing and research and development. The firm with the largest market share has the largest sales volume against which to charge marketing and R&D expenditures. Absolute dollar expenditures can be larger than those of competitors but a small percentage of sales, leading to improved profit margins. For reasons that were not clear, the strength of the relationship between market share and profitability was somewhat stronger for industrial products than for consumer goods.

A similar analysis of a more recent and larger version of the PIMS data-base confirmed these findings. Farris, Parry, and Webster performed a regression analysis on a PIMS sample of 2,124 industrial and consumer businesses. The results showed that almost all of the variation in return on investment associated with market share is due to variations in return on sales (profit divided by sales), not turnover (sales divided by investment)—which are the two components of return on investment—and that the largest portion of the variation in return on sales was associated with the ratio of purchasing expenditures to sales.[9]

[8] Sidney Schoeffler, Robert D. Buzzell, and Donald F. Heany, "Impact of Strategic Planning on Profit Performance," *Harvard Business Review*, **52**, 2 (March-April, 1974), 137–45; and Buzzell, Gale, and Sultan, *op. cit.*

[9] Paul W. Farris, Mark E. Parry, and Frederick E. Webster, Jr., *Accounting for the Market Share—ROI Relationship*, Technical Working Paper, Report No. 89–118, (Cambridge, Mass: Marketing Science Institute, November, 1989).

Another analysis of the PIMS data revealed that product quality is a key variable in explaining the relationship between profitability and sales volume. Whereas earlier explanations have focussed on the experience curve and the relationship between volume and cost as an explanation of profitability, the work of Phillips, Chang, and Buzzell has shifted the focus to product quality.[10]

They found that, across a range of industrial and consumer products businesses, product quality had both a direct and indirect influence on profitability. There was the direct effect that higher quality led to higher prices, with a positive impact on profit margins. Importantly, it was found that high price did *not* deter market penetration. This stands in sharp contrast to a commonly held assumption that high price means low share. Product quality also had an observable positive impact on market share—other things being equal, customers prefer higher quality products. Once again, it was observed that high share means high volume, which leads to lower per unit product costs. Thus, high quality can actually lead to lower costs, indirectly, through a favorable influence on market position. These findings serve to warn against a traditional line of reasoning that says that firms have only two basic strategic options—high quality, high price, and low volume; or high volume and low price, which generally implies lower quality. Most especially, these results suggest that it may be a serious strategic error to use low price as the weapon for achieving the large market share which traditional product portfolio-experience curve analysis suggests is the key to profitability. The reverse may be true—it is the combination of high quality, large share, *high* price, and low cost that characterizes the most profitable industrial firms.

We can conclude this brief introduction to the general concept of the product portfolio and its strategic implications by quickly noting a number of problems with the various product portfolio approaches based on the growth/share matrix:

1. Market definition is a subtle, critically important step in the analysis. The opportunities for self-deception in defining "served market" are very great. It is very difficult to know how to account for shared experience among businesses in the portfolio and other interdependencies. The whole concept of "systems selling" that characterizes many industrial businesses is a case in point.

---

[10] Lynn W. Phillips, Dae R. Chang, and Robert D. Buzzell, "Product Quality, Cost Position, and Business Performance: A Test of Some Key Hypotheses," *Journal of Marketing,* **47,** 2 (Spring, 1983), 26–13.

2. The assumption that relative market share is a good proxy for competitive position needs to be examined very carefully. The strongest positions may in fact be held by relatively small firms due to product differentiation, cost advantages due to design or manufacturing uniqueness, and so on.

3. The model assumes that market growth rate is a good proxy for cash requirements. Obviously, profitability and cash flow depend upon many things other than rate of market growth.

4. The models are probably most useful in the early stages of analysis, as a way of thinking about the competitive marketplace. Having positioned the business within the matrix doesn't say anything about the strategies appropriate to that position.

This introduction to the concept of the product portfolio has been intended to provide a framework within which to think about the development of new product strategies for industrial products. There is much more to be said about product portfolio analysis as a basic framework for planning corporate, business, and marketing strategy and we will return to that set of considerations in Chapter 11.

THE NEW PRODUCT DEVELOPMENT PROCESS

Every new product begins as an idea and reaches fruition as a bundle of physical attributes and services offered to a potential customer. The process by which ideas are generated, evaluated, directed, and turned into products is called the new product development process. This discussion will consider seven stages in the new product development process, but once again it should be remembered that this is a somewhat arbitrary description of a process that can be depicted in a variety of other ways, with more or fewer stages. The seven stages need not occur in sequential fashion. The seven stages are (1) new product strategy development; (2) new product idea generation; (3) initial screening; (4) business analysis; (5) development; (6) testing; and (7) commercialization.[11]

The point about the non-sequential nature of these steps can be confirmed by reference to the testing stage, which includes concept

[11] Booz · Allen & Hamilton, Inc., the management consulting firm, can be credited as the authors of this particular scheme in their report entitled *Management of New Products*, 1968. An updated version of this report was published in 1982 and is cited in footnote 1 of this chapter.

testing, laboratory testing, pilot plant operation, and test marketing. The first tests may occur as part of the screening process. Laboratory and pilot plant tests are part of the development process, and test marketing may be seen as the first step in commercialization. Similarly, market testing can also be regarded as part of the development process, and the last steps in business analysis cannot be completed until the final form of the product is known and all required investments can be accurately estimated. Nonetheless, it is true that the emphasis upon each of these seven steps follows the depicted order in more or less chronological fashion.

New Product Strategy Development

The first step in the development of new products is the development of a strategy relating to new products. A survey of company practice in new product development found that over three quarters of all firms have a specific new product development strategy guiding their new product development process.[12] This was a marked change from the practice found in a study in the late 1960's and is consistent with the trend toward formal strategic planning systems that characterized the 1970's. The effect of adding this step to the new product development process has been to link idea generation, screening and evaluation, and business analysis more closely together in the context of an overall strategic direction. It identifies the strategic requirements that new product ideas should satisfy, such as defending a market share position or maintaining a market position as a technical leader. Maintaining technological leadership was found to be a particularly important new product development objective for industrial firms. When the strategic roles that must be played by new products have been defined, financial performance criteria, or "hurdles" that new products must clear, can then be established, including sales volume, profit contribution, and return on investment.[13]

The effect of integrating an initial strategic planning step into the new product development process has been a dramatic improvement in "mortality" of new product ideas. In the 1968 study, it was found that 58 new product ideas were required to generate one successfully commercialized new product. In the 1982 data, only seven new product ideas were required to get one new product

[12] Booz · Allen & Hamilton, Inc., *op. cit,* 1982.
[13] *Ibid.,* pp. 10–11.

success. Industrial products firms typically require only about half as many new product ideas to get one successful new product as do consumer durables manufacturers. This was attributed to significant improvements in the process of segmenting industrial markets, bringing a much sharper focus on specific customer needs and market opportunities, making the new product development process much more efficient.[14]

Idea Generation

New product ideas are everywhere—in the minds of sales representatives, customers, distributors, and managers as well as secretaries, free-lance inventors, shareholders, suppliers, and so on. Scientists and engineers are frequently organized into departments with the specific purpose of generating, developing, and exploiting new product ideas.

In addition to systems for generating new product ideas,[15] it is equally important to have well-defined and well-publicized procedures for collecting new product ideas. Potential sources of new product ideas can only introduce them into the new product development process if these sources are familiar with that process. Furthermore, the availability of such collection systems can stimulate the development of new product ideas.

A new product idea collection system includes an informed sales force on the lookout for new product ideas from customers and distributors and a well-defined procedure for communicating these ideas to the appropriate collection point in the firm. Such procedures should include provision for feedback to the sources of new product ideas to thank them for their suggestions, to acknowledge their receipt, to encourage the continued flow of ideas, and to inform the source if the idea is judged to have merit warranting further development. There are important legal considerations relating to this process. Persons supplying unsolicited new product ideas are a potential source of major legal difficulties unless careful steps are taken to eliminate liability. The usual procedure is to write to the person promptly, noting that the idea was unsolicited and disclaiming any interest in the idea and any intent to develop it.

[14] *Ibid.*, pp. 13–15.
[15] For a more complete consideration of the issues relating to new products idea generation and creativity in general, see Frederick E. Webster, Jr., *Marketing for Managers* (New York: Harper & Row, Inc., 1974), esp. Chap. 7, "Managing Creativity in Marketing," pp. 123–37.

When an idea, solicited or unsolicited, is believed to have merit, then there is an equally urgent need to come to terms with the person responsible for the idea concerning its ownership and the sharing of whatever rewards may be forthcoming from its development.

Most industrial companies have routine procedures for establishing these terms as part of their contractual arrangements with employees, suppliers, distributors, consultants, and others. Usually these specified conditions and procedures are adequate, but by no means is this always so. A potential source of great difficulty in the buyer-seller relationship is a failure to resolve at the earliest moment the issue of how the firms will share the results of a technical development effort involving both companies. The customer may ask for a solution to a production problem, for example, and suggest broad parameters for an approach. Or a customer may be approached by a supplier for cooperation in the development of a new product idea that can only be completed in an actual production situation in the customer's plant. Some of the guidelines for negotiation spelled out in Chapter 3 have special significance in this situation.

Customers as Sources for New Product Ideas

There is strong research support for the proposition that industrial customers are a very important source of new product ideas. Professor von Hippel has studied the sources of new product ideas in several industries.[16] In those industries where suppliers do not control the technology of the manufacturing process in customer industries and customers do depend upon equipment and material suppliers for improvements in their production methods, it is common for the customer to be a major source of new product ideas. Von Hippel noted, however, that many supplier firms were poorly organized to collect and respond to such information and often overlooked it when it was presented to them. For example, a supplier market research study was focussed on getting information about customer needs and failed to recognize information about specific product design that was presented by customers in their responses. This can result in "reinventing the wheel," redeveloping design

[16] Eric A. von Hippel, "Has a Customer Already Developed Your Next Product?" *Sloan Management Review*, **18**, 2 (Winter, 1977), 63–74, and "Successful Industrial Products from Customer Ideas," *Journal of Marketing*, **42**, 1 (January, 1978), 39–49.

work that was available "for free." Furthermore, this study found that the same customers repeatedly serve as sources of new product ideas for supplier industries.

This user-dominated new product development process is an excellent example of the buyer-seller interdependence characteristic of industrial markets. In this process, the customer invents the product, develops the prototype, and demonstrates its feasibility in use before going to equipment suppliers and asking them to build multiple units. Von Hippel has confirmed the presence of this process in the scientific instrument industry and in the semiconductor and electronics subassembly process equipment industries and reports preliminary data supporting its existence in many other product areas including computer software and medical products. Like many other research findings in marketing, this appears to be "common sense" now that it has been discovered.

In these industries where the user dominates the product development process, it is common for the user to derive significant benefits from the innovation and, thus, to have major incentive to innovate. Von Hippel hypothesized that the relative expected return on investment in innovation to user and to manufacturer determined the relative importance of each in the innovation process. In some industries, it was a material supplier, rather than the end-user or the equipment manufacturer, who possessed the greatest incentive to innovate. Von Hippel cited the case of polyethylene producers' invention of the machine adapters necessary to replace cellophane in bread-wrapping, for example. Similarly, a supplier of fiberglass-reinforced plastics found it necessary to develop production equipment for the automobile industry, in order to generate new applications for fiberglass-reinforced plastics to replace steel. The custom molders serving the automotive industry were either unable or unwilling to do this.

To summarize, idea generation is the essential first stage in the new product development process. In industrial markets, the customer may be an important source of new product ideas, especially when the customer gains significant economic benefits and the supplier does not control the technology.

Screening

An effective idea generation and collection system will deliver many more new product ideas than the firm can use. Carefully specified criteria and procedures for screening the flow of new product ideas are called for. The resulting judgments need not be "yes" or "no" decisions but may range from outright rejection to a decision to develop the new product as quickly as possible using all available resources. Procedures for screening new product ideas may be highly organized and formalized, or they may be quite casual. A highly formalized system might include printed forms, a committee that meets regularly, and specified weights to be assigned to several clearly defined screening criteria.

The basic question in screening a new product idea is, "Does this new product idea have enough feasibility and desirability to warrant more careful analysis?" A central issue is that of feasibility and consistency, given the firm's resources and objectives. The purpose of the screening stage is not to accept or reject the idea as a project for development but to determine if the idea has enough merit to warrant the expense of business analysis.

New product idea screening requires, first of all, a statement of company strategy and marketing objectives relating to the business the firm wants to be in and the markets it wants to serve. The first check on any new product idea should concern its consistency with that strategy. Surprisingly, this step is often very difficult, precisely because the necessary sense of clear strategic direction is lacking. Developing such a statement of strategic objectives can be a real struggle for management, but once completed it can eliminate much of the uncertainty and pain in new product idea evaluation.

The second set of screening questions and criteria relates to the availability of resources necessary to develop and exploit the idea. The nature of this part of the analysis can be suggested by a series of questions, meant to be suggestive but not exhaustive:

1. Do we have or can we develop access to the necessary raw materials?
2. Is the project of a scope that is feasible within our existing financial capability?
3. Is there some synergy with our existing product line?
4. Is it likely that our present customers represent a potential market, or must we develop entirely new markets?
5. Could the product be marketed through our existing sales force and distributor organization?
6. Does the idea appear to be within the capability of our product development organization?
7. What impact would the successful development of this product have on our existing products, markets, and marketing organization?

8. Would the new product be capable of manufacture within our existing production facilities and with our existing skills?

Negative answers to several such questions or the recognition that significant new financial, managerial, marketing, production, or supplier resources would be required would obviously reduce the attractiveness of the idea. The likelihood of actually developing a product with the desired characteristics is a question that is more difficult, and no attempt should be made to answer it at this stage unless the technical impossibility of the idea is a forgone conclusion. The probability of success in the development process is usually related to the amount of investment in research and development, and that is to be estimated as part of the business analysis.

Screening is the first hurdle, the feasibility hurdle, for the new product idea. As noted earlier, it takes seven new product ideas to yield one successful new product in the marketplace. Furthermore, companies still spend almost half (46 percent) of their new product expenditures on products that are unsuccessful, a significant improvement from a figure of 70 percent in the 1968 study. Despite these improvements in the efficiency of the new product development process, only 65 percent of products introduced to the marketplace are ultimately successful in achieving the performance objectives established for them.[17]

There are two ways to look at these statistics. On one hand, they can be said to show inefficiency and poor management of the new product development process. Many ideas that should not pass into development do so and many development projects fail. As a general observation, there is certainly room for improvement in the management of the process. But, on the other hand, a certain failure rate is an inevitable consequence of the necessary risk taking. There are few sure things in new product development and marketing, given the complexities of research and development and of the marketplace. A firm with a very high batting average in the new product development process may have a too conservative screening process and may not be taking the risks necessary for continued growth and profitability.

Business Analysis

Business analysis is a much more detailed and substantial evaluation of a new product idea in terms of required investment, expected

[17] Booz · Allen & Hamilton, Inc., *op. cit.*, 1982, p. 15.

sales volume, prices, costs, profit margins, and projected return on investment. It includes a market analysis with a sales forecast. The analysis must assess present and potential competition, beginning with a study of present competitive conditions and an evaluation of the strengths and weaknesses of key competitors. The stronger the positions held by established firms, the less attractive the possibilities for market entry with a new product idea.

Business analysis, when properly done, requires the investment of time and money in the form of the efforts of qualified analysts, whose experience and skills should include finance, marketing, engineering, and production, as well as overall strategic planning expertise. The ultimate purpose of the business analysis is to develop a reasonable, thorough, and defensible estimate of the profitability of the proposed new product. The specific analyses include a market segmentation study, an estimate of market potential, a sales forecast, projected costs of product development, estimates of required investments in plant, equipment, working capital, and market development, costs of manufacturing and marketing the product, likely price levels, and profitability and return on investment over the product life cycle. Obviously, this requires a significant amount of effort and involves significant expense.

It is probably unwise to leave the task of business analysis to those persons who have proposed the new product idea or who are advocating its acceptance. Excessive optimism is a major danger in the business analysis. It is easy for these advocates to overestimate the attractiveness of the product to the customer, to underestimate development and production costs, and to underrate the strength of present and future competition. It is unfortunately common for persons with a vested interest in the success of the product, or with the enthusiasm that normally accompanies parenthood, to base their sales and profit forecast on an estimate of the volume required to achieve the firm's return on investment objectives, given some assumptions (probably also optimistic) about price levels and production costs. For these reasons, consultants or central staff personnel, because of their more objective viewpoint, can play a useful role in business analysis.

The final steps in the business analysis cannot be completed until pilot plant production runs have been completed. Then cost estimates can be refined and test marketing can be completed to assess price and revenue estimates and to judge customer reactions. With careful analysis by experienced professionals, however, the business analysis can, and should, be a major step for the development of new products. The costs of a bad judgment—accepting a bad idea or rejecting a good one—are so high in the new product development process that almost any sum of money invested productively in business analysis will be money well spent.

Development

Development is the part of the process in which scientists, engineers, and technicians create the desired product. A thorough consideration of this process is beyond the scope of the current discussion and involves the many issues related to the management of research and development, the nature of creativity in scientific work, technological forecasting, and so on.

In a firm with an ongoing research and development function, it is likely that the R&D group itself will be a major source of new product ideas. In fact, when an industrial firm is committed to a basic company strategy of advancing the state of technology, the R&D group has a clear mandate to submit new product ideas on a regular basis. When advancing the state-of-the-art is a stated corporate objective, the company is betting that higher profits can result if the company, through technical breakthroughs, can lead the competition in introducing new products. This is a strategy that involves higher risk and requires the willingness of the company to make its own products obsolete. Such a commitment virtually requires that the company adopt a product portfolio management approach, and have careful strategies for exploiting mature products as well as new ones. The R&D group becomes a key element of corporate strength, or weakness, with the company highly dependent on its ability to deliver significant new technology, when expected. As we will see in Chapter 7, a strategy of price leadership in an industrial market can be assumed to require a basic commitment to the advancement of technology and to market development, not only to assure that the firm has the products most attractive to the customer, but also to maintain a competitive cost structure.

In companies with a basic commitment to technology, the marketing function has a vital role to play to assure that the results of R&D are in tune with the needs of the marketplace. Without a good flow of information to the R&D function about needs in the marketplace and about reaction to initial product concepts, there is high risk that the products developed will not find acceptance among customers. New product ideas generated in the R&D group should be subjected to the same careful screening and business analysis as ideas from any other source. Improperly evaluated ideas committed to the development process are a major source of R&D waste.

The research and development process can be thought of as beginning with basic research and progressing through applied research to product development. Only the industrial firm with a commitment to advancing technology will spend money for basic research, research intended to explore the horizons of science and technology and not to search for a solution to specific problems. Recently, there have been some expressions of concern that American firms are underspending for basic research relative to quicker-payoff development of existing technology. The problem of managing the R&D process is partly one of having a proper portfolio of projects in the various stages of the process, with differing priorities and time pressure. Some development projects will represent ideas that have grown out of basic research. Others will be underway in response to ideas and requests for assistance from customers, sales reps, and distributors.

The regular review of the firm's product portfolio should include a review of development projects and a reassessment of priorities, reflecting the need for new products as well as initial reactions from testing in the field. Favorable responses are often good reasons to push a development project ahead with all reasonable speed.

It cannot be overstressed that information from the marketplace about customer needs and reaction of customers, sales reps, and distributors to product concepts in various stages of development is absolutely essential to the effectiveness and efficiency of the development process. It is not uncommon for hundreds of thousands or even millions of dollars to be spent on the development of products representing exciting technical challenges only to find that the market has virtually no interest in the product. The notion that R&D people do not care about market acceptance and are not interested in market information is erroneous. The overwhelming majority of scientists and engineers employed in industry want very much to do work that will have commercial value to their employers. Of course, they also want the technical challenge, but there is no reason why the two need be inconsistent. Obviously, the strength of the R&D function over a period of time is, in large measure, determined by the commercial success of the business.

Testing

Testing is the information gathering part of the new product development process. It begins with the testing of new product ideas or
"concepts," then moves to evaluation of various forms of the product
in the laboratory and in the field. When the product is finally in its
expected market form, it must be manufactured in a pilot production test and the results carefully judged for quality, cost, and other
considerations. Finally, the product will be presented to the market
under test conditions, including limited market scope, careful control of the elements of the marketing mix (price, promotion, and
distribution), and objective evaluation of results.

The testing stage in product development is by no means
straightforward. A classic demonstration was the market failure of
the Ford Motor Company's Edsel, one of the most thoroughly
researched new products in history. Part of the problem relates to
measurement errors in testing, but that is a relatively minor aspect.
Perhaps the most serious dimension of the problem is simply time,
the long time required to go from product concept to commercialization and the fact that market conditions are changing continually—
especially customer needs and preferences and competition. This
process of dynamic change in the marketplace can make initially
accurate information erroneous for future decision making.

Another problem in the testing stage is the risk of tipping the
firm's hand to competition in field tests. Research on customer
needs and preferences for various product parameters can be conducted without revealing anything about the firm's product development plans and does not require exposure of the product itself.
But the more complete the product concept, the more extensive the
research, and the more complete exposure of the product to the
persons interviewed, the higher the risk of serious competitive
response.

Analysis of buying decision criteria within the buying center of
representative firms in the market is a very significant part of
concept testing in industrial market research. It is a kind of research
from which the firm may benefit, regardless of product development plans. The results, moreover, can be of substantial assistance
to the product development process. It is vital to know which
dimensions of a product are most significant in the minds of those
who will evaluate them in the customer organization, and how these
criteria are weighted, as well as how the specific product concept
measures up against these criteria.

A practicing industrial market researcher and product planning consultant, Ronald Paul, has noted that there are seven marketing research techniques of potential value to the new product development process. He listed them in order of cost-value, the first being the least expensive:

1. Secondary research.
2. Focus group interviews.
3. Mail surveys.
4. Telephone interviewing.
5. Personal interviewing.
6. Product placement.
7. Test marketing.[18]

Secondary research is the use of published sources and probably represents a bare minimum of necessity for evaluating new products. Focus group interviews involve small groups of persons representing potential customers, who are asked to discuss product concepts and product usage under the guidance of a trained group leader. The leader must focus their attention on key issues. Paul noted that such groups have greatest information value when representatives of management can observe the discussion.

Surveys and interviews are likely to be useful in gathering such information as present purchase patterns, rates of usage, supplier preferences, and so on but will have limited usefulness in assessing reaction to the new product itself. For many industrial products it is necessary to commit to virtually full-scale production volume in order to have enough of the product to make it possible to do test marketing or even to place a few with customers. Placing samples of the product with a few key customers can be adequate to assess customer reaction in certain instances. In Paul's judgment, actual market tests, when feasible, can provide ten types of data:

1. Users' reactions to the product itself and to specific attributes.
2. Appropriate applications and intended usage levels.
3. Identification of key markets with significant potential.
4. Identification of key purchasing influences.
5. Estimation of market potential and profitability at various prices.

[18] Ronald Paul, "People Plus Organization Yield New Industrial Products," *Marketing News*, December 30, 1977, pp. 1 and 3.

6. Identification of possible points of sales resistance.
7. Determining buying habits and schedules, since they influence channel and distribution questions.
8. Testing alternative sales approaches and promotional techniques.
9. Assessing users' reaction to various price levels.
10. Assessing reactions to various warranty, maintenance, and service programs.[19]

Commercialization and Product Positioning

In the commercialization stage, the company makes a full commitment to marketing the new product. It becomes part of the company's promoted product line and takes its place alongside other products in catalogs, price lists, and dealer inventories. The new product marketing program requires careful definition of market segments, development of marketing objectives, short-term and long-term, and the training of the sales force and distributor organization. There is the need for painstaking attention to a large number of details, such as the creation of advertising, catalog pages, sales aids, display pieces, and so on.

Positioning is a central strategic issue in the marketing of new industrial products, although positioning is often thought to apply only in a consumer market context. Positioning means carving out a niche in the market by stressing certain product features *vis-a-vis* competition, defining the value proposition. In consumer marketing, positioning may be achieved principally through advertising and sales promotion strategy. In industrial marketing, positioning may involve primarily the tailoring of a bundle of services to accompany the actual product, although advertising and sales promotion can also be significant tools. The set of decisions represented by positioning is necessary to complete the design and development of the industrial product.

An extremely important aspect of industrial product positioning is the element of the entry level decision as part of the segmentation problem, the "vertical" segmentation decision identified first in Chapter 4. Most industrial markets consist of several levels, from raw materials through processed materials to component parts, subassemblies, and so on. The entry level problem is seen most clearly in the case of a materials supplier, who must decide how

[19] *op. cit.*, p. 3.

much value to add to a product and, therefore, at what level of the customer market to target his effort. An aluminum producer, for example, attempting to develop an end use, such as lawn furniture, could conceivably elect to sell ingot to extruders or extrusions to fabricators of aluminum furniture components or components to a firm that would assemble finished furniture or, at the extreme, to make furniture and sell it to retailers.

The industrial product positioning decision requires very careful segmentation analysis with each level of the using market being a macrosegment. Among the considerations of major importance are the presence or absence of established competitors at each level, the technical ability of segment members to do the required engineering and manufacturing, and the manufacturer's desire to maintain product quality through the various levels of the market to the end-use application. There is a risk that the producer will be impressed with the manufacturing profits available at several levels in the market structure but may overlook the marketing requirements for becoming a seller in an unfamiliar level of the market.

MANAGING THE MARKETING–R&D INTERFACE

Industrial marketers face a special challenge in managing the new product development process because of the often dominant technical-engineering-manufacturing culture of the industrial firm. To oversimplify slightly, the problem can be summarized as one of balancing the marketer's focus on customer needs and wants with the technical person's concern for creating a superior design or achieving a new and important technical breakthrough. Evidence of a problem in this regard is the many instances of development of technically impressive new products for which there proved to be nonexistent market potential and customer interest. The technical people may think of the technical possibilities as the real challenge and take the existence of a market opportunity as a given if they can only create the best product. They focus on product features, not benefits.[20]

The problems here can be best understood in the context of organizational structure and culture. Recent research, motivated by a concern with improving the efficiency and effectiveness of the new

[20] Deborah Dougherty, *Interpretive Barriers to Successful Product Innovation,* Working Paper, Report No. 89–114, (Cambridge, Mass.: Marketing Science Institute, September, 1989), p. 19.

product development process, has been concerned with understanding the interaction between the research and development function and other management functions, especially marketing, within the organization. Much of this research has been rooted in the discipline of cultural anthropology, looking at the fundamentally different "thought worlds" of the different business departments and functions. The key to effective new product development is to match the needs of the marketplace with the technological possibilities. To do so requires not only market analysis and forecasting but also attention to the behavioral and organizational mechanisms by which information about the marketplace can be merged with an understanding of the technological opportunities.

Dougherty examined 18 new product development projects in five firms, looking for factors that impede this process of matching market needs and technical possibilities. She found that each department tends to interpret available information in a qualitatively unique way that produces a sense of completeness that tends to close it off from the others. Each department tended to consider the same set of issues, so its analysis appeared to be complete, but it did so in a biased fashion—in terms of its own "thought world" that was in conflict with similar analysis by another department. This tendency was exacerbated by the normal organizational routines that tend to reinforce the separate thought worlds of each department. The successful new product development projects succeeding in breaking out of these established organizational routines, establishing new modes of communication that broke through the thought-world barriers. First, these new mechanisms were based on a recognition and acceptance of the fact that other departments had a unique way of looking at things, and by a deeper understanding and appreciation of the other's viewpoint, not just heightened interaction and a greater quantity of communication. Second, they also had a simplified definition of the product concept that everyone could understand without "stepping out of" their thought world. Third, the new routines included the development of new criteria to judge the new product, a process of reframing the issues that led to better organizational learning, vs. defense of the *status quo*.[21]

This notion of successful innovation requiring a breaking of the organizational rules is a familiar one. Quinn has found that big companies seem to stay innovative "by behaving like entrepre-

[21] *Ibid.*, pp. 15–29.

neurial small ventures."[22] He identified multiple bureaucratic barriers to innovation: top management isolation; intolerance of fanatics; short time horizons; accounting practices; excessive rationalization, excessive bureaucracy; and inappropriate incentives. But he also noted that successful innovation requires orientation to the market, multiple approaches, including "developmental shootouts" where multiple projects addressing the same opportunity move forward in parallel until a critical choice must be made, and flexible organizations such as the often talked about "skunk works."

Customer Visit Programs

Dougherty's research findings are consistent with management practice at Hewlett Packard, where customer visit programs are an important tool of market research and product development.[23] The objectives of these programs are to define and diagnose problems, to gauge customer satisfaction, to plan future product requirements and market strategy, and to understand new markets. In this program, customer visit teams are carefully constructed from multiple departments, trained, scheduled, managed, and debriefed. A written report is prepared by the team, with a summary analysis, and shared throughout the organization. Among the benefits cited for the customer visit programs are getting new product ideas, understanding buyer behavior, solving specific customer and product problems, defining market changes and trends, building partnerships with customers and across departments within the company, improving relations with customers and the field sales organization, and demonstrating how market research can be made meaningful and useful.

Successful customer visit programs are said to require clear objectives focussed on business issues, a trained and dedicated staff, "political buy-in" within the organization and on the part of customers, a strong champion or sponsor, and a supportive company

[22] James Brian Quinn, "Managing Innovation: Controlled Chaos," *Harvard Business Review*, **63**, 3 (May-June, 1985), 73–84.
[23] Katherine Tobin, "Hewlett-Packard's Customer Visit Program: Getting Closer to Customers," a presentation at the Marketing Science Institute Conference on Communicating with Industrial Customers, March 8–10, 1989 and summarized in Jakki Mohr (ed.), *"Communicating with Industrial Customers,"* Conference Summary, Report No. 89–112, (Cambridge, Mass.: Marketing Science Institute, August, 1989), pp. 14–15.

culture. Hewlett-Packard cites several positive outcomes from the customer visit program including:

- We have updated our knowledge of customer environments and their needs.
- We have updated our knowledge of our competitors' products.
- We have collected information to improve our product strategy.
- We have educated engineers to be more aware of market conditions.
- We have reinforced with our customers that we are concerned about their needs.
- We have enhanced cooperation between the R&D Lab and the Marketing organizations.
- We have fostered mutual understanding between the factory and the field. [24]

Note how the last four points are especially responsive to the problem of needs-linking and different thought worlds.

CAUSES OF INDUSTRIAL NEW PRODUCTS FAILURE

There are many reasons why industrial products fail. Many of these reasons are interrelated. Usually there are several reasons, not one, why a new product fails. By definition, every industrial new product failure could be avoided, either by not committing the tactical and strategic errors in product development and marketing, or by measuring market potential more carefully and not developing products for which there is inadequate potential. But the world of new product marketing is not risk-free, and willingness to take the necessary risks is an essential part of any new product program.

Certainly, many new products fail for technical reasons. They fail to perform as expected and intended. Most often this is not so much a failure by the technical people in solving the problem, but rather that the technical operation did not understand the customers' needs and the conditions under which the product would have been used. One aspect of this lack of understanding is a failure to anticipate the impact of the new product on the customers' production process, including the effect on existing investment in plant and equipment, the challenge to existing production skills and methods,

---

[24] These points were contained in the presentation by Dr. Tobin cited in the previous footnote, but are not part of the conference summary.

and questions of compatibility with existing production technology.[25] All of these represent significant causes of high perceived risk for adoption of new products by industrial buyers.

Another cause of industrial product failure is the introduction of an incomplete product to the market, one that lacks features required by customers or that fails to perform as expected. Very often, the physical product itself is good, but the necessary supporting services have not been developed, such as after-sale maintenance service, operator training, insuring the supply of necessary supporting materials, and so on. Sometimes, these service responsibilities are left to the distributor organization, but no steps are taken to prepare distributors to accept their responsibilities.

This relates to another reason for new product failure in industrial markets, inadequate preparation of customers and of the marketing organization. Unless the new product is fully accepted by sales reps and distributors, it obviously will not be presented enthusiastically to customers. Furthermore, if the product represents a substantial change for the customer, it cannot just be "introduced" to them. They must be prepared for its introduction with a careful program of communication and instruction. Such was the situation, for example, when Union Carbide introduced a new granular form of low density polyethylene to its customers, replacing a pellet form. The new product required customers to develop new materials handling systems.

All such matters must be carefully planned, if the new product is to be complete when it is introduced to the market. In Chapter 1, functional interdependence was said to be one of the distinguishing features of industrial marketing, meaning that the industrial marketing program requires the cooperation of many other parts of the business outside of the marketing function. There is no surer way to kill a new product, for example, than to be unable to deliver reliable quality and quantity after customers begin to order. Other necessary components of successful new product programs, besides manufacturing capability, are inventory control systems from factory production through the channel to end users, adequate credit and electronic data interchange arrangements to facilitate ordering, applications engineering to tailor the product to the customer's requirements, quick repair service and parts availability, and dependable delivery. Engineering work involving the customer's man-

[25] Some of these ideas were originally presented in Frederick E. Webster, Jr., "New Product Adoption in Industrial Markets: A Framework for Analysis," *Journal of Marketing*, **33**, 3 (July, 1969), 35–39.

ufacturing process is often necessary to assure that the customer derives the intended benefits from the new product.

Underlying all of these problems may be a basic failure to gather adequate information about customers' needs so that the marketing can be tailored to achieve maximum satisfaction of customer needs. Not only may this failure lead to an incomplete product offering, but also to inadequate macro- and microsegmentation. Poor definition of market targets and a failure to reach all relevant buying decision influences is always a reflection of this lack of information and understanding. Also, it may lead to a failure to provide the necessary information to identified buying influences, not gearing the sales presentation to their particular evaluation criteria.

SUMMARY

Developing and marketing new industrial products is a complex and difficult undertaking, one of the greatest challenges facing the marketing manager. But it is a vital task, necessary to sustain the profitable growth of the firm. Without it, the firm must struggle to keep mature and declining products alive, a fight that almost guarantees low profits. A strategic view of the product portfolio, identifying stars, cash cows, problem children, and dogs can help to lay out the options and to stimulate the development of new products. The new product development process was depicted in seven stages—strategy development, idea generation, screening, business analysis, development, testing, and commercialization. The next chapter will examine the diffusion of innovations and the development of markets for new industrial products in greater detail.

Bibliography

Booz · Allen & Hamilton, *New Products Management for the 1980s* (New York, 1982).

Cafarelli, Eugene J., *Developing New Products and Repositioning Mature Brands* (New York: John Wiley & Sons, Inc., 1980)

Choffray, Jean-Marie, and Gary L. Lilien, *Market Planning for New Industrial Products* (New York: John Wiley & Sons, Inc., 1980).

Corey, E. Raymond, *Industrial Marketing: Cases and Concepts,* 3rd ed., (Englewood Cliffs, N.J.: Prentice-Hall, Inc., 1983), esp. Chapter 2, "The Strategy of Market Selection and Product Planning," pp. 151–174.

Day, George S., "Diagnosing the Product Portfolio," *Journal of Marketing*, **41,** 2 (April, 1977), 29–38.

Thorelli, Hans B. and Stephen C. Burnett, "The Nature of Product Life Cycles for Industrial Goods Businesses," *Journal of Marketing*, **45,** 4 (Fall, 1981), 97–108.

Von Hippel, Eric, "Successful Industrial Products from Customer Ideas," *Journal of Marketing*, **42,** 1 (January, 1978), 39–49.

Webster, Frederick E., Jr., *Marketing for Managers* (New York: Harper & Row, Inc., 1974), esp. Chap. 7, "Managing Creativity in Marketing," pp. 123–37 and Chap. 8, "Product Policy and New Products," pp. 139–63.

Wind, Yoram, *Product Policy: Concepts, Methods and Strategy* (Reading, Mass.: Addison-Wesley Publishing Co., Inc., 1982).

6 Developing Markets for New Industrial Products

Commercialization, the final step in the new product development process, is really a separate process in itself. Commercialization can be redefined as the market development process. Its stages can be described in terms similar to the product life cycle concept, beginning with market introduction and moving to growth, maturity, saturation, and decline. In order to understand the process of market development for new industrial products, we must take into consideration the unique aspects of industrial marketing and, especially, the complexity of the buying process.

DIFFUSION OF INNOVATIONS

A market can be thought of as a kind of social system through which a new product diffuses over time. The elements of the social system in an industrial market are firms and their employees as well as individuals, such as consulting engineers, architects, management consultants and other professional change agents. In Chapter 2, the organizational buying process was described as both an individual decision-making process and a group process bringing together and integrating these individual perceptions and decisions. When we consider the nature of the influence process in the development of markets for new industrial products, we must recognize that both firms and individuals are influencing one another (see Figure 6-1).

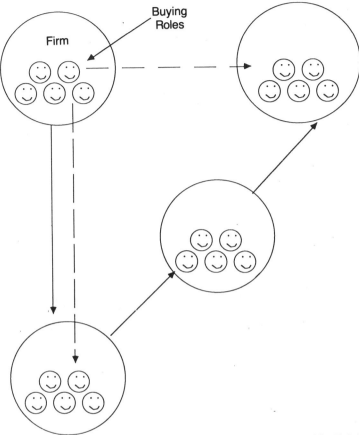

Firms Influence Other Firms (Solid lines)
Individuals in the Buying Center
are Influenced by
Individuals in Other Firms (Dotted lines)

Figure 6-1. The diffusion process—economic and social influences.

The new product, or innovation, can be thought of generally as a concept or idea that must gain acceptance if the market is to develop. Diffusion is a process in which the members of the social system influence one another in a variety of direct and subtle ways— through demonstration that creates awareness, through providing information that shows the viability of the new product in use, and through creating pressure to adopt the innovation. In industrial markets that pressure is likely to be derived in part from the need to compete with earlier adopters of the new product, who have improved their competitive effectiveness.

The process of diffusion of innovations in industrial markets is both a social influence process among the various actors in the social system (the using industry) and an economic process in which costs, revenues, and market structure and competitive conditions are altered. There are two rather distinct research traditions in the study of the diffusion of innovations in industrial markets, one stressing the social process and the other stressing economic consequences. These differing approaches have tended to merge in the marketing literature, where there has been a reasonably balanced concern for both the process and the results of diffusion.[1]

The Adoption Decision Process

The adoption decision process is an intrafirm process in which the firm builds an increasing commitment to use a new product or process. It is a "new task," an example of extensive problem solving, to use terminology introduced in Chapter 2, and, therefore, includes all stages in the buying decision process, beginning with need recognition.

For the new industrial product, the creation of need recognition by the prospective buyer is likely to call for a high degree of creative salesmanship by the seller. It is not likely that the prospective customer will be highly dissatisfied with the performance of whatever product or service the new product or service is intended to replace. Furthermore, a change from an established solution to an entirely new solution involves, by definition, a substantial degree of risk to the buyer in terms of unproven availability, quality, and price stability.

The stages in the new product adoption process have been de-

---

[1] These two research thrusts are examined more carefully in Frederick E. Webster, Jr., "Communication and Diffusion Processes in Industrial Markets," *European Journal of Marketing*, **5**, 4 (Winter, 1971), 178–88. A good summary of the economic literature is Edwin Mansfield, *Industrial Research and Technological Innovation* (New York: W. W. Norton & Co., Inc., 1968) and Mansfield et al., *The Production and Application of New Industrial Technology* (New York: W. W. Norton & Co., Inc., 1977). Sociological research has been summarized in Everett M. Rogers and F. Floyd Shoemaker, *Communication of Innovations: A Cross-Cultural Approach* (New York: The Free Press, 1971).

scribed as awareness, interest, evaluation, trial, and adoption.[2] These decision stages are best viewed as conceptual definitions, not empirical facts, describing an individual's decision-making process in the purchase of a new product. When applied to a firm, the stages in the adoption process can be regarded as characterizing individuals in the buying center, who may be in different stages.

Awareness is just what it says, becoming aware of the innovation. It can be a passive, unintentional act, or it can be the result of conscious search for a solution to a buying problem, a problem defined in terms permitting its solution through some purchasing action. Interest is a relatively more active stage in which the decision maker gathers information with which to evaluate the new product. In the evaluation stage the prospective buyer actually considers the purchase in his own situation, trying to carefully assess its advantages and disadvantages, mentally assessing the risk involved.

Trial is the actual use of the product or process on a limited scale. Trial is itself a risky decision, because it requires a commitment of time, money, and personnel. The trial may take several weeks or months, and the outcome may not indicate unambiguously whether the innovation should be purchased or not. Trials may be repeated several times until all members of the buying center are comfortable with the results. Obviously, the trial stage is in many respects the critical stage in the adoption process, leading to acceptance or rejection of the innovation.

In the adoption stage the purchaser becomes committed to full-scale use of the product. In industrial markets especially, the adoption decision often means the replacement of some portion of existing plant and equipment, as well as the development of a new buyer-seller relationship.

Uses of Information Sources by Adoption Decision Stage

Members of the buying center rely upon different information sources at the different stages of the adoption process. A critical dimension is the credibility of the information source, a determinant

[2] Everett M. Rogers, *Diffusion of Innovations* (New York: The Free Press, 1962), pp. 81–86. In the third edition of this book, Rogers has redefined the adoption process as the "innovation–decision process" and the five stages as: (1) knowledge, (2) persuasion, (3) decision, (4) implementation, and (5) confirmation. See *op. cit.*, 3rd ed., pp. 21–22. Note also that the book by Rogers and Shoemaker cited in the previous footnote as a new book in its 1971 edition subsequently came to be referred to as the second or revised edition of *Diffusion of Innovations*.

of its ability to help the decision maker reduce perceived risk. Information sources can be characterized as either personal or impersonal and as either commercial or non-commercial. Some examples include:

Personal—Commercial: Sales representatives, distributors.

Impersonal—Commercial: Advertising, catalogues, direct mail.

Personal—Noncommercial: Consultants, government agency personnel, employees of other companies.

Impersonal—Noncommercial: Technical journals, government publications.

Research findings from a broad variety of studies of the diffusion of innovations support a general conclusion that impersonal sources of information are most relied upon at the awareness stage. Personal sources become more important for the evaluation and trial stages. These general studies also lead to a conclusion that commercial sources are most important in the early stages, awareness and interest, but give way to non-commercial sources for evaluation. Friends and opinion leaders are believed to be more dependable sources of evaluation information. Personal, commercial sources are found to be more important at the trial and adoption stages, when personal demonstration and application, as well as persuasion and order writing, may be required.[3]

The underlying implication in much of this research is that commercial sources have relatively low credibility. Specifically, the sales representative is primarily a persuader, who will try to sell a new product even if adoption is not in the buyer's self-interest. This stereotype may have some validity for certain types of sales reps selling consumer products, although that can be debated. However, here is another instance where the uniqueness of industrial marketing must be taken into account and where conclusions from studies of consumer markets must be viewed with caution.

In addition to the four dimensions of uniqueness in industrial marketing defined in Chapter 1 (functional interdependence, product complexity, buyer-seller interdependence, and buying process complexity), it should be noted that personal selling is much more important than in consumer marketing. Furthermore, the functions

---

[3] For a review of these research findings, see Frederick E. Webster, Jr., *Marketing Communication* (New York: Ronald Press Co., 1971), pp. 166–74.

performed by advertising in industrial marketing are to a degree different from those in consumer marketing and include generating sales leads, supporting the sales rep, and creating an image of company capability and dependability.

Studies of the use of information sources by industrial buyers at different stages of the adoption process are limited. In one available study, manufacturers' sales reps were found to be the most important source of information for industrial buyers at all stages, except awareness, in the buying decision process. For awareness, trade journals were said to be slightly more important. Such journals were cited by 90 percent of those interviewed, compared to 84 percent citing sales reps. At the interest stage, reps were mentioned by 90 percent, compared to 38 percent mentioning trade journals and an equal number mentioning trade shows, the two next most important sources. Even at the evaluation stage, sales reps were most important. They were mentioned by 64 percent of respondents. Fifty-five percent mentioned engineers in other companies and 28 percent cited buyers in other companies as sources of information. The research being described here hypothesized that buyers and engineers in other companies would serve as important sources of word-of-mouth communication (opinion leadership) in industrial markets. As noted, the sales rep was found to be more important. Opinion leadership and word-of-mouth communication, it was suggested, may be less important in industrial markets than in consumer markets.[4] The implication for industrial marketers is quite clear. Development of markets for new industrial products requires heavy reliance on the sales representative. Although advertising and articles in technical and trade journals may help to create awareness and to support the sales rep, an adequately trained and carefully deployed salesforce is the backbone of new product marketing effectiveness.

Factors Influencing the Intrafirm Rate of Adoption

Some industrial firms (or, more precisely, buying centers) go through the stages of the adoption process more rapidly than others.

---

[4] Frederick E. Webster, Jr., "Informal Communication in Industrial Markets," *Journal of Marketing Research*, **VII**, 2 (May, 1970), 186–89. Similar findings and conclusions were reported by Urban B. Ozanne and Gilbert A. Churchill, "Adoption Research and Information Sources in the Industrial Purchasing Decision," in Robert L. King (ed.), *Marketing and the New Science of Planning* (Chicago: American Marketing Association, 1968), pp. 352–59.

The characteristics of firms that make decisions more quickly have been examined by Mansfield and his students. Innovations studied have included diesel locomotives, chemical processes, numerical controls for machine tools, plastics, textiles, electronics, and aircraft engines.[5] It has been learned, not surprisingly, that the larger the firm, the longer it takes to move through the adoption decision process. Similarly, the more people involved in the decision process, the more time required. Size of firm and size of buying center were correctly treated as separate variables, but it would obviously be expected that larger firms would have larger buying centers. Also, firms with larger market shares tend to take longer to move from awareness to adoption. It was also found that the later in the diffusion process a firm begins its own adoption decision process (i.e., the larger the number of firms that have already adopted), the more quickly it will tend to move through the process. Thus, earlier adopters tend to be more cautious. Later adopters tend to catch up more quickly, taking less time to substitute new technology for old.

The cautiousness of the earlier adopters is due, in part, to the fact that the innovation often is unfinished when it first appears on the market. As noted in the previous chapter, many new industrial products fail because they are "incomplete," leaving too much of the final application development to the customer. On the other hand, each customer may of necessity have to contribute to the ultimate development of the new technology in each specific application, especially in the early stages of market development. As Mansfield notes, "During the early stages of the diffusion process, the improvements in the new process or product may be almost as important as the new idea itself. Moreover, when a new product's design is finally stabilized, costs of production generally fall in accord with the so-called 'learning' curve."[6] In other words, the later adopters may receive a better product at lower cost.

In this section we have been considering the intrafirm rate of adoption, the speed with which a firm moves from awareness to fullscale adoption. We now turn to an examination of factors influencing the time at which a firm begins to consider adoption of an innovation, not how long it takes to make a decision.

[5] Mansfield et al., *The Production and Application of New Industrial Technology, op. cit.*

[6] *Ibid.*, p. 17. The influence of the experience curve was also examined in detail in the previous chapter.

Adopter Categories

Adopter categories in the diffusion research tradition are defined in terms of variation from the mean time of adoption for all firms in the using industry (see Figure 6-2). The first 2½ percent to adopt are called *innovators;* the next 13½ percent are called *early adopters;* and the next 34 percent are the *early majority*. They are followed by the *late majority,* 34 percent, and the *laggards,* 16 percent. These categories have provided standard definitions for diffusion studies of farming innovations, pharmaceuticals, and other consumer products. Because of the relatively smaller numbers of potential adopters in the typical industrial market, these precise categories may have variations, and industrial researchers have tended to use less precise or consistent definitions. In general, industrial diffusion research makes a distinction between earlier and later adopters with "earlier adopters" including both "innovators" and "early adopters" categories from the more traditional studies.

Research on diffusion of innovations in industrial markets supports a conclusion that an S-shaped logistic curve is a reasonably good description of the process over a period of time. The process described is one in which the number of firms adopting the innovation at first rises very slowly and then begins to rise at an increasing rate. When about half of the potential adopters are using the new product or process, the rate of acceptance is at its peak but then begins to slow down, with the late majority and eventually the laggards adopting at a slower rate. In very rough terms, studies

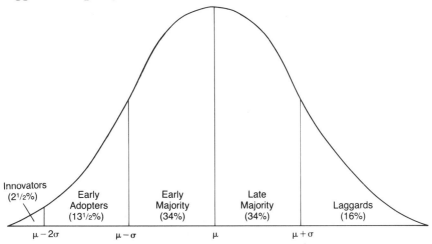

Figure 6-2. Definition of adopter categories.

show that the typical industrial innovation requires 5 to 10 years before half of the firms in an industry begin using it. The rate of diffusion over a period of time, according to this simple logistic curve model, is determined by two variables: the profitability of the innovation to the potential adopter relative to alternative investments and the investment required to adopt the innovation as a percentage of the total assets of the firm.[7]

A variety of studies have confirmed and supported this basic model, and its validity has been further confirmed by using it to forecast the rate of acceptance of numerically controlled machine tools.[8] Several other variables have been tested and incorporated into extensions and elaborations of the basic model including: (1) the R&D expenditures of adopter firms; (2) the market structure of the using industry; (3) the dispersion of the profitability of the innovation—an operational measure of perceived risk; (4) the length of time the innovation has been in use in other industries—one measure of the importance of a "demonstration effect;" and (5) the age of the chief executive officer of the adopting firm.

Characteristics of Earlier Adopters

One of the strongest generalizations emerging from the majority of these studies is that the earlier adopters tend to be the largest firms in the industry. The underlying reason seems to be that their greater financial resources make them better able to afford the required investment and to absorb the risk inherent in being an innovator or early adopter. In addition, larger firms; because of their size, may have greater replacement needs, as well as a broader range of potential applications. Larger firms may simply be in a better position because of scale and scope of operations, and market share, to derive economic benefit from an innovation. As noted earlier in the

---

[7] *Ibid.*, pp. 108–10. The formula for the logistic curve is

$$P_{ij}(t) = [1 + e^{-(1_{ij} + \theta_{ij} t)}]^{-1},$$

where $P_{ij}(t)$ is the proportion of firms in the using industry that have adopted the innovation at time (t). It can be shown that the rate of "imitation," as Mansfield calls it, depends only on θ_{ij}. According to Mansfield's model $\theta_{ij} = b_i + a_1 II_{ij} + a_2 S_{ij} + Z_{ij}$, where the a's and b's are parameters (to be estimated by means of regression analysis), II_{ij} is the profitability of the jth innovation to the ith industry, S_{ij} is the required investment, and Z_{ij} is an error term. The original model appeared in Edwin Mansfield, "Technical Change and the Rate of Imitation," *Econometrica*, **29**, 4 (October, 1961), 741–66.

[8] *Ibid.*, pp. 11–12.

discussion of the intrafirm rate of diffusion, however, the larger firms tend to have more complex buying centers and decision processes and, therefore, take longer to go from awareness to adoption. The effects of size of firm are less likely to appear when the costs of adoption are low.

The earlier adopters are also consistently those for whom the innovation offers the highest potential return on investment, or profitability. This is an understandable result that suggests the importance to the marketer of carefully analyzing the needs and economic structure of potential adopters before selecting target industries and companies for marketing effort. In addition, it suggests a direct relationship between price charged and the rate of diffusion. Other things being equal, higher price means lower profitability for potential adopters.

A study of the adoption of the first long-range jet aircraft, the Boeing 707 and the Douglas DC-8, by commercial airlines in the United States disclosed that total assets, as a measure of firm size, were significantly related to time of adoption. Also found to be significant were debt-to-equity ratio (a measure of the firm's ability to finance the required investment) and the predicted growth in revenues, as revealed by operating data in later years. These three variables combined in a regression analysis accounted for 75 percent of the variance among firms in time of adoption of the DC-8 and 707. The earlier adopters were larger, faster growing airlines and had more borrowing power than later adopters.

For the intermediate-range Boeing 720, these three variables explained only about half of the variability in time of adoption. One explanation for this is that the 720 was quite similar to the 707 and DC-8 in range and operating characteristics, and those firms that adopted the long-range jets first were not in the market for the 720, since the 707 and DC-8 were in fact, being used in intermediate-range service. For the Boeing 727, the relationship was somewhat stronger, ($R^2 = 0.60$), although the 720 further complicated the market for the intermediate-range 727 as well. For the short-range DC-9, the relationship was stronger again, ($R^2 = 0.74$). Total assets and debt-to-equity ratio were the most important. Predicted revenue growth was less so. In the later years of the analysis (1964–65), debt-to-equity ratio became a more important consideration, partly because earlier commitments to jets had significantly influenced the ability of the airlines to take on the additional debt required to finance the purchase of the newer, smaller models. The diffusion of these newer and smaller aircraft was much more rapid than for the long-range models, and this undoubtedly reflects both the smaller investments required for the smaller models and the fact that the risk of adoption had been significantly reduced as the industry was entering the second decade of the jet age.[9]

Another set of conclusions from this body of research can be summarized by relating speed of adoption to what can be called the managerial and technical progressiveness of the firm. Earlier adopters have been found to be firms that spend more on R&D, and have presidents who are younger and better educated. (No relationship has been found between the intrafirm rate of adoption and the age or education of the president.) Firms spending heavily on R&D may be more comfortable evaluating new technologies, as well as better informed about them, and more generally receptive to change. These characteristics of early adopters have clear implications for the definition of market segments.

A study of the adoption of continuous casting technology in the steel industry did not find the hypothesized relationship between firm size and early adoption. Size of firm was not significant, either positively or negatively. The earlier adopters tended to have fewer people involved in the buying center and a more open, less formalized and structured decision process. Furthermore, members of the buying center tended to have wider job experience. Earlier adopters also tended to be newer firms and to depend less heavily on outside agencies (suppliers) as sources of innovation.[10]

Influence of Customer Industry Market Structure

Earlier economics studies found that innovations diffuse more rapidly in less concentrated industries. Thus, the best market targets for new industrial products, assuming that the product is such that the marketer, in fact, has a choice to make, would appear to be industries that are not dominated by a few large firms. To a certain extent, these findings would seem to conflict with a widely held notion that industries composed of a few giant firms tend to be most progressive technologically.[11]

---

[9] Frederick E. Webster, Jr., "Communication and Diffusion Processes in Industrial Markets," *European Journal of Marketing*, 5, 4 (Winter, 1971), 178–88.
[10] John A. Czepiel, "Decision Group and Firm Characteristics in an Industrial Adoption Decision," in R. L. Bernhardt (ed.), *Marketing; 1776–1976 and Beyond* (Chicago: American Marketing Association, 1976), pp. 340–43.
[11] Mansfield *et al.*, *op. cit.*, p. 208.

In fact, more recent research supports a different conclusion—that earlier adopters are likely to be found in concentrated industries with limited price competition.[12] It would be fair to conclude, at this stage, that the relationship between rate of diffusion and customer industry concentration is not well understood.

COMPETITIVE EFFECTS ON DIFFUSION

The careful reader may well have noted that all of the previous discussion concerns the characteristics of potential customers as determinants of the rate with which a new product is accepted in the marketplace. However, a moment's reflection suggests the obvious point that actions taken by the marketer along with competition from other vendors in the marketer's industry will have an important impact on the diffusion process. Robertson and Gatignon in 1986 developed a series of propositions about the influence of both supply and demand side competitive effects on the rate of diffusion.[13] Their propositional inventory included the following:

Supply side competitive effects:
Rate and level of diffusion are positively influenced by the following factors, which are rather easily understood:

- Competitive intensity among suppliers
- The reputation of the supplier group
- Standardardization
- Vertical coordination between suppliers and customers
- R&D expenditures by the supplier group
- Marketing expenditures by the supplier group

Demand side competitive effects:
Rate and level of diffusion are associated with industry structural and communication factors, each of which requires a brief explanation:

[12] Hubert Gatignon and Thomas S. Robertson, "Technology Diffusion: An Empirical Test of Competitive Effects," *Journal of Marketing*, **53**, 1 (January, 1989), 35–49.
[13] Thomas S. Robertson and Hubert Gatignon, "Competitive Effects on Technology Diffusion," *Journal of Marketing*, **50**, 3 (July, 1986), 1–12.

- Adopter industry structural factors include:
  1. Industry "heterogeneity," the extent to which firms are similar to one another, where it is expected that an *intermediate* level of heterogeneity is best. If firms are very similar, the information potential of new technology is reduced; if they are very different, communication breaks down due to lack of common focus.
  2. Competitive intensity, where an *intermediate* level is best. Very intense competition reduces the potential benefit for the adopter; minimal competition removes the incentive to innovate. Also, highly competitive industries with low profit margins may not have the financial resources for adoption.
  3. Demand uncertainty, which is expected to be positively related to acceptance of innovations, which offer the possibility of preemption and differentiation in terms of costs or product features, including price reduction.
- Adopter industry communication factors include:
  4. Signal frequency and clarity, which should be positively related to speed and level of diffusion.
  5. Level of professionalization of employees, a key to the amount of social influence in the industry, which would have a positive influence.
  6. "Cosmopolitanism," the external orientation of firms in the industry, associated with such measurable characteristics as the percentage of employees who have worked in other industries and the percentage of sales derived from foreign markets, which should positively influence the industry's acceptance of innovations.

This set of propositions is a useful reminder that the adoption of technological innovations is a risky undertaking. Adopters need not only the incentive of improved competitive effectiveness from the innovation. They also need the assurance and support of a credible supplier group, vendors with proven track records who have committed the necessary technical and marketing resources to insure successful development of the new technology and sufficient competition on the supply side to insure availability, reasonable pricing, and continued improvement of the technology.

Robertson and Gatignon then began a program of research to test these propositions. They have studied the acceptance or rejection of lap-top computers for the sales force by sales managers in a variety of industries. In general, their research supports their propositions. The firms that adopted the innovation were in more concentrated industries with less intensive price competition, and therefore with opportunity to use the innovation as a competitive tool and with the financial resources (profit margins) necessary to afford it. However, the expected relationships with demand uncertainty and openness of communication were not confirmed. The amount of vertical coordination between vendors and customers, through key account relationships, for example, was also related to speed of adoption, as was the presence of supplier incentives, such as special discounts.

Although not clearly part of their initial propositions, they also tested for the effects of customer company centralization/standardization (hypothesized to be positive) and selling task complexity (hypothesized to be negative) on the rate of adoption, but could find no significant relationships here. Two other areas of inquiry had to do with decision maker information-processing characteristics and were also not part of the original framework. These variables were preference for negative information and access to personal or impersonal information. Here the results were mixed. The expected positive relationship between preference for negative information and likelihood of adoption was confirmed, supporting the notion that some decision makers have a greater tolerance for ambiguity and may actively seek out negative information, primarily through word-of-mouth, in order to make a more informed decision, and may also be correspondingly more receptive to innovation if they can be reassured in this manner. Likewise, it was found that individuals with more exposure to personal information sources were more likely to be adopters. However, they found no relationship with access to impersonal information sources such as advertising and sales promotion, suggesting perhaps that this information may have little impact because the net effect of exposure is confusing and contradictory. Finally, the evidence refuted the hypothesis that adopters would favor heterogeneous information sources, those beyond their immediate industry.[14]

The Gatignon and Robertson research is an important contribution in understanding the importance of competitive effects and in re-emphasizing the importance of supplier industry characteristics on the diffusion process. It can only be hoped that they, and others, will continue to explore the influence of such factors as supplier competition, marketing programs, standardization, and R&D support on the successful commercialization of new technologies. The available information about the influence of marketing effort is based

---

[14] Gatignon and Robertson, *op. cit.*

primarily on clinical and observational studies. More empirical and analytical research is needed.

Quality of Marketing Effort

The marketing literature, including both journal articles and case studies, is replete with examples of new industrial products that failed due to inadequate marketing effort, including lack of careful market analysis and a failure to define market segments with precision. Among the causes of new product failure in industrial markets, the following were mentioned in one study:

1. Failure to define precisely that segment of the total market in which the product is likely to have the greatest value for users.
2. Underestimation of the amount of marketing effort required, resulting in an inadequate deployment of resources.
3. Underestimation of the amount of new investment required by users and the extent to which production technology and skills were made obsolete.
4. Inadequate understanding of the composition of the buying center and of its decision process, causing an underestimation of the amount of time required for the intrafirm adoption process.
5. Lack of awareness of established relationships between potential customers and existing suppliers.
6. Lack of awareness of influence patterns and market structure in the potential customers' industry.[15]

Even though they were not focussing on the quality of marketing effort itself, Mansfield and his colleagues observed how critical marketing effort was to the success of industrial technological innovations. They stated a conclusion that " . . . our results indicate that the probability of commercialization (given technical completion) is directly related to the degree to which R&D and marketing are integrated."[16] In addition they cited evidence that industrial firms often underexploit the results of R&D, because marketing and production do not cooperate and coordinate their efforts with R&D. This can be interpreted as a failure of top management and of

[15] Frederick E. Webster, Jr., "New Product Adoption in Industrial Markets: A Framework for Analysis," *Journal of Marketing*, **33**, 3 (July, 1969), 35–39.
[16] Mansfield *et al.*, *op. cit.*, p. 197. These findings are also reviewed in Mansfield, Edwin, "How Economists See R&D," *Harvard Business Review*, **59**, 6 (November-December, 1981), 98–106, esp. 100.

marketing management to recognize functional interdependence and to bring about the necessary degree of interfunctional coordination. It also underscores the importance of managing the Marketing–R&D interface and the linking of market needs with technological opportunities, as stressed in Chapter 5.

Characteristics of the Innovation Influencing Rate of Diffusion

Traditional diffusion research has found that the speed with which an innovation is accepted is a function of:

1. Relative advantage—the degree to which the innovation is perceived as superior to the idea, practice, or product it replaces.
2. Compatibility—the degree to which the innovation is consistent with existing values and practices.
3. Complexity—the degree to which an innovation is easily understood and used.
4. Divisibility—the extent to which an innovation can be tried on a limited basis.
5. Communicability—the extent to which the results of using an innovation can be observed by or described to others.[17]

Relative advantage of the industrial innovation can be measured by the impact on the profitability and return on investment to the user, compared with alternative technologies. As noted, the work of Mansfield and his colleagues shows a strong relationship between profitability and speed of adoption.

While no data on the influence of *variability* in potential profitability to users have been reported, to my knowledge, Beardsley and Mansfield have published the results of studies of the accuracy of an important industrial firm's forecasts of the profitability of its product and process innovations. They concluded that forecast accuracy was initially quite low, with 50 to 60 percent of first-year forecasts of profitability over the life of the product either more than two times too high or more than 50 percent too low. It typically took four or five years for a firm to get reasonable forecasts of the discounted flow of profits over the life of the innovations.[18] It was found

[17] Rogers, *op. cit.*, pp. 124–54.
[18] George Beardsley and Edwin Mansfield, "A Note on the Accuracy of Forecasts of the Profitability of New Products and Processes," *Journal of Business*, 51, 1 (January, 1978), 127–35.

that the profitability of the very profitable products was consistently underestimated and that of the relatively unprofitable products was consistently overestimated, revealing a kind of conservatism or risk aversion on the part of the forecasters.

A variety of economic arguments have been put forth to explain the relationship between rate of diffusion and characteristics of the innovation. Essentially, they all boil down to a statement that the new product must satisfy the customer's needs and be feasible within the technical and economic constraints facing the user. Among the factors that have been considered are the costs of changing the technique of production, the divisibility of manufacturing facilities, and the reliability of existing sources of supply. If the potential customer is not aware of a problem with its existing methods and purchases, the marketer of the innovation has an uphill struggle. To understand the market development challenge, the marketer must view the innovation not as a technical achievement but, in dynamic relationship with the characteristics of the using firm, as a solution to a customer problem.

Adopter—Vendor Relationships

Remembering the importance of buyer-seller relationships in industrial marketing, the discussion to this point may seem strangely disjointed. First we looked at the characteristics of adopter firms; then we added a concern for supply-side competitive effects and the quality of marketing effort before we looked at the characteristics of the innovation itself. In fact, this is the way the problem has been approached by researchers and writers in the field. Only recently has there been an attempt to relate the new product development process, seen as something that happens under the total control of the marketer's organization, and the adoption decision process within the customer organization. Intellectually, the roots of this integration may be traced back to the work of von Hippel,[19] cited also in the previous chapter.

It has been suggested by More that the failure of new industrial products, often correctly attributed to weaknesses in the management of the new product development process, may often be the result of weakness in understanding and managing relationships

[19] Eric A. von Hippel, "Has a Customer Already Developed Your Next Product," *Sloan Management Review*, **18**, 2 (Winter, 1977), 63–74.

with potential adopting organizations.[20] He argued that the selling and buying organizations each go through a management decision process, which for the seller we call *development* and for the buyer *adoption*. As shown in Figure 6-3, adoption and development follow the same nine stages. These nine stages are an elaboration of the six-stage model of the new product development process presented in Chapter 5 and the five-stage model of the adoption decision process developed earlier in this chapter. More points out that the nine stages need not occur sequentially and each stage consists of multiple tasks, activities, and decisions.

More's model integrates the development and adoption processes in terms of interactions between the vendor and the adopter. Figure 6-4 illustrates, with the path labelled "A," the typical developer-driven serial relationship; path "B" might describe an adopter-proactive co-development relationship. In Figure 6-5, path "C" describes a developer-proactive development relationship, one where the marketer takes the initial leadership in developing new technology. Path "D" describes the process followed in the empirical example of the development of a computer-assisted learning system studied by More.

This conceptualization of an interactive new product development process brings to life the idea of value-added partnerships that we discussed in Chapter 3 and relates them nicely to issues of developing markets for new industrial products. It suggests that in a wide variety of situations, industrial marketers will want to work closely with potential adopters in all stages of the new product development process. Partnership may be the key to success.

MARKET SEGMENTATION STRATEGY FOR NEW PRODUCTS

By now we have established firmly that the product in industrial marketing strategy must be seen as a variable, not as a given. Products are a complex set of technical, economic, personal, and legal variables and relationships that must be tailored to the customer's needs. As discussed in the previous section, the new industrial product is often a flexible technical concept that continues to evolve in time as the result of the learning by innovators and earlier adopters. The industrial product is unfinished until it has been

[20] Roger A. More, "Developer/Adopter Relationships in New Industrial Product Situation," *Journal of Business Research*, 14 (December, 1986), 501–17.

Developing (Selling) Organization	Stage	Adopting (Buying) Organization
Analysis and definition of the internal organizational need and strategic rationale for developing new technology/product/market scenarios.	Problem Recognition	Analysis and definition of the internal organizational need and strategic rationale for adopting new technologies/products.
Analysis and definition of needs, payoffs, and risks of market segments in adopting a new product.	Need Analysis	Analysis and definition of needs, payoffs, and risks of adopting a new product.
Analysis and definition of the choices between alternative product performance dimensions and physical product features for different market segments.	Product Concept	Analysis and definition of required performance dimensions and physical features for the needed product.
Analysis, definition, choice, and linkage of alternative physical technologies for the product concept.	Technology Choice	Analysis, definition, choice, and linkage of alternative physical technologies-in-use for the product concept.
Analysis and definition of the financial viability of developing alternative new technology/product/market scenarios.	Financial Analysis	Analysis and definition of the financial viability of adopting alternative technologies/products.
Analysis, definition, and detailed translation of technologies and product concept into physical products for target market segments.	Product Design	Analysis and detailed definition of the required physical and performance attributes for a new product.
Analysis and planning of production process, sourcing, and logistics to produce product units.	Production Sourcing	Analysis and planning of sourcing, search for alternative technology/product suppliers, analysis of alternative technologies, products and suppliers.
Commitment of financial and human resources to produce and market product units.	Unit Commitment	Commitment of financial resources to purchase product units and choice of suppliers.
Testing of customer process implementation and integration of use of the new technology/product and modification of the product.	Use Implementation	Process implementation and integration of use of the new technology/product, analysis and evaluation of effectiveness and satisfaction, analysis of changes necessary, and repurchase.

Figure 6-3. Stages in the development and adoption processes. [Source: Roger A. More, *"Developer/Adopter Relationships in New Industrial Product Situations,"* Journal of Business Research, 14 *(December, 1986), 501–17, at 505.*] *Reproduced with permission.*

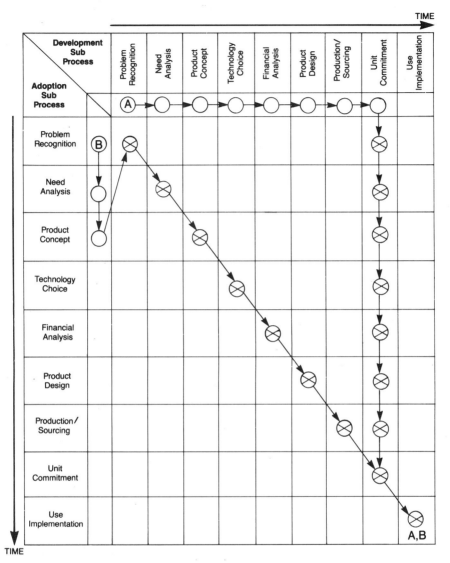

Figure 6-4. Examples of adopter-vendor relationships. A = Traditional developer-driven serial relationship; B = adopter-proactive co-development relationship; X = Interfacing; O = Non-interfacing. [Source: Roger A. More, "Developer/Adopter Relationships in New Industrial Product Situations," Journal of Business Research, 14 (December, 1986), 501–17, at 512.] Reproduced with permission.

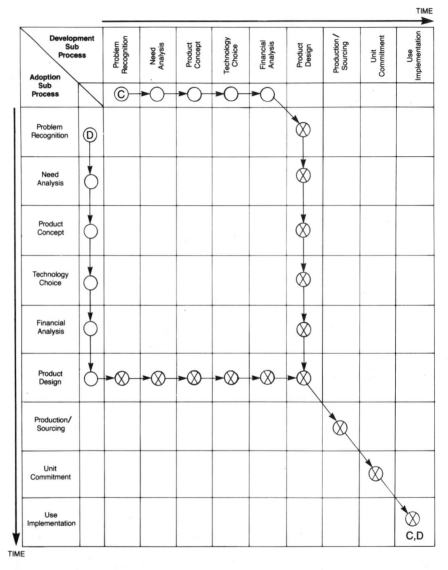

Figure 6-5. Examples of adopter-vendor relationships. C = Developer-Proactive Co-Development Relationship; D = an actual observed relationship; X = interfacing; O = non-interfacing. [Source: *Roger A. More, "Developer/Adopter Relationships in New Industrial Product Situations,"* Journal of Business Research, 14 (December, 1986), 501–17, at p. 513.] *Reproduced with permission.*

augmented with the necessary bundle of customer services, including application engineering, installation, a distribution system that will insure availability, production process assistance, credit and other financing arrangements, and so on.

Since the whole bundle of product and service attributes must be tailored to fit the customers' needs, it follows that the selection of customers, the market segmentation decision, is a necessary step before the final definition of the product. This does not mean that new products should not be born in the laboratory nor that firms should not follow strategies of technical leadership. What it does mean is that communication with carefully selected customers is necessary, if there is to be a reasonable probability of commercial success. The validity of this assertion was well established by the research reviewed earlier in this chapter.

Macrosegmentation

Macrosegments are defined by industry (S.I.C. code), by size, and by geographic parameters. The potential customer's type of business is a major determinant of the characteristics it requires in the new product. The relative profitability of the innovation will reflect cost conditions, competition, market structure, existing production technology, relationships with existing suppliers, and other key dimensions of the target industry, as they influence a specific potential customer. Accurate macrosegmentation should produce groupings of firms with similar needs and applications for the new technology.

The central question in selecting macrosegments is "For which firms in which industries does the product have the greatest potential value? Which firms have the greatest need?" Good answers to this question can only come from good market research and careful analysis. But it must be remembered that, at this stage in the marketing planning process, the product is still a variable. A major use of the market analysis will be to develop information with which to decide about the various dimensions of product design and the related service offering. Therefore, the analysis of company capabilities—"What can we do best?"—is also a key input to the macrosegmentation decision. These capabilities are dynamic, reflecting earlier commitments to segments and developing in new directions as a result of the new commitments. Commenting on the critical importance of the macrosegmentation decision, Professor Corey has stated:

Choice of market is a choice of the customers and of the competitive, technical, political, and social environments in which one elects to compete. It is not an easily reversed decision; having made the choice, the company develops skills and resources around the markets it has elected to serve. It builds a set of relationships with customers that are at once a major source of strength and a major commitment. The commitment carries with it the responsibility to serve customers well, to stay in the technical and product-development race, and to grow in pace with growing market demand.

Such choices are not made in a vacuum. They are influenced by the company's background; by its marketing, manufacturing, and technical strengths; by the fabric of its relations with existing customers, the scientific community, and competitors, and by other considerations.[21]

The macrosegmentation decision is a matching of company capabilities and goals with unfilled market needs and opportunities. Specific product attributes are defined by the intersection of company capabilities with customer needs. The result is a positioning of a new product within a market. Some of the important product attributes will be technological in nature. Others will relate to the service offering and to how the product is marketed, the features that are stressed in promotion.

Vertical Segmentation

Horizontal market segmentation is the process of defining and selecting customer targets from among different industries. Companies within a horizontal segment will have a similar end-use application for the product. *Vertical* market segmentation is the definition and selection of customer groupings at different levels within a target industry. Vertical market segmentation, or the market entry level decision, was discussed briefly in Chapter 4. Here we consider vertical market segmentation more carefully as a key issue in the commercialization of new industrial products.

The importance of the entry-level decision is most clear in the case of materials or components, products that are farthest removed from end users or consumers. Vertical market segmentation may be less of an issue for producers of capital equipment, although, even here, there may be important strategic questions about the target-

[21] E. Raymond Corey, "Key Options in Market Selection and Product Planning," *Harvard Business Review,* **53,** 5 (September-October, 1975), 119–28, at 121.

ing of marketing effort at different levels within an industry and within the distribution channel, especially when there are "value-added" resellers.

Vertical market segmentation takes specific notice of supplier-customer relationships within an industry and of how products are modified as they move from one level to the next. It also considers the nature of competition and the technical skills required at each stage of the process. These determine the value added and the profit opportunities at each stage. For the new product marketer there may also be different risks of product misapplication and failure at each stage.

In a classic study of market development for new industrial materials, Professor Corey concluded:

> To develop the markets for materials, the materials producer has found it necessary to undertake marketing programs of great breadth and complexity at two market levels. He has had to work extensively with his immediate customers, the end-product fabricators, to build an industry which will make and supply the new product to end users. In addition, he has had to undertake long-range promotional programs in the end-product market to create demand for the product among consumers and industrial purchasers.[22]

Very often, the new product marketer is faced with a dilemma. On one hand, he needs to invest time and money in the development of a strong fabricator group in order to insure adequate quality standards and reliable supply to end users. A major market development task, therefore, is to negotiate a clear understanding about the sharing of risks and rewards with the fabricators. On the other hand, extensive applications assistance and promotional effort must be expended for the end users to develop both their applications and their loyalties. The fabricator may view the supplier as competing for its customers, especially if the negotiation of an understanding about risks and rewards has been incompletely or poorly done. The dilemma for the new product marketer arises from the need to stimulate end-user demand and to control the quality of the end-use application, on one hand, and, on the other, to receive necessary compensation and to avoid the perception of competing with the fabricator for his customers' loyalty. Corey noted that the problem

[22] E. Raymond Corey, *The Development of Markets for New Materials* (Boston: Division of Research, Graduate School of Business Administration, Harvard University, 1956), p. 234.

was often exacerbated by the fact that materials suppliers focussed their attention initially on technical product development and related manufacturing problems with the fabricator group. Only when the market failed to develop as quickly as anticipated did the supplier turn its attention to the end users. Often this was perceived as implicitly critical of the fabricator's work with the end-user and as an attempt to capture control of the relationship with the end-user.

Corey found that fabricators evaluated new materials in terms of the required capital investment, the impact on the use of existing equipment, and the new materials' ability to help them strengthen their market positions.[23] These observations, based on extensive case studies, are completely consistent with the results of the statistical analyses of the diffusion of industrial innovations by Mansfield and his colleagues described earlier in this chapter. However, in contrast to Mansfield's findings about the influence of firm size, Corey suggested (but was careful to avoid a firm conclusion) that smaller fabricators might tend to be earlier adopters, because the innovation provides them with incentive to improve significantly their market position. Furthermore, the risk of loss of market position due to failure of the new product may be greater for the established market leader. An active technical development role by the materials producer, if it has an established reputation, can significantly reduce the perceived risk for end users.

The balance of marketing effort between end users and fabricators should be determined by the product benefits offered to each level. Effort should be concentrated where the benefits are greatest. The nature of the benefits to be derived at each level of the market is, of course, determined by a host of strategic decisions made by the producer, including pricing, product design in its broadest sense, the marketing support offered to firms at each level in the market structure, and so on.

The materials producer's assessment of the strengths and weaknesses of the end user and fabricator groups and of the market opportunities at each level may lead to a decision to establish itself as a competitor. In other words, the materials producer may decide that the only way to develop the market is to become a fabricator or · to actually make consumer products. This decision may result in complete alienation of the other firms at that level of the market, leaving the materials supplier with no choice but to assume full

[23] *Ibid.*, pp. 235–37.

responsibility for market development at that level. Competing with customers is always a risky undertaking.

Microsegmentation

Microsegments are homogeneous clusterings of firms within macrosegments. They display common patterns of response to marketing effort. In Chapter 4, microsegmentation variables were defined as behavioral in nature. They focussed on the composition and functioning of the buying center within the firm, rather than the characteristics of the firm itself. If all firms within a given macrosegment have similar buying center composition and decision making characteristics, then microsegmentation is an unnecessary step in market analysis and strategic planning.

For new product development and commercialization, it is critical to realize that microsegments are likely to have different buying center composition, leading to different criteria for evaluating a new product. Furthermore, different decision-making processes within each microsegment can lead to different decision outcomes, even for clusterings of firms with similar buying center composition and evaluation criteria.

Identification and analysis of microsegments can provide information with which to make decisions about product design, as well as to develop selling messages and to define target audiences. Trade-offs among product parameters can be resolved with information about the relative importance placed on specific product attributes by members of the buying center. In addition, the degree of influence of the various members of the buying center, and, therefore, the impact of their particular evaluation criteria, can be assessed.

A sophisticated methodology for microsegmentation analysis has been developed by Choffray and Lilien and has been referred to in Chapters 2 and 4.[24] To illustrate the application of the methodology, Choffray and Lilien have reported an analysis of the industrial market for solar powered air conditioning.[25] First, macrosegments were defined in a traditional way, using industry, geographic, and size variables and including electronics, food processing, pharmaceutical, printing, and apparel manufacture firms in specified geographic areas. Second, the need specification dimensions used

[24] See Chapter 2, pp. 49–53, and Chapter 4, pp. 112–114.
[25] A summary of the methodology appeared in Jean-Marie Choffray and Gary L. Lilien, "Assessing Response to Industrial Marketing Strategy," *Journal of Marketing*, **42**, 2 (April, 1978), 20–31.

to evaluate solar powered air conditioning were defined through interviews with three to five members of the buying centers of several potential customers. Third, a survey was conducted to determine the requirements of each firm in the sample along these dimensions. It was found that over 50 percent of the companies surveyed required:

1. An expected system life of more than 10 years.
2. Investment cost less than $988 per ton of capacity.
3. Warranty period greater than 12 months.
4. More than five prior successful applications.
5. Operating cost (per year) less than 10 percent of the initial cost.

The fourth step in the analysis was to determine the composition of the buying center in each firm and the organizational responsibilities of each member. This led to the development of a decision matrix specifying the degree of involvement of each decision participant at each stage of the decision process, as illustrated in Figure 6-6. These data also provided the necessary input for a cluster analysis leading to the definition of microsegments of relatively homogeneous groupings by buying center composition.[26] Within each microsegment, the composition of the buying center is carefully assessed.

The fifth step in the analysis concentrated on individual decision participants and assessed their awareness, perceptions, and preferences. The necessary data were obtained through interviews or mail surveys, asking respondents to evaluate product attributes. Summary measures of product awareness, perceptions, and preferences were then developed for each buying role. Media usage patterns were also developed at this stage. When this analysis was completed, measurements had been obtained for determining product awareness, for assessing the acceptability of various product attributes to a given organization, and for developing models of individual evaluation and preference formation, as a function of specific product attributes. Choffray and Lilien pointed out that these individual

[26] The specific methodology of microsegmentation is developed in Jean-Marie Choffray, "A Methodology for Investigating the Structure of the Industrial Adoption Process and the Differences in the Perceptions and Evaluation Criteria Among Potential Decision Participants," unpublished Ph.D. thesis, M.I.T., Sloan School of Management, April, 1977. It is also reported in detail in Jean-Marie Choffray and Gary L. Lilien, Market Planning for New Industrial Products, (New York: John Wiley & Sons, Inc., 1980), pp. 74–91 and 194–205.

	Decision Phases / Decision Participants	1 Evaluation of A/C Needs, Specification of System Requirements	2 Preliminary A/C Budget Approval	3 Search for Alternatives, Preparation of a Bid List	4 Equipment & Manufacturer Evaluation*	5 Equipment & Manufacturer Selection
	Production & Maintenance Engineers	%	%	%	%	%
	Plant or Factory Manager	60%	%	50%	30%	40%
Company Personnel	Financial Controller or Accountant	%	%	%	%	%
	Procurement or Purchasing Department	%	%	%	%	%
	Top Management	%	100%	%	%	20%
	HVAC/Engineering Firm	40%	%	50%	70%	40%
External Personnel	Architects & Building Contractor	%	%	%	%	%
	A/C Equipment Manufacturers	%	%	%	%	%
	Column Totals:	100%	100%	100%	100%	100%

* Decision Phase 4 generally involves evaluation of all alternative A/C systems that meet company needs while Decision Phase 5 involves only the alternatives (generally 2-3) retained for final selection.

Figure 6-6. Buying center composition and involvement by decision stage: industrial cooling study. [Source: Jean-Marie Choffray and Gary L. Lilien, op. cit., p. 28.] Reproduced with permission of the American Marketing Association.

evaluation models permitted the analysis of industrial market response to changes in product positioning as well as the development of marketing communication programs that addressed issues most relevant to each category of decision participant.

The final step in the analysis of market response to a new industrial product was to develop the group decision model that related the decision process in the buying center to the preferences of its members. Mentioned briefly in Chapter 2, the group decision models specified how individual preferences were summed in the buying center to produce organizational choice. Four group decision models were specified: (1) a weighted probability model; (2) a proportionality model; (3) a unanimity model; and (4) an acceptability model. It was left to the marketing manager to determine which of these four models of the group decision process best described the characteristic decision-making behavior of firms in a given microsegment. Simulation can be used to assess the sensitivity of the overall market response model to different assumptions about the nature of the group decision-making process.

To summarize, Choffray and Lilien have developed a sophisticated methodology that makes the general model of organizational buying behavior and the concept of the buying center operational and useful for predicting market response to new industrial products. Included in the methodology are specific procedures for defining and analyzing microsegments. The resulting analysis can be used to refine and improve the product design, to develop advertising and personal selling messages, and to target communication programs. In addition to the industrial solar powered air conditioning market study used, above, as an example, Choffray and Lilien report the successful application of the model and measurement procedures to the design of an intelligent computer terminal and a supporting marketing communication program, the evaluation of marketing strategies for copiers, and estimating the market potential for thermic diode solar panels. The model is continually being refined and improved.

MARKET PIONEERING

From a strategic perspective, one of the most important decisions facing the industrial marketer is whether, or more accurately, when to be a market leader or a follower in the introduction of new technology. Remember the old adage—"It's easy to recognize the pioneers; they're the guys with the arrows in their backs." It is by no means obvious that it is always wise to try to be the first to market with new technology.

The market pioneer faces the financial commitment, and associated risk, of product development, market development, and investment in plant and equipment. The pioneer assumes the risk of technological failure. By demonstrating the feasibility of the new technology, the pioneer encourages competitive imitation at much lower cost and risk, and often with product enhancements, unless he also can erect substantial barriers to market entry. Is the greater risk for the pioneer associated with greater economic returns for successful innovation?

Here is another area where available research has tended to emphasize consumer products to the exclusion of technology-based industrial products. Fortunately, there has recently been some research to begin to correct this imbalance. The analysis suggests that indeed, under certain conditions, industrial market pioneers do earn higher rates of return. Robinson has reported a sophisticated analysis finding that, in a broad cross-section of industrial businesses in the PIMS data base, pioneers have important market share advantages over later entrants. Pioneers were found to have higher product quality and broader product lines and broader served markets than later entrants. These results were strongest in industries where the value of the average transaction was highest. However, the advantages of quality are diminished by competition over time. Also, the advantages of market share for the pioneer tend to be strongest in those industries where there is high value added (i.e., low ratio of purchases to sales). Pioneering produces the smallest market share benefits when share is based on lower direct costs of manufacture and lower prices.[27] Notice the consistency of these results with those reported in Chapter 5 concerning the relationship between market share and profitability as revealed by analysis of the PIMS data base.

The most successful pioneers are those who have the resources to achieve a dominant position in the market, with superior product quality and a broad product line, before competitors can enter the business. Based on consumer market studies, but with common sense supporting the extension to industrial markets at least to a degree, it has been suggested that pioneering is most appropriate

[27] William T. Robinson, "Sources of Market Pioneer Advantages: The Case of Industrial Goods Industries," *Journal of Marketing Research*, **XXV**, 1 (February, 1988), 87–94.

when image and reputation are important to the customer; when cost-experience effects are important and not easily copied; when brand loyalty accrues to the pioneer; and when cost advantages can be obtained by early commitment to suppliers and to distribution channels.[28]

Later market entrants have the advantage of being able to learn from the pioneers' mistakes. They may be able to improve and refine the technology, develop product improvements, or do a superior job of market segmentation and product positioning. Effective price competition may be an important source of differentiation for the follower, especially if it is based on cost advantages associated with refined process technology or substantial economies of scale. If larger firms play the role of market follower, they may compete by building large scale production capacity, achieving lower costs and erecting effective barriers to competition. Especially if the market pioneer does not have the resources necessary to establish a dominant market position, fast followers may win the battle for profitable market share.

SUMMARY

Commercialization, the last step in new product development, has been viewed as a process of market development reflecting complex interaction between the characteristics of the product and the characteristics of potential customers. The product was viewed as a flexible concept gradually taking final shape as the customer influenced the final stages of product development.

The characteristics of firms most likely to be early adopters of a new industrial product or process were defined, based on several statistical studies of market response to technological innovation. Buyer behavior at the several stages of the new product adoption decision process, including differing use of information sources, was also analyzed.

The selection of target industries and the development of market entry level strategy were discussed as critical steps in the new product market development process. Empirical studies were seen to support a conclusion that the failure of new industrial products was often a failure to achieve adequate coordination of R&D and

[28] Steven P. Schnaars, "When Entering Growth Markets, Are Pioneers Better Than Poachers?," *Business Horizons*, **29**, 2 (March-April, 1986), 27–36.

marketing and, specifically, a failure to provide marketing input to the final design of product parameters and the related service offering. The Choffray and Lilien methodology provided the necessary information for this task, as well as for the development of the supporting marketing communication strategy.

Bibliography

Baker, Michael J., *Marketing New Industrial Products* (London: The Mac-Millan Press Ltd., 1975).

Choffray, Jean-Marie, and Gary L. Lilien, *Market Planning for New Industrial Products* (New York: John Wiley & Sons, Inc., 1980).

Corey, E. Raymond, *The Development of Markets for New Materials* (Boston: Division of Research, Graduate School of Business Administration, Harvard University, 1956).

Mansfield, Edwin, *The Economics of Technological Change* (New York: W. W. Norton & Co., Inc., 1968).

————, *Industrial Research and Technological Change* (New York: W. W. Norton & Co., Inc., 1968).

————, *et al.*, *The Production and Application of New Industrial Technology* (New York: W. W. Norton & Co., Inc., 1977).

————, *et al.*, *Research and Innovation in the Modern Corporation* (New York: W. W. Norton & Co., Inc., 1971).

More, Roger, A., "Developer/Adopter Relationships in New Industrial Product Situations," *Journal of Business Research*, **14**, 6 (December, 1986), 501–17.

Ozanne, Urban B., and Gilbert A. Churchill, "Adoption Research: Information Sources in the Industrial Purchasing Decision," in Robert L. King (ed.), Marketing and the New Science of Planning (Chicago: American Marketing Association, 1968), pp. 352–59.

Rogers, Everett M., Diffusion of Innovations, 3rd ed. (New York: The Free Press, 1983).

7 Pricing Strategy

Price is a critical element in the marketing strategy of the industrial marketer and should always be viewed in the context of that marketing strategy. Price interacts with all other elements of the marketing mix to determine the effectiveness of each and of the whole. The objectives that guide pricing strategy should be a subset of the objectives that guide overall marketing strategy. Thus, it is probably wrong to view price as an independent element of marketing strategy or to assert that price, by itself, is a central element in the marketing mix.

PRICE AS PART OF THE PRODUCT OFFERING

Price should be viewed as part of the product offering. Therefore, price strategy should be seen as an adjunct to product strategy.

First, it is an important variable in the buyer's perceptions and combines with his judgments about availability, quality, and other product attributes to determine his overall perception of value. Price is thus a key consideration in the strategic positioning of the product. Price to the industrial or institutional customer is obviously a major determinant on the economic impact of the purchased product on his cost structure.

Second, from the seller's viewpoint, the price charged for the product determines not only the profitability of the product, but also the margins that are available to support the costs associated with all other aspects of the product offering, including technical support, after-sale service, delivery, credit, and so forth. This suggests the danger in viewing price out of the context of product strategy. Unwise managerial pricing judgments may be the result of simplistic thinking about the relationship between price and sales volume, overlooking the interaction between price and other elements of the product offering. Lower price is likely to require some reduction in costs, resulting in subtle changes in the product offering and a diminution of the resources available for promotion and market development.

Third, price is a major strategic variable for exploiting the product life cycle. It is a characteristic of the product life cycle model that profit margins are highest in the growth stages of the cycle, reflecting relatively high prices in the absence of strong competition, a condition that changes as the product enters the mature stage. However, as pointed out in the consideration of the experience curve concept in Chapter 5, management may opt to pursue a strategy of low price and high volume at the beginning of the life cycle, hoping to achieve experience curve cost benefits more rapidly than the competition. This approach could discourage competitive entry and establish a commanding market position for the product innovator. Research was also cited in Chapter 5, however, which calls into question this basic low price → high volume → low cost strategy. Instead, this study showed that the most profitable firms were those that had high quality, strong market position, and *high*, not low, prices, and that high prices did not appear to deter market penetration. Product quality, not low price, appeared to be the driving force in establishing a profitable market position.[1]

These research findings suggest that it may be a strategic error to use low price as a vehicle for achieving the market dominance that traditional analysis of the product portfolio suggests is the key to profitability. Support for this viewpoint is found in the experiences of Texas Instruments, Inc. in its forays into consumer electronics and microcomputers. In each instance, TI was eventually forced to absorb millions of dollars of losses with massive write-offs on calculators in the mid-1970's and on watches in 1981. Its 99/4A home computer, which was selling at $950 in 1981, was reduced to a price of $199, after a $100 rebate offer, in September 1982. Shooting for the dominant position in a market whose total size TI appears to have badly overestimated, TI reduced its price by another $50, to $149 with the $100 rebate, in February 1983. Sales volume responded, but so did competition. When the rebate offer expired, TI dropped its regular price to $149 and its major competitor, Commodore Business Machines, Inc., responded with a price below $100,

[1] Lynn W. Philips, Dae R. Chang, and Robert D. Buzzell, "Product Quality, Cost Position, and Business Performance: A Test of Some Key Hypotheses," *Journal of Marketing*, **47,** 2 (Spring, 1983), 26–43.

and was reported to be outselling TI by as much as 10 to 1. TI planned to respond with another rebate offer which would have lowered the price of the 99/4A to $99. As one TI manager commented, "Our cost-reduction plans could not go that fast and that deep." TI decided to withdraw from the market at that stage. The personal computer operation reported a pre-tax loss of $183 million for the quarter that ended June 30, 1983, including write-offs and write-downs of inventory judged to be unsalable in the amount of $83 million.[2]

Despite these cautions about using price to achieve market dominance, the fact remains that price *is* an important variable for exploiting the product life cycle. The firm needs to consider relationships between prices and stage of market development, and to have specific pricing strategies appropriate to each stage of the life cycle. We return to this set of issues when we consider "skimming" and "penetration" pricing strategies.

These observations about the interdependence of pricing and the product offering have equal relevance in the case of undifferentiated commodity products, such as caustic soda, isopropanol, or sulphuric acid. If the supplier is selling only a commodity product and if there is no opportunity to differentiate the product offering with services, there is clearly no basis for trying to achieve a price premium in the marketplace. Company reputation will count for little unless it can be translated into specific customer benefits, such as guaranteed availability, consistent quality, or manufacturing process assistance. Even for commodity products, therefore, there is always an interdependence of price and product. A commodity product requires a commodity price. The challenge for the marketer is to upgrade the product from its commodity status by adding product features and augmenting the product with service. Those opportunities always exist and create the potential for higher prices and improved profit margins. As noted in Chapter 5, however, there is always the risk that customers will not perceive sufficient value in the service bundle to justify the marketer's cost to provide it.

FORMULATING PRICING STRATEGY

Two strategic decisions must be made before the determination of price. The first is the macrosegmentation decision, the selection of

[2] "Texas Instruments Cleans Up Its Act." *Business Week*, Number 2802 (September 19, 1983), 56–64.

customers to be served. We have stated repeatedly that the selection of customers is the single most important element in industrial marketing strategy. It is a creative act by management from which all other aspects of marketing strategy follow.

The second strategic decision required before developing pricing strategy is the definition of product strategy. The values for target customers must be defined in detail, and the product must be positioned among competitive offerings. The role of price within this product strategy can then be defined and will lead to the determination of pricing objectives consistent with overall marketing objectives.

Needless to say, careful analyses of customer needs and of market conditions are necessary inputs to both of these strategic decisions—the definition of macrosegments and of product positioning. For the specific purposes of pricing strategy, such analysis should include an examination of the full range of competitive product offerings and prices and careful assessment of the importance that customers attach to price compared with other elements of the product offering. This may require detailed analysis of customer operations, with emphasis on costs and how they would be influenced by adoption of the supplier's product at various prices. An assessment of competitive conditions in the customer's industry (macrosegment) should be part of the market and customer analyses.

The objective of these first two analytical steps is to estimate the value of the product to the customer, both economically and psychologically. Obviously, costs must eventually be considered, but the critical element in pricing strategy is *not* the cost of manufacturing and of providing the necessary supporting services. This assertion will be supported when the discussion considers cost-based approaches to pricing. Here, the point is to stress the overriding importance of customer value. As Professor Corey has aptly put it: "Customer value is to pricing what magnetic north is to a compass needle."[3]

PRICING OBJECTIVES

Many objectives guide pricing decisions in the industrial firm. Some firms emphasize certain objectives and give lesser priority to others,

[3] E. Raymond Corey, *Industrial Marketing; Cases and Concepts*, 2nd ed. (Englewood Cliffs, N.J.: Prentice-Hall, Inc., 1976), p. 170.

but in most situations, prices reflect the interplay of several objectives. The complexity of pricing objectives is a result of several factors, including the interaction of pricing with other elements of the marketing mix, the dynamic nature of market conditions (especially competition and the level of demand), and the specific impact of pricing actions on the financial aspects of the firm. The latter includes profit margins, the return on investment, volume of production, inventory investment, and so on. Because the effects of pricing are so pervasive, simplistic definitions of pricing objectives are dangerous and misleading.

In a classic study of pricing objectives in large corporations (a good portion of which were industrial firms), Lanzillotti found that the most typical pricing objectives were: (1) pricing to achieve a target return on investment; (2) stabilization of price and margin; (3) pricing to realize a target market share; and (4) pricing to meet or prevent competition. He noted that in any given company one of these goals was likely to be dominant but that pricing decisions in any one firm was not always ruled by a single pricing objective.[4]

At the time of his research, in the late 1950's, Lanzillotti noted that concern with return on investment was a relatively recent management development. The concept of target return pricing was quite new and even radical at that time, in contrast to the conventional economic wisdom that companies set prices to maximize profits. Lanzillotti's conclusions were very provocative, especially in their suggestion that management could exercise a large degree of control over prices, aiming toward an acceptable rate of return: "It seems reasonable to conclude that the pricing policies are in almost every case equivalent to a company policy that represents an order of priorities and choice from among competing objectives rather than policies tested by any simple concept of profits maximization."[5] Furthermore, it was suggested that price followers decided whether to follow industry price leaders according to whether or not the leader's target rate of return resulted in an acceptable rate of return to the follower. If this was the case the price follower would be content to hold market share and to adjust price accordingly.

Surprisingly, there has not been a large amount of research to test the conclusions espoused by Lanzillotti. A research program under

[4] Robert F. Lanzillotti, "Pricing Objectives in Large Companies," *American Economic Review*, **48**, 5 (December, 1958), 921–40. This article re-examined data previously analyzed in A. D. H. Kaplan, Joel B. Dirlam, and Robert F. Lanzillotti, *Pricing in Big Business* (Washington, D.C.: The Brookings Institution, 1958).
[5] *Ibid.*, p. 939.

the direction of Professor Weston at U.C.L.A. produced results that conflicted with Lanzillotti's interpretation of the data from the earlier study. Professor Weston's conclusions pointed to the complexity of factors influencing the pricing decision, of which target return was only one. Target rate of return serves as a checkpoint, Weston concluded, not an objective. Weston studied both industrial and consumer products firms and believed that his data suggested that firms use target return prices as a reference point, adjusting prices to reflect market conditions. In fact, Weston questioned whether firms could have "pricing policies" of any kind, because of the complex forces influencing the pricing decision.[6] It is not surprising that the research on pricing objectives has not produced clear-cut answers to the question of pricing objectives of major industrial corporations. The reasons have been discussed earlier in this chapter. Pricing is too complex an issue to have distinct objectives that can be ascertained independently of an analysis of corporate marketing strategies.

Flexible Pricing

Pricing objectives in the 1990's are much more complex than in the past, with customers exerting a much stronger influence on pricing. Most industrial markets are global in scope and customers have a wide range of procurement options. A large customer in a strategic buyer-seller relationship can suggest clearly and strongly a certain price target that the vendor will be expected to meet. The customer, facing its own set of global competitors, will be motivated primarily by a desire to control costs, with quality a given and assured availability a must. The final price for a procurement, often involving a one-year agreement, will be arrived at through negotiation. The marketer's objective in the negotiation will be to maintain a target share of this customer's business, in order to reach planned levels of total sales and profitability.

Professor Lanzillotti saw the OPEC oil crisis of the mid-1970's as the key event in shifting management away from target rate-of-return pricing. He commented that "target pricing just does not prove to be as viable as it once was," and acknowledged that "firms are becoming much more flexible in their price thinking now."[7] Large firms committed to target return pricing found their market

[6] Gilbert Burck, "The Myths and Realities of Corporate Pricing," *Fortune*, **85**, 4 (April, 1972), 85–89 and 125–26.
[7] "Flexible Pricing," *Business Week*, 2513 (December 12, 1977), 78–88, at 79.

shares eroding as aggressive competitors sought business with flexible pricing. Professor Lanzillotti added:

> The initial business response was a confused attempt to pass on cost increases in an unthinking way—an effort to retain target rates of return but in an atmosphere requiring higher and higher prices. But with unused capacity around the world, there was just too little demand and too much competition to allow target return pricing to work. Indeed, 1975 and 1976 were marked by repeated retreats from announced industrywide price boosts in steel, paper, aluminum, and chemicals.[8]

Flexible pricing to meet competition and to maintain market share is especially likely in industry situations where there is excess capacity and high fixed costs. Target rate-of-return pricing may be a meaningful objective only when planning new product introductions or deciding to enter distinct new market segments. In those instances, the question may be whether market conditions will allow the required return on investment, which becomes a "hurdle rate" for deciding whether to go forward.

"Skimming" Versus "Penetration" Strategies

One useful characterization of pricing objectives makes a distinction between "skimming" and "penetration" pricing strategies. In a skimming strategy, prices are set high in the initial stages of the product life cycle. The product is then aimed at segments of the market where demand is least price-elastic. (Price elasticity is measured by the ratio of the percentage change in sales revenue associated with a percentage change in price. The higher the ratio, the more "elastic" demand is said to be.) Thus, the new product is aimed initially at those market segments where the level of demand is least sensitive to price—where customers are willing to pay the most for the product. As time passes, prices will be lowered in stages to attract new buyers from other market segments.

The implicit objective in a skimming strategy is to maximize profit margin. Skimming strategies recognize differences in price elasticity among market segments and attempt to discriminate among those segments. This is exactly what the economist means by the phrase *price discrimination*, charging different prices to different

[8] *Ibid.*

types of customers. In this case the different prices are charged at different times.

A penetration strategy, in contrast, has the implicit objective of maximizing sales volume and market share. Prices are set as low as possible to realize the largest possible market share and to realize resulting "experience curve" cost advantages. It is assumed that a large market share will provide a degree of market control by providing the base necessary for promotional activities and by discouraging competitive entry. (One of the risks of a skimming strategy is that the high profit margins are likely to attract new competitors). We have already pointed out the potential shortcomings of a penetration strategy.

Both skimming and penetration strategies can be consistent with a long-term return on investment objective, and both can be used to exploit the product life cycle. Penetration strategies are aimed at gaining an early commanding market position as a means of maximizing the return on the investment in the new product and forestalling competitive entry. Skimming strategies attempt to get back new product investments in the earlier stages of the product life cycle with the expectation that competition will eventually force down prices and margins.

The attractiveness of a skimming strategy or a penetration strategy is determined by the nature of the product and by market conditions, including both demand and competitive conditions. Skimming strategies are not possible in markets where there are not reasonably clearly definable market segments. Obviously, a skimming strategy assumes that the product is different from competitive product offerings. One of the key considerations in a skimming strategy is the amount of time needed before competition develops and markets a similar product offering. Strong patent protection is a good argument in favor of skim pricing.

LIST PRICES AND DISCOUNTS

Part of the controversy over pricing objectives reflects the flexibility that often characterizes pricing. When firms have published list or book prices, significant price cutting may occur as the firm attempts to hold or gain market share in a competitive situation. The extent of price cutting is a function of economic conditions and the specifics of competition in a given market. Although much of the economists' research is concerned with book prices and how they were determined, actual market prices are likely to vary significantly from book prices. Actual market prices, of course, are a much better indication of the nature of competition in a given industry than are book prices.

In the markets of the 1990's, most industrial firms find it necessary to sell a significant portion of their volume below announced "list" prices. The willingness to negotiate discounts in competitive procurement situations sometimes goes by the colorful phrase "fishing behind the net." Firms that go to market primarily through distribution may get locked into a pattern of seasonal promotional discounts to encourage dealer stocking. Others may find it necessary to cut prices in order to reach quarterly or annual sales objectives. All of these practices have the potential to lead to serious and rather permanent price erosion, making so-called "list prices" a myth.

Day and Ryans have observed that price discount decisions are made reactively in most companies but, when discounts are part of a carefully planned marketing strategy combining price and non-price incentives, they can be very effective and difficult for competitors to match.[9] A straight price cut, in contrast, is easily copied. A tightly focussed niche competitor can offer discounts that cannot be matched by a larger competitor with high service and support costs required to serve a broader market. Market targeting is usually the key to profitable discounting.

Quantity Discounts

It is common practice to offer customers reduced unit prices with increased purchase quantities. The lower unit prices reflect the economies of scale possible with larger purchase quantities. Quantity discounts can be a key strategic weapon for securing a position with major customers. Legally, all competing customers must be offered similar terms and prices. Discount quantities cannot be set so high that only the largest customers can take advantage of them. (The effect would be to reduce competition in the customers' industry.) If quantity discounts are to be justified, legally, on a cost basis, then marketing cost efficiencies should be given major emphasis, not production costs. Firms can not argue that lower costs are possible because fixed costs were covered on "earlier" production allocated to other buyers. Obviously, there is no defensible argument to justify lower prices based on lower costs, when the key issue

[9] George S. Day and Adrian B. Ryans, "Using Price Discounts for a Competitive Advantage," *Industrial Marketing Management*, **17**, 1 (February, 1988), 1–14.

is how customers are assigned positions waiting for production output.

Large customers can exercise considerable power in the price negotiation when the supplier has excess capacity in a plant that has high fixed costs. Suppliers must be able to defend the prices that result from such negotiations, either in terms of meeting equally low prices offered by competitors, or in terms of cost reductions permitted by the larger volumes. Once again, it should be stressed that similar prices and other terms of sale must be available, at least potentially, to all competing customers.

Functional Discounts

Resellers in the marketing channel are offered reductions from list prices as compensation for the services, or functions, they perform. (In the next chapter, issues of marketing channel management and strategy, including the role of pricing in the marketing mix and the functions performed by channel members, will be treated in detail.) Discounts offered to channel members are called *trade* or *functional* discounts. The list price is the base from which discounts are calculated. Although the list price may be the suggested price for the resellers to charge his customers, the manufacturer can not now legally insist that he charge that price. Resellers are free to set whatever price they wish to charge for the product.

Discounts to Meet Competition

List prices can be reduced to meet competition. Such price reductions may take several forms—outright price cutting, variations in the terms of payment, elimination of charges for certain extras, such as product modifications and transportation charges, substitution of one quality of product for another, and so on. Marketers can offer lower prices to one customer and not to another competing customer, but only if it can be shown that the customer had been offered an equally low price by another supplier or that differences in price are justified by differences in costs of doing business and are available to all customers. The burden of proof is placed upon the seller under the law.

The most important piece of legislation in this area is the Robinson-Patman Act of 1936, an amendment to the Clayton Act of 1914. The Clayton Act was an amendment to the Sherman Antitrust Act of 1890. The latter was aimed at pricing and other collusive practices that tended to create monopoly. The Clayton Act made it unlawful to discriminate in price among purchasers, if the effect of such discrimination was likely to cause reduction of competition. The Robinson-Patman Act strengthened the provisions of the Clayton Act by extending the protection of the act to competition in buying industries, not just selling industries, and by extending the prohibition to situations where competition was merely "injured," not actually "substantially lessened."

To remain within the confines of these laws, the marketer must avoid opportunistic pricing where the objective is simply to get available business (to maximize sales volume or market share). If the marketer pursues opportunistic pricing, there is the possibility that competing customers will be offered different prices and terms. One of the advantages of delegating pricing authority to independent distributors is that they can have greater flexibility in meeting local competition. But there is a risk in delegating pricing authority to company sales representatives. If different sales reps offer different prices to competing customers, that is in violation of the law.

PRICING METHODS

Cost-Based Pricing

It is widely believed that most industrial marketers set prices on new products and adjust prices on old products predominantly on a cost-plus basis. Stated differently, the costs of producing a product are believed to be the major consideration in setting a price on that product in industrial markets. The procedure followed, in simple form, is to estimate all variable costs of production, allocate a reasonable portion of relevant fixed costs, and add on a customary allowance for profit given some assumptions or forecasts about the quantity that will be sold. Cost-based pricing is formalized in some situations, such as the procurement of technology by the military establishment on a cost-plus contractual basis.

The arguments in favor of cost-based pricing are well-known. It has an aura of fairness about it and can be easily justified to the customer who wants to know how prices are determined. The concept of a fair profit margin or return on investment is generally accepted among businessmen, although there may be some disagreement about how much profit is fair. Cost-based pricing avoids the difficult problem of estimating the relationship between price and demand and setting prices intended to achieve a maximum profit. Cost-based pricing is more secure in the sense that, if target projections of volume to be produced are correct, the firm is reasonably assured of earning its targeted return on investment.

As noted earlier, the economic conditions of the 1990's have made it much more difficult to realize those targeted prices and the related return on investment. There are a number of other difficulties with cost-based pricing. First, when there are fixed costs shared with other products, there is always a difficult judgment about the allocation of those costs among individual products. Thus, the justification of a cost-based price may still be quite difficult, especially if there is excess capacity and the allocation of fixed costs is based on less than full capacity utilization. Second, as noted before, there may be no firm basis of justification for a targeted return on investment or profit margin. Third, there is no attempt to relate price charged to quantity demanded in the market. This means that costs are based on some volumes that are projected and assumed independent of price. But given these volume assumptions, cost-based pricing requires fewer assumptions than does demand-oriented pricing. Of course, this can be a false sense of security, because the relationship between price and volume still exists, even if it is not considered explicitly in the price-setting.

THE EXPERIENCE CURVE

As noted before, prices are often set for industrial products based on some assumptions about how the cost of producing the product will decline as the volume of production increases over a period of time. It is well known that variable costs of production will decrease for a new product as greater quantities are produced and the accumulated volume of production increases. The experience curve is the relationship between the variable unit cost of production and the total quantity of the product that has been produced up to a point in time. It can also be described as a relationship between cost and time, although this is misleading, because time causes nothing. It is the accumulated experience of producing the product that influences costs.

Learning in a production process has two components. First, the people who are responsible for producing the product, either through actual production skills or through monitoring the production process and adjusting it as necessary, are gaining increased experience and familiarity with the product. Second the production process itself, as a system composed of interdependent subsystems, becomes more efficient in time as adjustments are made, machinery is refined to solve problems that appear in the initial stages, and so on.

The specific parameters of the experience curve will obviously vary from one situation to another, although the shape of the learning curve will stay more or less the same. One of the difficulties facing accounting and engineering staffs in the development of cost-based prices is to estimate the experience curve applying to a given new product. Previous experience with similar products will certainly be helpful but can only be used as a guideline, not a precise estimate. One formulation of the experience curve phenomenon is given by the equation, $T(n) = kn^{1-\lambda}$, where $T(n)$ is the cumulative time required to produce n units, consecutively; k is the time required to produce the first unit; n is the number of units made; and λ is the learning coefficient, $0 \leq \lambda \leq 1$.[10] The formula can be restated in terms of the average time required to produce a unit as follows:

$$\overline{T}(n) = \frac{T(n)}{n} = kn^{-\lambda}$$

In any given situation, the problem for the analyst is to estimate the value of the learning coefficient in the above formula. Studies by The Boston Consulting Group suggest that there is roughly a 25 percent reduction in unit costs of production for each doubling of production output. The formula applies only to that part of learning associated with improved labor efficiency. Other sources of improved efficiency identified by The Boston Consulting Group studies are the lower costs associated with economies of scale and overall systems effects where improvements in marketing, distribution, and production all benefit each other.[11]

One study of price changes for a total of 82 petrochemical products showed that the experience curve was the strongest influence on the downward trend in petrochemical prices. The research considered year-to-year price changes and also looked at price changes over a seven-year interval. Four independent variables were examined. Two were product life cycle variables—(1) the entrance of new

[10] Martin K. Starr, *Operations Management* (Englewood Cliffs, N.J.: Prentice-Hall, Inc., 1978), p. 479.
[11] *Ibid.*, pp. 28–29.

competitors and (2) product standardization (the degree to which competitive products were interchangeable with one another). Two were cost-reduction variables—(3) accumulated production (the experience curve) and (4) demand growth (economies of scale). With the dependent variable defined as the percentage change in price over the specified time interval, the influence of each of these four dependent variables was estimated using regression analysis. However, the model did not do a very good job of predicting price changes. For one-year intervals the coefficient of determination (R^2, which can be thought of as the percentage of variance in the dependent variable explained by the independent variables) was only .03. For seven-year intervals, this improved to .27. There was an average, time-related price decline of one to three percent per year independent of the variables in the model.[12]

There are a number of shortcomings in this model that should be noted. First, putting the data for 82 different petrochemicals into one model may obscure regularities that might appear if more homogeneous groupings of products had been made. Second, no marketing mix variables have been considered. The analysis in this chapter has strongly argued that price cannot be analyzed independent of such questions as product quality, the degree of product uniqueness (which is in the model), the importance of various elements of the service offering, the role played by distribution and availability, and so on. Third, the model does not include the critical variable of degree of capacity utilization, which has a major influence

---

[12] Robert B. Stobaugh and Phillip L. Townsend, "Price Forecasting and Strategic Planning: The Case of Petrochemicals," *Journal of Marketing Research*, 12, 1 (February, 1975), 19–29. For the interested reader the model used was as follows:

$$\frac{P_{i+r}}{P_i} = K \left\{ \frac{N_{i+r}}{N_i} \right\}^{\beta_1} \left\{ \begin{matrix} \text{Standard} = e \\ \text{Non-standard} = 0 \end{matrix} \right\}^{\beta_2} \left\{ \frac{\text{Cum } Q_{i+r}}{\text{Cum } Q_i} \right\}^{\beta_3} \left\{ \frac{S_{i+r}}{S_i} \right\}^{\beta_4}$$

which was restated as a log transform:

$$\log \left[\frac{P_{i+r}}{P_i} \right] = \log K + \beta_1 \left[\log \frac{N_{i+r}}{N_i} \right] + \beta_2 (0,1) + \beta_3 \left[\log \frac{\text{Cum } Q_{i+r}}{\text{Cum } Q_i} \right]$$
$$+ \beta_4 \left[\log \frac{S_{i+r}}{S_i} \right]$$

where P_i = the average price in year i; r = year of interval being considered; N_i = the number of producers in year i; the dummy variable = e for standard products (= 1 in the log transform) and 0 for nonstandard products; Cum Q_1 = cumulative production through year i; S_i = average production per producer in year i; and K, β_1, β_2, β_3, and β_4 = coefficients determined by regression.

on manufacturer's pricing policy. Fourth, the price trend (price as a function of time) was not included in the model, although, as noted, there was a strong trend downward in prices, independent of the other variables in the model. Nonetheless, the reason for citing this research here is that it did confirm the importance of the experience curve, and it does illustrate the application of management science techniques to the study of industrial marketing.[13]

Value-Based Pricing

Value-based approaches to pricing require careful assessment of the value of the product to the customer. Because different customers may value the same product differently, market segmentation is a key step in value-based pricing. Some market segments are likely to show much more price elasticity than others. Furthermore, the complete product offering may vary significantly from one market segment to another, as a function of the different service packages offered in each segment. Thus, value-based pricing may be quite complex.

Value-based approaches to pricing are built around the customer's perceptions of the value of the product in use in a particular application. One approach to value-based pricing has been outlined by Shapiro and Jackson as requiring the following steps:

1. Understand the total use situation of the customer.
2. Define and analyze the variables that determine the benefits to the customer in this use.
3. Define and analyze the variables that determine the customer's costs in using the product.
4. Determine the cost/benefit tradeoffs in the customer's use situation.[14]

Note that it is the customer's costs, not the seller's costs of producing the product, that are the central factors considered in value-based pricing. To implement their approach, Shapiro and Jackson propose developing a "product space" that graphically portrays relationships and tradeoffs between pairs of benefit variables that are known to be

[13] For a thorough review of empirical findings concerning experience curves and their use in strategy formulation, see George S. Day and David B. Montgomery, "Diagnosing the Experience Curve," *Journal of Marketing*, **47**, 2 (Spring, 1983), 44–58.

[14] Benson P. Shapiro and Barbara B. Jackson, "Industrial Pricing to Meet Customer Needs," *Harvard Business Review*, **56**, 6 (November-December, 1978), 119–27.

important to customers, such as horsepower and torque in the case of electric motors, and to array competitive products in this product space. Clustering of competitive products in this two-dimensional space may reveal visually the presence of clearly defined segments. Cost variables are next estimated, including acquisition costs plus all important costs of application and use, over the life of the product in this use. The tradeoffs between customer benefits and costs can be assessed in a variety of ways, one of the most useful being a graphical portrayal of price vs. performance in two-dimensional graphs, one graph for each performance dimension known to be important. This approach to pricing is completely consistent with the argument, introduced at the beginning of this chapter, that price should be viewed as part of the product offering. The customer views price in that framework and so should the marketer.

Research at Signode Corporation, a manufacturer of steel strapping, illustrates an effective approach to value-based pricing keyed to segments defined by differences in price and service elasticities. It also provides an excellent example of microsegmentation based on differences in buyer behavior as described in Chapter 4. Using sales reports and sales reps' judgments and hierarchical cluster analysis, Rangan and Moriarty were able to divide Signode's 174 national accounts into four distinct market segments with different patterns of response to changes in service and price levels. These segments were:

1. **Programmed Buying**—small customers who view the product as a routine purchase, divide the business among a few vendors, and are relatively insensitive to price and service level. They pay list price for below average service.

2. **Relationship Buying**—small customers who are very sensitive to price increases but demand higher service levels than Segment 1. The product is moderately significant in their operations. Buyers are well informed and would not hesitate to change vendors. They paid a lower price than Segment 1 but higher than Segments 3 and 4.

3. **Transaction-Oriented**—bigger customers with the highest sensitivity to changes in price and service levels. They averaged a 10.1 percent discount. They were highly knowledgeable about competitors' offerings and would not hesitate to switch vendors.

4. **Bargain Hunters**—large volume customers who got an average discount of 11.3 percent and the highest service levels. The product was very important in their operations. They were very well informed

about competitive product offerings and very sensitive to any changes in price and service levels.[15]

Demand Curve Pricing in Contrast to Value-Based Pricing

The realities of value-based pricing are in marked contrast to the simple assumptions underlying the economist's demand curve, which relates volume demanded to price charged, although the concept of the demand curve and price elasticity may be a useful starting point for thinking about the relationship between sales volume and price. To be a truly useful analytical concept, however, the demand curve must be estimated empirically. That is, the relationship between price and volume must be measured, through analysis of past sales and price data, through experimentation, or by use of management judgment. Because of the complex interactions of price with other marketing variables, it is difficult to estimate empirically the relationship between price, *in vacuo*, and quantity demanded.

The demand curve for an entire industry, as opposed to the demand curve for a given producer, may be easier to estimate, because it is not necessary to deal with such nuances as differences in the marketing approaches, product offerings, and customer preferences for individual producers that also cause changes in demand. The basic question in estimating the demand curve is the extent to which demand for the product of a total industry is influenced by price itself. In a surprisingly large portion of industrial markets, total demand may be relatively insensitive to price over a fairly wide range of prices. That is due in part to the fact that demand for industrial products is derived from the demand for OEM and consumer products. Demand for truck axles, for example, will be determined by customer demand for trucks, not by the price of axles. On the other hand, market share for an individual axle manufacturer may be very sensitive to its price relative to competitors' prices.

Although total industry demand for certain industrial products may be quite insensitive to changes in price within a certain range, it may suddenly become very price sensitive if prices go beyond that range, depending upon the availability of substitute products. Thus, demand for steel sheet used in automobiles and trucks may be

[15] V. Kasturi Rangan and Rowland T. Moriarty, "Segmenting National Accounts at Signode Corporation," unpublished working paper, Harvard Business School, June, 1990.

reasonably insensitive to price until a certain critical price level is reached. Beyond that point, aluminum or fiberglass may become economically attractive as substitutes for steel. Estimates of the price—volume relationship for the product of an industry must therefore be sensitive to the availability of substitute products from other industries.

Constraints on Value-Based Pricing

Just as cost considerations set a lower level on prices, so do the customer's perception of fair value and the workings of competition set an upper level. Figure 7-1 illustrates the forces shaping a customer's perception of value. Like a cloud, the customer's definition of value changes continually as it is shaped by both internal and external forces. Customers are defined and selected by the firm's market segmentation and targeting strategy. The served market is chosen in a manner intended to maximize the market value of the

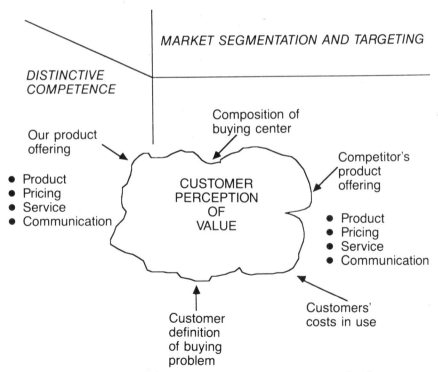

Figure 7-1. Forces shaping the customer's perception of value.

firm's distinctive competence as it is presented through the product offering. However, the customer is also exposed to competitors' product offerings and the interaction of the multiple product offerings sets the customer's expectations and definition of value. Internal to the firm and its buying process, the individuals in the buying center, their definition of the buying problem, and their estimates of the risks and costs in use will shape the final definition of value.

There are many constraints on the definition of value to the customer. The industrial buyer usually brings a wealth of experience and knowledge to an individual buying situation, and this creates a set of expectations of what is going to be reasonable. Industrial buyers, through trade associations and informal contacts, are likely to talk with one another and seek advice and counsel when there is uncertainty about the reasonableness of the price of a given commodity. Engineering and production personnel in the purchasing organization can often make reasonable estimates of the manufacturer's cost of producing the product. There is always the market price of similar or substitute products as a source of comparative data. Clearly, then, the definition of a fair price is often possible and puts considerable pressure on the manufacturer who wishes to price his product according to the value perceived by the customer. Figure 7-2 illustrates a range of factors within which a "fair price" is defined.

Careful analysis of the impact of the purchased product on the customer's cost structure and revenue-producing ability is called for in value-based pricing. The sales representative has a critical role to play in gathering the necessary information for the seller's cost accounting, engineering, production, and other personnel, who may help to determine the price that will be charged. As observed earlier, different market segments may obtain significantly different values from a given product. If prices in different segments have been set to reflect value to the customer, there will be a tendency for a product aimed at the lowest value segment to find its way into the greater value segments, unless the product can be differentiated significantly and in functional terms. These realities of the marketplace make price discrimination among market segments difficult in practice, although not impossible if there is true product differentiation and if marketing channels used to reach the different segments are distinct. The key to value-based pricing is knowledge of customers' product use systems, costs, and strategy for profitability.

WHAT IS A "FAIR PRICE" FOR THE CUSTOMER?

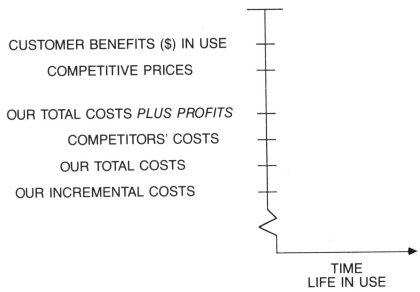

CUSTOMER BENEFITS ($) IN USE

COMPETITIVE PRICES

OUR TOTAL COSTS *PLUS PROFITS*

COMPETITORS' COSTS

OUR TOTAL COSTS

OUR INCREMENTAL COSTS

TIME
LIFE IN USE

Figure 7-2. The range within which a "fair price is defined."

COMPETITIVE BIDDING AND NEGOTIATION

Competitive bidding and the negotiation of prices are common practices in industrial markets, especially in procurement by governmental agencies and institutions. The prevalence of competitive bidding and negotiation of prices in industrial markets is a major reason why book or list prices often have little significance, except as communication devices and reference points.

Competitive bidding may take several forms. In *closed* bidding, potential vendors are invited to submit written, sealed bids. All bids are opened at a previously announced time, often in a public meeting to which all bidders are invited, and the lowest bidder, assuming the bid meets specifications, receives the award. In *open* bidding, a more informal process, the buyer announces that bids would be welcome up to a certain date. Offers are often made in verbal form and the buyer continues discussion with potential vendors, perhaps providing clues to each about its relative standing in terms of price. Open bidding may be preferable to closed bidding where competing sellers have different products and services and in other situations where detailed specifications are hard to develop.

Negotiated pricing is similar to open bidding. The product offering is typically hard to define and price is negotiated along with details of the product offering. Although list price may be the starting point in negotiated pricing, it is likely to be modified considerably along with other terms of sale, including quantity to be purchased, time period to be covered by the contract, payment terms, delivery and packaging requirements, sharing of rights to product improvements, minimum and maximum quantities to be sold, and so on. Negotiated pricing may be the only viable alternative in a complex procurement where all of these details must be negotiated.

The use of closed bidding requires the development of detailed procurement specifications and their incorporation into a request for quotation (RFQ) or request for proposal (RFP). The RFQ or RFP may only be sent to qualified bidders, potential vendors who have participated in an evaluation procedure employed by the purchaser. In markets where competitive bidding is commonplace, placement on the list of qualified bidders is a critical strategic objective.

Not all bids submitted will necessarily be responsive to the RFQ. Significant differences between the product offering and the bid specifications will result in a bid being disqualified or rejected. In a related vein, a common selling strategy is to get procurement specifications developed in such a way that the seller's product offering will be favored. Such a strategy is feasible if the vendor's product has some unique, important features not found in competitors' products. In contrast, procurement managers will strive hard to avoid specifications that *de facto* result in a sole source or limited competition.

Bidding Models

The expected value to the marketer of a given bid is a function of the amount of the bid and the probability of being awarded the business. Obviously, the lower the bid price, the higher the probability of winning the award. But as prices go down and the probability of winning the award goes up, so does the potential profitability of the business go down. The probability of winning the competition is also a function of the number of other bidders and their bid strategies.

An extremely important input to the seller's bidding strategy is knowledge about potential competitors and their likely bidding strategies. Sales representatives and distributors can be very helpful in making these assessments. Public information, available through business journals, trade associations, and other sources, can also be useful in estimating such things as the competitors' current capacity and backlog situation, pricing actions on other recent procurements, and the strength of their product offerings. The seller must also assess its own capacity and backlog situation and make some conscious determination of how badly it needs a given piece of available business. Bidding strategy can not be determined until specific pricing objectives have been established.

The task of estimating the probabilities of various competitive actions and outcomes and the profitability of the business at various prices can become exceptionally complex. Substantial calculations must be performed, especially if the marketer wishes to trace through the implications of different assumptions about the probabilities of winning the contract award at various prices. To assist in this analysis, simple competitive bidding models have been developed that can be of assistance to the marketing manager with little technical training.

One such model has been described by Sewall. His model was developed for use by a small construction firm to determine bid prices in competition for local government construction projects. The model allows the contractor to test the implications of various subjective estimates of the probability of winning the award at various prices. The model included historical data about a set of core competitors, who frequently competed against this contractor, and another set of data for peripheral competitors, who were treated in aggregate. For each competitor in the core and for the peripheral group, the contractor estimated the probability that the competitor would bid at all. If the competitor did bid, the contractor also estimated the probability that he would bid below a given proposed bid price. The pattern of previous bidding was a key input to this judgment, and the model expressed this as a ratio (in percentage) of the competitors' bid prices on previous contracts of varying sizes to the contractor's estimated costs of fulfilling the contracts. These distributions were expressed as normal distributions of specified mean and standard deviation. The computer told the model user what the range (the mean plus and minus two standard deviations) was for each competitor. The user of the model was given several options for modifying the assumptions of the model and for displaying the results of the analysis.[16] This simple model could be adapted relatively easily to the needs of any marketer who must bid against several competitors with a known history of bidding behavior.

This competitive bidding model is an excellent illustration of the benefits of the so-called decision calculus approach to model building developed by Professor John D. C. Little.[17] The hallmark of the decision calculus approach is that it permits the incorporation of subjective probability estimates by the user of the model, and it typically permits the user of the model to interact with the model directly through a computer terminal. The models used in the decision calculus approach are usually quite simple and easy to understand, and they place a premium on describing the problem in terms familiar to the user. These characteristics of the decision calculus approach make it particularly attractive to the industrial marketer. It is responsive to the complexity of the industrial marketing problem, as well as to the fact that subjective managerial judgments must often be substituted for the larger, aggregate data bases used by consumer marketers.[18]

PRICE LEADERSHIP

An oligopoly is a market in which there are relatively few sellers and each can influence the price of the product. In fact, oligopoly is the characteristic market condition for most markets of interest to the student of industrial marketing. In oligopolistic markets, each firm's price is influenced by, and influences, the prices of all other sellers. It is this interdependence of sellers' prices that constrains the pricing behavior of any individual seller, rather than the market of the perfectly competitive market model, in which forces of supply and demand determine the price of the product. Perhaps the only examples of reasonably pure, perfectly competitive market situations are markets for the products of forest, farm, and sea where

[16] Murphy A. Sewall, "A Decision Calculus Model for Contract Bidding." *Journal of Marketing*, **40**, 4 (October, 1976), 92–98. For an earlier treatment of the problem of estimating the probability of winning an award at various bid prices, see Arleigh W. Walker, "How to Price Industrial Products," *Harvard Business Review*, **45**, 5 (September-October, 1967), 127–32.
[17] John D. C. Little, "Models and Managers: The Concept of a Decision Calculus," *Management Science, 16* 8 (April, 1970), B466–B485.
[18] Frederick E. Webster, Jr., "Management Science in Industrial Marketing," *Journal of Marketing*, **42**, 1 (January, 1978), 21–27.

many, many sellers offer a product that is virtually undifferentiated from the product of all other sellers.

In an oligopolistic market, there may be a condition in which one or a few sellers consistently set prices that others in the industry follow. When such a condition exists, the firms that set prices are called price leaders. The remaining firms in the industry are called price followers. In simplest terms, a price leader is simply a firm whose pricing actions tend to be copied by other firms in the industry. Price leaders are really elected by the actions of their followers as much as by their own initiatives. There can be no price leader if there are no followers.

Sultan's study of pricing in the electrical equipment oligopoly is an excellent examination of the conditions favoring price leadership.[19] This study was made possible by the trials, in the early 1960's, of several executives from the three largest electrical equipment firms, on charges of price fixing. As a result of these court actions, company records describing production and pricing behavior over a period of many years came into the public sector, permitting the extensive econometric analysis performed by Sultan.

Sultan's analysis concluded that the decision to lead or follow was a critical strategic choice for the marketer. A decision to be a market price leader required a commitment to several other strategic actions, including technological leadership gained through above average (for the industry) investments in research and development and a commitment to lead the industry in cost reduction. Large market share is a necessary condition for price leadership, although the price leader need not have the largest share. Large market share means that the seller has relatively large sales volume. This should contribute to below average direct costs of production (due to economies of scale and experience curve effects). High market share also means that the marketer has access to a large portion of all available transactions and a high probability of being invited to bid on most available business. This high level of participation in market activity provides the information necessary to keep track of market price trends and competitors' behavior, permitting better prediction of competitive activity in any particular situation.

The lower direct costs of the market leader also provide above average profit margins, which means that the firm can keep price pressure on competitors, discouraging competitive entry, as well as

---

[19] Ralph G. M. Sultan, *Pricing in the Electrical Oligopoly; Vol. 1: Competition or Collusion; Vol. II: Business Strategy* (Boston: Division of Research, Graduate School of Business Administration, Harvard University, 1974).

providing a larger pool of funds for research and development and marketing activities, and other forms of staff support that enhance chances of maintaining market leadership. Therefore, the market leader should have large market share, lower direct costs, greater marketing resources, and a leadership position in technology. All of these conditions give the market leader the ability to manage its market share. Sultan also pointed out that effective market leadership required that management must have the will and the capacity to lead. Conversely, followers typically had smaller market shares, higher costs, limited overhead resources, and a second-best technology.

Not all oligopolistic markets have price leaders and the leadership position in a given market may not be very clear, especially if one firm has cost leadership and another firm has technological product leadership. Such conditions can easily exist if firms have followed different research and development priorities, one focussing on process and cost improvements, another looking for new products. In these conditions of unclear advantage, an ongoing struggle for market leadership can easily occur. Market leadership can also be hard to discern in those market situations where an historical market leader has made a conscious decision to abandon its leadership position as a way of maximizing short-term profits. Such a strategic choice could make sense with a mature product where significant gains in market share were possible through selective price cutting, turning the product into a "cash cow" to support the development of new products and markets.

Strategic Options

Sultan's analysis led him to suggest that industrial firms in oligopolistic markets had four strategic options, as depicted in Figure 7-3. There are two long-term pricing strategies—*pressure pricing*, in which the market leader tries to hold prices at reasonable levels even when demand is surging, discouraging competitive entry, and permitting prices to rise slowly in a disciplined fashion, and *opportunistic pricing*, in which prices are increased to the limit of customer goodwill when demand is strong, then cut back when business is not good. Likewise, there are two short-term pricing options—*gold-standard pricing*, in which all customers are quoted one price, regardless of the competitive situation, and *negotiated pricing*, in which each transaction is priced according to the competitive and customer situation. Both leaders and followers have these four

Pricing Individual Transactions

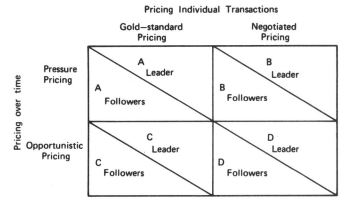

Figure 7-3. Strategic options for pricing in oligopolistic industrial markets. Reprinted by permission of Harvard University Press from Pricing in the Electrical Oligopoly, Volume 1, *By Ralph G. M. Sultan, Boston, Mass.: Division of Research, Harvard Graduate School of Business Administration, Copyright © 1974 by the President and Fellows of Harvard College.*

options, making possible, theoretically, a total of 16 pairs of strategies. Sultan's analysis suggests, however, that over a period of time, only two strategy pairs are stable conditions. Either leaders and followers use pressure pricing on the gold-standard (strategy pair A-A), or both leaders and followers use negotiated-opportunistic pricing (strategy pair D-D). All other strategic combinations are unstable. For example, a market leader attempting to price on the gold-standard can quickly be undercut by competitors who are using negotiated, opportunistic pricing. Sultan expressed a preference for pressure pricing on the gold-standard, because it provides stability over the long run, permitting continued development of technology and avoiding problems of customer ill-will. However, he also noted that this might present an appearance of collusive behavior and attract attention from antitrust law enforcement officials.

A firm wishing to follow a pricing strategy of pressure pricing on the gold-standard must commit itself to several objectives and tactics in order to maintain its market leadership. It must be committed to increasing capacity, slowly but surely, in line with increases in the size of the market, if it is to maintain its market share and leadership position. It must be willing to punish recalcitrant followers when they resort to opportunistic pricing actions. This can be done by significantly underbidding them on an important piece of business or by forcing prices lower and holding them there, a tactic possible for the market leader because of its favorable cost position. It must contribute to good industry information and announce all price moves clearly, carefully, and broadly, especially with key customers. Book or list prices may be used as communication devices, although today it is possible that any broadcasting of prices, through distribution of price lists or through dissemination of price announcements to the news media, can be seen as an attempt to coerce competitors into accepting the new prices. Such dissemination may be viewed as a form of implicit collusion and challenged by the antitrust authorities. The regulatory environment, as well as the instability and economic uncertainty that characterize many industrial markets, makes effective price leadership increasingly difficult.

The key long-run strategic choice in maintaining a strategy of market price leadership may very well be the decision to add capacity. Failure of a company to keep up with industry demand will obviously lead to an erosion of market share, undermining the resource base necessary for a leadership position. On the other hand, increasing capacity too quickly can lead to industry excess capacity with an almost certain result that prices will tumble. Capacity expansion may also be necessary in order to maintain a leadership position in technological innovation and cost reduction. Once again, current and complete information about industry conditions is essential, if individual firms within the industry are to avoid the problems that come with too rapid expansion of capacity. The seriousness of the problems that result have been seen in many industries, including synthetic fibers, agricultural fertilizers, polyolefins, and airlines.

SUMMARY

Although pricing is a critical variable in industrial marketing strategy, it cannot be analyzed independently of other strategic variables: In this chapter we have looked at a number of issues related to pricing, including the interaction of various pricing objectives, such as maintaining or increasing market share, earning a target rate of return, and maintaining the proper levels of order backlogs and capacity utilization. A distinction was drawn between book or list prices and the actual prices that result in the marketplace after quantity discounts, functional discounts, and discounts to meet competition. Cost-based and value-based pricing approaches were compared and the influence of the experience curve was described. Competitive bidding and negotiated pricing were described briefly, and one bidding model was reviewed. Finally, the phenomenon of market or price leadership was considered and the strategic options facing the marketer were defined, based on Sultan's extensive study of pricing behavior in the electrical equipment industry.

From this review of issues in pricing strategy and the relationship of pricing to overall marketing and corporate strategies some general guidelines for setting prices can be drawn. A balance between cost and production considerations, on the one hand, and customer value and marketing considerations, on the other, must be found, with the latter having some priority in the typical competitive situation.

As in other areas of marketing decision making, the pricing analysis should begin with a precise definition of market targets, the macrosegmentation strategy. Market potential in these segments should be determined as accurately as possible, and the relationship between industry price levels and the level of demand in those segments carefully estimated. Then the analyst must develop the firm's product positioning in those segments and design a total product offering and marketing mix consistent with that positioning.

The next step should be estimation of all relevant costs, assuming certain levels of demand and production, including both production costs (fixed and variable) and marketing costs. The competitive environment in each segment should be examined in detail, including not only the seller's competition but competition among firms in the macrosegment, trends influencing their business, their cost structures, and demand in the markets that they serve. Relevant legal and regulatory matters should also be assessed, especially as they relate directly to pricing and antitrust considerations.

When all these considerations have been analyzed, the marketer can then set specific pricing objectives that will be consistent with overall marketing objectives in that segment, as well as consistent with production and legal requirements. Out of this statement of objectives and a definition of the role of price in the product offering and in the marketing mix, a specific price structure, including book prices and discounting policies, can be defined, and tactics for meeting price competition developed. An appropriately long-term view, provided by the definition of pressure pricing on the gold-standard, for example, can help to avoid the mistakes of short-term opportunistic reactions to particular customer demands and competitive conditions. Such unplanned pricing action can destroy market leadership positions and can significantly reduce the chances of achieving corporate objectives relating to technological leadership, expansion, and return on investment. The importance of good market information, both from and to customers and competitors, cannot be overstated in the development of sound pricing strategy.

Bibliography

Lanzillotti, Robert F., "Pricing Objectives in Large Companies," *American Economic Review*, **48**, 5 (December, 1958), 921–40.

Monroe, Kent B., *Pricing: Making Profitable Decisions* (New York: McGraw-Hill, 1979).

Nagle, Thomas T., *The Strategy and Tactics of Pricing* (Englewood Cliffs, NJ: Prentice-Hall, Inc., 1987).

Ross, Elliot B., "Making Money with Proactive Pricing," *Harvard Business Review*, **62**, 6 (November-December, 1984), 145–55.

Seymour, Daniel T., (ed.), *The Pricing Decision: A Strategic Planner for Marketing Professionals*, (Chicago: Probus Publishing Co., 1989).

Shapiro, Benson P., and Barbara B. Jackson, "Industrial Pricing to Meet Customer Needs," *Harvard Business Review*, **56**, 6 (November-December, 1978), 119–27.

Sultan, Ralph M., *Pricing in the Electrical Equipment Oligopoly; Vol. I: Competition or Collusion; Vol. II: Business Strategy* (Boston: Division of Research, Graduate School of Business Administration, Harvard University, 1974).

8 Industrial Distribution Strategy

Distribution is an essential element in the product offering of the industrial marketer, reflecting the importance of availability and reliability of supply as purchasing objectives for the industrial buyer. Distribution has two related but distinct meanings in industrial marketing. First, distribution includes *resellers* who buy and sell the product as it moves along the channel of distribution. Second, distribution includes *physical distribution*, the movement and storage of products as they proceed from the manufacturer to the end user. The first aspect is often called the *marketing channel*; the latter is known as *logistics*.

The decade of the 1990's will see heightened interest in industrial distribution strategy and management as marketers search for increased cost effectiveness and opportunities for differentiation based on service levels. In mature and increasingly fragmented markets, marketers face increased competition and higher customer expectations for, and sensitivity to, price and service levels.

Professor Louis Stern, a leading authority on distribution channels, has described the evolution of distribution strategy from the 1960's to the 1990's. He characterized the environment of the 1960's and early 1970's as product-oriented firms focussed on domestic markets with distribution offering essentially *random* market coverage. Manufacturers and their distributors tended to view one another as adversaries. The late 1970's and 1980's he saw as typified by market-oriented firms facing slower growth markets. This was accompanied by a shift to multinational marketing and a battle for market share, with distribution designed to achieve *maximum* market coverage. Suppliers saw distributors as customers; distributors saw suppliers and their product lines as cost centers. Stern expects the 1990's to be characterized by intense competition for both customers and marketing channel support, global marketing systems with a local market focus, and distribution designed to achieve *selective* market coverage. Suppliers and distributors will see one another as strategic partners.[1]

Thus, the trend toward strategic partnerships in industrial marketing is found in relationships with distributors as well as with customers and vendors. In many instances, the strategic focus is shifting toward the three-way partnership of vendors, distributors, and end-users in a strategic view of supply chain management.

Traditional models for studying industrial distribution channels were built around the presumed inherent conflict between manufacturers and dealers as they divided up the value they attempted to create jointly in the marketplace.[2] Ideally, each party's share of the reward should be based upon its contribution in the flow of the product from producer to consumer. Such a standard of equity might be found in the manufacturer-reseller relationship when it is first designed and agreed to by the two parties. As market conditions change, however, the appropriate roles of the parties change but compensation tends to be based on tradition and past practice, leading to conflict. In general, distribution arrangements tend to lag behind the changing marketplace because they are based on contractual and interpersonal relationships that are hard to alter. The resulting inefficiency, ineffectiveness, and misunderstanding are a major source of conflict between manufacturers and resellers.

Today's models of the role of the distributor are shifting to a focus on communication, cooperation, and trust as the key elements in effective relationships.[3] Distributors are increasingly seen as partners and strategic collaborators, in flexible relationships that evolve over time in response to changing market conditions. In this chapter, we will find it helpful to integrate both viewpoints, conflict and cooperation, as they help understand different aspects of manufacturer-reseller relationships.

[1] Presentation to the Marketing Seminar on Distribution Channels at the Amos Tuck School of Business Administration at Dartmouth College, Hanover, NH, on May 16, 1990.

[2] Allan J. Magrath and Kenneth G. Hardy, *A Strategic Framework for Diagnosing Manufacturer-Reseller Conflict*, Working Paper, Report No. 88-101 (Cambridge, Mass.: Marketing Science Institute, March, 1988).

[3] James C. Anderson and James A. Narus, "A Model of Distributor Firm and Manufacturer Firm Working Partnerships," *Journal of Marketing*, **54**, (January, 1990), 42–56.

The Nature of Industrial Distribution

Industrial products tend to have fewer customer outlets than consumer products. The number of retail outlets for such consumer products as food, clothing, sporting goods, books, furniture, and so on, is many, many times greater than the available outlets for the typical industrial product, many thousands compared to several hundred or less. There are several reasons for this. First, industrial customers are fewer in number and, with a few exceptions for such products as office supplies, there is simply no need for such extensive distribution. Second, manufacturer-direct-to-user marketing channels are much more prevalent than in consumer markets. Third, purchase quantities are often large and can frequently be handled more efficiently on a direct shipment basis. Fourth, industrial distribution often requires a high level of technical expertise that demands investment in training and physical facilities and can only be made on a reasonably selective basis.

These factors affect not only the number of resellers required to cover the industrial market, but also the quality of the relationship between the manufacturer and the reseller. Industrial resellers will tend to have closer relationships with their suppliers than consumer resellers. Similarly the industrial manufacturer will tend to depend more heavily on each member of the channel and may do more to support that channel member. The industrial reseller may have a critical role to play, not only in assuring availability of the product, but also in completing the process of tailoring it to the customer's needs.

Push Versus Pull Strategies

It is helpful to characterize two kinds of marketing strategies, *push* and *pull*. The critical difference is the role of the reseller. In the push strategy, the reseller has a very active role. In the pull strategy the role tends to be passive. In the pull strategy, the manufacturer takes major responsibility for creating end-user demand through advertising and personal selling activities aimed directly at end-users. In the push strategy, personal selling is used to stimulate demand at all levels of the marketing channel, from manufacturer to reseller and from reseller to end-user, with perhaps several layers of resellers in between. In the push strategy, the reseller has an active responsibility for creating demand, but he is primarily responsible for servicing demand in the pull strategy. Before going further with the distinction between push and pull strategies, it should be noted that it is usually a matter of relative emphasis on push versus pull. Rather than being a true dichotomy, the typical manufacturer's marketing strategy includes elements of both.

In a push strategy, all elements of the marketing mix must be adjusted to reflect the reliance on resellers and the active role assigned to them. Prices and trade margins must be adequate to insure their willingness to assume that role. The promotional mix of advertising and personal selling (including the matter of sales force compensation) must be adjusted to reflect the importance of resellers and the need to support them. Push strategies tend to be accompanied by selective distribution. Broad, extensive distribution is characteristic of pull strategies. Advertising and sales promotion tend to dominate the communications budget in a pull strategy, but personal selling is the major promotional variable in a push strategy. In a push strategy, the reseller may have some responsibility for product adjustment to fit the individual customer's needs. The product is usually sold off the shelf without modification in a pull strategy. Push strategies tend to be characteristic of industrial markets, but consumer markets are more frequently the battleground of competing pull strategies.

The concept of push and pull strategies makes a useful analytical distinction between active and passive roles for the reseller serving the manufacturer and the end-user. It helps to understand the varying role of the industrial reseller in marketing strategy and the differences between industrial and consumer markets.

FUNCTIONS OF THE RESELLER

Classical marketing theory identifies ten different functions that are performed in the marketing channel: buying, selling, assorting, financing, storage, sorting, grading, transportation, market information, and risk-taking. This definition of marketing functions reflects the early development of marketing theory from the field of agricultural economics. It puts an emphasis on commodity products, but the list of functions, with a couple of minor exceptions, fits the marketing of any product. We can elaborate briefly upon each of those functions for the purpose of providing more complete definitions:

Buying—every reseller must purchase products for resale or contract as an agent to receive a supply of product.

Selling—every reseller must contact potential customers, promote the product, and solicit orders.

Assorting—the typical reseller brings together an assortment of merchandise, usually of related items, from several sources to better serve his potential customers.

Financing—by investing in inventory and by extending credit to customers, the reseller helps to finance the exchange process.

Storage—products must be assembled in a convenient location to assure availability and must be protected to prevent deterioration and loss.

Sorting—in some situations, the reseller provides the important function of buying in large quantities and breaking the bulk purchase into smaller quantities for resale.

Grading—it may be necessary for the reseller to inspect, test, or judge the products he receives for quality and to assign distinct quality grades to them.

Transportation—this is the logistics function, managing the physical flow of the product.

Market Information—the reseller typically has some responsibility for providing market information both to his customers and to his suppliers, including information about availability, product quality, competitive conditions, customer needs, and so on.

Risk-taking—risk is inherent in the ownership of an inventory of product than can deteriorate or become obsolete.

The design of a marketing channel is an attempt to get each of these functions performed as efficiently and effectively as possible. With the possible exceptions of sorting and grading, every one of these functions must be performed someplace in the marketing channel between manufacturer and end-user. This is the key point to remember about the functions of the reseller—somebody must perform these steps, since they are essential to the exchange process. In a direct-to-end-user channel, the manufacturer assumes most of the responsibility, although some functions, such as financing and assorting, may be left primarily to the customer. In other situations, the manufacturer may leave the performance of these functions to the end-user, such as when the product is picked up at the factory by the customer who pays cash upon receipt.

In the typical industrial marketing channel, however, resellers are depended upon to perform many of these functions, because they are specialists with established customers and sources of supply and the necessary physical facilities and expertise. They can perform these functions more effectively and at a lower cost than the manufacturer could.

The availability of resellers is only one factor to consider in the design of channel strategy, however. Channel strategy must be related to overall marketing strategy before the role of distribution can be properly defined and objectives established for the distribution function. Among the issues that the manufacturer must consider are the degree of control desired in the relationship with the customer, whether the manufacturer or the distributors have better knowledge of the market, the manufacturer's financial ability to perform the various distribution functions (including deploying a sales force, maintaining branch offices, establishing warehouses with inventories, and extending credit), and the competitive opportunity to achieve distinctiveness of product through the offering of superior distribution service.

HYBRID MARKETING CHANNELS

The complexity of industrial markets creates some interesting opportunities for the use of information technology to supplement and extend traditional industrial distribution channels. Traditional industrial marketing systems have consisted of a direct sales force, often with a national account organization embedded in it, perhaps with industrial distributors and some direct mail. Each of these four elements was responsible for all of the marketing functions including generating sales leads, qualifying and pre-selling those leads, closing the sale, and maintaining the account relationship over time. Which of the four marketing communication tools was used would depend primarily on the sales potential of the customer, with each tool more or less dedicated to a particular class of customer. Thus, distributors might be prevented by policy from calling on large potential customers while sales people were not supposed to call on medium or low potential accounts.

Clearly, such a system is likely to be suboptimal, to lack flexibility in responding to customer needs and market conditions, and to lead to conflict between direct sales forces and resellers. It is not likely that a single tool in the marketing and distribution tool kit will be equally effective at all stages of the buying-selling process, or that a single customer will always be well served by a single communication vehicle. For example, direct mail by itself is not likely to be terribly effective in maintaining account relationships over time. Direct sales to low potential accounts will never be cost effective. Small accounts may need direct sales coverage from time to time, however. Large accounts may prefer the efficiency of telemarketing and direct mail or catalogue ordering to spending time with a sales representative for routine buying.

Moriarty, Swartz, and Khuen have illustrated the problem nicely, and the opportunity for addressing it with information technology, with their concept of hybrid channel systems, as shown in Figure 8-1. The top part of the figure shows a traditional marketing system. The lower part depicts the concept of a hybrid marketing system with marketing channels tailored to the potential of the customer.

The concept of hybrid channel systems makes a good deal of sense, but it should be tempered by some appreciation of the complexity of the strategic and management issues that can result. There is a greater potential for conflict because of the overlapping of functions and responsibilities among previously independent channel entities. Also, there will be an increased need for communication and cooperation between the marketing managers responsible for each of the distinct functions—direct sales, distribution, direct mail, telemarketing, etc. Finally, the complexity of hybrid channel systems increases the difficulty of measuring results and controlling performance.[4]

TYPES OF INDUSTRIAL RESELLERS

Resellers can be categorized according to the number of functions they perform and the extent to which they specialize in the performance of certain functions. Perhaps the major distinction that should be made is whether a particular member of the marketing channel does or does not take legal title to the merchandise as it passes from the manufacturer to the user. Another important distinction is whether the reseller takes physical possession of the

[4] Rowland T. Moriarty, Gordon S. Swartz, and Charles A. Khuen, "Managing Hybrid Marketing Channels with Automation," Working Paper, Report No. 88-113, (Cambridge, Mass.: Marketing Science Institute, December, 1988), p. 6.

Traditional Marketing Systems*

Customer/Prospect Sales Potential	Generate Lead	Qualify and Presell	Close	Maintain Over Time
Very High	□	□	□	□
High	●	●	●	●
Medium	‡	‡	‡	‡
Low	◆	◆	◆	◆

Time

Modern Hybrid Marketing Systems with Custom Channels*

Customer/Prospect Sales Potential	Generate Lead	Qualify and Presell	Close	Maintain Over Time If Potential Remains/ Migrates to		
				Same	Lower	Higher
Very High	●◇	●	□●	□	●◇	□
Med-High	●◇	‡◇	●	●◇	◇◆	□●
Medium	‡◇◆	‡◇◆	‡◇	◇◆	◆○	●‡
Med-Low	◇◆	◇◆	◇◆	◆○	○	◇◆○
Low	◆○	◆○	◇◆○	◆○		◇◆○

Time

---

*Symbols represent use of different marketing systems to achieve stated objective. Multiple symbols indicate simultaneous use. Explanation of symbols:

□ = National Account Management		◇ = Telemarketing	
● = Direct Sales		◆ = Tailored Direct Mail	
‡ = Industrial Store		○ = Catalog	

Figure 8-1. Traditional and hybrid marketing channel systems. [Source: *Rowland T. Moriarty, Gordon S. Swartz, and Charles A Khuen,* Managing Hybrid Marketing Channels with Automation, *Working Paper, Report No. 88-113, (Cambridge, Mass.: Marketing Science Institute, December, 1988), p. 5.] Reproduced with permission.*

merchandise. A third distinction is whether the channel member exerts active selling effort to create demand for the product. Finally, some channel members specialize in the performance of a single function such as transportation (truckers, barge lines, airfreight forwarders), storage (public warehouses), or financing the transaction (banks and credit companies). A "full-function" reseller is one that performs most of the distribution functions, such as an industrial distributor or a retailer. Brief definitions of some common terms for types of industrial marketing channel members are as follows:

1. **Agents**—including sales agents and manufacturers' agents or manufacturers' representatives, focus on the selling function and do not take physical possession or title and seldom finance the transaction. They may perform a market information function for the manufacturer.
2. **Brokers**—a type of agent who does not take title and may operate on behalf of both buyers and sellers, to create a market and manage price negotiations, in areas such as raw materials and other standardized products. They seldom physically handle the product or get involved in the payment process.
3. **Jobber**—a general term for a type of wholesaler or distributor who may tend to specialize more than an industrial distributor and who may serve other channel members who are closer to the user. For example, a jobber might specialize in electrical equipment and sell to both contractors and industrial distributors.
4. **Merchant wholesaler**—another general term for a channel member who takes legal title and physical possession and performs most of the other channel functions.
5. **Drop shipper**—a merchant wholesaler who performs selling, credit, market information, and other functions but who does *not* physically handle the product, but instead arranges for direct shipment to the customer from the manufacturer.

In industrial markets, two types of resellers tend to be most common—the manufacturers' representative, who is a type of agent, and the industrial distributor, a type of merchant wholesaler. The functions of each are now examined in detail.

Manufacturers' Representatives

The manufacturers' representative, commonly called a rep, operates as an independent business with a contractual agreement with the manufacturer to sell its products in a specified geographic area. The terms manufacturers' representative and manufacturers' agent are synonymous. The former is preferred in industrial marketing usage. The manufacturers' representative is likely to handle the products of several related, but non-competing, manufacturers. The rep is paid on a straight commission basis, which means that the manufacturers' selling costs are variable with volume. The successful manufacturers' representative may do several million dollars worth of business a year, operate many branches, and field a large sales force. However, the single-person firm is not uncommon.

The manufacturers' representative usually does not take legal title to the products it sells, operating as an agent for the manufacturer, but may in fact keep a small supply of the product on its premises on a consignment basis. Reps tend to have ongoing, long-term relationships with their principals, in contrast with brokers and sales agents, whose dealings are more likely to be short-term and opportunistic. Brokers are also commission agents, but they tend to shop around for product lines available on an attractive basis from time to time, usually calling on the same customers. Brokers and sales agents are much more common in consumer products and in the garment trades than in industrial marketing. In industrial markets their principal use is for undifferentiated commodity products, such as raw and processed materials, where they can guarantee their clientele a reliable supply from a variety of sources. Sales agents have the same short-term orientation and usually contract to sell the total output of a manufacturer for a stated period of time. Sales agents tend to specialize in sales to a given class of trade.

The manufacturers' representative is used as an alternative to company-employed sales representatives. Some companies use a combination of reps and sales reps, but such arrangements tend to be awkward and difficult to manage. Because of the specialized nature of manufacturers' representatives, their use still requires that the manufacturer perform many of the distribution functions either through the use of other resellers or directly, including financing, storage, transportation, and risk taking.

Manufacturers' representatives offer many advantages to the manufacturer, including their market knowledge and established relationships with potential customers, the incentive value of working on a straight commission basis, their attractiveness to the customer by offering a more complete line of products, the low investment required to achieve market coverage, and, frequently, their product knowledge. Manufacturers' representatives are a necessity for the manufacturer without sufficient volume to justify the expense of its own sales force.

A disadvantage to using manufacturers' representatives is the limited degree of control over their activities and over their relationship with customers. In a sense, the manufacturer is at the mercy of the manufacturers' representative who may or may not elect to push its product line with sufficient vigor. They may be less knowledgeable about the product than would be the company-employed sales representative. These disadvantages can be managed by careful programs that give the manufacturers' representatives full support through sales promotion, sales training, product knowledge, and so on.

Although the variable nature of sales expense is an advantage in the use of manufacturers' representatives by manufacturers with small volume, it can become a disadvantage as volume grows and sales expense increases in linear fashion. In one instance, a manufacturer of electronic instruments converted to a direct sales force and achieved an immediate reduction in sales expense to less than 6 percent of sales revenue compared with the straight 10 percent that had been paid to several manufacturers' representatives to achieve national coverage. There is frequently suspicion on the part of the manufacturer that the manufacturers' representative will hold sales volume below the level at which the rep thinks the manufacturer will switch to direct sales coverage, even though additional volume is reasonably easily available. At the same time, manufacturers' representatives tend to fear that manufacturers will take away their lines after the rep has developed the territory and made it large enough to be profitable for direct coverage. Each party in the relationship must work hard to create an atmosphere of mutual trust and respect.

Industrial Distributors

Whether the firm relies upon its own sales force or manufacturers' representatives to obtain sales coverage, a number of other marketing functions must be performed that neither the sales representative nor the manufacturers' representative can provide. Very often, these functions are performed by the industrial distributor.[5]

---

[5] The following material is based upon research conducted by the author under a grant from The Marketing Science Institute. A good portion of the text in this section is taken directly from the report of this research: Frederick E. Webster, Jr., *The Changing Role of the Industrial Distributor*, Report No. 75-121 (Cambridge, Mass.: The Marketing Science Institute, 1975), and is used with permission.

The industrial distributor is a specific type of reseller who sells primarily to manufacturers. He stocks the products that he sells, has at least one outside sales representative as well as inside telephone and/or counter sales personnel, and performs a broad variety of marketing channel functions, including customer contact, credit, stocking, delivery, and providing a full product assortment. The products stocked may be maintenance, repair, and operating (MRO) supplies; original equipment manufacturer (OEM) supplies, such as fasteners, power transmission components, fluid power equipment, and small rubber parts, which become part of the manufacturer's finished product; equipment used in the operation of the business, such as hand tools, power tools, and conveyors; machinery used to machine raw materials and semifinished goods into finished products.

There are three types of industrial distributor. *General line distributors*, or mill supply houses, stock a broad range of products and are often referred to as the supermarkets of industry. *Specialist firms* carry a narrow line of related products, such as bearings, power transmission equipment and supplies, or abrasives and cutting tools. The distinction between these two types has been blurred in recent years by a growing tendency for general line houses to develop specialist departments. Less common is a tendency for specialist firms to broaden their product offerings in order to provide more complete service to customers. For example, some bearing specialists are moving into the broader field of power transmission. The third type of industrial distributor, the *combination house*, is either a specialist *and* a generalist *combined* or engages in other forms of wholesaling in addition to industrial distribution. An example is an electrical distributor who sells to retailers and institutions as well as to the construction industry and to manufacturers. Specialists and combination houses tend to be more profitable than generalists.

Most firms going to market through distribution will find it necessary to use some combination of generalist and specialist firms. As a general rule, general line distributors tend to be somewhat larger than specialists and to carry larger inventories, although the reverse could be true in a particular situation; some specialist distributors are very large.

Some Trends Influencing Industrial Distribution

For the past two decades there appears to have been a trend toward consolidation of smaller firms and branching by larger firms, but the typical firm is still an independently owned business, managed by the owner, doing business at a single location. Approximately one third of all firms do business in more than one sales location. A typical firm might have 25 or so employees, six outside sales representatives, four or five inside (telephone and counter) sales people, average order size of $250, and sales of $150,000 to $200,000 per employee—and about $300,000 to $400,000 per *sales* employee.

Analysis of trade association data and published surveys of industrial distribution operations show that industrial distributor firms are becoming somewhat larger on average. The larger firms have grown by acquisition. The pressures of competitive markets and increasing costs of operation have favored firms large enough to achieve available economies of scale in operations, especially through computerized ordering, inventory management, and billing systems.

The increased size of the distributor firm produces a number of qualitative changes in the nature of the distributor. Larger firm size provides increased opportunities for the general line distributor to develop specialist departments and to offer systems purchasing contracts to customers. Larger, computerized operations permit lower costs, tighter control, and better customer service. Better, more up-to-date information on customers and their ordering and usage patterns makes the distributor a better partner for both the manufacturer and the end-user and gives the distributor more control over its sales and marketing operations. Customers can be offered stockless purchasing arrangements with guaranteed overnight delivery. Despite increased size, there also appears to be a trend for distributors to carry smaller inventories as they attempt to reduce their costs.

Another identifiable trend is increasing importance and power for the industrial distributor in the marketing channel. A number of factors have combined to increase the importance of the distributor:

- Inflationary cost pressures, plus a general increase in financial management sophistication and concern for cost efficiencies, have forced industrial manufacturers to look harder at the costs of physical distribution, including order processing, field inventories, delivery, and production scheduling. In many cases this review has resulted in manufacturers shifting more physical distribution responsibilities to the distributor.
- Increased standardization of many products (bearings are a good example) has given the distributor relatively more control over the relation-

ship with the end-user customer, because the customer has fewer reasons to favor the brands of a specific manufacturer.

- A large number of distributors are performing special services, such as assembly, submanufacturing (cutting, welding, fabrication, etc.), and contract purchasing, for their customers. For example, a saw manufacturer selling entirely through distributors ships rolled band saw stock which the distributor cuts, welds, and finishes to customer specifications for each order. It appears that most distributors perform these additional services as an accommodation for customers rather than as a carefully designed, active element of marketing strategy. Nonetheless, the availability of these services makes the distributor more attractive to both manufacturer and end-user.

- Increased purchasing sophistication among end-users, especially for MRO and other frequently used standard items, has resulted in more efficient, more routinized purchasing of the standard "80 percent of the orders that account for 20 percent of our dollar purchases." The local distributor is usually in an advantageous position to service blanket purchase orders and systems contracting purchasing agreements, as well as to provide necessary safety stocks. Some distributors are making systems contracting a central element in their marketing strategies.

There is also an observable trend toward increased product specialization by industrial distributors. The trend toward specialization has generally been associated with increased technical competence and product knowledge. The specialist can offer greater depth, including multiple brands, in a given product area. Some general line distributors have agreed to set up specialist departments as a condition for obtaining a leading product line. In other cases, manufacturers report that they are being forced to go to the specialist distributors, because of their wide acceptance in certain product areas.

Thus, there are a number of forces and trends shaping the industrial distributor. It must be emphasized, however, that these trends are evolutionary, not revolutionary. As average firm size increases and the industrial distributor performs more functions for both the manufacturer and the end-user, his control over the marketing channel will increase, his trade margins should increase, and his management should become more sophisticated.

Value-Added Resellers

A relatively recent development is the value-added reseller, or VAR, found especially in markets for computers and other forms of information technology. Antecedents of today's VARs are found in industries where final alterations in the physical form of the product are made by the distributor. For example, the steel distributor may cut, bend, and weld final shapes and subassemblies; an electrical equipment distributor may combine gauges, pumps, valves, and controls to create fluid-handling systems.

Value-added resellers are common in the computer industry as they integrate hardware and software to create systems uniquely tailored to a given customer's problems. These VARs are often specialized by industry, such as firms serving hospitals, hotels, law firms, engineering and design companies, or even industrial distributors of various kinds. It is their ability to develop specialized software for applications market segments that might be too small to be attractive to a large equipment manufacturer that represents the VARs' source of competitive advantage. Thus, for the hardware manufacturer, the VAR may be a valuable ally in reaching these market niches.

However, value-added resellers offer a special opportunity for channel conflict. Seldom can market boundaries be so clearly drawn that VARs can avoid competing with their manufacturer suppliers. Legally, the manufacturer cannot preclude the VAR from soliciting business from certain potential customers. The company's marketing strategy may state quite clearly which market segments it intends to serve through VARs. These segments will tend to consist of specialized applications in smaller end-user firms. However, the company's direct sales reps may be reluctant to turn over potential leads to a VAR until it becomes very clear that they are not going to be able to make the sale by themselves. Likewise, the VARs may solicit business from prospects that they are not qualified to serve as well as the manufacturer because of the narrow hardware line available to the VAR.

Also, VARs may develop systems using hardware from several competing vendors, thus increasing the likelihood of conflict with a particular supplier. If the sales rep turns over a lead to the VAR, there is always the chance that the VAR will end up selling the competitor's products. On many requests for proposals, the manufacturer may find itself competing with one or more of its own VARs.

Value-added resellers will likely continue to develop in markets where customers buy integrated systems of hardware and software, especially where the latter is developed for specific market niches and applications. VARs are not limited to computer systems, but might be found in any information-technology-based industry, and even beyond that to markets where applications require the combination of products and services from multiple sources. The creative design of distribution channels using VARs of various kinds can be a key source of competitive advantage, especially in highly fragmented markets.

Channel Conflict and Channel Management

We have made frequent reference to the concept of channel conflict, and it is now time to define it and analyze it more carefully as background to understanding some of the issues involved in managing manufacturer-reseller relationships. Channel conflict is the natural result of the interdependence of reseller and manufacturer and the fact that there is overlap among the marketing functions they perform and limited resources for performing them. Even though each party is aware of the interdependence, it struggles to maintain its own autonomy and control over its own operations as it strives to achieve it goals. For conflict to occur in this interdependent state, the parties must become aware of specific issues in the relationship—for example, the relative sizes of gross margins, responsibilities for maintaining inventories, restrictions on account solicitation, overlapping territories, or the amount of cooperative advertising allowances. The next step is often to personalize the conflict and to develop hostile feelings to the other party. That in turn leads to specific behavior, often in the form of reduced cooperation or, more positively, attempts to resolve the conflict through communication and negotiation.[6]

The roots of potential conflict are found in the differing perceptions that each party has for itself and for the other party, in differing goals and objectives, and in ambiguity about the strategic roles of the distributor and the manufacturer. As the marketplace evolves, a failure to adjust strategy can lead to channel conflict. Unfortunately, the process of diagnosing channel conflict may not recognize its strategic roots at first. Initial problem definitions might be in terms of the attitudes of individuals or problems and inefficiencies in the other party's operations. Blame might be directed toward personnel, policies, or procedures when the real problem is that the

---

[6] Louis W. Stern, Adel L. El-Ansary, and James R. Brown, *Management in Marketing Channels* (Englewood Cliffs, N.J.: Prentice-Hall, Inc., 1989), pp. 358–64.

manufacturer's strategy, and the defined role of the distributor in that strategy, are flawed.[7]

PERCEPTIONS OF THE INDUSTRIAL DISTRIBUTOR

How the Distributor Views Himself

Interviews with distributors and review of the trade literature of industrial distribution show that the industrial distributor has a rather clear self-concept. He sees himself as an independent businessman and is proud of his industry and the service role it plays in the economy. He emphasizes his ability to provide full sales coverage, broad product lines, and a full range of customer services. He regards his customers as just that—*his* customers—and it is his ability to contact and service these customers that he offers to the selling manufacturer. Although the typical industrial distributor may be small compared to national marketers, he may be one of the largest independently owned and managed businesses in the local community. His local acceptance he regards as one of the major strengths he offers to his suppliers.

The industrial distributor thinks of himself, at least in part, as a customer, and a very desirable one for his suppliers, one to be catered to and served. He has freedom to decide which lines he will handle. He judges suppliers in terms of the quality and availability of their sales reps and the support they offer, and by their ability to service his orders promptly, accurately, and predictably. He tends to be more customer-oriented than supplier-oriented. He listens patiently to the supplier's attempts to get better representation of his product line but remains firm in his conviction that his main obligation is to serve customer needs. In fact, some distributors speak with pride of the fact that their sales reps can provide better customer service because they don't have to spend so much time begging for orders.

How the Manufacturer Sees the Distributor

The manufacturer views the industrial distributor as a member of her sales and physical distribution organization. She is frustrated by the distributor's relatively low level of management competence and

[7]Allan J. Magrath and Kenneth G. Hardy, *A Strategic Framework for Diagnosing Manufacturer-Reseller Conflict*, Working Paper, Report No. 88-101, (Cambridge, Mass.: Marketing Science Institute, March, 1988).

lack of management depth, as well as by inadequate financial management and the frequent lack of provision for management succession. The distributor is seen as financially successful and, therefore, somewhat complacent, rather uninterested in innovation or improved management practices.

Industrial distributors are seen as best able to handle small accounts and to perform physical distribution functions, and less competent to handle large accounts, sales, and technical service functions. The distributor's sales personnel are seen as more order-takers than creative sales reps and are judged weak in finding new accounts and aggressively promoting new products. The distributor's key function is to provide the right product to the customer when and where it is needed. He must be urged to carry full inventories, which he is sometimes reluctant to do. The supplier thinks of end-users as *her* customers, not the distributor's.

Suppliers tend to regard industrial distributors as unwilling to provide information about their operations and both unwilling and unable to provide information about market areas and individual accounts. A lack of willingness to solicit new accounts is seen as a lack of awareness of available business, and generally low interest in market research.

In describing these two sets of perceptions, overstatement of differences has conscientiously been avoided. These generalizations are based on interviews and are intended to be accurate descriptions of how the industrial distributor sees himself and how he is seen by the manufacturer-supplier. Both are true to the limits of our research validity and reliability, not only as statements of subjective perceptions, but also in large measure as statements of fact. These markedly different perceptions can not be said to be right or wrong. Rather, the marketer must consider what these different perceptions mean for effective management of the distributor-supplier relationship. These differing perceptions are the root cause of a number of management issues in the relationship.

DEFINING THE DISTRIBUTOR'S ROLE IN MARKETING STRATEGY

No single marketing strategy is characteristic of those industrial firms that rely heavily upon the industrial distributor. Rather, the distributor's role will vary as a function of several interrelated factors, including:

1. The manufacturer's marketing strategy and especially the means she chooses to achieve unique competitive advantage—quality, price, availability, applications engineering and technical service, full line, technical product leadership, and so on.
2. The strength of the manufacturer's market position, whether she is a market leader or a minor brand.
3. The technical characteristics of the product, especially the presence of strongly differentiating product features among brands and the need to make technical judgments about the best response to customer requirements.
4. The importance of immediate product availability to the customer or, conversely, the extent to which requirements can be forecasted and planned for.

Products sold through industrial distributors tend to be established products with broad and large demand. Thus, industrial distributors fit better into a pull strategy, where they have the important function of servicing existing demand. Industrial distributors generally do not have the ability to aggressively develop markets for new products or to serve narrow market segments with specialized product needs. Even the specialist distributor of such products as bearings, power transmission equipment, or high technology fasteners serves customers from a broad range of manufacturing industries. One source outlines the characteristics of products best sold through industrial distributors as follows:

1. They have a large base of potential customers.
2. They can be easily stocked and serviced locally.
3. The quantity per transaction is relatively small.
4. Responsibility for the buying decision is located at lower levels of the organization.
5. Rapid delivery and service are of major value to the customer.[8]

The Role of the Manufacturer's Sales Representatives

Companies using industrial distributors must maintain their own field sales forces as well. While manufacturers' representatives may be helpful in developing market demand for new or established

[8] James D. Hlavacek and Tommy J. McCuistion, "Industrial Distributors—When, Who and How?," *Harvard Business Review,* **61,** 2 (March-April, 1983), 96–101, at 97.

products, they are not well suited to managing the company's relationships with distributors. Typically, the sales reps' major function is to solicit orders from, service, and support the distributor organization. They may frequently make customer calls with distributors' sales reps, especially for technical service. In other cases, the manufacturer's sales representative is responsible for customer contact and order generation, while the distributor mainly handles physical distribution. Not uncommonly, the manufacturer's sales rep is responsible both for working with the distributor on most accounts and for direct service to large accounts.

In considering the many different marketing strategies employed by industrial manufacturers, there are several major distributor functions which tend, in varying degrees depending upon the market circumstances of the manufacturer, to characterize the role of the industrial distributor in the manufacturer's marketing strategy. These functions are (1) to provide market coverage and product availability, (2) to develop markets and to solicit accounts, (3) to provide customers with technical advice and product service, and (4) to provide market information.

Market Coverage and Product Availability

The key responsibility of the industrial distributor is always to contact present and potential customers and to make the product available, with the necessary supporting services (e.g., delivery, credit, or technical advice) as quickly as economically feasible. In some cases, for example abrasives, market coverage and availability require several hundred general-line distributors. In other cases, such as fluid power equipment, 25 to 30 distributors may insure adequate coverage and availability. The number of distributors required to cover the market and insure availability depends upon several variables, most notably:

1. Total market potential and geographic concentration.
2. The manufacturer's current market share and the intensity of competition.
3. Frequency of purchase and whether the product is an MRO item or an OEM item.
4. Whether lack of availability could interrupt the customer's production process.

5. Amount of technical knowledge required to sell or service the product.

6. The extent of product differentiation, determining how important immediate availability is as a competitive variable.

Market Development and Account Solicitation

Although the industrial distributor tends to be responsible primarily for servicing existing demand, in some cases the distributor can play a major role in soliciting new accounts and expanding the size of the market. For example, a manufacturer of saw blades gave distributors major responsibility for soliciting new business from potential customers identified by the manufacturer after thorough and expensive market studies in the distributor's assigned territory. Or, to cite another example, a manufacturer of pop rivets expected distributors to aggressively solicit customers away from sheet metal screw manufacturers.

When the distributor takes on major responsibility for promoting a product line, it is likely to be a line that provides a large share of his total volume. In such circumstances, the promotional responsibility often encompasses sales promotion (especially direct mail), advertising, and field sales coverage.

Technical Advice and Service

Even for product categories where the technology is rather stable, the technical nature of the product is usually such that many customers need advice in determining optimum product specifications for a given application. The distributor's sales reps must have adequate product knowledge to render necessary assistance. Technical expertise is important even for such products as fasteners (threaded products, rivets, etc.), abrasives, and saws and files. In the case of grinding wheels, for example, minor differences in wheel composition can produce major cost differences in the grinding operation.

Market Information

The large majority of manufacturers find that their distributors are of virtually no help as a source of market information. Notable exceptions are cases where a technical product is distributed mainly through specialists and where the manufacturer's line accounts for more than half the distributor's volume. In these cases, the distributor's market scope is narrow enough to encourage his development of some expertise, and he has real incentive to participate effectively with the manufacturer in market development. Nevertheless, in most cases the distributor does not have current or complete market data. Even distributors with electronic data processing seem to neglect the market analysis and planning function.

ISSUES IN THE SUPPLIER-DISTRIBUTOR RELATIONSHIP

Direct Accounts

A perennial source of strain in the supplier-distributor relationship is manufacturers' establishment of direct accounts with end-user customers. Often, direct accounts are an exception, rather than part of a planned pattern of combined direct and distributor account coverage. The problem usually arises when a major customer, often one with multiple buying locations, threatens to do business with another manufacturer unless she receives a lower price than the manufacturer can provide through a distributor. In other cases, the customer may demand direct coverage because she wants better technical advice or the recognition and higher service level of direct dealing. Since such powerful accounts are often a major portion of the distributor's volume, the solution is often a difficult one. Complicated commission or fee arrangements for distributor's service on direct accounts may be negotiated, or the supplier may arbitrarily withdraw the account from the distributor. Only a minority of manufacturers have steadfastly been able to refuse to deal directly with major, national accounts, and, thereby, avoid becoming competitors for their distributors.

Distributor Management

The distributor owner-manager is often not a well-trained professional manager. As a successful small business, she may reach a point where she has little interest in opening new territories, soliciting new accounts, or developing new product lines. The distributor's lack of a growth motivation is frequently mentioned as a source of frustration by manufacturers wishing to improve their competitive position.

A related issue is the problem of management succession. The retirement or death of a distributor owner-manager can seriously reduce the effectiveness of the distributorship. Suppliers attempt to cope with this problem by working with the distributor to assure smooth transitions and by incorporating contract provisions for terminating the relationship if there is a change in ownership.

In general, the quality, or lack of it, of distributor management is a pervasive issue. Although increasing firm size can lead to more professional management, lack of planning, inadequate financing, poor managerial and administrative control systems, cash flow problems, and haphazard inventory policies remain common problems for the industrial distributor. Distributor management often has inadequate information with which to determine product line profitability, order processing costs, or optimum stocking levels.

Inventory Levels

Manufacturers usually must employ a great deal of persuasion to get distributors to increase inventory levels, an increase often seen by the manufacturer as essential to effective customer service. One method of persuasion is to increase distributors' profit margins. Manufacturers usually wish to be among the most profitable lines stocked by their distributors. In line with the distributor's characteristically strained financial condition, the manufacturer may find it necessary to finance distributors' inventory expansion by delayed billing, consignment sale, or even cash loan. The manufacturer's sales rep can often show how larger inventories can improve the distributor's profitability but may find the process of developing this analysis lengthy, because of distributor reluctance to share cost data or a general lack of such data.

Second Lines

Manufacturers would obviously prefer that their distributors not carry competing product lines, although they cannot legally prohibit them from doing so. (The manufacturer can, in most cases, legally require the distributor to carry his full line.) On the other hand, distributors often want a second line in order to have a broader price range or a wider variety of product types. Some manufacturers compete for available distributors by positioning themselves as a second-line supplier, but this may lead to a catch-as-catch-can distributor organization, leaving the distributor in control of the relationship.

One incentive used to encourage the distributor to concentrate its purchases in a single line is quantity discounts on purchases. The presence of second lines is especially annoying to those firms that make major commitments to and major investments in their distributors, such as training programs, market development expenses, and so on. Such programs are undertaken in an attempt to become the distributor's most important and profitable line. Second lines frustrate the achievement of this objective.

Adding Distributors and Overlapping Territories

As markets and distributors change, existing distributor coverage patterns may prove inadequate. When it is determined that the existing distributor is incapable of covering its assigned territory, it may be replaced or a new distributor may be added. Since nearby distributors seldom assign exactly the same geographical limits to what they regard as their territories, overlapping territories may result. Furthermore, this overlapping may be the conscious intention of the supplier, if it determines that different distributors have strengths in different market segments. Obviously, considerable controversy can arise from such arrangements and most distributors will seek to avoid them. When such arrangements are made, the manufacturer clearly runs the risk of losing the older distributor, a risk often deliberately taken.

To summarize this discussion of the role of the industrial distributor in industrial marketing strategy, many manufacturers have actively reviewed their distributor policies and organizations in recent years. On balance, there is a clear trend toward greater reliance upon fewer, larger, and better-managed distributors, although, of course, there will always be firms moving in the other direction. In the process, weak, marginal distributor firms have been weeded out. A variety of market-related and economic forces have stimulated this trend. Manufacturers faced with tight money, increased competition (often price competition from overseas), and rapidly increasing transportation costs are forced to search hard for ways to increase the efficiency of the physical distribution system and marketing program effectiveness.

THE MANUFACTURER'S RESPONSIBILITY
TO THE DISTRIBUTOR

Even though industrial distributors are becoming stronger and more effective, they still depend heavily upon the manufacturer for their strength and effectiveness. On the other hand, the distributor is an independent business. It is unlikely that a single supplier can substantially change the distributor's operation. The idea of partnership remains essential. When the manufacturer turns to the distributor for more help, the manufacturer does not give up its own responsibility for effective marketing, nor can it expect the distributor to respond positively to all suggestions. Rather, the manufacturer assumes new responsibilities for making the distributor more effective through programs of product development, careful pricing, promotional support, technical assistance, order servicing, and training for distributor sales personnel and management. Not surprisingly, the manufacturers held in highest regard by the distributor are those with the most complete programs of distributor support and who give distributors the most complete responsibility for their product line. These programs typically have several features.

First, the distributor's role is carefully and thoroughly defined in the supplier's marketing strategy. The functions to be performed are clearly understood and margins reflect fairly the value of these marketing functions to the manufacturer and the cost to the distributor of performing them well. These clearly defined policies guiding the supplier's relationship with distributors are carefully communicated to all members of the company's sales force and distributor organization.

Second, the company's own sales reps are told that maintaining an effective relationship with the distributor is their primary responsibility. The sales reps are trained, supervised, and compensated accordingly. The distributor sees the sales rep as a source of product knowledge, an expert on technical applications, and a solver of problems with the factory on orders and delivery.

Third, the company must have an active program for building up the competence of the distributor organization. Distributor management is offered training of various kinds, with opportunities for supplier and distributor personnel to get to know each other better. Sales reps are trained not only in knowledge of the supplier's product, but also in basic points of salesmanship, account management, and technical background. Distributors are provided with analytical methods and aids for dealing with inventory level decisions, product line profitability analysis, and market area analysis. In sum, the distributor is given help in analyzing business opportunities and managing resources efficiently.

Fourth, instead of asking distributors to do something beyond their capabilities, the manufacturer often does it for them. As one manufacturer marketing manager stated it, "If it is not worthwhile for us to do it, it probably wasn't worthwhile at all." Direct mail sales promotions, local advertising, and sales rep training sessions are not only planned but also executed by the supplier. This helps to build morale and renew interest in the product line, while assuring that the details of implementation are effectively controlled. (Attention to detail is especially important for programs designed to develop consistent information on market area potentials and to build a data base for helping distributors allocate sales effort efficiently.)

Most manufacturers have developed a variety of training programs and supporting services to make the distributor as effective as possible, thus strengthening the distributors and their commitment. There is emphasis upon adding market development and account solicitation functions to the distributor's more traditional functions of market coverage and product availability. Thus, the process of improving industrial distribution seems to be one that will sustain itself, producing larger, more effective, better managed industrial distributors who perform a broader variety of functions for their suppliers. For the typical manufacturer, the result will be fewer but better distributors to work with and a stronger, more effective partnership. Another result will be that firms that wish to move from direct sales and service coverage to industrial distributors will find it much harder to locate available and qualified distributors who are not committed to existing manufacturers.

PHYSICAL DISTRIBUTION—LOGISTICS

Whether the manufacturer uses distributors or goes direct, it retains some degree of responsibility for physical distribution of the product, including replacement parts where applicable, to the end-user. Without reliable distribution arrangements, the product offering is incomplete. Customer service is often defined primarily in physical distribution terms.

Physical distribution must be factored into the design of marketing strategy. When availability is a key consideration for the customer, then the manufacturer must establish specific standards for customer service, such as the percentage of all orders that will be shipped within a stated time period following receipt—e.g., 95 percent shipped within 24 hours—or for the length of time between receipt of an order and the customer's receipt of the goods. For fungible items, such as office supplies, abrasives, or lubricating oil, the standard of customer service may also be specified in terms of broad market coverage and available inventories near all major customer concentrations.

Effective management of the logistics function as part of the marketing mix has been hindered in many industrial firms by viewing it as part of the manufacturing function. One side effect of this has been a tendency to view logistics as a cost element (involving inventory investments and transportation expense) and to regard cost reduction and control as the major dimensions of effectiveness, rather than thinking in terms of customer service. Very often, the objectives of maximizing customer service and minimizing distribution cost are in direct conflict. This means that real conflict can exist between manufacturing and marketing in their views of the distribution function.

The Total Distribution Cost Concept

An important step toward resolution of this conflict was the development of the so-called total distribution cost concept, an extension of systems thinking, already mentioned briefly in Chapter 2 in our discussion of the materials management concept.

The total distribution cost concept recognizes that several individual cost elements interact in complex ways to determine total distribution cost and that an attempt to minimize any single cost element can actually increase total cost. The individual cost elements include transportation, inventory investment, warehousing, packaging, obsolescence and deterioration, order processing, and the cost of lost business. The last element is an opportunity cost reflecting the loss of sales volume attributable to poor customer service. Reducing any single cost to its absolute minimum is almost certain to cause more than offsetting increases in other cost elements. For example, using lowest cost transportation, such as barge or rail transport, may require larger investments in inventory and packaging, and entail loss of business that cannot be served well by these low-cost means. Analysis of the complex interactions among the elements of distribution cost often requires the tools of the operations researcher, including computer simulation.

The logic of the total distribution cost concept suggests why the manufacturing manager's view of the physical distribution function may be inadequate. In some industrial firms, the adoption of the total distribution approach to the analysis of customer service has led to the creation of a high level management position responsible for the distribution function, with organizational authority equal to that of marketing and manufacturing. Titles include Manager of Customer Service and Vice President for Physical Distribution. Other companies have adopted the approach of using a distribution committee, with representatives from marketing, manufacturing, finance, and perhaps purchasing, to develop distribution policy and to coordinate and control the logistics function.

A well known management consulting firm developed a six-step approach to managing the customer service function consistent with the total distribution cost concept and its integration into the marketing mix. These steps are:

1. Define the elements of customer service, such as order processing time, order assembly time, delivery time, inventory reliability (stockouts, back orders, percent of orders shipped complete, etc.), order size constraints, consolidation of items from several locations, and consistency in each of these items.

2. Determine the customer's view of service, defining which elements are most important to the customer and the economic significance of each element, as well as the customer's view of the service levels offered by the firm and its competitors.

3. Develop a service package, viewing distribution as part of the product offering responsive to the customer's needs and perceptions. Creativity at this stage, looking at trade-offs among distribution cost elements, is as important as in the design of the physical product itself and may lead to both improved service and lower cost—such as the use of airfreight to ship repair parts from a central location, rather than tying up investment in inventory at many locations and shipping by truck.

4. Develop a program to sell service, remembering that the service offering, like the product, will seldom sell itself.

5. Market test the service package, offering it, with the selling program, to actual customers for their reaction.

6. Develop performance standards and controls, measuring actual distribution system performance and taking corrective action where necessary.[9]

[9] William M. Hutchinson, Jr., and John F. Stolle, "How to Manage Customer Service," *Harvard Business Review,* **46,** 6 (November-December, 1968), 85–96.

The authors emphasized that this approach was applicable to all elements of customer service including sales reps' calls, engineering advice, notification of shipments, the invoice, and other aspects, not just to the commonly recognized elements, such as transportation and warehousing.

Logistics must be viewed in a long-term, strategic context.[10] If logistics is treated only as a short-term, operational problem, then the industrial firm may miss major opportunities for achieving unique competitive advantage with its service offering and avoiding unnecessary distribution expense. In the interest of developing valuable long-term vendor relationships, the customer may be willing to adjust its requirements for service to help the supplier achieve economies for the benefit of both parties.

SUMMARY

Distribution is part of the total product offered to the customer, a major dimension of service. The functions of resellers in the marketing channel and of physical distribution, as part of the service package, must be carefully defined in the context of overall marketing strategy. Designing the marketing channel is the task of assigning responsibility for the performance of those functions to those firms that can perform them most efficiently and effectively. Typical resellers in the industrial market channel are the manufacturers' representative and the industrial distributor, but "hybrid" channel systems are becoming more common.

A number of trends affecting the evolution of the industrial distributor were identified and their impact on the distributor's role in industrial marketing strategy was assessed in some detail. Several management issues in the distributor-manufacturer relationship were reviewed with an emphasis on developing effective, cooperative manufacturer-reseller partnerships. Finally, the long-term, strategic role of physical distribution, or logistics, in industrial customer service was emphasized.

[10] James L. Heskett, "Logistics—Essential to Strategy," *Harvard Business Review*, **55**, 6 (November-December, 1977), 85–98.

Bibliography

Anderson, James C., and James A. Narus, "A Model of Distributor Firm and Manufacturer Firm Working Partnerships," *Journal of Marketing*, **54**, 1 (January, 1990), 42–58.

Cady, John F., "Reasonable Rules and Rules of Reason: Vertical Restrictions on Distributors," *Journal of Marketing*, **46**, 3 (Summer, 1982), 27–37.

Corey, E. Raymond, Frank V. Cespedes, and V. Kasturi Rangan, *Going to Market: Distribution Systems for Industrial Products* (Boston: Harvard Business School Press, 1989).

Hardy, Kenneth G., and Allan J. Magrath, *Marketing Channel Management: Strategic Planning and Tactics* (Glenview, Ill.: Scott, Foresman and Co., 1988).

Hlavacek, James D., and Tommy J. McQuistion, "Industrial Distributors—When, Who, and How?," *Harvard Business Review*, **61**, 2 (March-April, 1983), 96–101.

Magrath, Allan J., and Kenneth G. Hardy, *A Strategic Framework for Diagnosing Manufacturer-Reseller Conflict,* working paper, Report No. 88-101, (Cambridge, Mass.: Marketing Science Institute, March, 1988).

Moriarty, Rowland T., and Gordon S. Swartz, "Automation and Marketing to Boost Sales and Marketing," *Harvard Business Review*, **67**, 1 (January-February, 1989), 100–108.

————,————, and Charles A. Khuen, *Managing Hybrid Marketing Channels with Automation*, working paper, Report No. 88-113, (Cambridge, Mass.: Marketing Science Institute, December, 1988).

Narus, James A., and James C. Anderson, "Turn Your Industrial Distributors into Partners," *Harvard Business Review*, **64**, 2 (March-April, 1986), 66–71.

Shapiro, Roy D., and James L. Heskett, *Logistics Strategy* (St. Paul, Minn.: West, 1985).

Stern, Louis W., Adel I. El-Ansary, and James R. Brown, *Management in Marketing Channels* (Englewood Cliffs, N.J.: Prentice-Hall, Inc., 1989).

Webster, Frederick E., Jr., "Perceptions of the Industrial Distributor," *Industrial Marketing Management*, **4**, 5 (October, 1975), 257–64.

————, "The Role of the Industrial Distributor in Marketing Strategy," *Journal of Marketing*, **40**, 3 (July, 1976), 10–16.

9 Managing the Industrial Sales Force

Industrial marketing strategies are characterized by their reliance on personal selling as the primary tool of communication, compared with consumer marketing's emphasis on advertising and sales promotion. The reasons for this, to be explored more carefully in a moment, relate to the nature of the customer's buying decision process and the buyer-seller relationship. The sales representative can also be an essential part of the company's capability for solving customer problems. The foundation for the following analysis of the role of personal selling in the industrial marketing strategy was laid in Chapter 3 in the discussion of industrial buyer-seller relationships and the nature of buyer-sales rep interaction.

THE INDUSTRIAL SALES MANAGEMENT PROGRAM

There are three rather distinct sets of decision problems in the development of industrial sales management programs. First, the role of personal selling in the marketing mix must be defined. Second, there is a set of decisions relating to the management and organization of the sales force, including issues of the size and structure of the organization, recruitment, selection, training, supervision, motivation, compensation, evaluation, and control. Third, sales effort must be deployed and allocated to specific assignments including geographic territories, product lines, and customer accounts. We will look at each of these decision areas in turn. A useful overview of the decisions required in the design and management of the sales program, is given in Figure 9-1.

The sales management program

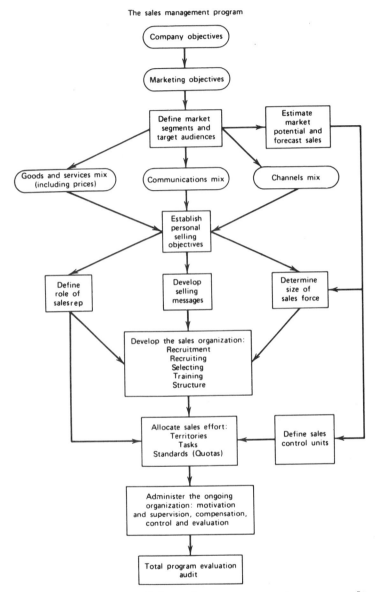

Figure 9-1. An overview of the sales management program. [Source: *Kenneth R. Davis and Frederick E. Webster, Jr.,* Sales Force Management: Text and Cases *(New York: Ronald Press Co., 1968). p. 727.*] *Reproduced with permission.*

DEFINING THE ROLE OF PERSONAL SELLING

The purpose of all marketing effort is to create a satisfied customer, and the sales rep is ultimately responsible for the degree of customer satisfaction. Industrial marketing is different from consumer marketing in the extent to which the sales rep is part of the company's total capability for solving customer problems and creating satisfied customers. This aspect of industrial selling relates to buyer-seller interdependence, one of the four dimensions of uniqueness in industrial marketing identified in Chapter 1. Stated differently, the sales rep is part of the company's product offering. The role of personal selling must be defined in that light.

In addition, the sales rep is also part of the company's communications mix or promotional strategy. That is, the sales rep is responsible for conveying selling messages to potential customers and for keeping existing customers informed about products and services, as well as generating revenue from these existing accounts. As a communicator, the sales rep's effectiveness is also influenced by the other elements of the company's communications mix, including advertising, direct mail, product display, catalogues, trade shows, and other forms of sales promotion.

Both roles, that of providing the product or capability, and that of communicator or promotional agent, must be considered in defining the role of the sales rep in the company's marketing strategy. All aspects of the sales management program must be consistent with this definition of the sales representative's role.

As Part of the Product Offering

The idea that the sales rep is part of the company's product offering needs to be explored and developed more completely. There are several dimensions to this part of the sales rep's role.

First, the sales rep has an important job to perform in helping the customer to define the buying problem. The rep must show the customer how the purchase of particular goods or services can contribute to the accomplishment of the customer's objectives. In technology-oriented product lines, this calls for expert product knowledge and technical skill. In less technically oriented product situations, the sales rep may be much more of a business consultant, focussing the customer's attention on the economic consequences of various purchase alternatives, looking at the potential impact on costs and revenues. The sales rep's ability to help the customer define and solve these problems is an extremely important part of the capability that the customer purchases from suppliers.

Second, the sales rep may have important responsibilities relating to the installation and maintenance of the product, as in the case of capital equipment purchases. In the purchase of materials and OEM items, the sales rep's responsibility for assistance to the customer may relate more to the customer's production process and the integration of the purchased materials and components into the production system, including issues of inventory planning and control. All of these aspects—installation, applications engineering, maintenance and repair, and inventory planning and control—can be grouped under the label of customer service. Many companies will maintain a separate field service organization along with a sales organization to provide these functions. Very often, especially for undifferentiated products, this service component is more important in determining the value of the buyer-seller relationship to the customer than is the physical product itself. For example, for decades the marketing strategy of IBM has been based on a recognition that the customer is not buying the physical hardware of a computer system so much as the service package that accompanies it.

Third, in a marketing-oriented company, as opposed to a sales-oriented one, the sales representative has a responsibility for "representing the customer to the factory." This is the ultimate in application of the marketing concept, assuring that the business is truly customer-oriented. It is an extremely important capability for assuring competitive advantage in the marketplace, given that the industrial product is often a variable that must be tailored to the customer's needs. The sales rep's influence may not be limited to defining product parameters in the somewhat narrow technical sense, but it can relate to such aspects of the total product and service offering as credit terms, contractual terms of various kinds, delivery planning and expediting, and so forth. This function can be especially important in those situations where the industrial marketer thinks of the distributor as its customer.

In all of these functions—helping the customer to define the buying situation, providing customer service, and representing the customer to the factory—the sales rep is working with other people in his or her company. Some are part of the marketing organization, such as customer service specialists, applications engineers, and order processing personnel. Others are from the operations and financial functions of the business, including product planners, production schedulers, credit managers, and so on. It takes careful planning of organizational relationships to make sure that all of these people cooperate as an effective team. It also takes planning and interpersonal skills on the part of the sales rep to put together and manage the necessary relationships.

The sales rep's role as part of the company's product offering or problem-solving capability was highlighted in Chapter 3, in the examination of the sales representative as a "boundary role" person. Functioning on the perimeter of the organization, managing the interface with the customer organization, the sales representative faces a number of pressures from both directions. In the boundary role, the sales rep may come to be distrusted or disliked by those within the seller's organization whose duties are defined and evaluated in such a way that they resist changes in operations and procedures requested by the sales rep who is trying to respond to customer demands and the competitive situation. The sales rep is likely to be quite aware of these attitudes and they may be a source of anxiety and role conflict for the rep.

Figure 9-2 illustrates one company's attempt to feature its sales representative as part of its product offering in an advertising program. Here, we see the stress on the sales rep's ability to help define the buying problem and to tailor the product and service to the customer's needs.

As Part of the Communications Mix

The sales rep is also responsible for delivering sales messages and for generating sales volume, for writing orders. Therefore, a rep must be skilled in interpersonal interaction. In Chapter 2 we developed a view of the industrial buying process that stressed the importance of identifying the members of the buying center and defining their individual needs and wants, in order to target communications at individuals, not at the abstract organization. In Chapter 3, buyer-sales rep interaction was examined in detail. As a form of communication, personal selling is more efficient, because the sales rep can adjust selling messages based on feedback received during the interaction. It was noted in Chapter 3 that empathy, the ability to sense the reaction one produces in another person, is believed to be a critical ability for the sales rep.

In the previous chapter we considered the role of personal selling in the industrial marketing mix when the distinction between push and pull marketing strategies was discussed. An evaluation of buying patterns and preferences in the relevant market segments is the

Figure 9-2. An advertisement for Computer Sciences Corporation, featuring the sales representatives as part of the company's product offering. Reproduced by courtesy of Rieser & Williams, Inc., Costa Mesa, California.

starting point for considering the relative merits of push and pull strategies. The result of that analysis is to define either an active role for the sales rep in stimulating demand—a push strategy—or a more passive role of servicing demand (either among end users or distributors) that has been stimulated by other means such as advertising and sales promotion—a pull strategy. Industrial marketing strategies, as often noted before, are much more likely to be of the push variety, with a vital role assigned to the sales rep for stimulating demand, as well as servicing it.

Thus, several previous chapters have examined aspects of the sales rep's role that are relevant for considering his responsibilities as a communicator.

The Job Description

These two dimensions of the sales rep's role, as part of the product capability and as a communicator, must be incorporated in the industrial sales representative's job description. A written description of the sales rep's responsibilities, and a statement derived from it that describes the skills, knowledge, and attitudes required to execute those responsibilities, is an essential building block for all other parts of the sales management program. The job description specifies the work that the sales rep must do, and, therefore, the criteria by which she should be evaluated. Implicit therein is a statement of what she is to be paid for and even how she is to be compensated, as well as the training that is required and the activities that must be planned. Figure 9-3 is an illustration of an industrial sales rep's job description. That illustration should be examined carefully, since it provides a useful summary of this section on defining the role of personal selling, and of the sales rep in industrial marketing strategy.

SALES FORCE ORGANIZATION AND MANAGEMENT

As a critical resource in the development and implementation of the industrial marketing strategy, the sales force must be carefully planned, organized, and managed. It is essential that the management of the firm recognize the vital importance of the sales organization and devote the necessary money and management attention to the development of the organization as an entity and of the people in that organization. Decisions to invest in the development of sales

Title: Account Manager   **Date:**
Incumbent: **Interviewer:**
Reports To: District Sales Manager   **Approvals:** (1)
      (2)

Accountability Objective

Generate sales volumes in the assigned territory and achieve market participation within divisional strategies, goals, objectives, prescribed budgetary limits and established cost constraints, in order to sustain the AMG's leadership position in the industry.

Principal End Results

1. Increase sales volume for assigned products to assure consistency with divisional marketing strategies, goals and targets.
2. Maintain and enhance good working relationships with distributors' management, sales personnel, and all large, key account personnel in the territory, to advance the AMG's selling efforts.
3. Demonstrate expertise and mastery of the timely utilization of Norton's engineering technology in the course of solving customer problems relative to the application of abrasive products.
4. Organize and conduct distributor meetings to insure that the distributor sales force is knowledgeable of the technical attributes and applications of the Norton product lines which they sell.
5. Maintain excellent, up-to-date record system for accounts, products, and distributors and to have a territory continuity strategy on file.
6. Analyze and provide timely, accurate market information to the District Sales Manager, such as pricing situations and status of competitive activities and products, relative to the success of marketing strategies and programs for the territory.

The Account Manager reports to a Distict Sales Manager, along with Sales Representatives, Sales Supervisors, Territory Managers, other Account Managers, Sr. Account Managers, and District Product Supervisors. There are no positions reporting to the incumbent, although a Sales Representative may be assigned to work with the incumbent for a period of time for training purposes.

The incumbent covers a sales territory which may vary in size from several counties to an entire state. He/she sells a variety of products, such as coated,

Figure 9-3. An industrial sales rep's job description. Reproduced courtesy of Norton Company.

vitrified, organic and diamond abrasives, loose grain, diamond dressing tools and coolant. The Account Manager sells products through various market channels, including distributors, direct accounts, and Original Equipment Manufacturer (OEM) accounts. Product applications are found in many industries such as automotive, foundries, steel, glass and ceramic, and bearing. The incumbent must exhibit current awareness of innovations, customer processing systems and future expansion plans in diverse industries, in order to respond to increased sales opportunities. The primary responsibility is to consistently increase territory sales and market share in the assigned area and to provide assistance in other areas when required. Norton distributors do most of the maintenance selling, although the incumbent is involved with major accounts and assists the District Sales Manager in special projects.

To sell to the customer, the incumbent analyzes customer manufacturing systems and develops engineering data which supports his/her proposal for either a custom or a standard product to satisfy customer requirements. In many cases, custom products require special moulding and design at Norton, Worcester. The incumbent is recognized for his/her expertise in analyzing accounts and key buying influences that will result in increased sales.

In the course of selling abrasive products through distributors, the Account Manager works closely with distributor sales personnel. He/she accompanies them when calling on accounts and assists in the solution of technical and adminsitrative problems, such as application of Norton products, teaching selling skills, and territory management. Additionally, he/she recommends changes and assists the distributor in the selection and maintenance of adequate stock to meet customer requirements. The incumbent consistently manages orders and inventories to maximize sales and minimize obsolescence and makes recommendations to manufacturing for future sales needs. The Account Manager motivates distributors throughout the territory for maximum effectiveness and continues to develop meetings for the distributors to respond to their needs. In an effort to maintain the most effective sales channel in his/her assigned territory, the incumbent analyzes competitive and present distribution and develops strategies for the territory. He/she develops a continuity plan for distribution to comply with the future needs of the marketplace.

In order to ensure continued market position, the incumbent analyzes market needs and relates them to the effect they will have on the Company's business. He/she develops an action plan and makes recommendations to the District Sales Manager to assist him and the marketing group in the development of strong and objective sales strategies and market programs. The incumbent maintains a consistent and up-to-date awareness of new and existing potentials for abrasive products and is able to serve on advisory councils for the Company.

Figure 9-3. (Continued)

In the course of selling Norton products, the incumbent is in contact with people at various management levels at the customer site. These individuals include engineers, superintendents, purchasing agents, and top management. Usually, more than one of these individuals are involved in the selling process and buying decision, requiring the incumbent to establish and develop personal relationships using his/her excellent entertainment and human relations skills for a maximum return on investment, and to assure that customers gain and maintain a favorable attitude toward Norton Company and its products. The incumbent also has frequent contact with kindred line manufacturers in a variety of industries. Within the Company, the incumbent often deals with Customer Service, Price Administration, Quality Assurance, Product Management and Plant Management. The incumbent is required to travel within the assigned territory. The amount and duration of the travel varies according to the territory. In addition, the Account Manager travels to classes and seminars and to two annual district meetings.

The incumbent requires practically no direct supervision in this position and is capable of handling all the sales or territory problems that occur in his/her area. Frequently, the incumbent provides assistance for the District Sales Manager on critical special assignments in the district. They communicate regularly in order to ensure a constant flow of information about happenings in the district. The incumbent uses an acquired mastery of planning to arrange a time schedule that will ensure the best return on investment. He/she demonstrates expertise in handling and following through on all complaints and in maintaining up-to-date records which will provide for territory continuity. He/she maintains a desirable call level on customers and other personnel and continues to maximize the total sales potential of major accounts.

The position requires successful completion of the Sales Supervisor and Territory Manager positions, and a mastery of the Company's product lines and technical information. The incumbent must have a complete knowledge of industry management practices and must use this knowledge to the best advantage. He/she must display an expertise in all selling, communication, human relations, and entertainment skills, and must also effectively administrate marketing and promotional material and plans and suggest new ideas to sales and marketing personnel. The incumbent is expected to have a mastery of competitive products; to develop strategies to counteract competitive products and marketing trends; and to communicate these strategies to management. High degrees of self-discipline, self-motivation, enthusiasm and professionalism are absolutely essential. The incumbent normally has approximately seven years of selling experience and is a recognized expert in abrasive technology and sales.

Figure 9-3. (Continued)

259

reps, support personnel, and the organization itself, should be made with the same careful analysis that characterizes other capital budgeting decisions. Only with a sound organization in place can an effective selling strategy be designed and executed.

Types of Sales Organizations

There are three distinct types of sales force organizations, although elements of all three types can be found in some organizations that are large enough to permit multiple types of specialization at various levels of the organization. Which type of organization is best for a given firm depends upon the size of the firm and the resources available to it, the nature of the product being sold, the nature of the market, including distinct segments and buying patterns in each, the role assigned to resellers and the relationship of the firm's sales organization to its distributors, the skills, abilities, and knowledge of the people employed in the sales organization, the breadth of the product line, and a host of financial considerations, including profit margins that determine the funds available to support promotional effort.

Geographic organizations are the most common in industrial marketing. A sales rep is assigned responsibility for a given geographic area and promotes all of the company's products to all of the customers located within those geographic boundaries. Other things being equal, the geographic organization is likely to be the most economical, permitting one person to minimize the travel times and distances from customer to customer. Geographic assignments help to insure that all customers in the territory are covered, since there can be no disagreement about which customers should be covered by which sales rep. Measures of market potential are often available on a geographic basis, assisting the process of managerial control.

Geographic organizations also have distinct benefits for the customer. One sales rep for the selling company represents the full range of products offered by the company, permitting more efficient ordering. The product line can be sold as a total system, which can be an important advantage for the customer who wants the benefits of buying interrelated products from the same supplier, including whatever design and technical assistance is required to put together the total product system.

In companies with multiple product lines, often organized as separate product divisions, so-called pooled sales organizations are sometimes found. The pooled sales organization is a form of geo-graphic organization. One sales rep sells the products of two or more separate product divisions to the customers in that area. Pooled sales organizations have all the benefits of geographic specialization, including economic efficiency. They can present a number of man-agement problems, however, including a suspicion by the product manager that the sales force devotes more attention to some prod-ucts at the expense of others, or that the sales force is more qualified to sell certain products to the detriment of others.

Product organizations permit the sales force to specialize in a relatively narrow part of the total product line. Product sales organi-zations can be efficient, if the total sales volume of the company is large enough to permit such specialization and if the selling require-ments for distinct product groups are quite different. Not only may different products require different types of product knowledge and selling skills, but also customer buying patterns for those products may be different enough to be a major reason for product specializa-tion. For example, IBM data processing systems and office equip-ment are sold through distinct marketing and sales organizations. Although many customers could very well purchase both types of products, the two markets are quite distinct, and the buying centers and buying processes, even within the same customer organization, are also likely to be very different.

The major advantage of the product sales organization is the greater product knowledge permitted by specialization, leading to enhanced competitive effectiveness. Ultimately, the sales of each product group can be expected to be somewhat greater because of greater concentration offered by the sales organization. Develop-ment of new markets is generally believed to be more effective when the sales representatives have specific product responsibility.

The disadvantages of product specialization are possibly greater sales expense resulting from two or more sales reps selling in the same geographic area, and the frustration sometimes experienced by industrial buyers because they cannot purchase all of a company's products from one sales representative. Most companies with prod-uct-specialized sales organizations will still find it necessary to have geographic specialization within the product organizations. Because of the organizational duplication that results from multiple product sales organizations, it is likely that not only will sales reps' travel expenses be higher than in a non-product-specialized sales organi-zation, but also other costs of sales management, including recruit-ing, selection, training, and supervision, will be higher. The greater costs of product specialization must be compared with the benefits of specialization that can lead to higher sales and profit margins for each product line.

Market or *customer* specialization is the basis for the third type of sales organization. Like product specialization, it usually is combined with geographic specialization. Market or customer specialization in the sales force is found where distinct customer groups are large enough and have markedly different buying needs and processes to warrant the specialization. If the sales rep must develop detailed knowledge about customers, this form of specialization makes sense. With customer or market specialization, the different sales forces may sell virtually the same products, but the service offering, methods of sale, and buyer-seller relationship may all vary markedly from one customer group to another. For example, aircraft manufacturers usually maintain separate sales organizations for military and commercial sales, and for domestic and foreign customers. To take another example, manufacturers of industrial coatings may have distinct sales organizations for railroads, ship owners, automotive customers, appliance manufacturers, and the packaging industry.

National Account Programs

When a single large customer buys at multiple locations, the marketer may serve that customer through a national account program. Such programs (also called house accounts, corporate accounts, or major accounts) respond to the complexity of the procurement situation but they also introduce a dimension of complexity into the sales organization. One motivator for such arrangements is the customer's desire to receive the benefits of the combined purchasing activity at multiple locations, in the form of enhanced service levels and favorable pricing terms.

A common element of these programs is the need to coordinate activities at the customer's headquarters with those at the local and regional levels. Thus, a national account manager may need to work through local sales representatives who also report through a traditional geographic organization hierarchy. In very large companies, there may be a separate national accounts organization that includes sales reps in geographic territories. In smaller companies, national account programs may consist simply of assigning key executives to liaison roles with major customers.

In an extensive program of research on national account organizations, Shapiro and Moriarty concluded that there is no perfect solution. There are many organizational options, each of which has advantages and disadvantages. However, properly designed, national account programs can be a major source of competitive advantage in terms of superior service and responsiveness to large, strategically important customers. They observed that organization structure *per se* is not the answer, but must be combined with appropriate management systems and processes.[1]

A major responsibility for the national account manager is developing and coordinating the account support necessary from functions other than sales management. For strategic buyer-seller relationships, the success of the national account manager's efforts will determine account satisfaction and performance—and profitability. Support systems for national account management involve eleven management areas: information systems; billing and accounts receivable; field and technical service; logistics; manufacturing/operations management; applications engineering; development, design, and product engineering; finance, especially pricing and credit; legal; control—in the sense of accounting systems for evaluating national account profitability; and marketing. Shapiro and Moriarty concluded that information systems provided the single greatest point of leverage in the relationship, drawing attention to the competitive value of investments in information technology. Finally, their interviews with managers in a variety of firms led them to observe that the success of national account programs depended upon not only having a competent national account organization but also a culture of customer orientation and internal cooperation and top management commitment to the program.[2]

The Organizational Hierarchy

Regardless of the form of specialization (it should be repeated that a combination of geographic and product or market specialization is very common), the sales force will consist of a hierarchy of selling and managerial positions, each of which has a critical role to play in

[1] Benson P. Shapiro and Rowland T. Moriarty, *Organizing the National Account Force,* working paper, Report No. 84-101 (Cambridge, Mass.: Marketing Science Institute, April, 1984).
[2] Benson P. Shapiro and Rowland T. Moriarty, *Support Systems for National Account Management Programs: Promises Made, Promises Kept,* Working Paper, Report No. 84-102 (Cambridge, Mass.: Marketing Science Institute, April, 1984).

the execution of marketing strategy. Typically, the sales representatives report to a first-line supervisor called a district manager. In very large sales organizations, the district manager may have a variety of responsibilities in addition to managing the sales representatives, including managing an office, managing the service organization, representing the company to the community, and so on. If this is true, then day-to-day supervisory tasks may be handled by a sales supervisor.

The number of levels of management in the hierarchy between the sales reps and the chief sales executive will depend upon the size of the organization and is dictated largely by the concept of span of control—the number of persons that a manager can effectively manage. Although hard and fast rules about the optimum span of control are now obsolete in management theory, it is generally believed that six or seven is a reasonable maximum number of people to have reporting to a manager. Wide variation around this norm should be carefully examined for reasonableness.

To illustrate the span of control concept, and to indicate some common sales management job titles, imagine a sales organization with 120 field sales representatives. A span of control of six would give an organization of approximately 20 district managers, reporting to approximately three regional managers. These regional managers would report to a vice president-sales or a national sales manager. District managers in large organizations may have several branch managers reporting to them. The title area manager is sometimes used and can refer to any of several levels of the sales organization, but usually applies to a relatively small geographic area and lower-level management. Company practice in this matter of naming the organizational levels varies widely.

We will be better able to understand the responsibilities of these field sales managers after we have considered the remaining parts of the sales management program and discussed the problems of allocation and deployment.

Recruitment and Selection

The development of an effective industrial sales organization begins with a careful process for recruiting and selecting sales representatives, guided by a carefully prepared description of the sales rep's job. Responsibility for recruiting and selecting sales reps can rest with the district manager, or it may be coordinated through a central sales personnel office. This depends upon the size of the organization, its policies, and the professionalism of its management. Typically, sales force recruiting and selection is part of the local managers' responsibility, although the procedures followed are carefully planned and controlled by a central staff.

The typical industrial sales rep must be fairly well educated and trained. Whether or not technical training, such as an undergraduate degree in engineering, is required depends upon a variety of factors, including the technical complexity of the product and the product knowledge required to sell it effectively. Many companies do rely upon colleges and universities as a major source for new sales talent. Sales trainees are likely to be assigned to product or engineering departments for periods up to two years as part of their training. Regardless of their education, new sales reps will have to be carefully trained to acquire the necessary product knowledge.

There is a kind of tradeoff to consider between the selection process and the training program. A company can reduce its training costs by hiring sales reps with the necessary knowledge and skills. This typically means hiring experienced sales reps from competitors, distributors, and customers. A narrower search is therefore possible, and the company probably will have to pay higher salaries to attract such people. If the company is willing to invest in the necessary training, however, then younger, less experienced, and less expensive personnel can be hired from a broader variety of sources.

A well organized recruiting program will be ongoing and will provide a pool of potential sales personnel. Planned additions to the sales force can be made smoothly, avoiding the expense and error of rushing to replace a lost sales rep or to add a needed new person. Care in the recruiting and selection process can be the most effective way of reducing sales force turnover, which can be a major expense for the firm.

Selection is the process of evaluating the candidates against the criteria provided by the job description. Data with which to make the evaluation can come from three sources—the application form, personal interviews, and tests.

There are many different types of tests available from commercial sources to assist in the sales representative selection process. Such tests can also be developed internally by the hiring company. Among the most popular are tests of interests, intelligence, aptitudes, and knowledge. So-called personality tests, which attempt to measure the emotional, social, and motivational aspects of behavior, although perhaps somewhat useful in particular situations, are generally believed to be the least valid and reliable of all psychological tests. Measures of interests and aptitudes are more straightforward and can be especially helpful when the company has developed a data base that relates job success in the company to particular dimensions measured by such tests. Thus, psychological tests should be used somewhat cautiously and require specific validation within the hiring company.

Application forms can be a very important source of data and should be constructed with great care. Knowledge about education, previous experience, and career objectives are all important in assessing the suitability of an applicant for the sales job and can provide the basis for the personal interview. The objective of the interview should be to permit two-way communication between the applicant and a company representative, so that both can reach suitable assessments of the other. To use the interview for such purposes as seeing the applicant's behavior under pressure or ability to cope with an unexpected question on an unfamiliar topic, is a misuse of the interview. Two or more people can conduct the interviewing in particular situations, but too many people present can put the applicant under excessive pressure. In a good interview, the applicant has the opportunity to ask questions and to learn a good deal about the company, its markets, its products, and the nature of the selling job. A good applicant will have prepared for the interview and will ask questions against this background of information. The two-way nature of communication in an effective job interview can not be overemphasized.

Training

What does the sales rep need to be effective? That question has been answered in the job description. Among the categories of attributes required for effectiveness are product knowledge, company knowledge, customer knowledge, knowledge of markets and competitors, selling skills, and favorable attitudes toward the company, the product, and the job itself. Each of these attributes can be the subject of training. There may be a tendency in industrial firms to emphasize the knowledge component, especially product knowledge, and to underestimate the importance of the other attributes. Some firms have the tendency to fill sales positions with people from the product engineering department, persons with only minimal preparation in the necessary customer knowledge and salesmanship skills.

A traditional and problematic approach to sales representative training is to assign the new recruit to work in the field with an experienced sales rep. This "mother hen" approach has the advantage of immersion in the actual field situation, but it is often conducted by sales reps who are not adequately prepared to assume the responsibilities of being sales trainers. Too often, the approach is essentially one of "watch what I do and do what I do." This has a number of obvious problems, including the fact that it may not be at all clear why the senior sales rep is effective, or even what he is doing. Furthermore, a senior sales rep may not be a very sound model.

A number of consulting firms and commercial organizations now offer very effective sales training programs tailored to the needs of the individual client firm. These organizations usually use a number of advanced and fairly sophisticated techniques, including video-tape feedback, role-playing, programmed instruction, and so on. The professionalism of these firms often justifies the somewhat greater expense involved compared with a do-it-yourself program developed by the firm for its own sales reps.

Supervision and Motivation

Supervision is the process of directing the sales reps in the daily performance of the selling job and of providing them with the necessary resources, including continued training and personal development. Supervision is by definition carried out in the context of the superior-subordinate relationship. Each manager has supervisory responsibility for the people who report directly to her. Supervision includes responsibility for directing the efforts of the sales reps, but it involves a good deal more than that. The functions of the supervisor include interpreting and enforcing company policy, acting as a two-way communication link between the sales reps and higher levels of the organization, establishing standards of performance, both through formal setting of goals and through informal setting of an example, creating a favorable work environment, and providing for continued development of sales personnel.[3]

Motivation is not something that managers do. It is something existing within the individual sales representative. Thus, it is wrong to say that a sales manager motivates the sales rep. Rather, through

[3] Kenneth R. Davis and Frederick E. Webster, Jr., *Sales Force Management: Text and Cases* (New York: Ronald Press Company, 1968), pp. 564–70.

providing a favorable work environment, establishing standards of performance, and so on, the manager can heighten and direct the motivation of the sales people. In the case of monetary compensation and other forms of sales incentives such as contests, the manager is providing incentives designed to stimulate the motivation of the sales reps.

For industrial sales reps, the nature of the work itself can be highly motivating. First, there is the challenge found in all selling of trying to get the sale, of trying to convince the prospective customer to buy the product. Second, there is the nature of the customer problem, the intellectual challenge of understanding the customer's needs, the nature of the buying decision process, and the development of solutions to problems. There is the related intellectual challenge of mastering a body of knowledge relating to the product, the customer's industry, and the competitive environment and applying that knowledge to the particular buying situation.

One of the major features of the typical selling job is that it is conducted by the individual alone in the field, outside the presence of direct supervision. This makes the issues of sales rep motivation and supervision quite distinct from those that characterize other situations where superior and subordinate work in close physical proximity and interact with one another on a regular basis. Because of their physical isolation from supervisors and colleagues, and because of the nature of the work itself, industrial sales reps are known to experience broad fluctuations in morale and motivation, from the lows of repeated negative responses from customers and the frustrations of the selling process to the highs of obtaining major orders and achieving important breakthroughs in solving customer problems.

There have been some interesting studies of supervisory practices and environmental factors that influence sales reps' job performance and satisfaction. One study by Churchill, Ford, and Walker of a cross section of industrial sales reps confirmed many prior findings as well as adding new insights. Several interrelated components of job satisfaction were identified, including the job itself, fellow workers, supervision, company policies and support, pay, opportunities for promotion and advancement, and the nature of the customers called on. Among the conclusions of this study were the following:

> Industrial sales reps' job satisfaction is positively related to the closeness of the supervision that they receive. Sales reps appear to prefer

that their performance be watched and directed closely and carefully. When there is close supervision the sales reps feel that they understand their jobs and company policies better and that they know more clearly what is expected of them. This finding contradicts a belief held by some that sales people prefer independence and autonomy. That is apparently not true for industrial sales reps.

Industrial sales reps' job satisfaction is strongly related to the amount of influence they believe they have in determining the standards by which their performance is evaluated. Likewise, industrial sales reps show more job satisfaction when they feel that they have an input to the determination of company policies and procedures that have an influence on their jobs.

The innovativeness required of the sales rep in doing the job has some positive relationship to satisfaction with the job itself but has a negative relationship with attitudes toward supervision and company policies. Thus, while the sales rep enjoys the challenge of finding his own solutions to customer problems, he still wants close supervision and support.

Job satisfaction is directly related to the extent the sales rep feels she understands clearly what is expected, and how to satisfy those expectations. This conclusion supports the assertions about the importance of the job description that were made early in this chapter.

The relationship between length of time in job and job satisfaction was interesting. Sales reps who had been in the job between five and fifteen years were less satisfied than those who had been industrial sales reps either fewer or more years. The most satisfied had held their jobs two years or less. The reason for the older sales reps' relatively high degree of job satisfaction could not be adequately assessed because of the small size of the sample of people in that experience range. The younger people perceived a good opportunity for promotion and advancement. The major source of job satisfaction was, perhaps, viewing their current jobs as only a means to an end.

Frequency of contact with the supervisor was not an important determinant of job satisfaction. Quality of the relationship was more important than frequency of communication.

Industrial sales reps appear willing to accept direction and authority from a number of departments in the company without a significant negative influence on their job satisfaction. This finding is consistent with the nature of industrial selling—the need for the industrial sales rep to work with many different departments to find and deliver solutions to customer problems—but it is contrary to the commonly

270 MANAGING THE INDUSTRIAL SALES FORCE

accepted notion of the importance of unity of command, the notion that people do not like to take direction from more than one source.[4]

These interesting and important research findings contribute significantly to our understanding of the nature of industrial sales force motivation and performance and underline the critical role played by the first-line supervisor. Churchill, Ford, and Walker have developed a model of sales force motivation and performance in industrial selling from which they derived a total of 37 testable propositions as targets for further research. In this model, a sales rep's performance is seen as a function of her motivation, aptitude, and role perceptions. Each of these three components is influenced by personal, organizational, and environmental variables. The sales rep's motivation is strongly influenced by perceptions of rewards—externally mediated rewards, those controlled by other people, such as pay, security, and recognition, and internally mediated rewards, which the sales rep largely attains for herself, such as feelings of accomplishment, career advancement, personal growth, and self worth. These rewards interact with the sales rep's role perceptions (and the degree of role uncertainty and conflict) to determine job satisfaction. Unclearly defined role assignments and a perception of conflicting expectations among customers and supervisors can create psychological discomfort and significantly reduce job satisfaction. This theoretical formulation was based in part on the findings about job satisfaction mentioned earlier. A thorough testing of the many propositions developed from this model will require extensive research.[5]

Compensation

A sales rep's compensation usually consists of some combination of three types of pay—salary, commission, and bonus. Compensation plans can be found that range from all salary to all commission, but the typical pay plan includes some elements of both fixed and variable compensation. For all sales reps, both for industrial products and for consumer products, a very crude estimate of the aver-

[4] Gilbert A. Churchill, Jr., Neil M. Ford, and Orville C. Walker, Jr., "Organizational Climate and Job Satisfaction in the Salesforce," *Journal of Marketing Research*, **XIII**, 4 (November, 1976), 323–32.
[5] Orville C. Walker, Jr., Gilbert A. Churchill, Jr., and Neil M. Ford, "Motivation and Performance in Industrial Selling: Present Knowledge and Needed Research," *Journal of Marketing Research*, **XIV**, 2 (May, 1977), 156–68.

age ratio of fixed to variable compensation might be about 65 percent fixed and 35 percent commission and bonus. In industrial sales compensation plans, salary is generally a much larger part of the total package, say 75 to 90 percent. Straight salary plans, perhaps with a small bonus tied to particular performance objectives, are not uncommon.

To reward the sales rep with commissions is believed to be valuable in providing an incentive, stimulating motivation to make the sale, and tying compensation directly to achievement. The nature of the industrial selling job argues against a large variable component in the sales compensation package. Several factors reduce the usefulness and effectiveness of commissions as part of the industrial sales compensation package.

First, the nature of the buying process is such that there is often a long time lag between selling effort and sales results. The sales rep may be doing the job extremely well without a sales result for months or even years. Thus, it can be unfair to tie compensation directly to sales results. Second, many factors other than the sales rep's own efforts at a particular point in time contribute to the sales result, including previous sales effort, product quality, pricing, and distribution. Other parts of the promotional program include advertising and promotional literature of all kinds, customer service, and so on. A sales rep might work diligently for months only to lose the sale on the basis of a lower bid by competition. Third, it may be inappropriate for the sales rep to actually push for an order at a given point. Incentive compensation can cause the sales rep to be too aggressive and to attempt closure of the sale before the buying process and the selling job have been completed.

However, some modest amount of incentive compensation probably has value in most situations. It can stimulate the sales rep to exert incremental effort in some situations, and it can serve to focus his attention on the ultimately desired result of all effort—creating a sale. The nature of the variable component of compensation can be either a commission, paid as a percentage of sales, or a bonus in the form of a lump sum payment for the achievement of certain specified objectives. Thus, bonuses can be related to the opening of new accounts, achieving some predetermined total level of sales, either by the sales rep individually or by the district as a whole, maintaining a specified level of gross margin contribution, and so on.

Some companies attempt to achieve balanced selling across the product line by offering commissions or bonuses related to the mix of products sold. The specific methods for doing this vary widely, from offering variable commissions—with higher commissions on more profitable products or on products that are believed to be harder to sell—to bonuses that require achieving some minimum sales level for each and all of the product lines.

The particular compensation plan used by a company should reflect specific objectives for sales activity. Salary, usually the most important element of the compensation package, is paid for the performance of specific duties that may or may not produce a definable sales result. The higher the salary component, the more control the sales manager has over the sales reps. Sales reps will be reluctant to perform tasks that do not produce a more or less immediate sales result, if they are paid primarily on commissions. Thus, salary rewards the sales rep for developing new accounts, for developing new markets, for introducing new products, for gathering market information, for representing the customer at the factory, and doing all of those other important tasks that do not yield immediate and measurable sales revenue results.

The objective of any sound sales compensation plan is to attract and retain qualified sales reps and to reward them fairly for their efforts. The level of pay required to achieve these objectives is a function of the amount of education, training, and experience represented by the individual and of competitive conditions in the local labor market and in the industry employing the rep. The method of pay should reflect the nature of the job and the objectives of the company.

One way of thinking about the design of the sales compensation program is to list the sales rep's tasks down the side of a matrix and the components of the compensation scheme (salary, commission, bonus) across the top. Each component of the job can be assessed in terms of whether fixed or variable compensation is most appropriate as a reward for that task. Such an analysis can also help to assess the appropriate balance between fixed and variable compensation. It is important that the system be clear enough for the sales reps to understand how it works and how they will be rewarded. The sales reps must see the connection between their efforts and the rewards provided by the system.

The administration of any compensation plan requires an evaluation system to determine the extent to which the sales rep has performed the tasks for which she is to be rewarded.

Evaluation and Control

Specific and measurable objectives are the key to an effective and fair system of sales force evaluation, control, and rewards. Evaluation is the process of comparing actual performance with previously established standards. Control is feedback of the evaluation results to the operating system so that adjustments can be made to better obtain the objectives. Thus, evaluation is backward-looking but the control process is essentially forward-looking.

The standards by which sales reps are evaluated can take two general forms. First, there are numerical standards, sales quotas that are based on sales forecasts and measures of market potential, for entire geographic areas, for specific accounts, for customer groupings, by products, and so forth. Second, there are more subjective standards and objectives, established by the sales manager in consultation with the sales rep. Such qualitative objectives might include developing improved product knowledge, attending a sales training seminar, developing a stated number of new accounts, learning more about competitive activities, and so on.

In consumer markets, measures of market potential relate to the buying power of consumers in that geographic area. Market potential is relatively easy to estimate in consumer markets, because the necessary data on population, income, other household characteristics, and total retail sales, are quite readily available from governmental and commercial sources. In industrial markets, the estimates of market potential are likely to be based on such data as number of firms in target industries (defined by S.I.C. code), number of employees per firm, sales volume of potential customers, or other measures of production activity. Such data are not always available in secondary sources and the company may have to spend for market research or depend on its sales force to gather the necessary information. Industry trade associations, as well as governmental agencies, are also important sources of information on market potential. These variables will have to be studied, using regression analysis and other statistical techniques to find the relationship with demand for the firm's products.

Often, an aggregate sales forecast for the company as a whole is allocated to geographic territories according to the percentage of market potential each territory is believed to represent. A common scheme is for the national sales manager to allocate the forecast among regions, for the regional sales manager to determine the portion of the sales forecast assigned to each district, and for the district manager to set quotas for each of his sales reps. At all stages of this process, it is important that the people receiving the quotas feel that they have participated in the setting of the quotas, by providing information and in discussion and negotiation.[6]

A system of performance appraisal and management by objectives (MBO) can also be a valuable aid in the development of the sales rep and the sales organization. In this process, the sales manager conducts an in-depth discussion with the sales rep about the latter's needs and goals for the coming period and how these relate to the company's needs, goals, and plans. The results of the discussion are put into writing and become the basis for evaluating the forthcoming period's activities. At the end of the period (at least annually and sometimes semi-annually or even quarterly), the sales manager and the sales rep once again have a discussion in which the sales rep's performance is evaluated against those previously defined objectives, and new goals are set for the coming period. Needless to say, frank and open discussion is a necessary basis for the operation of such a system of MBO and performance appraisal. The sales manager must be trained to use such a system and *his* performance evaluation must be based in part on how well he is able to execute this responsibility.

A system of performance appraisal and MBO is often part of a total personnel development and career planning system intended to identify and develop management potential within the ranks of the sales reps, as well as to insure that all sales people are evaluated and rewarded fairly. Without a career planning system, the sales representatives can become trapped in their jobs and advancement opportunities can be significantly reduced.[7]

SALES EFFORT ALLOCATION

The assignment of sales reps to territories, products, and specific accounts is a major responsibility for the industrial sales manager and requires a large measure of analytical ability, if it is to be done properly. The outcome of the allocation decision determines the efficiency of the sales operation—the relationship between effort

---

[6] Francis E. Hummel, *Market and Sales Potentials* (New York: The Ronald Press Co., 1961) remains an excellent reference on this subject of measures of industrial market potential and their uses.

[7] Andrall E. Pearson, "Sales Power Through Planned Careers," *Harvard Business Review,* **44,** 1 (January-February, 1966), 105–16.

and results, inputs and outputs. It also is a major determinant of the effectiveness of the sales operation, the extent to which it achieves its objectives.

The conditions for optimal allocation of sales effort will be familiar to anyone who has studied basic economics. An optimal allocation is one in which the marginal rates of response to sales effort are equal among the units receiving effort. In other words, shifting effort from one account to another, from one territory to another, or from one product to another will not increase the total response and may in fact decrease it. In order to make this determination, the manager obviously needs some assessment of how customers and combinations of customers respond to sales effort.

The Sales Response Function

At the heart of the analytical problem facing the sales manager is the need to estimate the relationship between sales effort (almost always measured by number of sales calls) and sales results. This is obviously an extremely difficult problem, especially in those buying situations so often characteristic of industrial markets where sales effort precedes sales results by several months. Conceptually, one can consider the sales response of individual customers or of larger aggregates of customers, such as geographic territories. The dependent variable in the relationship can take many forms, such as total dollar or unit sales during the specified time period, the percentage of a given customer's requirements that the seller is supplying at a point in time, the probability of obtaining an order on the next sales call, and so on.

The sales manager may think about the sales response function on an unstructured, intuitive basis, or the problem may be approached in a highly analytical fashion, perhaps assisted by a staff of management scientists.[8] Regardless of the degree of analytical sophistication, the manager must make some estimate of the sales response function in order to make allocation decisions. A well trained sales manager will be able to think about alternative mathematical formulations of the sales response function and is likely to be able to visualize the process of terms of the probabilities of certain out-

[8] For a review of the problems and opportunities represented by cooperation between sales managers and management scientists, and for a review of several applications of management science to selling strategy, see David B. Montgomery and Frederick E. Webster, Jr., "Application of Operations Research to Personal Selling Strategy," *Journal of Marketing*, 32, 1 (January, 1968), 50–57.

comes. Sales response functions can be estimated by statistical analysis of the relationship between past effort and results, or an experiment can be conducted under controlled conditions in which sales effort is systematically varied among like customers or with the same customers over a period of time. The differences in sales response can be carefully monitored and analyzed. The resulting knowledge will be very valuable and should be worth the expense involved. Lagged relationships between dependent and independent variables, that is, models in which sales response in a given period is expressed as a function of sales effort, not only in the current period, but also in previous periods, will probably prove more accurate than single period models.

In situations where the lag between sales effort and sales results is too long to permit any reasonably accurate measurement of the relationship, the sales manager may wish to consider substitution of some intermediate measure of results rather than sales, such as changes in levels of customer awareness or attitudes. Hughes has proposed a method for obtaining such measures.[9]

The CALLPLAN Model

One rather sophisticated model of the sales effort allocation problem has been developed and refined by Lodish.[10] The CALLPLAN model is an example of the decision calculus approach developed by Little.[11] In it the model user's own subjective judgments are an important input to the interactive, computer-based analysis. Thus, the manager can assess the implications of various assumptions and estimates of probabilities. (The decision calculus approach was also described earlier in our discussion of pricing decisions and a contract bidding model.)

The CALLPLAN model asks the sales rep and/or the sales manager to estimate how customers will respond to various sales call frequencies. The model also considers travel time between customers, time per call, and account profitability. The frequency of calls during a stated period (i.e., x calls per month, quarterly, or

[9] G. David Hughes, "A New Tool for Sales Managers," *Journal of Marketing Research*, I, 2 (May, 1964), 32–38.

[10] Leonard M. Lodish, "CALLPLAN: An Interactive Salesman's Call Planning System," *Management Science*, 18, 4, Part II (December, 1971), 25–40.

[11] John D. C. Little, "Models and Managers: The Concept of a Decision Calculus," *Management Science*, 16, 8 (April, 1970), 466–85.

most typically, annually) is the decision variable in the CALLPLAN model. A distinction is made between present customers and prospects, and the sales representative or manager specifies the maximum and minimum sales calls to be made on any account during the period. The user of the model must estimate the response function, first in general form for all accounts $[r_i(x_i)]$ and then with an account adjustment factor a_i for each type of account, reflecting profit contribution of the product mix purchased by the account or management priorities by account type. The objective is to maximize $\Sigma_{i=1}^{I} a_i r_i(x_i)$ for all I accounts.

A given sales rep's territory is divided into J geographic subareas, representing as closely as possible areas covered on the same trip from home or office; g_i designates the area in which a given account is located. In a specified area, it is assumed that an average sales call requires an amount of time equal to t_i. Each trip to an area j is assumed to take an average of u_j time units (usually expressed as hours or quarter hours) and to cost c_j in out-of-pocket expenses. NT_j is the total number of trips made to area j during an average effort period, and e is the number of effort periods in each response period. The number of trips made to an area during a response period is therefore e times NT_j. The objective of the model is then to find call frequencies for all accounts (I) in order to maximize z, the total adjusted sales from all accounts and prospects, minus travel costs over the response period where

$$z = \Sigma_{i=1}^{I} a_i r_i(x_i) - e\Sigma_{j-1}^{J} NT_j c_j$$

The constraint on total time available for selling and travel T is expressed

$$\Sigma_{i=1}^{I} t_i x_i + \Sigma_{j=1}^{J} NT_j u_j \leqslant T$$

The number of trips to an area is a function of the number of calls made to each account in the area

$$NT_j = \text{Max}\{x_I \text{ such that } g_j{}^{=j}\} \text{ for } j = 1, \ldots, J$$

and the maxima and minima on calls per account per effort period are expressed as

$$\text{Min}_i \leqslant x_i \leqslant \text{Max}_i \text{ for } i = 1, \ldots, I$$

After formulating the problem in this fashion, Lodish was able to develop a very efficient incremental search procedure that finds a very good solution to the problem, although the procedure can not guarantee that the solution is optimal in the strict sense. Sales reps using the model can assess the frequencies, time per call, travel times, and so on. The significance of different assumptions about response functions can also be assessed.

The results of the analysis can be used to realign sales territories into more homogeneous and manageable groupings of accounts that permit better allocation of sales rep's time. Lodish developed a mathematical programming model for integrating the CALLPLAN analysis into a restructuring of sales territories and reported that five firms had used it successfully.[12] Other scholars have reported successful development and implementation of extensions of the Lodish model. Continued refinement and elaboration can be anticipated.[13]

It is obvious that the development of the CALLPLAN model was a major step forward in the field of industrial sales force allocation. The success of the model in actual use demonstrates the viability of the decision calculus approach. The approach overcomes many of the problems inherent in the application of management science and computers to actual managerial decision making. Successful use of such models still requires a good dose of managerial judgment and common sense.

Assigning Sales Reps to Territories and Accounts

The allocation problem has been cast in quantitative terms, the number of calls to make on an account in a given period, the length of the call, the cost, travel time, and so on. Implicit in this approach was an assumption that all sales reps are equally effective and interchangeable. After assessing the allocation problem and coming up with reasonably optimal allocations of time and effort, the manager must make further adjustments to reflect the strengths and weaknesses of individual sales people, their experience, training, preferences, and so on. This is the assignment problem. It becomes

[12] Leonard M. Lodish, "Sales Territory Alignment to Maximize Profit," *Journal of Marketing Research*, **XII**, 1 (February, 1975), 30–36.
[13] Andris A. Zoltners, "Integer Programming Models for Sales Territory Alignment to Maximize Profit," *Journal of Marketing Research*, **XIII**, 4 (November, 1976), 426–30.

especially important in strategic buyer-seller partnerships and national account programs.

A good deal of judgment is required to assign sales reps to accounts, but a somewhat more rigorous analysis may help to trace the consequences of these judgments. Some sales reps will get along with some customers better than others, and customers may express strong preferences to the sales manager to have certain sales reps call on them. A sales rep's education, job experience, and training may make her especially qualified to work with a given customer.

Once again, Lodish has addressed this problem with an extension of the CALLPLAN model. In this extension, the manager makes judgments about the effectiveness of each sales rep with each account and incorporates these judgments into the analysis of call frequencies and territory alignment. In addition to any questions about the fit of the sales rep's personality with that of key people in the customer buying center, the manager can assess the importance of a large number of customer characteristics, including size, composition of the buying center, technical sophistication and complexity, and industry affiliation. In the Lodish model, the sales manager makes these estimates of efficiency for each sales rep and for each account in a large matrix. Average effectiveness with an account is given a 1.0 weight, and downward and upward adjustments are made in a range of 0.0 to 2.0. The solution involves a combination of mathematical programming and linear programming procedures. After a solution is found, the manager can adjust his judgments, shift some accounts, and assess the resulting changes in profitability. The model has been successfully implemented in a sales force selling to advertisers, advertising agencies, and media buying services.[14]

ACCOUNT MANAGEMENT

Buyer-seller relationships in industrial markets tend to be long-term affairs. The purchasing manager is concerned with developing vendors on whom he can depend. The manager must insure a reliable supply of quality products and services when needed. Similarly, the amount of selling effort required to attract a new customer, frequently taking that customer away from the competi-

[14] Leonard M. Lodish, "Assigning Salesmen to Accounts to Maximize Profit," *Journal of Marketing Research*, **XIII**, 4 (November, 1976), 440–44.

tion, often means that a long-term relationship is necessary to justify the costs of account development. For these reasons, the immediate sale is not likely to be as important as the quality of the relationship between buyer and seller over the long run.

Thus, sales reps should view their task as one of developing and maintaining long-term relationships, not just making the sale. Thinking in these terms, sales managers need to develop a fairly complex set of criteria for evaluating sales reps. In addition to measures of sales volume, the manager needs to consider how effectively the sales reps have planned their activities with major customers, how well they understand their buying organizations and decision-making processes, and how well they represent that customer at the factory in order that the full range of company capabilities can be brought to bear in finding solutions to customer problems.[15]

Automation, initially identified solely with manufacturing and logistics, has moved into industrial sales and marketing, especially in the form of *telemarketing*, defined simply as the use of the telephone to contact customers and prospects. For some companies, telemarketing is an extension of, and support for, the field sales organization. For others, it is a distinct marketing channel. Telemarketing also requires the use of computers to maintain lists of prospects and customers, to provide sales and service personnel with up-to-the-minute information about product availability and pricing, to present selling scripts to calling personnel, and for order entry. Other types of sales and marketing automation include support systems for sales reps and managers such as call reporting, expense reporting, order entry, inventory checking, and lead tracking, as well as direct mail and fulfillment systems, and analytical and reporting tools for sales and marketing managers.

Moriarty and Swartz have developed the concept of marketing and sales productivity (MSP) systems, which they see as offering two sets of benefits: (1) improving efficiency by automating repetitive support tasks such as answering requests for product literature; and (2) reducing the time sales people spend on non-selling tasks like order entry and call scheduling. Among the industrial marketers they report as developing successful MSP systems are Xerox, Excelan (a marketer of circuit boards and software), Hewlett-Packard,

---

[15] Benson P. Shapiro, "Manage the Customer. Not Just the Sales Force," *Harvard Business Review,* **52,** 5 (September–October, 1974), 127–36.

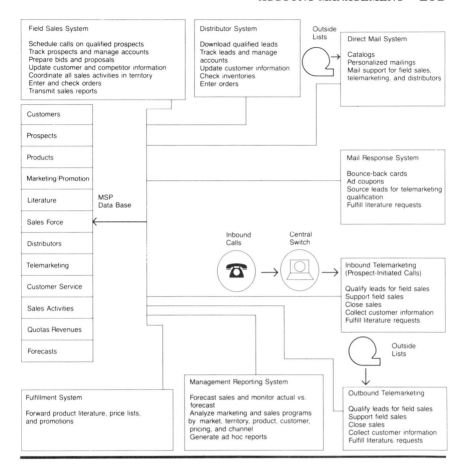

Field Sales System

Schedule calls on qualified prospects
Track prospects and manage accounts
Prepare bids and proposals
Update customer and competitor information
Coordinate all sales activities in territory
Enter and check orders
Transmit sales reports

Distributor System

Download qualified leads
Track leads and manage accounts
Update customer information
Check inventories
Enter orders

Outside Lists

Direct Mail System

Catalogs
Personalized mailings
Mail support for field sales, telemarketing, and distributors

MSP Data Base

Customers
Prospects
Products
Marketing/Promotion
Literature
Sales Force
Distributors
Telemarketing
Customer Service
Sales Activities
Quotas Revenues
Forecasts

Mail Response System

Bounce-back cards
Ad coupons
Source leads for telemarketing qualification
Fulfill literature requests

Inbound Calls → Central Switch →

Inbound Telemarketing (Prospect-Initiated Calls)

Qualify leads for field sales
Support field sales
Close sales
Collect customer information
Fulfill literature requests

Outside Lists

Management Reporting System

Forecast sales and monitor actual vs. forecast
Analyze marketing and sales programs by market, territory, product, customer, pricing, and channel
Generate ad hoc reports

Fulfillment System

Forward product literature, price lists, and promotions

Outbound Telemarketing

Qualify leads for field sales
Support field sales
Close sales
Collect customer information
Fulfill literature requests

Figure 9-4. An integrated MSP system for an office automation company. [Source: *Rowland T. Moriarty and Gordon S. Swartz, "Automation to Boost Sales and Marketing,"* Harvard Business Review, *67, 1 (January–February, 1989), 106.*] **Reprinted by permission of** Harvard Business Review. *Copyright © 1989 by the President and Fellows of Harvard College; all rights reserved.*

and Chevron Chemical.[16] Figure 9-4 illustrates an integrated MSP system.

A common application of MSP systems is seen in the increasing use of laptop computers by sales reps to access the company's data base on product availability, applications information, production

[16] Rowland T. Moriarty and Gordon S. Swartz, "Automation to Boost Sales and Marketing," *Harvard Business Review,* **67,** 1 (January-February, 1989), 100–108.

schedules, price lists, customer information, and more. Often, distributors are also tied into the system. Both sales reps and distributors can enter orders directly and give customers firm commitments on availability and delivery. The length of the order cycle is usually shortened dramatically, reducing costs and improving service levels.

MSP systems are not cheap and they require sophisticated information management skills. Moriarty and Swartz estimated the cost of hardware and software at $4,000 to $7,000 per sales rep, and direct mail and telemarketing systems at $30,000 to $100,000 per installation, with further significant investments required to integrate all of these pieces into an MSP system. A fully integrated and smoothly functioning system might cost $10,000 or more per sales rep, but can be both a key success factor and a barrier to competitive entry. Such investments in information technology have become as important as investments in manufacturing capacity as sources of competitive advantage in the industrial markets of the 1990's.[17]

The combination of telephone, telecommunications, and database technologies not only reduces the costs of direct selling and account maintenance but also frees up sales reps for creative selling, problem solving, and new account solicitation. A Conference Board report highlighted multiple benefits in reducing sales costs, diagnosing sales activity, qualifying leads generated by advertising and direct mail, and converting prospects to customers.[18] Among the leading companies that have reported successful telemarketing program are Hercules, Ingersoll-Rand, SPSS, DuPont, Pinkerton's, General Electric, 3M, and Digital Equipment.

Customers seem to appreciate the convenience and efficiency of being able to place routine orders via telephone on a regularized basis rather than having to commit time to a sales rep's visit, as well as the opportunity to initiate the call when necessary. This allows the field rep to concentrate on non-routine problem solving and developing new business with both new and established accounts. Costs of telemarketing calls have been estimated at $18 vs. $400 for a

---

[17] Rashi Glazer, *Marketing and the Changing Information Environment*, Working Paper, Report No. 89-108 (Cambridge, Mass.: Marketing Science Institute, March, 1989), p. 43.

[18] Earl L. Bailey (ed.), A Growing Role for Business-to-Business Telemarketing, Conference Board Research Report No. 912 (New York: The Conference Board, Inc., 1988).

personal sales visit. Telemarketing also usually improves service quality and enhances the value of the buyer-seller relationship.[19]

SUMMARY

The essential nature of the sales rep's activities and the importance of long-term buyer-seller relationships place a major responsibility on the sales manager in the industrial company. He is responsible for generating sales in the short term in order to reach quota and for developing an effective sales organization that maximizes the opportunities for profitable sales growth over the long run.

Among the critical decisions made by sales managers are those relating to the role of personal selling in the marketing mix and the specification of the sales rep's responsibilities and the required abilities that results from this definition of the selling role. These specifications are formalized in a job description that serves as the basis for decisions relating to recruitment, selection, training, supervision, evaluation, compensation, and control. The field sales manager must serve as a first-line supervisor and as a communication link between the sales reps and higher levels of the sales and marketing organization. She must represent the company to the district and to the local community, and must analyze the local market and plan market coverage. The field sales manager may also have major responsibility for calling on certain accounts. When this is the case, there is a significant danger that the manager will focus attention on the short-term problems relating to generating sales from those accounts and will tend to overlook the longer term responsibilities for developing the sales reps and the organization as a whole.

The allocation of sales effort to accounts, to products, and to territories requires that the manager think analytically about how customers respond to sales effort. Some relatively recent developments in the application of management science techniques to sales effort allocation and territory design were reviewed as aids to managerial decision making. These rigorous approaches were seen to extend management judgment, not to serve as a substitute for it. The problems of determining the optimal call frequency, of design-

[19] Harry Davis, Richard Huether, and Terry Brophy, "Optimizing the Telemarketing Resource," in Jakki Mohr (ed.), *Communicating with Industrial Customers*, Conference Summary, Report No. 89-112 (Cambridge, Mass.: Marketing Science Institute, August, 1989), pp. 9–11.

ing sales territories, and of assigning sales reps to specific accounts were examined. These are the details of the successful implementation of industrial marketing strategy.

Finally, it was stressed that industrial selling requires a long-term view in which the sales representative's and the sales manager's responsibilities are defined as managing the buyer-seller relationship, not just making the sale. Information technology as employed in sales and marketing productivity systems is a key to enhanced sales force effectiveness and efficiency and improved service levels for the customer.

Bibliography

Beswick, Charles A., and David W. Cravens, "A Multistage Decision Model for Salesforce Management," *Journal of Marketing Research,* **XIV,** 2 (May, 1977), 135–44.

Churchill, Gilbert A., Jr., Neil M. Ford, and Orville C. Walker, Jr., *Sales Force Management* (Homewood, Ill.: Richard D. Irwin, Inc., 1981).

Hughes, G. David, "Computerized Sales Management," *Harvard Business Review,* **61,** 2 (March-April, 1983), 102–12.

Moriarty, Rowland T., and Gordon S. Swartz, "Automation to Boost Sales and Marketing," *Harvard Business Review,* **67,** 1 (January-February, 1989), 100–108.

Webster, Frederick E., Jr., *Field Sales Management* (New York: John Wiley & Sons, Inc., 1983).

10 Industrial Marketing Communications

Industrial marketing communications are a mix of personal and impersonal communications aimed at the industrial buyer. They include personal selling, catalogues and product literature, advertising, direct mail, trade shows, publicity and public relations, and promotional novelties and gifts. The effect of any one of these promotional tools is a function of its interaction with the others, although each has a distinct role to play in moving the potential customer from unawareness of the company and its products through several stages of the buying decision process to buying action. The industrial marketing strategist must plan communications strategy with a keen eye on the specific functions of each element of the communications mix and the interactions, or synergy, among them.

The reader is by now more than familiar with the fact that industrial marketing communication strategies are very likely to have personal selling as the principal component. The reasons for this have been thoroughly presented in earlier chapters. In the present chapter, we will look at those other elements of the marketing communications mix that are primarily impersonal, such as advertising and direct mail, although some others, such as trade shows, are still essentially personal communication. But, because personal selling is such an important part of the industrial marketing communications mix, we will often be evaluating a given form of communication primarily in terms of its interaction with the personal selling function. Thus, the concept of an integrated, interacting mix of communications is the central thread through the analysis that follows.

THE HIERARCHY OF EFFECTS

The purpose of the marketing communications program is to move the potential buyer from unawareness to buying action. There are a number of ways of characterizing the mental stages through which individual members of the buying center must pass in order to get to the buying action stage. In Chapter 2, we examined an eight-stage model of the buying decision, beginning with need recognition and ending with performance feedback and evaluation. This eight-stage model is most appropriate as a description of organizational decision making, that is, of the buying center. For purposes of communication strategy, however, we must think in terms of the changes in the *individual's* levels of awareness and attitudes, and of specific buying behaviors that are the ultimate objective of marketing communication.

The marketing communication literature usually talks about the buyer's mental stages as a hierarchy of effects of communications, although there is some disagreement about the nature of the hierarchy and whether the steps are valid descriptions of actual buyer behavior. One hierarchy-of-effects model is the adoption process model (awareness, interest, evaluation, trial, and adoption) presented in the discussion of the new product adoption decision process in Chapter 6. There we noted that the adoption process model is a description of the decision stages of individuals in the buying center, not of the buying center in aggregate.

Another description of the hierarchy of effects is a six-stage model proposed by Lavidge and Steiner: (1) awareness; (2) knowledge; (3) liking; (4) preference; (5) conviction; and (6) purchase.[1] This six-stage model is consistent with a classical psychological model that divides behavior into three components—a *cognitive* component (awareness and knowledge), dealing with the rational, knowing, intellectual parts of behavior; an *affective* component (liking and preference), dealing with the emotional or feeling aspects of behavior; and a *conative* or motivational component (conviction and purchase), describing the striving aspects of behavior, in which objects are treated as positive or negative goals. Howard and Sheth used a similar formulation in their theory of buyer behavior: (1) attention; (2) comprehension; (3) attitudes; (4) intention; and (5) purchase behavior.[2]

Each of these models is a hierarchy-of-effects model. For our purposes, it is the similarities among the models, not the differences, that are important. All describe response to communication in terms of a progression of mental stages from initial awareness (cognition) through the development of favorable attitudes (preference) to buying action (motivation). Those who dispute the validity

[1] Robert J. Lavidge and Gary A. Steiner, "A Model for Predictive Measurements of Advertising Effectiveness," *Journal of Marketing*, **25**, 6 (October, 1961), 59–62.
[2] John A. Howard and Jagdish N. Sheth, *The Theory of Buyer Behavior* (New York: John Wiley & Sons, Inc., 1969).

of the hierarchy-of-effects models do so on two grounds, one essentially managerial and the other theoretical and empirical. The managerial critics argue that the model has limited usefulness for management, since only the final stages of purchase action are relevant communication goals. This viewpoint is basically wrong. This will become clear when we discuss the matter of communication objectives. The theoretical and empirical critics have a somewhat more solid argument. They point out that there is no firm empirical support, and no particular theoretical justification, for the assertion of the model that awareness leads to the development of attitudes, favorable or unfavorable, nor that favorable attitudes will lead to buying action. Thus, they dispute the implied causative relationships in the model.

In response to those who criticize the hierarchy-of-effects models on theoretical and empirical grounds, however, it must be said that the model really does not assert that movement through the various stages is an inevitable process. In fact, any marketing practitioner is keenly aware that making people familiar with a company and its products by no means leads inevitably to buying action. But awareness is a necessary precondition to the development of favorable attitudes, and favorable attitudes are usually, but not always, necessary before buying action can occur. Each stage in the hierarchy of effects presents its own challenges to the marketer as its attempts to move potential customers to actual buying behavior. The basic value of the hierarchy-of-effects models resides in their ability to help marketing communication strategists think clearly about the objectives of specific communication tools and how they will evaluate the results of communication effort. This brings us to the central question of objectives.

MARKETING COMMUNICATION OBJECTIVES

The question of objectives is central in the formulation of marketing communication strategy, as it is in all strategic decision making. The concept of a hierarchy of effects becomes an extremely helpful analytical tool for developing industrial marketing communication strategy. The planning of communication effort and, equally important, the subsequent evaluation of that effort as a prelude to the next round of planning, depend heavily on the precise statement of communication goals in terms that permit measurement of accomplishment.

The managerial critics of the hierarchy-of-effects models are correct to this extent—the ultimate objective of all marketing activity is to create a sale. They are fundamentally wrong, however, when they argue that the specific, operational objective of each communication activity should be to create a sale. The nature of the industrial buying decision process is such that this would be an unreasonable objective for each and every sales call, advertisement, direct mail piece, and so on. In fact, as we have argued before, it may be a strategic error to try to create a specific sales result with every sales call or other communication.

Should a given marketing communication strategy emphasize awareness, attitudes, or buying action? The answer obviously depends upon many factors. For a new product, the problem may be to get awareness. For established products, the problem is more often to develop favorable attitudes or to overcome unfavorable attitudes. However, whether for new products or old, seldom are buying action (sales) objectives appropriate for mass communications, such as advertising and publicity.

The first step in the development of marketing communication objectives is for the marketing strategist to define the communication problem. The role of communication within the overall marketing strategy must be specified. This problem-definition process can often be assisted by the collection of data on existing levels of awareness and attitudes among customers and potential customers. Without such data on predispositions within the relevant market segments, the formulation of communication strategy is a case of seat-of-the-pants decision making. Unless clear, quantitative benchmarks can be established, evaluation will be difficult, if not impossible. With such data, the marketing communications strategist can specify objectives, such as "to increase awareness of our product from 17 percent to 65 percent among process engineers in the chemical industry."

Specific communications media will be more effective in accomplishing some communication objectives and less effective in others. As we saw in our discussion in Chapter 6 of the differential use of media by members of the buying center according to stage in the new product adoption decision process, advertising may be most effective in creating awareness. Personal sources of communication become more important in the later stages of the process. Because media effectiveness depends upon stage in the decision process, and because buyers have different habits of media exposure and usage, a mix of marketing communications is required in almost every marketing situation. Thus, the marketing communication strategist must think about two kinds of objectives—objectives for the overall marketing communication strategy (which will indicate a reliance on some media more than others) and objectives for each specific medium during the planning period. For example, the primary objective of the total communication program may be to create a preference for the company's products over those of a specified competitor. This indicates a heavy reliance on the field sales force, and some use of industry trade journals and attendance at key trade shows. A secondary objective might be to create awareness among prospective customers and the establishment of a market presence in some new market segments. The latter calls for advertising in general business media, and some use of direct mail.

THE INDUSTRIAL MARKETING COMMUNICATIONS MIX

An integrated approach to the development of marketing communication strategy has been advocated in the literature for many years.[3] This position is based on the fact that different modes of communication have specific advantages, and that they interact with one another in such a way that the strategist must consider those interactions in order to develop the most effective and efficient total mix of promotional variables. Furthermore, it is obvious that most marketers do in fact use a blend of promotional weapons. Therefore, the concept of the communications mix is not a great deal more than a recognition of the obvious fact that the mix is more than the sum of its parts and should be planned and managed accordingly. One additional feature of the marketing communication approach is the integration of knowledge about buyer behavior, and especially about the effects of communication, into the decision-making process.

That is easier said than done, however, for to make the concept of the communications mix operational, the strategist must be able to isolate the effects of each communication element, as well as the interactions among them. This calls for a sophisticated analytical approach, based on careful measurement of communication effects.

[3] See, for example, Frederick E. Webster, Jr., *Marketing Communication: Modern Promotional Strategy* (New York: The Ronald Press Co., 1971); Edgar Crane, *Marketing Communications: A Behavioral Approach to Men, Messages, and Media* (John Wiley & Sons, Inc., 1965), and Michael L. Ray, "A Decision Sequence Analysis of Developments in Marketing Communication," *Journal of Marketing*, **37**, 1 (January, 1973), 119–24.

An optimal mix of communications for a given total level of expenditure is one in which the marginal response rates for all are equal. As in the case of sales force allocation decisions, the marketing communications strategist needs to know the response function describing how customers respond to each element of expenditure. The dependent variable may be some measure of awareness, attitudes, or sales.

Information Sources Used by Industrial Buyers

In Chapter 6, we reviewed some research on the use of information by buyers during the new product adoption process. In general, that research showed that impersonal sources are more important at earlier stages of the process whereas personal sources become more important for evaluation, trial, and adoption. Moriarty and Spekman have reported a study that looked at buyer's uses of information during the buying process in general, as opposed to the adoption process narrowly defined, but produced similar conclusions.[4] They studied the relative importance of 14 different information sources for the purchase of non-intelligent data terminals. At least two respondents were surveyed from each of 319 companies. On a scale of 1 (not important) to 6 (most important), these sources were ranked as follows:

	Mean	Standard Deviation
Information systems department	5.011	1.257
Using department	4.688	1.406
Top management	4.213	1.528
Salespeople from manufacturer	3.862	1.454
Actual terminal operators	3.767	1.543
Sales literature	3.446	1.504
Colleagues in other companies	3.220	1.505
Rating services	2.848	1.672
New stories in trade publications	2.684	1.424
Trade association data	2.510	1.478
Trade shows	2.473	1.513
Advertising in trade publications	2.290	1.290
Outside consultants	2.090	1.489
Purchasing department	1.675	1.086

[4] Rowland T. Moriarty and Robert E. Spekman, "An Empirical Investigation of the Information Sources Used During the Industrial Buying Process," *Journal of Marketing Research*, **XXI**, 2 (February, 1984), 137–47.

The next step was to look at factors influencing usage patterns. This analysis concluded that phase in the decision process was the most important consideration, with sales reps becoming most important at the recognition-of-need and search-for-alternative-vendors stages. Buyers also depend more upon *commercial* personal sources of information (that is, sales reps and dealers) when the amount of perceived risk and the amount of investment are higher. Rate of technical change in the product category could be a major risk factor. However, as the amount of conflict and risk increase, respondents also relied more on *non-commercial* personal sources, such as colleagues and opinion leaders within the company. *Commercial* impersonal sources, such as advertising and sales literature, are used to search for potential vendors and tend to be relied upon more heavily by data-processing personnel than by users or administrators, probably reflecting the technical nature of these materials. *Non-commercial* impersonal sources, such as rating services, were used primarily at the early problem definition and search-for-vendors stages but less so for actual choice among vendors, a result that was not expected. These sources are also relied upon more heavily in high risk situations, which was expected.

These research results have several important managerial implications. First, they point to the importance of thinking of a total, integrated mix of communications tailored to specific objectives and specific steps in the buying process. Second, they suggest that impersonal, commercial sources have a role to play that goes beyond awareness creation. Third, they suggest the potential value of market segmentation based on such considerations as perceived risk, as well as size of customer, with relatively inexpensive impersonal media being an effective way of taking smaller potential customers through all stages of the buying process in relatively low-risk buying situations. Conversely, the research also points to a role for non-commercial, personal sources at all stages of the process; this suggests that the cultivation of favorable word-of-mouth via publicity and the nurturing of satisfied users can pay significant dividends. Finally, the results also underscore earlier research findings that the sales rep becomes more influential as the importance and perceived risk of the buying situation increase.

It is hard to generalize about the mix of communications actually used by industrial marketers, because different products and different markets create some fundamentally different requirements for marketing communication strategy. One study of the communications practices of producers of ferrous components showed the following mix of communications (excluding personal selling):

Promotional gifts	32%
Advertising	24%
Catalogues	19%
Trade shows and exhibits	11%
Direct mail	5%
Other	10%

In this industry, it was found that the typical firm spent only an average of $2^{1}/_{2}$ percent of sales, excluding sales service, on all marketing communications activities, including personal selling, a figure that is very low in comparison with normal industrial marketing practice. This same study found that expenditures for personal selling were two-thirds of the total communications budget. The remaining 33 percent of marketing costs were divided, 23 percent spent on preparing quotations and delivering bids and only 10 percent on the mass communications listed above. The author of this research concluded that industrial marketing communication managers based their allocation decisions on their own attitudes and subjective judgments about each of the media, and that "the concept of an integrated marketing communications system is a long way from being implemented, or indeed recognized, in the industry researched."[5]

Other studies have also supported the notion that the level of expenditure for marketing communication in industrial markets may not be adequate to justify the level of analytical sophistication called for by the total communication concept.

The ADVISOR Studies

This is one of the conclusions from the ADVISOR studies at M.I.T. (ADVISOR stands for *AD*Vertising *I*ndustrial products: *S*tudy of *O*perating *R*elationships.) In ADVISOR 1, the marketing communications expenditures of 12 companies for a total of 66 products were analyzed for relationships between expenditure levels and certain characteristics of products and markets. The word *advertising* was used in this study to represent all marketing communications other

[5] Peter W. Turnbull, "The Allocation of Resources of Marketing Communication in Industrial Markets," *Industrial Marketing Management*, 3, 5 (October, 1974), 297–309, at 308.

than personal selling, including print media, direct mail, trade shows, catalogues, and various forms of sales promotion.

These companies spent an average of 6.9 percent of sales volume on all marketing activities, including personal selling and technical service as well as advertising, with most products falling in a range of 3 to 14 percent. Advertising represented an average of 9.9 percent of the total marketing budget, with the range of 5 to 19 percent for most products. The median figure for advertising as a percentage of sales was 0.6 percent with a range for most products of 0.1 to 1.8 percent. The study suggested that managers conceptualize the advertising-to-sales (A/S) ratio, not as a single entity, but as a result of a two-step process. First, the ratio of marketing expenditures to total sales (M/S) is established, and then a decision is made to allocate a certain portion of the marketing budget to advertising (A/M). The results of the ADVISOR analysis are all consistent with this two-step model.

A large number of variables describing product and market were examined in the ADVISOR study to determine if they were related to expenditure patterns, either to the marketing-expense-to-sales (M/S) ratio or the advertising-to-marketing expense (A/M) ratio. Six factors were found to be important: (1) stage in product life cycle: (2) frequency of purchase; (3) degree of product differentiation (i.e., product quality, uniqueness, and identification with the company); (4) market share; (5) concentration of sales; and (6) growth in total numbers of customers. Both the M/S and A/S ratios had a strong negative relationship to product life cycle, but the A/M ratio did not seem to be effected. New products were found to have higher ratios of expenditure for marketing, including advertising.

More frequently purchased products appeared to have a higher ratio of advertising to marketing expense, but the ratio of marketing to sales did not appear to be influenced by the frequency of purchase. More highly differentiated products also tended to have higher A/M ratios, although the degree of product differentiation did not have a significant influence on the M/S ratio. A differentiated product means that there is a story that can be told through advertising. Thus advertising can assume a more important role in the communication mix.

Market share was negatively related to the M/S ratio. The M/S ratio decreased as market share increased. The A/M ratio was not strongly influenced by market share, but the A/S ratio decreased. Thus, there appear to be economies of scale in industrial marketing budgets. Industrial marketers with large market shares may be able to have large marketing communications budgets relative to their competitors and still spend a lower percentage of revenues to accomplish their communication objectives.

When sales were concentrated among fewer customers, the M/S ratio went down, but the A/M ratio went up, and the A/S ratio did not change significantly. Although it seems consistent with common sense that marketing expenditures went down as customer concentration increased, one might have expected that advertising would become less important when there were relatively fewer customers.

Finally, as the total number of customers increased over a period of time, so did the M/S ratio and the A/M ratio. The A/S ratio tended to increase as well, although the influence of growth in number of customers was relatively slight compared with the other variables. To summarize, the factors of stage in product life cycle, concentration of sales, and market share were found to influence primarily the M/S ratio. Purchase frequency and product differentiation influence primarily the A/M ratio. Interestingly, differences among product categories (e.g., machinery versus chemicals) were not found to be significant. These results were made part of a computer-based interactive model that permitted managers to compare their own expenditure patterns with some norms and ranges developed from the data.

Within the advertising (i.e., marketing communication) expenditures examined, there were four types of media: (1) space (41%); (2) sales promotion (24%); (3) direct mail (24%); and (4) trade shows and exhibitions (11%). The numbers in parentheses are the allocations to the media for all 66 products in the sample. Allocation of the advertising budget among these various media was influenced by sales volume, stage in product life cycle, sales concentration, and growth in total number of customers. As sales volume increased, companies tended to spend less on direct mail and space advertising and more on trade shows and sales promotion. As products became more mature, companies tended to spend more on direct mail and less on sales promotion with little effect on expenditures for shows. If sales were concentrated on a few customers, trade shows were less likely to be used. As the number of customers increased, less use was made of direct mail. The only factor that seemed to have any relationship to expenditures on media space advertising was the sales volume variable, but even there the relationship seemed to be quite weak.

These results also became part of the interactive computer program. A program user answers a series of questions about her product and its markets. The model output is a set of marketing and advertising budget guidelines based on what a typical industry allocation would be. It is not intended to be optimal in any sense but simply a guideline, based on industry norms, from which the manager can draw her own conclusions and take whatever action she believes is appropriate.[6]

ADVISOR 2 is an extension and elaboration of the first ADVISOR study with a larger data base—22 companies (19 new and 3 from ADVISOR 1) and a total of 125 products. In ADVISOR 2, more complex functional relationships were examined (log-linear versus linear), and models were developed for year-to-year changes in expenditures as well as for the norms of the various types of expenditures. In most respects, the results of ADVISOR 2 are consistent with those of ADVISOR 1. The median A/S ratio in ADVISOR 2 was 0.7 percent compared with 0.6 percent in ADVISOR 1. The median A/M ratio was 10 percent versus 9.9 percent in ADVISOR 1, and the median M/S ratio was 7.0 percent compared with 6.9 percent. In ADVISOR 2, eight categories of variables, mostly similar to those in ADVISOR 1, were analyzed for their impact on marketing communications expenditures:

1. Sales level.
2. Number of customers and their concentration.
3. Stage in the product life cycle.
4. Product plans and objectives (replacing "growth in total customers" in ADVISOR 1).
5. Product made to order (versus carried in inventory).
6. Product complexity (defined primarily in technical terms).
7. Product perceptions (how actual customers rank the product compared to prospective customers).
8. Distribution channels used.

In ADVISOR 2, the variable called purchase frequency in ADVISOR 1 was found to be ambiguous (the confusion relates to the distinction between order frequency and decision frequency) and was therefore dropped. Generally, the results of ADVISOR 2 confirmed the conclusions of ADVISOR 1. The major difference was

---

[6] Gary L. Lilien and John D. C. Little, "The ADVISOR Project. A Study of Industrial Marketing Budgets," *Sloan Management Review,* **17,** 3 (Spring, 1976), 17–32.

that in ADVISOR 2 no relationship was found between expenditure ratios and market share, but this was due to a difference in the estimation procedures used. To explain this discrepancy, the researchers suggested that if ADVISOR 1 procedures had been used on ADVISOR 2 data, a strong relationship between expenditure ratios and market share would have been found.

As in ADVISOR 1, the weakest models were the media allocation models attempting to explain how advertising was allocated among the four classes of media. The explanation for these weak relationships is simply that product- and market specific-factors (e.g., the number of trade journals available) are likely to be the most important determinants of the allocation of advertising dollars among space, direct mail, trade shows, and promotion, whereas the generalizable relationships are quite weak.

To summarize the significant results of ADVISOR 2, a strong positive relationship was found between sales volume and both the M/S and A/S ratios. In other words, products with larger sales volumes had a larger percentage of dollar sales going to both marketing and advertising. Also, as product sales volume went up, advertising received relatively less of the marketing dollar. As the number of users increased, both the M/S and A/S ratios tended to increase, but there was no effect on A/M. When sales were concentrated on relatively fewer customers, both the M/S and A/S ratios went down, but the A/M ratio was unaffected. If a large share of a firm's sales were made to order, then marketing and advertising expenditures tended to be lower. Products in the growth stage had larger M/S and A/S ratios than those in the mature stage, while the A/M ratio was not significantly influenced. Expenditure ratios were higher when companies had aggressive plans for increasing product sales volume and number of customers. A/M there was unaffected. The M/S ratio tended to be higher when products were more complex and there was a difficult, technical story to tell to prospective customers. Again, there was little effect on A/M. When current customers ranked product quality higher than prospects (this is how the product perceptions variable was defined), this was found to be associated with a relatively low M/S ratio and with a higher A/M ratio, but the A/S ratio was unaffected. What this appeared to indicate was a relatively low level of use of the sales force, more reliance on advertising, and a general underspending for marketing. Conversely, if the level of sales direct to users was high (rather than through distributors—the channel strategy variable), then M/S tended to be higher, A/M tended to be lower, and A/S was once again unaffected.[7]

Thus, the ADVISOR studies have brought to bear a reasonably rigorous level of econometric analysis on the question of how industrial firms' levels of expenditure for marketing communication are related to various product and market factors. The results are a valuable description of industry practice. Equally valuable are the methodological breakthroughs made by ADVISOR in measuring these relationships and putting them into a form (following the decision calculus approach) that permits managers to compare the results of their decision making with the norms in the model. These norms are strictly descriptive and do not imply optimality in any sense, but they do provide useful benchmarks and guidelines.

SOURCE EFFECT: THE IMPORTANCE OF IMAGE

The effects of industrial marketing communication are synergistic (i.e., the communication modes interact with one another and produce an effect that is more than a simple summation of the individual effects) and cumulative over a period of time. Because personal selling expenditures tend to dominate the industrial marketing budget, accounting for an estimated 90 percent of the expenditures, the most important interactions in the marketing communications mix are those between personal selling and the other individual elements. If a customer or prospect has contact with a company's sales representative, then it is likely that impressions formed on the basis of those interactions will be the major determinant of the customer's view of that supplier firm. But if there is no direct contact with a sales rep, then the customer's or prospect's perceptions of the firm will be based on a general image formed by a variety of other sources of information, including word-of-mouth, public relations and publicity, and media advertising.

The Concept of Company Image

Every company, large or small, has an image—good or bad, clear or indistinct—in the minds of actual and potential buyers. The image will exist whether the company has done anything to cultivate it or

---

[7] Gary L. Lilien, *ADVISOR 2: A Study of Industrial Marketing Budgeting, Descriptive Analysis—Final Report*, Sloan School of Management, M.I.T., February, 1978.

not. If the image has been created largely by accident and generally without direction, it is less likely to be an image that is consistent with the firm's marketing and communication objectives.

Company image is the sum total of the effects of communications about the company in the mind of the receiver. It is the personality or reputation of the company viewed by customers, prospects, employers, suppliers, shareholders, and the general public, each of whom may have a different image of the company. Individual products and brands sold by the company may have images that are distinct and different from the overall company image. A good company image can enhance the effects of the company's various marketing communications activities.

Source Credibility

If we think of the company as a communication source, then the company will have a certain degree of credibility as a communicator. Credibility is synonymous with believability, the extent to which receivers perceive that the communicator possesses such characteristics as honesty, trustworthiness, and expertise. A good reputation in the minds of the intended audience enhances the effectiveness of individual messages from a given source, while an unfavorable reputation reduces message effectiveness. *Source effect* is a measure of the extent to which the effectiveness of a given message is enhanced or hindered by the reputation of the source. It can be measured by an experiment in which the message stays constant and the source is varied by attributing the message to different sources. By this means, the presence of source effect has been well established in communication in general[8] as well as in industrial marketing in particular.[9]

In Chapter 3, we discussed the determinants of an industrial sales rep's effectiveness in the buyer-seller interaction. Levitt's well-known research on source effect in industrial selling concluded that sales reps for industrial companies with good reputations always get a more favorable response than sales reps for companies that are unknown or have poor reputations. For industrial marketers, technical expertise is often an important dimension of source credibility. Levitt's high credibility source was the Monsanto Chemical Company,

[8] Carl I. Hovland, Irving L. Janis, and Harold H. Kelley, *Communication and Persuasion* (New Haven: Yale University Press, 1953).
[9] Theodore Levitt, *Industrial Purchasing Behavior: A Study of Communications Effects* (Boston: Division of Research, Graduate School of Business Administration, Harvard University, 1965).

"I don't know who you are.

I don't know your company.

I don't know your company's product.

I don't know what your company stands for.

I don't know your company's customers.

I don't know your company's record.

I don't know your company's reputation.

Now—what was it you wanted to sell me?"

MORAL: Sales start **before** your salesman calls—with business publication advertising.

Figure 10-1. An advertisement stressing the value of advertising to the industrial sales representative. Reproduced by courtesy of McGraw-Hill Publishing Company.

a firm with a solid technical reputation. Thus, there is reasonably good scientific evidence that company reputation, created through advertising and other forms of mass communication, can enhance the effectiveness of the sales rep.[10] There is less evidence that company reputation influences the effectiveness of other media, such as direct mail, sales promotions, and trade shows. Figure 10-1 is an advertisement stressing the value of industrial advertising.

[10] *Ibid.*

Influence of Advertising on Sales Reps' Effectiveness

One report of a series of studies by Morrill of the influence of industrial product advertising on the effectiveness of sales representatives concluded that the cost of selling was 10 to 30 percent lower to customer groups exposed to the company's advertising compared with unexposed customer groups. It was suggested that advertising did change opinions and attitudes and that this led to improvements in both share of customers and share of market dollars, empirical support for the hierarchy-of-effects model. These data were based on nearly 100,000 interviews covering about 1,000 advertising schedules for 26 different product lines sold in 90 product markets at 30,000 different buying locations.

Morrill suggested that, when such a company could not see clear results from its advertising, a major reason was usually inadequate advertising frequency. He concluded that a minimum of five pages of advertising in a given magazine in a year was necessary to achieve impact. Not only did the analysis show that advertising above this minimum level produced increased sales and reduced selling costs for the advertiser, but it seemed to increase the selling difficulties and marketing costs faced by the advertiser's competitors by as much as 20 to 40 percent. For companies selling through distributors, a combination of advertising and missionary calls by the company's own sales reps was found to be more effective than either advertising or missionary selling by itself. The effect was greatest when the distributor sales reps' call frequency was relatively low, suggesting that the reps were not able to reach key buying influences with adequate frequency, a clear case where advertising and missionary selling have important roles to play.[11]

The Morrill study lends support to the notion of source credibility as well as to the hierarchy-of-effects hypothesis. Although one can be critical of some aspects of his research methodology, and his conclusions should be regarded as general tendencies, not as precise measures of effect, the Morrill analysis indicates for the marketing communication strategist the value of careful collection and analysis of data relating advertising exposure, sales call frequency, distribution activity, share of customer orders and dollars, and competitors' advertising activity. Industrial advertising has been shown to reduce selling costs by opening doors for the sales rep, by creating

[11] John E. Morrill, "Industrial Advertising Pays Off," *Harvard Business Review*, **48**, 4 (March–April, 1970), 4–14, 159–69.

a favorable company reputation, and by reaching decision influences not readily accessible by the sales rep.

Developing the Industrial Marketing Communication Program

There are six distinct elements in the marketing communication program: (1) objectives; (2) audience; (3) budget; (4) message; (5) media; and (6) evaluation. The manager of marketing communication must analyze each element, make decisions about each for the coming period, and integrate them into a total program. In this section, each of these elements will be discussed briefly.

Setting Communication Objectives

In an earlier section of this chapter, the question of objectives was considered in terms of the hierarchy-of-effects model. The conclusion there was that the manager must be specific about whether the program is intended to influence awareness, attitudes, or buying action and that the objectives must be set in specific, quantitative terms permitting both pre- and post-measurement.

Two kinds of analysis must precede the setting of communication objectives. First, there must be the analysis of the company, its products, previous marketing effort, and planned marketing objectives. Which products are in good position in the marketplace and which are weak? What is to be the relative emphasis on new versus old products and new versus established customers? What are the company's strengths and weaknesses compared with the competition in product, pricing, and distribution? And so on.

Second, there must be an analysis of customers and conditions in the market. As observed earlier, this part of the analysis requires data about customer perceptions and preferences. How is the company viewed by present and prospective customers in comparison with competition? What do customers consider the company's major strengths and weaknesses as a vendor? How satisfied are customers with their present suppliers, including both the company and its competitors? Do customers have good knowledge about the company's products? Are they aware of the full range of the product offering? How are the company's sales reps and distributors compared with those of competitors? Answers to questions like these will define the range of marketing problems and opportunities to which the company must address itself in its planning of marketing strategy. Some subset of those problems will be communication problems—problems that can be corrected through communication. Other problems, of course, will not be amenable to a communication approach—problems with product quality, delivery, and pricing, for example, or inadequacies in the present dealer organization.

As we saw in Chapter 4, the concept of product positioning is just as relevant in industrial marketing as it is in consumer marketing. Product positioning is the use of communication to emphasize certain aspects of the product offering relative to the offerings of competitors. It is part of the process of creating an image for the product or brand. The opportunities for positioning a given industrial product are, of course, defined and constrained by the technical features and qualities of the product, but within those constraints a variety of market positions might be possible. Through the analysis of customer needs and predispositions and of competitive offerings, the industrial marketer can define an opportunity in the market to stress certain benefits and characteristics of the product, giving it what one advertising authority called a "unique selling proposition" or "USP," a reason for being in the competitive marketplace. The concept of product positioning is an important aspect of the marketer's search for competitive advantage and the definition of a product positioning has direct impact on the definition of communication objectives.

Defining the Target Audience

The definition of the target audience for the marketing communication program is a subset of the company's market segmentation strategy. Target audiences can be defined at both the macrosegment and microsegment levels. It will be recalled that the first defines types of buying organizations according to industry affiliation, type of product produced, end use for the marketer's products, and so on. The second defines buying centers according to composition, characteristic decision-making styles, and buying criteria used.

Not all market segments are of equal value to the company, and not all represent equal communication opportunities at any point in time. Thus, the definition of target audiences can focus on relatively short-term communication problems and opportunities compared with the longer-term orientation of the market segmentation strategy. The value attached to a particular target audience should be a reflection of fairly short-term marketing and communication objectives.

One of the most common errors in industrial marketing communication strategy is to give inadequate attention to the precise definition of target audiences. The most extreme case is when every exposure—a message delivered to a receiver—regardless of the characteristics of the receiver is assumed to be of equal value. Quite clearly, however, messages delivered to persons who are neither actual nor prospective customers have virtually no value to the marketer as part of his marketing program (although they may have some small value in the development of "goodwill" among the public at large). We can define an *effective exposure* as a message delivered once to a member of the target audience. A *wasted exposure* is a message delivered to a person not in the target audience. This distinction between effective and wasted exposures is important in evaluating various media. Media with the largest total audiences may be able to deliver the lowest cost per thousand total exposures but may be relatively inefficient when costs per thousand effective exposures are compared.

In the preceding discussion of setting communication objectives, it was stressed that data on predispositions in the target audience can be a very useful input to the planning process. Obviously, those data can also help to refine the definition of the target audience. Existing levels of awareness, attitudes, and buying action are important factors in the target audience and help to define the targets more specifically. It is unlikely, however, that it will be possible to develop a media strategy that can differentiate target audiences according to the levels of their predispositions. To illustrate, the target audience may be defined as purchasing agents and production supervisors in metal-working firms, who presently have low levels of awareness of the company's products. Although their low awareness level is important to consider in developing communication objectives, it can not help the strategist in selecting among media. One important exception is the case where a company has been using certain media and has been able to reach only a subset of the target audience and needs to develop a new media mix in order to reach a wider audience.

Determining the Budget Level

Economic theory tells us that a firm should continue to spend additional dollars for marketing communication until the incremental return, say a dollar of gross margin contribution, is just equal to the incremental cost. These ideal conditions for the optimum level of spending assume that the firm is realizing decreasing returns to its communication expenditures (that is, each dollar spent produces a somewhat smaller return), which may or may not be true in actual practice. The major difficulty in applying this analytical line of reasoning for establishing communication budgets, however, is the difficulty of estimating the market response function, the relationship between money spent and buyer response in terms of changes in awareness, attitudes, or buying action (sales). Furthermore, if communication objectives are phrased in terms of communication results—changes in levels of awareness or attitudes—rather than sales results, then economic analysis of the return on marketing communication expenditures requires that the manager be able to assign some economic value to changes in levels of awareness or attitudes. This is always a very difficult task, given the uncertainties about the hierarchy of effects. The Morrill study, described earlier, suggests, however, that the task is not impossible.

There are three different approaches to the setting of communication budgets.

Most common are a variety of guideline methods. Guidelines are rather arbitrary rules of thumb often used by managers, such as a specified percentage of sales or some norm established on the basis of a review of industry practice. Trade associations sometimes gather and report such information so that association members know, for example, that firms of a given size typically spend so many dollars or a given percentage of sales on advertising, or on total marketing activity. The ADVISOR studies generated such guidelines for the managers of communication in the participating firms, although the ADVISOR guidelines were developed on the basis of rather complex analysis of the product and market characteristics cited there—sales volume, stage in product life cycle, customer concentration, and so forth.

The most common guidelines rely on percentage of sales, either sales in the previous period or in the sales forecast. In this sense, sales volume causes advertising, rather than advertising causing sales. The many problems with the use of guidelines methods are probably obvious to the reader, but one particular problem should be highlighted. In this approach, the marketer is not asking what marketing communication can accomplish and what it is worthwhile to spend, the more appropriate bases for setting the budget level. Rather, in the guidelines methods, the manager is asking "What are other companies doing?" and "What can we afford?" This can lead to underspending or overspending, but the manager never really knows whether the budget level is optimal. The defense of the guidelines methods is that they are probably better than nothing.

Guidelines relate the company's spending levels to those of competition, and they can be explained rather quickly to those who inquire about the company's spending level. One of the side effects of this rather casual approach to budget-setting, however, is that the defense of a given budget level is rather weak, and the communications budget may be hard to protect against the predations of management looking for ways to reduce expenses and improve the bottom line of the profit-and-loss statement. When budget levels are set arbitrarily, they can be cut arbitrarily as well. It is therefore probably true that companies that rely exclusively on guidelines methods for setting their communication budgets often end up underspending for marketing communications.

A second set of methods for setting marketing communication budgets can be called objective-and-task methods. Using this approach, the manager attempts to specify in some detail the communication objectives that must be met, such as increasing awareness levels in the target audience from X to Y percent. From these objectives, the strategist attempts to work backwards to establish a budget by first defining the number of messages (effective exposures multiplied by desired frequency of exposure) and then calculates the cost of attaining that number of exposures in the various media being considered for use. This cost becomes the budget. The application of the objective-and-task method can be reasonably sophisticated conceptually, if the manager is considering such issues as stage in product life cycle, the nature of competitive response, reactions of the target audience to various message frequencies, and so on. The major difficulty, as indicated earlier, is in establishing the causal links in the hierarchy of effects—from exposures to awareness to attitudes to action. It should be noted, however, that these problems may also be present in the application of more rigorous analytical techniques, although they may be disguised by the elegance of the models used. Given these measurement difficulties, the objective-and-task method may represent the best approach to setting marketing communication budget levels in many situations.

The third set of budgeting methods, and the least commonly used, are rigorous budgeting procedures based on explicit modelling of market response, and the use of experimentation or sophisticated statistical analysis to estimate the parameters of the models. As we have noted before, the marketing communication budget levels of most industrial marketers may not be large enough to justify the expense of developing, setting parameters for, and maintaining these models. Furthermore, operating management may lack the analytical sophistication required to use these models well. Those models that have been developed and reported in the literature have been almost exclusively phrased in terms of consumer products, although most of them could be adapted to industrial marketing conditions.[12]

A combination of the objective-and-task method and the type of analytical approach developed by Morrill, cited earlier, is probably best for most industrial marketers. The Morrill analysis was facilitated by a much larger data base than the typical marketer may have, but the basic approach is feasible for any industrial marketer. An approach like Morrill's calls for the use of company records and market surveys to estimate rates of exposure in target audiences (to advertising and to other forms of marketing communication) and then attempts to relate these through statistical analysis to measures of sales response and to intermediate measures of buyer response to communication, such as changes in levels of awareness and attitudes. These data can then be used to guide the analysis necessary in the objective-and-task method—relating communication activity measures to changes in buyer behavior. This degree of analytical sophistication, while not very great when compared with the state of the art in management science, is a significant improvement over the most commonly used guidelines methods. The ADVISOR model falls into this range—a reasonably sophisticated version of the objective-and-task method. It is probably more useful to a manager than the more rigorous and elegant models that are available.

Developing Message Strategy

A reasonably clear definition of message strategy should be evident from the statement of communication objectives. There are two aspects to the problem of developing message strategy. We can call these the general and the specific message. The general message strategy is essentially the positioning statement considered in our discussion of objectives. In advertising management, it is often referred to as the copy platform, the basis on which specific selling messages are developed.

The general message strategy defines what is to be said about the company, its products, its general capabilities, its sales reps and

---

[12] For a review of a selection of these models, see Webster, *op. cit.*, 391–414.

distributors, and so on. In a narrow sense, the general message strategy is a statement of marketing communication objectives that specifies how the company wants to be known to its customers and prospective customers. In this sense, then, the message strategy must be consistent with the company's product strategy, since its stresses particular product features and company capabilities. However, the general message strategy must go beyond product features and company capabilities and translate these into specific customer benefits and the satisfaction of customer needs.

Specific message strategy consists of the creation and execution of specific messages to be placed in media. It means writing copy, developing illustrations, and testing the impact of alternative executions. The development of specific messages is often the responsibility of outside suppliers of creative services, such as advertising agencies, public relations firms, direct mail houses, and firms that specialize in the planning and construction of trade show exhibits. Needless to say, these firms can only do their jobs well if they are guided by a careful statement of the general message strategy. Any good supplier of creative services needs the freedom to bring to bear the best creative judgment on the problem that has been assigned. Stated simply, the marketer who retains the services of a creative agency should not then proceed to create its own marketing communications in competition with the agency. David Ogilvy, the legendary advertising executive, asked simply "Why keep a dog and bark yourself?"

The quality of the specific messages developed will reflect many factors, not the least important of which is the quality of the market research and management analysis that has gone into the development of communication objectives, the specification of the target audience, and the definition of the general message strategy. All relevant market studies and management planning documents should be available to the department or agency responsible for creating messages.

Many industrial firms prefer to retain the responsibility for the development of messages, rather than to assign the responsibility to an outside agency. These in-house agencies are often created because the company is not able to find satisfactory services from outsiders. While most advertising agencies emphasize the marketing of consumer products, there are several excellent agencies that specialize in industrial marketing communications. One of the difficulties in industrial marketing communications is that expenditures in traditional advertising media are likely to be relatively low. The standard method for compensating advertising agencies is to pay them 15 percent of the company's billings in so-called commissionable media, specifically magazines, newspapers, radio, and television. Because industrial marketers use many other media, such as sales promotion, trade shows, and direct mail more heavily than space advertising, industrial advertising agencies are usually compensated on the basis of negotiated fees. Furthermore, industrial advertising agencies must have the experience and skills required to work effectively with this broad range of communication media, not just with traditional print and broadcast media. Each of the specialized media of industrial marketing is likely to have its own unique requirements for message effectiveness. Therefore, the creative people assigned to an industrial account must understand the requirements for developing effective messages in such diverse media as direct mail, catalogues and product specification sheets, industrial trade journals, exhibitions and trade shows, sales promotions, and sales reps' presentations.

An interesting study of message strategy in industrial markets suggested that industrial marketers often did not have a good understanding of their audiences and what was important to them. Four industrial market segments were examined—consulting engineers, architects, electrical contractors, and nonresidential building contractors. Several hundred respondents to a mailed questionnaire were asked to assess the relative strength of 48 distinct appeals. Responses of each segment were examined and then these were compared with the appeals used by advertisers attempting to influence buying decisions in these segments. This analysis disclosed that advertisers were using appeals that were not particularly responsive to the needs and preferences of their audiences. Using his findings, the author was able to develop 12 different advertising appeals and to predict correctly in each case how they would be evaluated in the four market segments. The results of this research stress the importance of data on audience predispositions and buying criteria as the basis for developing effective messages.[13]

Selecting Media

Each of the industrial marketing communication media has a somewhat distinctive role to play in the execution of total strategy. The

[13] Gordon McAller, "Do Industrial Advertisers Understand What Influences Their Markets?," *Journal of Marketing,* **38,** 1 (January, 1974), 15–23.

selection of specific media to be used at a given point must be derived from the definition of the target audience and the statement of communication objectives. In our previous discussion of communication objectives, major attention was devoted to the concept that different media have differential effectiveness as a function of the type of response desired from the receiver and the stage in the product life cycle (diffusion process).

Once again, the problem can be broken into two components, a general and a specific. The general media problem is to specify which of the classes of communication media, or modes, to use. The modes of industrial communication, as we have seen, include general business publications (such as *Business Week, Fortune, Forbes, Barrons,* and the *Wall Street Journal*); trade journals (such as *Iron and Steel Age* or *Modern Packaging*); direct mail; trade shows and exhibitions; sales reps' aids, such as catalogues, technical product specification sheets, and slide presentations; sales promotion items such as displays and gifts (including desk accessories, calendars, clothing items bearing the company's identification, ballpoint pens, etc.); and public relations and publicity, usually in either the trade press or general business publications. The distinction between advertising and publicity is simply that the former is paid for and is clearly identifiable as advertising. Publicity is usually free and appears as part of the editorial content of the media.

Earlier sections of this chapter have presented evidence concerning how industrial marketers allocate their communication budgets among the various media. A somewhat different type of ranking was provided by one study that asked respondents to evaluate the effectiveness of the various media. Their rankings are presented in Table 10-1. It should be emphasized that these are the opinions of industrial marketers rather than either an objective measurement of media effectiveness or a measure of actual dollar allocations.

This study was intended primarily to assess the use of industrial trade shows and exhibitions as part of the total communication strategy. (For many firms, especially those in capital goods businesses, trade shows are generally the second most important marketing communication expenditure, after personal selling.) Data were gathered by means of mail survey. There were 255 respondents, 147 of whom were industrial products manufacturers; 44 were manufacturers of consumer products; and 64 were non-manufacturing firms. Thus, industrial firms are most important in the data base although the presence of consumer manufacturers could have

TABLE 10–1

Industrial Marketers' Ranking of the Effectiveness of Promotional Media

	Index of Perceived Effectiveness
Sales calls	100
Catalogues, manuals, specification sheets	46
Direct mail	39
Advertising	38
Trade shows	35
Samples, trial use, demonstration	34
Publicity and public relations	31
Customer entertainment	26
Promotional novelties (gifts)	24

Source: Peter M. Banting and David L. Blenkhorn, "The Role of Industrial Trade Shows," *Industrialized Marketing Management*, **3**, 5 (October, 1974), 285–95, at 292.

distorted the data in some cases. In order of importance, respondents saw the following benefits from trade shows:

1. An opportunity to introduce new products.
2. An opportunity to establish personal contacts with prospective buyers.
3. An opportunity to maintain visibility of the company's products and name.
4. An opportunity to establish contact with members of the buying center who can not otherwise be reached.
5. An opportunity to make direct sales.
6. The ability to display non-portable products.
7. A method of developing a list of prospects.
8. An opportunity to recruit new distributors.
9. A method of determining potential customer requirements.
10. An opportunity to evaluate competitors' products.
11. The possibility of discovering new applications for existing products.
12. An opportunity to obtain new product ideas from customers, distributors, and competitors.
13. An opportunity to discover new suppliers.

14. An opportunity to evaluate competitors' marketing tactics.
15. A good training opportunity for new sales personnel.
16. An opportunity to meet customers in a more relaxed atmosphere.

Despite this rather long list of potential benefits, however, most respondents expressed reservations about the value of trade shows and exhibits, primarily because of cost. Many respondents reported that their enthusiasm for trade shows had diminished in recent years due to increasing costs of constructing and running trade show exhibits. Related to these cost considerations were increased labor costs (often not a function of wage rates so much as labor rules and requirements), a proliferation of trade shows, the lack of selectivity in audience attracted and a large number of sightseers, as well as a lack of selectivity in exhibitors. Other problems mentioned included an insufficient supply of new products to warrant the number of shows, poor show publicity, and the lack of audited attendance. An earlier study, cited by these authors, put the cost of attending a trade show at $31 per prospect or customer reached (the figure is for 1972), which would seem to be quite high. Even though marketers may doubt the value of trade shows, they fear the consequences of not attending and thereby losing the visibility maintained by competitors. Customers and distributors may have strong expectations that the marketer will be attending the important trade shows in the industry.[14]

An assessment of industrial trade shows by Bonoma takes a somewhat more analytical approach and considers what steps management can take to enhance the benefits of participation. The apparent trend toward somewhat reduced interest in trade shows by industrial marketing managers was seen as caused, in part, by the escalating costs of participation and the difficulties inherent in measuring trade show benefits. Bonoma argued that managers should evaluate and select trade shows based on specific selling and non-selling benefits offered by each show. Selling benefits were defined to include identification of and contact with prospects, access to key members of the buying center not easily reached by sales reps, the opportunity to offer customer service, and actually writing orders. Non-selling benefits included maintaining the company image, access to competitive intelligence, a chance to test customer reaction to new products, and boosting employee morale.

[14] Peter M. Banting and David L. Blenkhorn, "The Role of Industrial Trade Shows." *Industrial Marketing Management*, 3, 5 (October, 1974), 285–95.

Following the general approach outlined in this chapter, stressing the central importance of clearly defined objectives, Bonoma proposed that the issue of trade show participation be approached in a four-step process:

1. Define the functions performed and objectives to be achieved by trade shows in the company's marketing communications program.
2. Define the target audience/market to be reached through trade shows.
3. Evaluate the shows available in terms of both selling and non-selling objectives, and put together a selection that best achieves the objectives and reaches the defined audience.
4. In the context of the firm's total marketing program, develop a procedure for auditing the results of trade show participation, assessing the return on the investment that has been made, and planning future investments.[15]

The above review of the advantages and problems of trade shows illustrates the claim often made throughout this chapter that each communication mode has a special set of benefits and requirements. It seems unnecessary to review the advantages and limitations of each of the other communication modes we have been considering. The basic objective of all marketing communication is to support the sales rep, to enhance her effectiveness, and to reduce total selling cost as a percentage of sales. The importance of thinking in terms of an integrated mix of communications, each contributing to the accomplishment of specific objectives, can not be overstated.

Up to this point, we have been considering the problem of selecting among the various modes of marketing communication. The other level of the media decision problem is to select among specific media vehicles within a given mode—which trade journals to use, which trade shows to attend, and so on. In this part of the decision process, the marketing communication strategist needs to look at two dimensions, the cost of each vehicle and the extent to which the audience delivered by the media vehicle matches the definition of the target audience. Here the concept of effective exposure becomes relevant and is the basis for comparing the various cost figures. Other factors that the strategist must consider

[15] Thomas V. Bonoma, "Get More Out of Your Trade Shows," *Harvard Business Review,* **61,** 1 (January-February, 1983), 75–83.

include the extent of duplication among the audiences delivered by specific media vehicles, the qualitative values of the media vehicle (their reputation, image, and credibility), and mechanical requirements for messages delivered in that medium.

For the marketer interested in bringing the highest reasonable level of analytical sophistication to judgments about the communication strategy, it is especially important to consider the quality of the data that the media vehicle provides about its audience. A good data base will aid both the planning process and subsequent campaign evaluation.

Once again, the conditions for an optimal allocation of the communication budget among the various modes of communication are the classic conditions from economic theory—the marginal rates of return to each of the modes of communication must be equal. For a given budget level, the firm should reallocate funds from those modes with lower rates of return into those modes with a higher rate of return until these conditions of optimality are achieved. Given the difficulties of measuring the marginal returns in each communication mode, however, these optimal conditions can at best be approximated by careful management judgment.

Evaluating Results

The planning process is not complete until evaluation has been carefully planned. Money spent in obtaining initial benchmark data and in subsequent planning and execution of the evaluation process can significantly increase the effectiveness of the money spent on media and message development. The evaluation task can be relatively straightforward, if data have been collected on existing awareness and attitudes and if objectives have been stated in terms that permit measurement.

In the best of all possible worlds, it would be feasible to state objectives in sales and profit terms and thereafter to trace the influence of the various elements of the total communications program on sales and profits, over whatever number of planning periods was necessary to account for the effects of communication expenditure. This ideal can be approximated at some expense, if the firm has a large enough promotional budget to justify the expenditure required and is willing to construct and refine the experimental procedures necessary. Only through experimentation is it possible to isolate the influence of various elements of the communication program on sales and profits.[16]

A more reasonable approach is usually to measure changes in audience predispositions by obtaining measurements of levels of awareness and attitudes. Even in this more easily attainable type of measurement, however, the effects of current communication activity may be hard to estimate, given the many influences on customers' levels of awareness and attitudes and given normal sources of error in marketing research techniques.

In addition to measurements of the results of communication activity, campaign evaluation can also be facilitated by an audit of the process of planning the campaign itself. The evaluator should look at such areas as the care with which objectives were stated, the quality of data available to management and the extent to which it was used, and the degree to which objectives for message strategy and media strategy were clearly delineated.

Other measures of communication program effectiveness can be called measures of communication activity or exposure. Sales rep's call reports can be tabulated for measures of sales call activity on new and old accounts. Circulation data for the various print media used can be tabulated. Attendance figures for trade shows can be examined. Such measures are obviously most appropriate for evaluating the media strategy, rather than the total communication program.

Another kind of measurement relies on opinion, reports of people who are in a position to evaluate the various parts of the communication program. Most important will be the opinions of customers, distributors, and sales reps. If they are favorably inclined to the communications, it can be assumed that they have been exposed to the communication, remembered it, and probably been favorably influenced by it. An increased probability of purchase can logically be expected to result. More directly, if one of the objectives of some elements of the communication program, such as trade journal advertising or sales promotions, has been to improve salesforce and distributor morale, then favorable opinions reported by those audiences can be regarded as one reasonable indication of the success of the program.

A pragmatic solution to the problem of evaluation relies on as many different types of measurement as can be obtained at reason-

---

[16] For a sophisticated model to evaluate communication expenditures, based on continuous experimentation, see John D. C. Little, "A Model for Adaptive Control of Promotional Spending," *Operations Research,* **14** (November-December, 1966), 175–97.

able cost. There can be no argument against looking at alternative measures of effectiveness, only against looking at too few or measures that have nothing to do with the objectives of the campaign. Of course, the fundamental error in evaluation is a failure to state objectives in a form that permits evaluation of the campaign. Equally serious is the failure to plan evaluation at all. In that case, the manager is unable to learn from his experience and is likely to repeat his errors in the future.

SUMMARY

Industrial marketing communications account for a lower portion of total marketing expenditures than is characteristic of consumer marketing. The importance of communication in the accomplishment of overall marketing objectives cannot be ignored, however. The central role played by the industrial sales representative must be supported by a blend of other communications tools, including advertising, catalogues, product specification sheets, direct mail, sales promotion, trade shows, publicity, and public relations. In the concept of an integrated mix of marketing communications, special attention must be devoted to the interaction of each mode of communication with the salesforce activity, because the latter is the central element in the communication budget.

Several studies of the allocation of communication budgets among the various modes of communication were examined in this chapter. Most important were the ADVISOR studies and Morrill's study of the influence of advertising on salesforce effectiveness and cost. The ADVISOR studies established a relationship between marketing and advertising budgets and a number of product and market characteristics, including sales volume, customer concentration, growth in number of customers, the aggressiveness of the marketer's plans, customers' perceptions of differences among competing products, stage in the product life cycle, and the role assigned to the distributor. The results of the ADVISOR studies have been used to develop models that provide norms against which a user of the computer-based model can assess his own plans for the total marketing communication budget and for the allocation of that budget among the various modes of communication.

Six steps in the development of the industrial marketing communication program were examined—setting objectives, defining the target audience, setting the communication budget, developing messages, selecting media, and evaluating the campaign. The strong connection between objectives and the evaluation process was stressed throughout the chapter, as was the need for economical measurement of audience predispositions and of the effects of communication on those predispositions.

Bibliography

Bonoma, Thomas V., "Get More Out of Your Trade Shows," *Harvard Business Review,* **61,** 1 (January-February, 1983), 75–83.

Lilien, Gary L., and John D. C. Little, "The ADVISOR Project: A Study of Industrial Marketing Budgets," *Sloan Management Review,* **17,** 3 (Spring, 1976), 17–32.

Lilien, Gary L., Alvin J. Silk, Jean-Marie Choffray, and Murlidhar Rao, "Industrial Advertising Effects and Budgeting Practices," *Journal of Marketing,* **40,** 1 (January, 1976), 16–24.

Moriarty, Rowland T., and Robert E. Spekman, "An Empirical Investigation of the Information Sources Used During the Industrial Buying Process," *Journal of Marketing Research,* **XXI,** 2 (May, 1984), 137–47.

Ray, Michael L., *Advertising and Communication Management* (Englewood Cliffs, N.J.: Prentice-Hall, Inc., 1982).

Webster, Frederick E., Jr., *Marketing Communication: Modern Promotional Strategy* (New York: The Ronald Press Co., 1974).

11 Industrial Marketing Planning

Several central ideas about the requirements for effectiveness in industrial marketing strategy have been developed in this text. In this last chapter, these ideas will be summarized and integrated into a consideration of strategic planning for industrial marketing activities.

A distinction among levels of strategy was introduced early in Chapter 1. Marketing strategy was seen as one of the areas of *functional* strategy, which also includes manufacturing, finance, R&D, procurement, and human resources strategies. Functional strategies must be designed in a manner consistent with, and in order to implement, *business unit* strategy, which answers the question "How do we want to compete?" Likewise, business unit strategy must be consistent with and implement *corporate* strategy, which answers the question "What business do we want to be in?" and views the company's distinct product/market commitments as an interacting portfolio of businesses. At the top of the strategic hierarchy is *enterprise* strategy, which defines the mission of the business in the society it serves and incorporates value judgments that must be made by management.

In this chapter, we will examine the relationships among marketing, business unit, and corporate strategies, with an emphasis on the role played by marketing managers in developing and implementing strategies at each level. It is essential to the success of the business that the entire process be informed by a very current and complete understanding of the customer—his needs, problems, perceptions, and buying decision process. Marketing management's major responsibility is to bring that competent understanding of the customer and her problems to all aspects of strategic planning, to be "expert" on the customer.

The most important strategic decision any firm makes is the selection of customers and markets to be served, the market segmentation and targeting decision. It is followed closely in importance by the choice of products to be offered to those markets and their positioning. The customer, it has been argued throughout this text, is the "given" in industrial marketing strategy, with the product being a "variable" that gets tailored to fit the chosen customers' needs. These market/product combinations define "businesses" in the strategic sense, and they define the business that the company is in. Here is another way of stressing that, especially in industrial marketing firms, marketing must be a general management responsibility. Thus, while the distinction among corporate, business unit, and marketing strategies is an important one, it is also true that marketing management has a critical role to play in the planning process at each level of strategy. To avoid repetition and confusion, the discussion will not treat each level of strategic planning as a separate process, however. Instead, we will begin with an overview of the strategic planning process in general terms, making the necessary distinctions among the different levels of strategy at later stages in the discussion as appropriate.

THE VALUE PROPOSITION—THE SEARCH FOR POSITIONAL ADVANTAGE

A central strategic concept in marketing, used often in this text, is that of *the value proposition*—the firm's unique way of delivering value to customers. It is a key part of the firm's positioning statement, the "why" part of the who-what-why paradigm of positioning presented in Chapter 4. The value proposition answers the question "Why should customers buy from us rather than our competitors?"

In Chapter 7, our consideration of value-based pricing was built around a dynamic view of customer perceptions of value, recognizing that customers keep changing their expectations and requirements in response to our product offering *and our competitors' product offerings,* which interact with one another in shaping the customer's expectations. The strategy formulation problem is built around the search for unique, sustainable competitive advantage in a market that keeps changing.

Thus, the firm's value proposition must be based upon an assessment of its strengths and weaknesses *vis-a-vis* competition as seen through the eyes of the customer. Day and Wensley report that most firms tend to define positional advantage either in terms of competitors or in terms of customers, not both. Competitor analysis looks at the strengths and weaknesses of the resources and skills of the firm relative to competition and tends to be internally focussed. Customer analysis emphasizes customers' perceptions, needs, and wants without adequately considering what the firm can do better than its competitors. Day and Wensley conclude that effective strategic planning requires a balanced mix of customer and competitor analysis. Then, the firm's resources and skills must be blended into a positioning statement that captures its strengths relative to competition in a way meaningful to customers. Finally, the firm must develop strategy, programs, systems, and tactics for implementing the positioning and achieving the desired performance outcomes—customer satisfaction, loyalty, market share, and profits.[1]

Note that our distinction between good and bad customers in Chapter 4 was an attempt to define market targets based on the firm's ability to have a unique value proposition for those customers. Good customers value what the firm can do well. A sound statement of the firm's value proposition is a key resource for communicating the strategy throughout the firm, for achieving a consensus about the firm's strengths, and its commitments to serving its target market. It can help all employees to understand requirements for success in the competitive marketplace. It becomes a key part of the corporate culture.

THE CONCEPT OF STRATEGIC PLANNING

Strategic planning is the process of defining company capabilities and matching these to opportunities in a changing environment. The purpose of a strategy is to allocate the firm's resources optimally. Strategic planning is forward looking and adaptive, requiring that management make forecasts and develop organizational and operational plans that will allow the firm to anticipate changes in the

[1] George F. Day and Robin Wensley, "Assessing Advantage: A Framework for Diagnosing Competitive Superiority," *Journal of Marketing*, **52**, 2 (April, 1988), 1–20.

environment (rather than to react after they have occurred) and adapt to those changes.

There are seven rather distinct components in the strategic planning process:

1. An appraisal of the strengths and weaknesses of the firm.
2. The creative definition of the firm's distinctive competence.
3. An assessment of the economic market environment and how it is changing.
4. The definition of long-term goals.
5. The identification of specific market and product opportunities available to the firm, given its capabilities, and the selection of those to be pursued.
6. The setting of specific, measurable objectives required to achieve long-term goals.
7. The development of programs for exploiting defined opportunities and meeting those objectives.

Each of these seven components of the planning process can be examined in more depth, although it should be clear that the process does not proceed step-by-step in chronological fashion. Large firms may have professional planners on their staffs, but in most firms the top functional and general managers carry the burden of the planning responsibility. In fact, one of the clearly identifiable management trends of the 1980's was a move to decentralize strategic planning responsibility, to push it down to operational levels of the business, and to integrate it with other aspects of the strategic management process, including budgeting and organization development. In many large corporations, like General Electric, noted for their sophisticated strategic planning systems, the corporate planning staff role has been fundamentally redefined to one of supporting and advising the planning process at the operating level, not that of developing the plans.

APPRAISAL OF STRENGTHS AND WEAKNESSES

Strategic planning begins with an appraisal of the firm's strengths and weaknesses. All areas of the firm must be assessed, including organization, financial capabilities, technical competence, location, production skills, physical plant and equipment, management and other personnel (especially those possessing scarce competence and skill), distribution patterns and distributor relationships, the sales force, image, customers, customer loyalty, cost advantages, advertising and sales promotion skills, and so on. Typically, competing firms provide a reference point, a basis for comparison, but a variety of criteria must be used in assessing strengths and weaknesses, including objective criteria, such as number of employees in various functions, and appropriate financial measures as well as more subjective criteria, such as the quality of the firm's relationships with customers and distributors.

Identification of strategic, administrative, and operational weaknesses may be more difficult, politically, than gaining management consensus around the definition of strengths. Definition of weaknesses often appears to be a placing of blame, and responsible managers are likely to deny that there is a problem in their area, or to argue that it will be corrected. It is often true that the definition of weakness is contingent on a particular market or product positioning for the firm. This must be made as specific as possible. A strength in one product/market area can be a weakness in another. For example, high product quality if associated with high unit cost could become a weakness in a market area characterized by heavy price competition and aggressive use of sales promotion. Another type of strategic weakness that may be hard to define is that due to a lack of some critical skills—e.g., lack of necessary advertising and sales promotion skills. It is often difficult to define precisely what these skills are that are lacking, or to get agreement that present management is not likely to be able to develop such skills.

Strategic planning is motivated by a desire to maximize exposure of the firm's strengths, while minimizing the exposure of the weaknesses. But that does not mean that the weaknesses have to be accepted or that new strengths cannot be acquired. The central concern of strategic planning is to allocate the firm's resources as effectively as possible. Clearly, one purpose of the analysis of strengths and weaknesses is to define areas in which the firm should commit resources that will improve its capabilities.

The Marketing Audit

Turning specifically to the marketing part of the organization, the strategic planning process may be facilitated by the use of a marketing audit. A marketing audit is simply an in-depth, comprehensive analysis of all aspects of the firm's marketing activities. It should be conducted by a team of observers who are not part of the operation being audited, although they could come from other parts of a larger company, for example. The audit looks at six areas of the marketing function: (1) environment; (2) strategy; (3) organization; (4) systems; (5) productivity; and (6) specific functions or decision areas. The scope of a marketing audit is suggested by the list of questions in Figure 11-1. The audit itself should be carefully planned and executed and should be done periodically, if it is to be effective, so that

---

THE MARKETING ENVIRONMENT AUDIT

I. Macro-Environment

Economic-Demographic

1. What does the company expect in the way of inflation, material shortages, unemployment, and credit availability in the short run, intermediate run, and long run?
2. What effect will forecasted trends in the size, age distribution, and regional distribution of population have on the business?

Technology

1. What major changes are occurring in product technology? In process technology?
2. What are the major generic substitutes that might replace this product?

Political-Legal

1. What laws are being proposed that may affect marketing strategy and tactics?
2. What federal, state, and local agency actions should be watched? What is happening in the areas of pollution control, equal employment opportunity, product safety, advertising, price control, etc., that is relevant to marketing planning?

Social-Cultural

1. What attitude is the public taking toward business and toward products such as those produced by the company?

Figure 11–1. Components of a marketing audit. (Figure continues on following pages.) [Source: *Philip Kotler, William Gregor, and William Rodgers, "The Marketing Audit Comes of Age,"* Sloan Management Review, *18, 2 (Winter, 1977), 25–43, at 39–43.*] *Reproduced with permission.*

II. Task Environment

Markets

1. What is happening to market size, growth, geographical distribution, and profits?

2. What are the major market segments? What are their expected rates of growth? Which are high opportunity and low opportunity segments?

Customers

1. How do current customers and prospects rate the company and its competitors, particularly with respect to reputation, product quality, service, sales force, and price?

2. How do different classes of customers make their buying decisions?

3. What are the evolving needs and satisfactions being sought by the buyers in this market?

Competitors

1. Who are the major competitors? What are the objectives and strategy of each major competitor? What are their strengths and weaknesses? What are the sizes and trends in market shares?

2. What trends can be foreseen in future competition and substitutes for this product?

Distribution and Dealers

1. What are the main trade channels bringing products to customers?

2. What are the efficiency levels and growth potentials of the different trade channels?

Suppliers

1. What is the outlook for the availability of different key resources used in production?

2. What trends are occurring among suppliers in their pattern of selling?

Facilitators

1. What is the outlook for the cost and availability of transportation services?

2. What is the outlook for the cost and availability of warehousing facilities?

3. What is the outlook for the cost and availability of financial resources?

4. How effectively is the advertising agency performing? What trends are occurring in advertising agency services?

Figure 11–1. (Continued)

MARKETING STRATEGY AUDIT

Marketing Objectives

1. Are the corporate objectives clearly stated and do they lead logically to the marketing objectives?
2. Are the marketing objectives stated in a clear form to guide marketing planning and subsequent performance measurement?
3. Are the marketing objectives appropriate, given the company's competitive position, resources, and opportunities? Is the appropriate strategic objective to build, hold, harvest, or terminate this business?

Strategy

1. What is the core marketing strategy for achieving the objectives? Is it a sound marketing strategy?
2. Are enough resources (or too many resources) budgeted to accomplish the marketing objectives?
3. Are the marketing resources allocated optimally to prime market segments, territories, and products of the organization?
4. Are the marketing resources allocated optimally to the major elements of the marketing mix, i.e., product quality, service, sales force, advertising, promotion, and distribution?

MARKETING ORGANIZATION AUDIT

Formal Structure

1. Is there a high level marketing officer with adequate authority and responsibility over those company activities that affect the customer's satisfaction?
2. Are the marketing responsibilities optimally structured along functional, product, end user, and territorial lines?

Functional Efficiency

1. Are there good communication and working relations between marketing and sales?
2. Is the product management system working effectively? Are the product managers able to plan profits or only sales volume?
3. Are there any groups in marketing that need more training, motivation, supervision, or evaluation?

Figure 11–1. (Continued)

Interface Efficiency

1. Are there any problems between marketing and manufacturing that need attention?
2. What about marketing and R&D?
3. What about marketing and financial management?
4. What about marketing and purchasing?

MARKETING SYSTEMS AUDIT

Marketing Information System

1. Is the marketing intelligence system producing accurate, sufficient, and timely information about developments in the marketplace?
2. Is marketing research being adequately used by company decision makers?

Marketing Planning System

1. Is the marketing planning system well-conceived and effective?
2. Is sales forecasting and market potential measurement soundly carried out?
3. Are sales quotas set on a proper basis?

Marketing Control System

1. Are the control procedures (monthly, quarterly, etc.) adequate to insure that the annual plan objectives are being achieved?
2. Is provision made to analyze periodically the profitability of different products, markets, territories, and channels of distribution?
3. Is provision made to examine and validate periodically various marketing costs?

New Product Development System

1. Is the company well-organized to gather, generate, and screen new product ideas?
2. Does the company do adequate concept research and business analysis before investing heavily in a new idea?
3. Does the company carry out adequate product and marketing testing before launching a new product?

Figure 11–1. (Continued)

MARKETING PRODUCTIVITY AUDIT

Profitability Analysis

1. What is the profitability of the company's different products, served markets, territories, and channels of distribution?
2. Should the company enter, expand, contract, or withdraw from any business segments and what would be the short- and long-run profit consequences?

Cost-Effectiveness Analysis

1. Do any marketing activities seem to have excessive costs? Are these costs valid? Can cost-reducing steps be taken?

MARKETING FUNCTION AUDITS

Products

1. What are the product line objectives? Are these objectives sound? Is the current product line meeting these objectives?
2. Are there particular products that should be phased out?
3. Are there new products that are worth adding?
4. Are any products able to benefit from quality, feature, or style improvements?

Price

1. What are the pricing objectives, policies, strategies, and procedures? To what extent are prices set on sound cost, demand, and competitive criteria?
2. Do the customers see the company's prices as being in line or out of line with the perceived value of its offer?
3. Does the company use price promotions effectively?

Distribution

1. What are the distribution objectives and strategies?
2. Is there adequate market coverage and service?
3. Should the company consider changing its degree of reliance on distributors, sales reps, and direct selling?

Figure 11–1. (Continued)

Sales Force

1. What are the organization's sales force objectives?

2. Is the sales force large enough to accomplish the company's objectives?

3. Is the sales force organized along the proper principle(s) of specialization (territory, market, product)?

4. Does the sales force show high morale, ability, and effort? Are they sufficiently trained and incentivized?

5. Are the procedures adequate for setting quotas and evaluating performances?

6. How is the company's sales force perceived in relation to competitors' sales forces?

Advertising, Promotion, and Publicity

1. What are the organization's advertising objectives? Are they sound?

2. Is the right amount being spent on advertising? How is the budget determined?

3. Are the ad themes and copy effective? What do customers and the public think about the advertising?

4. Are the advertising media well chosen?

5. Is sales promotion used effectively?

6. Is there a well-conceived publicity program?

Figure 11-1. (Continued)

changes in the pattern of strengths and weaknesses over a period of time can be observed.[2]

DEFINITION OF DISTINCTIVE COMPETENCE

Stepping back from the details of the marketing audit and the analysis of company strengths and weaknesses, the strategist needs to find a creative answer to the most important question of all that can be asked about a competitive enterprise: "What is the firm's distinctive competence?" A distinctive competence may be found in any area of the firm's operations—R&D, engineering, production, marketing, or distribution—and may come from synergy among

[2] Philip Kotler, William Gregor, and William Rodgers, "The Marketing Audit Comes of Age," *Sloan Management Review*, 18, 2 (Winter, 1977), 25–43.

several elements of the operation. The firm's distinctive competence is that set of capabilities that translates into a product-market strategy distinguishing the firm from its competitors in a way that is important to its customers.

One approach to defining the firm's distinctive competence focuses on the customers served and the nature of the needs that are satisfied and the role of the firm's product and service offering in satisfying that set of needs. This is often phrased as the question "What business are we in?" The answer is phrased in terms of customer need satisfaction.

This viewpoint on the matter of defining distinctive competence is at the heart of the so-called marketing concept with its emphasis on customer orientation. It is identified with Peter Drucker, who stated flatly that the one valid definition of business purpose was to create a customer,[3] and with Theodore Levitt who argued that any business must be viewed as a customer-satisfying process, not a goods-producing process.[4] For the industrial marketer especially, this may be an oversimplified view.

It is an extremely useful exercise for any marketing manager to try to view the business, and especially products, through the customers' eyes. Throughout this text, at several points, we have defined a product in terms of what it does for the customer, not in terms of what the seller sells, but in terms of what the buyer buys. But it is often unreasonably constraining and sometimes impossible to define a firm's distinctive competence in terms of the customer need satisfied. The firm's unique competence, especially for an industrial marketer, may be defined more appropriately by its internal strengths, and especially its technical competence, rather than its market relationships.

In other words, there is more to marketing than simply identifying and satisfying existing customer needs, although that is always part of the equation. Not all customer needs have been discovered and are being served in the marketplace as it is presently defined. From time to time, new technology and innovative products and services can create entirely new markets. Examples of truly new markets are hard to find, but among the classics are Xerox for photocopying; Federal Express for the guaranteed overnight delivery of small parcels; Apple for the personal computer (although IBM was the first to target business markets specifically); VisiCalc for

[3] Peter F. Drucker, *The Practice of Management* (New York: Harper & Row, Publishers, Inc., 1954), p. 37.
[4] Theodore Levitt, "Marketing Myopia," *Harvard Business Review*, **38**, 4 (July-August, 1960), 45–56.

spreadsheet software; and 3M's "Post-It" notes for the office. The point of these examples is that the firm's distinctive technical competence must be assessed along with what the market apparently wants in defining opportunity. Creating a market usually presents a much larger opportunity than battling for a share of a market that already exists, although it almost always requires major investments and carries high risk.

The firm's distinctive competence may not reside with its technical capabilities but can be found in virtually any area of its operations, such as:

Basic scientific knowledge in the R&D group, giving the ability to invent effective solutions to customer problems.

Access to critically important raw materials or components.

Patents and the related technical expertise.

Production skills relating to machinery or processes that allow better quality or cost savings.

Fixed plant, location and technology, that produces cost savings or unique product characteristics.

Distribution relationships that provide access to specific markets and customers not so readily available to competition.

Definition of the core competence of the firm defines the business it is in, which is the key step in the definition of *corporate* level strategy and leads directly to the specification of the basic product/ market or *business* level strategy. There are two different sets of implications for the marketing strategist in the definition of the firm's core competence. First, defining the core competence focuses the planning process on specific product/market opportunities for the firm and positions it in the competitive marketplace (business strategy). Second, and equally important, it defines those areas where the firm must allocate resources and develop functional strategies to maintain its competence and protect itself against competitive inroads. A failure to spend adequately for R&D, for example, or a failure to nurture the distributor organization, can lead to a loss of unique competitive advantage.

Definition of distinctive competence is not just straight analysis of the firm's strengths and weaknesses versus competition. It also requires management creativity and insight. The definition must be in terms basic enough for long-term viability. Success in defining distinctive competence is critically important to strategic planning, therefore, because it leads to the definition of product/market opportunities and to the commitment of company resources to the continued development of that basic competence. That definition of distinctive competence must be fitted to the changing competitive market environment. It will do no good to maintain an internal competence that is no longer desired by customers or that has been replaced by another competitor's different kind of competence—the classic buggy whip manufacturer's problem.

ENVIRONMENTAL ANALYSIS

If the environment was static, there would be no need for the strategic planning process. If the firm could define a proper set of goals, objectives, and plans once, then there would be no need for continual analysis of strengths and weaknesses, appraisal of product/ market strategies, and so forth. The environment obviously changes continually, however, as do the firm's capabilities. There are three distinct elements of the environment that are relevant for the marketing strategist: (1) the broad scope of economic, political, social, and legal forces that are beyond the influence or control of the firm; (2) competition in the markets in which the firm has elected to compete, including direct competitors who are following similar product/market strategies and indirect competitors who offer substitute products and services, broadly defined; and (3) customers, their needs and goals, and the environmental and competitive conditions in the customers' industries and markets that are shaping the customers' strategic problems.

The purpose of environmental analysis is to identify and assess threats and opportunities as they are evolving in the marketplace. The company itself is part of the changing environment, especially since it develops and refines its basic competence in interaction with its customers' evolving needs. Generally, virtually every aspect of the firm's marketing activities, and competitive and customer response to them, will have some effect on the structure and functioning of the marketplace, especially its pricing policies, distributor strategies, and new product marketing efforts. This is one aspect of buyer-seller interdependence, which we have defined as one of the unique dimensions of industrial marketing.

Environmental analysis requires a constant flow of information from a potentially limitless array of sources. Any piece of information has value if it contributes to increased management awareness and understanding of the forces shaping the economy, the industry, and the market. The typical manager relies on a number of regular reports and publications for this kind of information. From these information sources, she shapes a set of assumptions about the future that provides the basis for setting objectives and the development of plans and programs. Among the most obvious sources of information are sales representatives, customers, distributors, trade associations, management associations, universities, the general business press, government publications, management consultants, trade journals and professional publications, and other managers within the firm.

In addition to this general analysis of the environment performed by every manager, there is usually a need for more detailed analyses and measurements, including forecasts. Management consultants, corporate planning groups, or line managers may be charged with responsibility for developing analyses of particular industries or markets and for providing precise estimates of the future growth of specific market segments. Quantitative estimates may be developed for total sales volume, number of competitors, number of customers in various size categories, price levels, profit margins, and so on. The likely direction in the development of relevant technology, both product and production process technology, may also be forecasted.

The accuracy of all forecasts used as the basis for planning should be checked periodically for the obvious reason that actual experience can diverge significantly, even if the original forecast was reasonable. Long-range forecasts for periods of two to five years, and longer, can be revised on an annual basis and still be useful for longer range planning. A variety of sophisticated techniques are available to the analyst who has responsibility for preparing sales forecasts.[5] The marketing strategist need not be expert in the use of these techniques, but he should know the basic assumptions, strengths, and weaknesses of each, especially those that are being used by the staff people who provide him with forecasts and reports.

GOAL DEFINITION

Goals are statements of long-term business focus and purpose that are not usually modified in the annual planning cycle. These represent long-term commitments of company resources to certain management values, the development of a distinctive competence, and the satisfaction of specified customer needs. The importance of the values and personal goals of management in the definition of long-

[5] For an excellent review of forecasting methods, see Spyros Makridakis, Steven C. Wheelwright, and Victor E. McGee, *Forecasting: Methods and Applications*, 2nd ed. (New York: John Wiley & Sons, Inc., 1983).

term corporate goals is sometimes overlooked in academic discussions of strategic planning. The point is simply that goal definition is not just an answer to the question "What business should we be in?," given the firm's strengths and weaknesses, but equally important, "What business do we *want* to be in?"

For many authors who have written on the subject of strategic planning, goal definition is virtually the same as the definition of the distinctive competence of the firm. It is easy to agree that these two phases of the strategic planning process are very similar, but it is also useful to delineate the definition of distinctive competence as a bridge between the more analytical process of defining company strengths and weaknesses and the truly creative process of goal definition.

The statement of goals is a function not only of the definition of distinctive competence, but also of the definition of long-range competitive market opportunities that is an outcome of environmental analysis. Typically, goal definition revolves around the desire of management to achieve a leadership position in some area of product technology, market share, or response to customer needs. Some aspect of the goal statement should focus on customers and their needs. Goals that focus on such internal criteria as return on investment or profit as a percentage of sales are likely to lack the force that comes from defining business purpose in terms of distinctive competence or customer need satisfaction, although they may be useful as short-term objectives against which to assess performance.

The most useful goals are those that relate to the definition of the business (i.e., product/market strategy) that the firm is in, but do so in a way that permits a flexible response to the market over a period of time. Sound goal statements provide implicit criteria for selecting among various product/market opportunities in terms of their consistency with the basic competence of the firm. Conversely, goals phrased strictly in terms of return on investment or profit criteria may not be very helpful when it comes to assessing specific business opportunities.

IDENTIFYING AND SELECTING PRODUCT/MARKET OPPORTUNITIES

A business is defined by product/market combinations. One large company can be in many different businesses at the same time. It has been asserted repeatedly in this book that the selection of customers is the critical choice made by any industrial marketer, especially because the product is a variable in industrial marketing strategy and must be tailored, with its service offering, to fit the requirements of the customer. The industrial firm's product/market strategy is therefore largely determined by its distinctive competence and its macrosegmentation strategy.

The Product Portfolio

In modern management practice, the identification and selection of product/market opportunities is often aided by the application of product portfolio analysis. Product portfolio analysis looks at product-market combinations in terms of company capabilities and profit opportunities defined by rate of market growth and other market conditions. The latter usually are phrased in terms of some model of the product life cycle. The inputs for the product portfolio analysis are data and conclusions from earlier stages in the strategic planning process—especially the appraisal of strengths and weaknesses and environmental analysis. The output is a pattern for committing financial, production, and marketing resources to businesses (product/market combinations).

Basic concepts relating to the product portfolio and the experience curve were introduced in Chapter 5 as part of our consideration of product strategy. It will be recalled that the Boston Consulting Group (BCG) product portfolio approach presents a matrix using two dimensions—market growth rate, a measure of stage in the product life cycle, and market dominance, the market share held by the firm compared with that of the largest competitor. The importance of the experience curve was traced to the basic assumption that all competitors face the same experience curve, which leads to the logical conclusion that the firm with the largest market share will be the lowest cost producer in the industry, a source of great competitive advantage.

Given this fact, many management authorities have argued that any firm faces two broad classes of strategic options—either a strategy of product differentiation and market niching based on product quality, which is assumed to be a high cost strategy; or a strategy of low price, average quality, low cost, and high volume. We also took a critical look at the experience curve assumption and this simple strategic dichotomy, however, and cited strong research evidence to support the argument that high product quality, not low price, is typically associated with high market share. There is strong evidence of a positive relationship between market share and profitability. It appears, however, that it is the combination of high quality, *high* price, and low cost that explains the relationship, *not* low price and high volume. In fact, high quality with its favorable impact on sales volume and, therefore, market share can have a favorable, indirect effect on contribution margin.[6]

The basic purpose of a product portfolio analysis is to achieve a balanced commitment of resources, especially financial resources (i.e., cash), among the various businesses or product/market combinations served by the firm. In order to fund the development of the business opportunities of the future, some of the more mature businesses in the portfolio may be asked to play the role of generating cash. One very useful illustration of the process of balancing the product portfolio, using the BCG growth/share matrix, was developed by Day and is shown in Figure 11-2.[7]

The BCG approach does not clearly define strategies appropriate to each product category but indicates broadly that:

1. Stars require additional, continuing commitment of resources to their full development—i.e., *growth* strategies. Stars are likely to be heavy *users* of cash.
2. Problem Children are also heavy users of cash and may have unrealized potential in a fast growth market, but the firm may or may not be able to develop the required competence to exploit it—i.e., a variety of strategies are possible; all are risky.
3. Dogs are using resources and have little potential and should therefore be dropped unless they can be repositioned—i.e., a liquidation strategy.
4. Cash Cows dominate their market but have reached their peak and can be used to generate cash for other ventures, by pulling back on resource commitments—i.e., strategies for maintaining share or slowly liquidating the business.

While the BCG approach concentrates on rate of growth in the market and the company's competitive position in terms of market share, a more complex approach has been developed by Arthur D. Little, Inc. (ADL). In the ADL model, four stages in the product life cycle are defined and market position is given five distinct categories, leading to a 4 × 5 matrix as follows:

[6] Lynn W. Phillips, Dae R. Chang, and Robert D. Buzzell, "Product Quality, Cost Position, and Business Performance: A Test of Some Key Hypotheses," *Journal of Marketing*, **47**, 2 (Spring, 1983), 26–43.
[7] George S. Day, "Diagnosing the Product Portfolio," *Journal of Marketing*, **41**, 2 (April, 1977), 29–38.

Product Life Cycle State

		Embryonic	Growth	Mature	Aging
Market	Dominant				
	Strong				
	Favorable				
Position	Tenable				
	Weak				

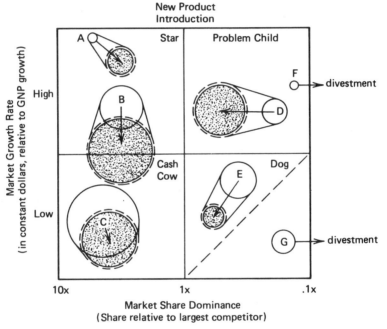

New Product
Introduction

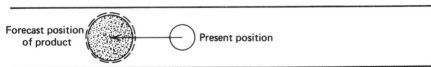

Forecast position of product   Present position

(Diameter of circle is proportional to product's contribution to total company sales volume)

Figure 11-2. Balancing the product portfolio. Source:*George S. Day,* "Diagnosing the Product Portfolio," Journal of Marketing, *41, 2 (April, 1977), 29–38, at p. 34.] Reproduced with permission of the American Marketing Association.*

Risk increases as products get older and as market position becomes weaker. ADL argues that there are certain natural strategies for each stage in the product life cycle and for each box in the matrix. For example, a strategy of market penetration could be sensible in the embryonic and growth stages. Strategies of backward or forward integration are appropriate for mature products. Altogether, the ADL approach defines 24 strategies appropriate for one or more of the boxes in the matrix.

Like ADL, Shell Chemical International also believes that there are certain natural strategies, given a company's current market position and the stage in market development. The Shell approach uses a somewhat simpler (3 × 3) matrix and defines nine types of strategies, as shown in Figure 11-3.

Perhaps the most sophisticated of the product portfolio models is that developed by General Electric, working with McKinsey & Company. Called the "Company Position/Industry Attractiveness Matrix," it is a 3 × 3 matrix, the dimensions of which are Business Unit Position, an elaboration of the basic idea of market dominance; and Industry Attractiveness, an expansion of the market growth rate or stage in the product life cycle dimension in the BCG model. Such a matrix is illustrated in Figure 11-4. The use of the GE/McKinsey model requires the analyst to make much more sophisticated and complex judgments about a variety of factors influencing both company position and industry attractiveness. These are outlined in the illustration. Positioning each business in the matrix, judgments can be made concerning whether the business should be one in which the firm invests for growth, harvests or divests, or selectively maintains through modest additional investment with an emphasis on maximizing earnings.

The value of any of these product portfolio approaches depends in large measure on management's ability to properly position each of its businesses within the matrix. This means that both market growth rate and company capability must be accurately assessed. Wishful thinking, rather than realistic appraisal, can cause disastrous misallocation of company resources.

We have presented an oversimplified description of each of these four product portfolio approaches with the intent of showing their usefulness to management in thinking about strategic options. More detailed measurements and analysis, such as estimation of the relevant experience curves in the BCG approach, are necessary, of course, to actually apply each of these approaches. A critically important step in the process is that of defining the market to be

Prospects for business profitability

	No good	Average	Attractive
Weak	Disinvest Unload now and redeploy assets	Phased withdrawal Cash out over time	Double or quit Tomorrows stars— need large cash infusion or get out
Average	Phased withdrawal Cash out over time	Custodial Maximize cash generation—no major commitment of resources	Avis Try harder, though you may be doomed to #2 status
Strong	Cash generator Use cash for growth elsewhere	Growth Where there is no leader — stay with the competition— grow with the market	Leader Give absolute priority to the product—spend all resources necessary to hold market position—invest in capacity

(Company's competitive capabilities — Weak / Average / Strong)

Figure 11-3. The Shell Chemical International approach to product portfolio analysis, defining strategic options. [Source: *Robert T. Davis,* "Strategic Planning," *unpublished paper circulated privately, p. 18.*]

analyzed; management can deceive itself about the strength of its market position if it defines the served market too narrowly. The focus on competitive market position and market growth in these product portfolio approaches is valuable, but the management team that is identifying and selecting among product/market opportunities has several other factors to consider in setting long-term corporate strategy.

A major consideration is how the firm's distinctive competence matches the requirements for competitive effectiveness in the product/market under consideration. This appraisal requires some reasonably complete understanding of competitive conditions in the industry being examined. Sometimes the factors that relate to business success are quite subtle, such as established relationships with the technical personnel in customer organizations or the ability to get commitment of field effort from distributor sales personnel.

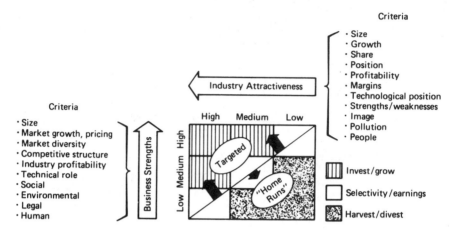

Figure 11-4. The General Electric–McKinsey & Company "Company Position/Industry Attractiveness Matrix." [Source: *General Electric Company.*] *Reproduced with permission.*

Related to this issue of distinctive competence are a number of other features of the firm, such as financial resources, organizational flexibility, management availability, access to sources of supply, and other capabilities. These, too, must be assessed in relationship to requirements of the business being analyzed.

A second consideration is whether the business being evaluated is consistent with the firm's goal definition, especially with its definition of the customer needs to be served over the long-run. If there is no obvious relationship to the firm's present customer orientation, there is a need for caution, but it is not a need for rejecting an opportunity out of hand. It does suggest, however, that the firm's existing knowledge of customers, and its general approach to the marketplace, may not be terribly useful in the new business. However, its distinctive competence may still be relevant. If neither the distinctive competence nor the existing customer orientation are likely to be relevant, it is highly unlikely that the firm's present management will be able to manage the new venture intelligently. Awareness of this truth, and of the unexpected difficulties faced by many managements in the acquisitions-and-mergers mania of the 1970's and 1980's, has underscored the wisdom of the dictum "Stick to your knitting!"—in other words, know, grow, and defend your basic competence.

A third set of considerations in the assessment of product/market opportunities relates to environmental conditions influencing the market and industry. Among the most important may be governmental regulations of various kinds, both state and federal, including those relating to product standards, regulation of competition, product standards relating to safety and air or water pollution, and the like. The availability of government funds to finance purchase may also be important. Labor unions may be an important factor in determining future cost structures. The state of technology and the speed with which it is changing can be considered an environmental factor as well.

Fourth, the nature of the market itself should be considered. We have already devoted a good deal of attention to the dimension of market growth rate. Other aspects to be considered include degree of concentration (number of firms and the spread of market shares), cyclicality and seasonality of demand, investment required per dollar in sales, presence of price cutting, unique product engineering requirements, availability of distributors, spending by competitors for marketing and advertising as a percent of sales volume, degree of customer satisfaction with existing brands and suppliers, and the strength of existing customer loyalties.

Such considerations can be incorporated into a product portfolio approach. Relevant dimensions for analysis can be defined by the analyst and a five-point scale can be used to assess each existing and potential business opportunity. Each can then be positioned in the matrix according to total points on two summary measures, one relating to company capabilities and one relating to market attractiveness.

The Importance of Market Share

How important is market share? Much of the foregoing has been concerned with the ability of the firm to obtain a fairly significant share of the target market. This question was raised for the first time in Chapter 5 when the product portfolio model was introduced as an aid in the product planning process. In our analysis of pricing strategy (Chapter 7), market share was said to be a prerequisite for effective price leadership, especially since it provided the necessary basis for investments in marketing and R&D expenses, as well as economies of scale in production. Similarly, in our consideration of marketing communication strategy (Chapter 10), the analysis of marketing communication budgets showed that the ratio of marketing expenditures to sales tended to decrease as market share increased. Thus, large market share has a two-fold impact on marketing expenditures—first, by increasing the base of sales revenue and, second, by decreasing the percentage of that base necessary for marketing communications—personal selling, advertising, direct mail, trade shows, and so on. As sales volume increases, the total spent for marketing communications can increase, while the ratio of expenditures to sales actually decreases.

As noted before, studies by the Strategic Planning Institute have confirmed the importance of market share as a factor influencing the profitability of a business. Their studies are called the PIMS Project (*Profit Impact of Marketing Strategy*) and were originated within the General Electric Company by Sidney Schoeffler. The data base now consists of financial and strategic information for around 3,000 business units. Using the statistical techniques of regression analysis, the PIMS project analyzed 37 variables that might be expected to have some influence on business profitability. One of the strongest conclusions from the early research was that there was a strong relationship between market share and profitability, as measured by return-on-investment (ROI).[8]

Today, the Strategic Planning Institute puts another conclusion first among the PIMS Principles—"In the long run, the most important single factor affecting a business unit's performance is the quality of its products and services, relative to those of competitors."[9] This line of analysis was presented in the research of Phillips, Chang, and Buzzell mentioned earlier.[10]

Initial thinking about the market share-profitability relationship focussed on the purchases-to-sales ratio as the primary reason why market share and its correlate, sales volume, would produce economies of scale in purchasing, leading to better profit margins. Subsequent analysis suggested the more complicated relationship to quality and other economies of scale, including lower direct costs of production and lower expenditures for R&D and marketing (as a percentage of revenues), but also cautioned against the simpleminded notion that higher market share was always more profitable. Using price cutting to attain share, or spending excessively on

[8] Robert D. Buzzell, Bradley T. Gale, and Ralph G. M. Sultan, "Market Share—A Key to Profitability," *Harvard Business Review* **53**, 1 (January-February, 1975), 97–106.
[9] Robert D. Buzzell and Bradley T. Gale, *The PIMS Principles: Linking Strategy to Performance*, (New York: The Free Press, 1987), p. 7.
[10] Phillips, Chang, Buzzell, *op. cit.*, 26–43.

advertising and sales promotion, or making inefficient investments in capacity to support greater market share, could all produce the opposite result. In fact, the third PIMS principle has been stated as "High investment intensity acts as a powerful drag on profitability."[11]

Nonetheless, the PIMS studies support a general conclusion that an increase of 10 percentage points in market share is associated with about a 3½-percentage-point increase in return on investment.[12] Such a crude generalization must be viewed with extreme caution, however, as the circumstances under which the relationship exists undoubtedly vary significantly from business to business.

Prescott, Kohli, and Venkatraman used the PIMS data base to look more carefully at the relationship between market share and profitability and determined that it was specific to particular businesses and market conditions, and that it could be either direct or spurious depending on those conditions. Among the critical variables influencing the nature and extent of the market share-ROI relationship were investment intensity, relative product quality, stage in product life cycle, direct cost relative to competitors, and degree of market fragmentation.[13]

The Strategic Planning Institute studies suggest that increases in market share lead to (if not "cause," strictly speaking) improvements in profitability. Anterasian and Phillips have analyzed the PIMS data along with another data base, the Federal Trade Commission's "Line of Business" data, and offer a different set of conclusions.[14] They point out that many low-share niche players are very profitable and that the relationship between market share and rate of return may be spurious, a statistical artifact, with both share and ROI driven by other variables like product quality, marketing expenditures, stage in product life cycle, management skill, or luck.

Sorting through the data, Anterasian and Phillips used a different conceptual framework, which they called "the value delivery theory of competitive advantage." Instead of looking at the simple statisti-

---

[11] Buzzell and Gale, *op. cit.*, p. 10.

[12] Ibid., p. 8 and pp. 70–102.

[13] John E. Prescott, Ajay K. Kohli, and N. Venkatraman, "The Market Share-Profitability Relationship: An Empirical Assessment of Major Assertions and Contradictions," *Strategic Management Journal*, **7** (1986), 377–394.

[14] Cathy Anterasian and Lynn W. Phillips, *Discontinuities, Value Delivery, and the Share-Returns Association: A Re-Examination of the "Share-Causes-Profits" Controversy*, Research Program Monograph, Report No. 88–109, (Cambridge, Mass.: Marketing Science Institute, October, 1988).

cal relationships between market share and ROI, they posited that sustainable competitive advantage is rooted in the firm's ability to deliver superior value to customers, not in the structural barriers to competition that are at the base of the argument about a direct relationship between market share and ROI. They see market share as a result of the ability to deliver superior value. Both ROI and market share are "caused" by the management skills and resources of the firm. Environmental "shocks" or "discontinuities" such as the entry of new competitors, the advent of new technology, or directional changes in the business cycle, change the requirements for competitive effectiveness by shifting customers' preference structures ("value hierarchies") and/or the skills necessary to deliver superior value to customers at a profitable cost. Such shocks actually provide an opportunity for good management to make a difference. A key management skill, therefore, is the ability to detect and adjust to these discontinuities by redefining strategy and reconfiguring the value chain of the firm. This view is certainly consistent with the emphasis on delivering superior value to customers that has been the theme of this text.

In their analysis, Anterasian and Phillips could find no significant, positive, and temporally prior (i.e., causative) impact of market share on profitability. Industry discontinuities had a strong negative impact on market share and profitability. There was no predictable relationship between business size or market share and its ability to react to discontinuities. The smaller firms did not seem to have an advantage in their flexibility or lack of inertia, as sometimes argued. However, financial resources, a correlate of business size, did seem to have a favorable impact on the firm's ability to adapt to environmental change. The larger, more profitable firms seemed to be better able to gain share after a market shock. A more profitable firm has the resources to spend in order to take advantage of market discontinuities and to improve its competitive position. In this sense, *profits may cause share* rather than the other way around!

These results serve to make a thoughtful manager cautious in applying uncritically the simple notion that increases in market share will bring increases in profitability. Market share is probably best seen not as an objective, but as a reward, as a measure of how well the firm has delivered superior value to customers, which is also how profit is seen under the marketing concept. In their reflective commentary on these findings, Anterasian and Phillips offered these thoughtful observations:

. . . we think that a belief in law-like patterns of marketplace performance generalizable to the population of businesses should be relin-
quished, and the idea that certain patterns of behavior and outcomes
reveal themselves on a contingency basis should be embraced. Understanding what those contingencies are and how value delivery,
competitive advantage, market share, and profits can vary under
each, is a current challenge for both strategy researchers and managers. There is no single, foolproof way, no algorithm, to set strategy.
The only constants are anticipation, flexibility, and the willingness to
develop new skills at value delivery.[15]

In analysis of product/market opportunities, and in applying the
logic of product portfolio analysis, therefore, dominant market share
and rate of market growth are only two of the many variables that the
marketing strategist must consider.
To summarize this part of the strategic planning process dealing
with the identification and selection of product/market opportunities, the following questions should be asked in the appraisal of
specific businesses, and most of them answered in the affirmative if
the firm is to commit resources to a given opportunity:

1. Is the business growing?
2. Are other market conditions (e.g., cyclicality, seasonality, etc.) generally favorable? Does the market lack a strong leader?
3. Does the company's distinctive competence have applicability in this
   product/market?
4. Does the company have the resources required to match the demands
   for competitive effectiveness in this business?
5. Is this opportunity consistent with our goals and especially with our
   existing customer orientation?
6. Is it likely that the company can capture a significant market share,
   given existing competition?
7. Are environmental conditions favorable in this business?
8. If the company is significantly diversifying, can it acquire the necessary management skills?

The outcome of the analysis of product/market opportunities is a set
of commitments to distinct businesses—aiding those with the best
potential by aggressive plans and spending, maintaining market
share for established products, using mature products with strong

[15] *Ibid.*, p. 53.

market positions to generate cash to support other ventures, and liquidating those that are using resources in markets with little or no growth potential.

SETTING OBJECTIVES

Objectives are relatively short-term targets (one year to perhaps as long as five years) against which to measure the progress of the firm in achieving its goals. Unique but interlocking sets of objectives must be established at each level of strategic planning—corporate, business unit, and functional. Among the most common and useful corporate and business objectives are those relating to profit margins, sales revenue, market share, return on investment, and production costs as a percentage of sales. More specific functional objectives can be established for particular aspects of the company's pricing, distribution, and communications activities. Such detailed objectives are necessary to direct the efforts of functional managers, to coordinate their activities toward the accomplishment of broader corporate and business objectives, and to evaluate their performance.

Objectives represent a bringing together of what is desired, given goals and the selection of product/market opportunities, and what is possible, given the firm's current resources of financing, technology, management, marketing, and production capabilities. To be meaningful and useful, objectives must be attainable, although they should also challenge the capabilities of the organization to the fullest. Objectives have both a present and a future orientation. They provide targets for accomplishment during the planning period, and they provide standards against which to subsequently measure performance at the end of the period.

Objectives are examined and revised at the end of the planning period. They may be set higher or lower, or remain the same, depending on what was accomplished, and what was learned, during the period. Variations between objectives and actual performance measures must be examined carefully to determine the causes. The process of setting objectives is typically a collaborative effort, across management at the top, and then vertically through the organization hierarchy as functional managers work with their subordinates and superiors to set specific performance objectives. It is one of the cardinal rules of management that people will accept objectives as reasonable only if they feel they have participated in the setting of those objectives. And they must accept those objectives if they are to agree to have their performance measured against them. These behavioral considerations provide one major set of reasons why management cannot leave the planning task to a corporate planning staff. Top management must bear the ultimate responsibility for the formulation of corporate objectives, and it must secure the participation of line managers in defining those objectives.

DEVELOPING MARKETING PROGRAMS

After corporate objectives and the definition of the business (product/market) strategy have been set, the industrial marketing manager is responsible for developing the marketing program. The marketing program is a plan for achieving specified corporate and business objectives (market share, sales volume, R.O.I., etc.) and consists of five distinct elements: (1) definition of market segments; (2) products; (3) pricing; (4) distribution; and (5) communications. As has often been pointed out, the marketing program is more than the sum of its parts. The marketing strategist must blend these five decision elements to achieve balance and consistency. Product strategy must be consistent with the segmentation strategy. Distribution and pricing must be consistent with the product strategy, and communication must be consistent with the distribution strategy. Coordination among the elements of the marketing program is a key element in industrial marketing effectiveness.

We have often referred to functional interdependence, a recognition of the fact that the industrial marketer, in contrast to her consumer marketing counterpart, depends much more heavily on other parts of the business—especially R&D, engineering, and production—for the accomplishment of his task. This fact was recognized by Ames in his study of the marketing planning process in 50 industrial companies. A failure of marketing planning was often attributable to a failure to fit the concept of strategic planning to the unique requirements of the industrial marketing task including:

1. The recognition that industrial marketers usually operate in a multiplicity of product/markets and marketing channels (versus the single channel usually found in consumer products firms, even for multiple brands).

2. The need to plan around the constraints imposed by other functions. In Ames' words, the role of the marketing planner is as follows: "Rather than developing self-contained marketing plans, he analyzes and interprets market requirements so that top and operating management can decide how best to respond."[16]

Thus, marketing planning is a general management responsibility, as well as the responsibility of the marketing manager, although the latter is likely to have detailed planning and programming responsibility. Top management, in addition to specifying corporate objectives, must establish the organization arrangements and provide for interfunctional coordination as necessary to develop and execute the marketing plans. Ames concluded that the most successful marketing planning was based on solid information and understanding of economic facts and market trends in each of the product/market businesses that the firm was in. Planning cannot be based solely on desired outcomes and good intentions. It also requires market data and sound analysis.

The marketing manager has a critical role to play at each level of strategic planning. At the level of *corporate* strategy, where the fundamental question is "What business are we in or do we want to be in?," the marketing manager must be sure that the definition of the basic customer needs satisfied in the marketplace is one of the principal components of the definition of business purpose. Customer satisfaction must be the highest priority of the firm, for only if customers are satisfied can the firm maximize its performance for other stakeholders such as shareowners, employees, managers, and suppliers.

At the level of *business unit* strategy, marketing management must provide the most accurate and complete understanding possible of customer needs and competitive conditions in the marketplace, in order for the firm to select its market targets carefully and to define business strategies that will position the firm effectively against its competition. By being the expert on customers and competition in the ever-changing market, the marketing manager can take the lead in answering the question "How should we compete in the chosen market?" which captures the essential challenge of business strategy definition.

Clearly, at the level of *functional* marketing strategy the marketing manager must define the most skillful combination of segmenta-

[16] B. Charles Ames, "Marketing Planning for Industrial Products," *Harvard Business Review*, **46**, 5 (September-October, 1968), 100–11 at 102.

tion, product, price, distribution, and promotion strategies for implementing the planned business strategy. Marketing effectiveness depends in large part on the ability of marketing management to make the case for a customer orientation strongly enough that top management is willing to commit the resources necessary to get the job done. Part of this task, as Anderson has persuasively argued, is to convince all the other parts of the business, all of the other functional managers in finance, manufacturing, research and development, purchasing, and organizational development, of the reasons that the customer's viewpoint must have precedence over all the constituencies which they represent as managers, to convince them of the "survival value" of a customer orientation:

> Marketing's objective, therefore, remains long-run customer support through customer satisfaction. Paradoxically, perhaps, this approach requires marketers to have an even greater grasp of the technologies, perspectives, and limitations of the other functional areas. Only in this way can marketing effectively negotiate the implementation of its strategies.[17]

The marketing manager's major challenge and responsibility, then, especially in an industrial firm that depends on a total response from the entire organization to provide solutions to customer problems, is to make the whole firm and every actor in the system customer-oriented. As one Chief Executive Officer so aptly put it, "Marketing is too important to be left to the marketing people!"

The overriding mandate in developing industrial marketing strategy is *Know the customer!* But there are several other mandates as well: "Know your distinctive competence!" "Know your competition!" "Know your customer's customer!" "Know your customer's industry and competition!" "And know your own organization well enough to be able to make it work in delivering solutions to customer problems."

SUMMARY

Industrial marketing strategy poses a set of requirements for effective marketing planning that are distinctive, because of the unique-

---

[17] Paul F. Anderson, "Marketing, Strategic Planning, and the Theory of the Firm," *Journal of Marketing*, **46**, 2 (Spring, 1982), 15–26, at 24.

ness of industrial marketing. The dimensions of uniqueness include functional interdependence, product complexity, buyer-seller interdependence, and buying process complexity. Successful marketing planning has a set of general requirements as well, however, in both industrial and consumer companies: the need to put the customer at the center of the planning process; to know the customer and the marketplace in depth; and to define business goals in terms of the satisfaction of customer needs to the maximum extent possible without losing sight of the internal (often technical) basis for the firm's distinctive competence. In both consumer and industrial companies, the critical strategic decision is the choice of markets defined in terms of the customer needs to be served.

In this chapter, a seven-step planning process was defined: (1) appraisal of strengths and weaknesses; (2) definition of distinctive competence; (3) environmental analysis; (4) goal definition; (5) identification and selection of product/market opportunities; (6) setting objectives; and (7) developing the marketing program. Product portfolio analysis was described as a creative analytical approach for assessing alternative product/market opportunities.

Throughout this text an attempt has been made to integrate the results of recent research studies, theoretical and empirical, descriptive and normative, that have looked at the unique requirements for effectiveness in industrial marketing strategy. The intent has been to stress what is new and to define the directions in which the field is developing, both in theory and in practice, rather than to describe all of the institutions and operating problems of industrial marketing or to review the basics of marketing management. Such names as Corey, Lilien, Moriarty, Jackson, Little, Sultan, Wind, Bonoma, Shapiro, Cardozo, Buzzell, Spekman, and Phillips should be familiar. Through the efforts of these scholars and with the essential cooperation of industry, industrial marketing has developed as a body of knowledge that has significance and relevance for the industrial marketing decision maker.

Bibliography

Aaker, David A., *Developing Business Strategies*, 2nd ed. (New York: John Wiley & Sons, Inc., 1988).

Abell, Derek, and John Hammond, *Strategic Market Planning* (Englewood Cliffs, N.J.: Prentice-Hall, Inc., 1979).

Anderson, Paul F., "Marketing, Strategic Planning, and the Theory of the Firm," *Journal of Marketing*, **46**, 2 (Spring, 1982), 15–26.

Anterasian, Cathy, and Lynn W. Phillips, *Discontinuities, Value Delivery, and the Share-Returns Association: A Re-examination of the "Share-Causes-Profits" Controversy*, Research Program Monograph, Report No. 88–109 (Cambridge, Mass.: Marketing Science Institute, October, 1988).

Buzzell, Robert D., and Bradley T. Gale, *The PIMS Principles: Linking Strategy to Performance* (New York: The Free Press, 1987).

Day, George S., "Diagnosing the Product Portfolio," *Journal of Marketing*, **41**, 2 (April, 1977), 29–38.

———, and David B. Montgomery, "Diagnosing the Experience Curve," *Journal of Marketing*, **47**, 2 (Spring, 1983), 44–58.

———, and Robin Wensley, "Assessing Advantage: A Framework for Diagnosing Competitive Superiority," *Journal of Marketing*, **53**, 2 (April, 1988), 1–20.

Deshpandé, Rohit and Frederick E. Webster, Jr., "Organizational Culture and Marketing: Defining the Research Agenda," *Journal of Marketing*, **53**, 1 (January, 1989), 3–15.

Haspeslagh, Philippe, "Portfolio Planning: Uses and Limits," *Harvard Business Review*, **60**, 1 (January-February, 1982), 58–73.

Kotler, Philip, William Gregor, and William Rodgers, "The Marketing Audit Comes of Age," *Sloan Management Review*, **18**, 2 (Winter, 1977), 25–43.

Phillips, Lynn W., Dae R. Chang, and Robert D. Buzzell, "Product Quality, Cost Position, and Business Performance: A Test of Some Key Hypotheses," *Journal of Marketing*, **47**, 1 (Spring, 1983), 26–43.

Porter, Michael E., *Competitive Strategy* (New York: The Free Press, 1980).

———, *Competitive Advantage* (New York: The Free Press, 1985).

Rothschild, William E., *How to Gain (and Maintain) the Competitive Advantage in Business* (New York: McGraw-Hill, 1984).

Webster, Frederick E., Jr., "The Rediscovery of the Marketing Concept," *Business Horizons*, **31**, 3 (May-June, 1988), 29–39.

Index